Entrepreneurship Ecosystems and Their Opportunities and Challenges

Mohammed El Amine Abdelli
University of Brest, France

Shajara Ul-Durar
University for Creative Arts, UK

Hala Wasef Hattab
British University in Egypt, Egypt

A volume in the Advances in Logistics, Operations, and Management Science (ALOMS) Book Series

IGI Global
PUBLISHER of TIMELY KNOWLEDGE

Published in the United States of America by
IGI Global
Business Science Reference (an imprint of IGI Global)
701 E. Chocolate Avenue
Hershey PA, USA 17033
Tel: 717-533-8845
Fax: 717-533-8661
E-mail: cust@igi-global.com
Web site: http://www.igi-global.com

Library of Congress Cataloging-in-Publication Data

Names: Abdelli, Mohammed El Amine, editor. | Ul-Durar, Shajara, 1976- editor.
Title: Entrepreneurship ecosystems and their opportunities and challenges / edited by Mohammed El Amine Abdelli and Shajara Ul-Durar.
Description: Hershey, PA : Business Science Reference, [2023] | Includes bibliographical references and index. | Summary: "Entrepreneurship Ecosystems and Their Opportunities and Challenges explores and examines the importance of these factors in establishing a virtuous cycle of long-term sustainability in countries worldwide. The book promotes global communities to acquire an entrepreneurial mindset. Covering topics such as crowdfunding experiences, financial solutions, and social enterprises, this premier reference source is an excellent resource for entrepreneurs, business leaders, government officials, students and educators of higher education, researchers, and academicians"-- Provided by publisher.
Identifiers: LCCN 2023004844 (print) | LCCN 2023004845 (ebook) | ISBN 9781668471401 (hardcover) | ISBN 9781668471418 (paperback) | ISBN 9781668471425 (ebook)
Subjects: LCSH: Entrepreneurship--Environmental aspects. | Social entrepreneurship. | Strategic planning--Environmental aspects.
Classification: LCC HB615 .E5778828 2023 (print) | LCC HB615 (ebook) | DDC 338/.04--dc23/eng/20230202
LC record available at https://lccn.loc.gov/2023004844
LC ebook record available at https://lccn.loc.gov/2023004845

This book is published in the IGI Global book series Advances in Logistics, Operations, and Management Science (ALOMS) (ISSN: 2327-350X; eISSN: 2327-3518)

British Cataloguing in Publication Data
A Cataloguing in Publication record for this book is available from the British Library.
All work contributed to this book is new, previously-unpublished material.
The views expressed in this book are those of the authors, but not necessarily of the publisher.
For electronic access to this publication, please contact: eresources@igi-global.com.

Advances in Logistics, Operations, and Management Science (ALOMS) Book Series

John Wang
Montclair State University, USA

ISSN:2327-350X
EISSN:2327-3518

MISSION

Operations research and management science continue to influence business processes, administration, and management information systems, particularly in covering the application methods for decision-making processes. New case studies and applications on management science, operations management, social sciences, and other behavioral sciences have been incorporated into business and organizations real-world objectives.

The **Advances in Logistics, Operations, and Management Science** (ALOMS) Book Series provides a collection of reference publications on the current trends, applications, theories, and practices in the management science field. Providing relevant and current research, this series and its individual publications would be useful for academics, researchers, scholars, and practitioners interested in improving decision making models and business functions.

COVERAGE

- Marketing engineering
- Finance
- Decision analysis and decision support
- Networks
- Computing and information technologies
- Political Science
- Organizational Behavior
- Services management
- Production Management
- Risk management

IGI Global is currently accepting manuscripts for publication within this series. To submit a proposal for a volume in this series, please contact our Acquisition Editors at Acquisitions@igi-global.com or visit: http://www.igi-global.com/publish/.

The Advances in Logistics, Operations, and Management Science (ALOMS) Book Series (ISSN 2327-350X) is published by IGI Global, 701 E. Chocolate Avenue, Hershey, PA 17033-1240, USA, www.igi-global.com. This series is composed of titles available for purchase individually; each title is edited to be contextually exclusive from any other title within the series. For pricing and ordering information please visit http://www.igi-global.com/book-series/advances-logistics-operations-management-science/37170. Postmaster: Send all address changes to above address.

Titles in this Series

For a list of additional titles in this series, please visit: http://www.igi-global.com/book-series/

Emerging Technologies and Digital Transformation in the Manufacturing Industry
Fernando Ortiz-Rodriguez (Tamaulipas Autonomous University, Mexico) Sanju Tiwari (Tamaulipas Autonomous University, Mexico) Luis Manuel Hernández-González (INDEX, Mexico) and Agustin Tiburcio (INDEX, Mexico)
Business Science Reference • © 2023 • 300pp • H/C (ISBN: 9781668480885) • US $250.00

Transformational Leadership Styles, Management Strategies, and Communication for Global Leaders
Darcia Ann Marie Roache (University of Saskatchewan, Canada)
Business Science Reference • © 2023 • 532pp • H/C (ISBN: 9781668488225) • US $250.00

Black Women's Formal and Informal Ways of Leadership Actualizing the Vision of a More Equitable Workplace
Audrey D. Bowser (Arkansas State University, USA) Kimberley M. Davis (University of Arkansas at Pine Bluff, USA) and Natalie A. Johnson-Leslie (Arkansas State University, USA)
Information Science Reference • © 2023 • 340pp • H/C (ISBN: 9781668438275) • US $215.00

Multidisciplinary Approaches to Organizational Governance During Health Crises
Carla Sofia Vicente Negrão (CeBER, University of Coimbra, Portugal) Isabel Guerreiro Pimentel Maia (Centre for Business and Economics Research, University of Coimbra, Portugal) and João António Furtado Brito (University of Cape Verde, Cape Verde)
Business Science Reference • © 2023 • 300pp • H/C (ISBN: 9781799892137) • US $250.00

New Perspectives and Possibilities in Strategic Management in the 21st Century Between Tradition and Modernity
Javier Martínez-Falcó (University of Alicante, Spain & Stellenbosch University, South Africa) Bartolomé Marco-Lajara (University of Alicante, Spain) Eduardo Sánchez-García (University of Alicante, Spain) and Luis A. Millan-Tudela (University of Alicante, Spain)
Business Science Reference • © 2023 • 514pp • H/C (ISBN: 9781668492611) • US $315.00

IGI Global
PUBLISHER of TIMELY KNOWLEDGE

701 East Chocolate Avenue, Hershey, PA 17033, USA
Tel: 717-533-8845 x100 • Fax: 717-533-8661
E-Mail: cust@igi-global.com • www.igi-global.com

Table of Contents

Detailed Table of Contents

The pursuit of financial stability as a goal for entrepreneurs/enterprises is no more underscored than the shocks created by the COVID-19 pandemic. Up till the end of 2019, more attention to measuring and strategizing for financial stability has been largely limited to the national economy and the financial sector. However, the COVID-19 impacts which include forcing a large number of enterprises out of the market necessitates a focus on enterprise financial stability. This chapter adopts the CAMELS framework to explain the concept of enterprise financial stability. It further expatiated the concept from the perspectives of shocks arising from global, regional, national or industry disruptions. The chapter concludes with cornerstones for strategising and maintaining an enterprise's financial stability in the event of disruptions.

Entrepreneurial ventures are the only way through which unemployment can be handled effectively. Emerging economies such as India knows their strength, but its searching ways to effectively cash it out. The present helps in finding the mediating effect of entrepreneurial attitude (i.e., achievement, innovation, personal control, and self-esteem) in the link between entrepreneurial characteristics and self-employment intention among technical undergraduates of different government and private technical institutions of Chhattisgarh. Stratified random sampling was used to collect 1000 responses from technical undergraduates. Regression and confirmatory factor analysis were applied to analyse the data. The findings explained that entrepreneurial attitude dimensions were found partially mediated between entrepreneurial characteristics and self-employment intention among engineering undergraduates.

Social enterprises are oriented towards reversing an imbalance in the social system by creating a positive social change. Ethical issues and dilemmas are, therefore, of prime importance to achieve social objectives. This theoretical chapter's core purpose was to identify the ethical issues and dilemmas faced by social enterprises. Variances in the ethical issues concerning geographical and cultural factors have also been highlighted. This study will discuss the organizational theory and its concept. Secondly, this study evaluates the functions of social enterprises and their aims and objectives; and, thirdly, it identifies the shift of social enterprises towards hybrid organizations to achieve both social and economic objectives. The study concludes with a discussion on how ethical challenges impact organizations' performance and sustainability. The results have implications for future research on social entrepreneurship and hybrid organizations.

implementing a specific policy direction indicates the entrepreneurial ecosystem stage covered by each region. Results highlight measures employed at different stages of the entrepreneurial ecosystem - nascent, strengthening, and resilient - and identify three policy directions: recovery, reinforcing, and shooting.

Preface

Entrepreneurs, the driving force behind innovation and economic growth, possess a unique blend of vision, resourcefulness, and courage. In the ever-evolving landscape of modern business, where change is constant and technology reigns supreme, the role of entrepreneurs becomes increasingly pivotal. Governments across the globe have recognized this fact and are actively fostering environments conducive to entrepreneurship, particularly by nurturing small and medium-sized enterprises (SMEs). However, the path to entrepreneurial success is not without its hurdles, including the perennial challenges of securing working capital and navigating the complexities of marketing in a digital age.

Entrepreneurship, as a discipline, defies easy definition and teaching. It encompasses a medley of skills, attitudes, and knowledge that can be cultivated and honed over time. In this reference book, we delve into the multifaceted concept of Entrepreneurship Ecosystems, exploring the intricate web of factors that interplay to foster a sustainable entrepreneurial environment in countries around the world.

Our mission in compiling this book is twofold: first, to equip individuals with the mindset and tools necessary to embark on entrepreneurial journeys, and second, to serve as a valuable resource for a diverse audience. Whether you are a dedicated researcher seeking the latest insights, a student eager to expand your knowledge, a seasoned professional seeking fresh perspectives, or a decision-maker charting the course for your organization, you will find valuable insights within these pages.

This comprehensive reference work covers a wide range of topics, including:

- Social business and women entrepreneurship development.
- The impact of environmental factors on entrepreneurship development.
- Strategies for entrepreneurship development and the growth of enterprises.
- The role of entrepreneurship in the era of economic globalization.
- Harnessing green tourism for rural entrepreneurship development.
- The intersection of social entrepreneurship and sustainable development.
- Competencies required for entrepreneurial leadership.

- The crucial link between entrepreneurship education and economic development.
- Navigating the unique challenges faced by family firms in the entrepreneurial landscape.
- The intricate relationship between entrepreneurship, management, and sustainable development.
- A deep dive into entrepreneurship ecosystems, their dynamics, and impact.
- Exploring the challenges encountered by silent minority entrepreneurs.
- Ethical dilemmas and ethical challenges confronted by social enterprises in their quest for societal betterment.

Our goal is to provide you with a holistic understanding of the intricate world of entrepreneurship ecosystems and their pivotal role in shaping our global economic landscape. We hope this book serves as a beacon of knowledge and inspiration, guiding you through the ever-evolving terrain of entrepreneurship.

As editors, we extend our gratitude to the contributors who have shared their expertise and insights, making this book a reality. We invite you to embark on this intellectual journey with us, as we explore the opportunities and challenges that define the fascinating world of entrepreneurship ecosystems.

CHAPTER OVERVIEW

Chapter 1: Entrepreneurship [Enterprise] Financial Stability

In the wake of the COVID-19 pandemic, the importance of financial stability for entrepreneurs and enterprises has taken center stage. Chapter 1 introduces the concept of enterprise financial stability, using the CAMELS framework as a foundation. It explores the shifting landscape of financial stability, particularly in the face of disruptions caused by global, regional, national, or industry-specific shocks. The chapter not only defines the concept but also provides strategic insights on how enterprises can maintain their financial stability amidst these challenges.

Chapter 2: Consumers' Perception of the Innovation Capacity - The Role of the Services at SMEs

Chapter 2 dives into the unique perspective of consumers, examining how Small and Medium-sized Businesses (SMEs) perceive their own innovation capacity. This chapter addresses a gap in the literature by shedding light on this critical aspect. Through quantitative analysis and surveys, it explores how customers perceive innovation in the services sector, considering sociodemographic factors, types of innovation, and the impact of marketing innovation. The chapter reveals how various factors influence the ability of SMEs to innovate and how these perceptions can shape competitive advantages.

Chapter 3: Conditional Mediation of Entrepreneurial Self-Efficacy and Global Mindset in International Individual Entrepreneurial Intention of SME's Entrepreneurs

Chapter 3 delves into the international entrepreneurial intentions of small and medium-sized enterprises (SMEs) in Brazil. Using data from 794 entrepreneurs, the chapter examines the conditional mediation of global mindset and entrepreneurial self-efficacy in this context. It explores how these factors impact the international entrepreneurial orientation of SMEs. The findings suggest intriguing possibilities for future research and implications for those aspiring to become international entrepreneurs.

Chapter 4: Examining Technical Undergraduates' Entrepreneurial Attitude as Mediator between Entrepreneurial Characteristics and Self-Employment Intention Authors: Pushkar Dubey, Kailash Kumar Sahu, Parul Dube

Chapter 4 investigates the role of entrepreneurial attitude in mediating the relationship between entrepreneurial characteristics and self-employment intention among technical undergraduates in Chhattisgarh, India. Through rigorous analysis, this chapter uncovers the complex interplay of factors that influence the decision to pursue self-employment among engineering undergraduates. It offers valuable insights for policymakers and educational institutions seeking to nurture entrepreneurship in emerging economies.

Chapter 5: The Impact of Geographical and Cultural Factors on Ethical Issues and Dilemmas: An Investigation from Social Enterprises

Chapter 5 explores the ethical challenges faced by social enterprises, with a specific focus on how geographical and cultural factors influence these dilemmas. This theoretical chapter delves into the organizational theory, objectives of social enterprises, and their shift towards hybrid models. It underscores the importance of ethical considerations for organizational performance and sustainability, making it a valuable resource for those interested in social entrepreneurship and hybrid organizations.

Chapter 6: Policy Implications from a Selected Countries for Sustainable Future of the Society Through Green Entrepreneurship and Economic Development

Chapter 6 presents a critical analysis of green entrepreneurship's potential to contribute to a sustainable future for society. The authors introduce the Green Entrepreneurship Index (GEI) as a means of measuring progress in green entrepreneurship across 34 selected countries. They explore the causal relationship between green entrepreneurship and economic development, offering policy proposals to foster green growth and a sustainable future.

Chapter 7: Entrepreneurial Alertness in the perusal of New Venture Creation

Chapter 7 provides a roadmap for aspiring entrepreneurs by examining the role of entrepreneurial alertness in new venture creation. This research paper explores the serial mediation of opportunity creation, opportunity discovery, and entrepreneurial recognition in the context of entrepreneurship theory. With data collected from 575 respondents across South Asia and South Europe, this chapter sheds light on the key factors that influence the entrepreneurial journey.

Chapter 8: Concept of Microenterprises' Supply Chain Management and Active Flexibility of Micro-Organizations in Bangladesh.

Chapter 8 delves into the importance of supply chain management and dynamic flexibility for micro-organizations in Bangladesh. It assesses the current state of supply chain management and highlights areas for improvement. The chapter emphasizes the need for collaboration between the public and private sectors to enhance supply chain efficiency, ultimately contributing to economic development and sustainability.

Chapter 9: How Policies Foster Regional Development: An Italian Entrepreneurial Ecosystem Analysis

Chapter 9 explores the impact of policies on the evolution of regional entrepreneurial ecosystems, with a focus on three Italian regions: Lombardy, Campania, and Calabria. This chapter fills a gap in the literature by analyzing the role of policies in shaping entrepreneurial ecosystems at different stages of development. It identifies policy directions and their implications for regional development, offering valuable insights for policymakers and researchers.

IN SUMMARY

As we conclude this comprehensive reference book *Entrepreneurship Ecosystems and Their Opportunities and Challenges,* we reflect on the diverse and dynamic landscape of entrepreneurship explored within its pages. The chapters within this book have illuminated key aspects of entrepreneurship, offering fresh insights, empirical findings, and theoretical perspectives that contribute to our collective understanding of this vital field.

From the foundational discussions on enterprise financial stability in Chapter 1 to the innovative exploration of play-based approaches for Arab family businesses in Chapter 10, each chapter represents a unique facet of entrepreneurship's multifaceted landscape. We've journeyed through the lenses of consumers, researchers, entrepreneurs, and policymakers, gaining valuable perspectives on the challenges and opportunities that shape the entrepreneurial ecosystem.

This reference book not only reinforces the importance of entrepreneurship in driving economic growth, social change, and innovation but also highlights the critical role of factors like financial stability, innovation capacity, self-efficacy, and ethical considerations in shaping the entrepreneurial journey. The exploration of policies, regional dynamics, and cultural influences adds depth to our understanding of entrepreneurship ecosystems' complexities.

The diverse topics covered in this book serve as a testament to the breadth of entrepreneurship research and practice, offering a wealth of knowledge to researchers, students, professionals, and policymakers alike. Whether you seek to enhance your entrepreneurial mindset, delve into cutting-edge research, or formulate policies for sustainable economic development, this book is a valuable resource.

As editors, our hope is that this book inspires continued exploration, innovation, and collaboration in the field of entrepreneurship. We encourage readers to engage with the chapters, sparking conversations, and generating new ideas that will contribute to the ever-evolving entrepreneurial landscape.

In closing, we extend our heartfelt gratitude to the authors who generously shared their expertise and insights, making this book possible. We also thank the readers for embarking on this intellectual journey with us. May the knowledge and perspectives presented within these pages serve as a beacon, guiding us toward a future filled with entrepreneurial opportunities, growth, and positive change.

Warm regards,
Mohammed El Amine Abdelli
Shajara Ul-Durar
Hala Wasef Hattab
Editors

Section 1
Entrepreneurial Ecosystem Factors

Chapter 1
Entrepreneurship (Enterprise) Financial Stability

Ayansola Olatunji Ayandibu
https://orcid.org/0000-0001-5870-2388
University of Zululand, South Africa

Samuel Olutuase
https://orcid.org/0000-0002-3110-4449
Leicester Castle Business School, De Montfort University, Leicester, UK

ABSTRACT

The pursuit of financial stability as a goal for entrepreneurs/enterprises is no more underscored than the shocks created by the COVID-19 pandemic. Up till the end of 2019, more attention to measuring and strategizing for financial stability has been largely limited to the national economy and the financial sector. However, the COVID-19 impacts which include forcing a large number of enterprises out of the market necessitates a focus on enterprise financial stability. This chapter adopts the CAMELS framework to explain the concept of enterprise financial stability. It further expatiated the concept from the perspectives of shocks arising from global, regional, national or industry disruptions. The chapter concludes with cornerstones for strategising and maintaining an enterprise's financial stability in the event of disruptions.

"True stability results when presumed order and presumed disorder are balanced. A truly stable system expects the unexpected, is prepared to be disrupted, waits to be transformed." —Tom Robbins

DOI: 10.4018/978-1-6684-7140-1.ch001

1. INTRODUCTION

The aftermath of the global financial crisis is a renewed interest in financial stability that is elevated as a goal for an economy or enterprise (Yağcı, 2017). The global financial crisis, like the global pandemic (i.e., COVID-19), is "the unexpected" or "presumed disorder" spoken of by Tom Robbins. It, therefore, follows that the unexpected or presumed disorder *disrupts* established patterns, expectations and other status quo in a financial system, and the results can either be a significant change or collapse in the system. This truism applies to either the national, international or regional economy, and of course, to an enterprise of whatever scale. Concerning actual or presumed disruptions and their impact on the stability of a financial system, literature has focused attention on how to maintain or at least, regain financial stability in the event of adverse situations. Much of this attention has been on financial stability either in the banking system (Slater, 2020), financial markets (Gadanecz & Jayaram, 2009), or financial assets. Owing to the established nexus between the stability of an economy's financial system and micro-units such as individual firms and households, (Babajide et al., 2020), it becomes imperative to direct more attention to the enterprise [entrepreneurship] financial stability. This is more imperative given that enterprises, either micro, small or medium, are critical actors in creating wealth (Small Enterprise Development Agency (SEDA), 2016), catalysing economic growth (Wennekers & Thurik, 1999) and in turn, providing some sort of internal stability to a national or regional economy. The changing dynamics and emerging realities posed by the COVID-19 pandemic (Slater, 2020) especially necessitate renewed attention to enterprise financial stability.

2. UNDERSTANDING FINANCIAL STABILITY: MACRO AND MICRO-LEVEL PERSPECTIVES

Though the concept of financial stability is ubiquitous, it lacks a universally accepted definition. This is partly because financial stability is multi-faceted. For instance, at the macro-level (which may be national, regional or global), financial stability is viewed as a critical mechanism for maintaining price stability and assuring smooth and healthy development of the economy. This mechanism is underscored by the fact that high price volatility within the financial system accounts for variability in economic resource allocation which in turn stifles economic development and growth. Against this backdrop Schinasi (2004) as cited in Babajide et al (2020) conceives financial stability as "the strength of the financial system to enable resource allocation that leads to wealth transfer and economic prosperity of individuals and the state". The idea of "strength" in this definition, implies efficiency in managing well-articulated financial risks (what Robbins called presumed disorder) arising from incidence of external (and not to undermine the internal) shocks and volatility. This picture of financial stability is well corroborated by other definitions given by Korepanov et al (2020); Ozili (2019); and Savchina et al (2019). However, Schinasi (2004)'s definition of financial stability does not only imply efficiently managing financial risks within the economy. The definition also entails enhancing the flexibility and resilience of an economy to absorb some internal socio-economic disparities which may develop into economic threats thereby, causing some disruptions in the system. These two implications form the bedrock for financial stability goal at the macro level – smoothly facilitating economic activities, while dealing with imbalances arising from internal or external disruptions.

At the micro-level, financial stability can be viewed differently for obvious reasons. One, the specific issues hitherto not looked at, come into focus about individuals and firms. Two, the behaviour of these micro-units in response to the financial system disruptions also becomes a matter of interest, not only to the individual investors, and entrepreneurs but also to financial and economic experts, as well as policymakers. In the traditional financial stability literature, significant attention is focused on financial institutions, markets, infrastructure, assets, and investors. Institutional and financial theories would normally form the bedrock of such intellectual discourse. In this chapter, however, it is pertinent to state at this juncture that the focus is not on financial institutions' stability or the financial stability of corporate organisations. Our focus is on the financial stability of the entrepreneur and/or the enterprise they run.

3. HOW COVID-19 IS RE-SHAPING ENTREPRENEURIAL [ENTERPRISE] FINANCIAL STABILITY

It is no doubt that the COVID-19 pandemic has reshaped almost everything, including financial stability at the level of entrepreneurship. To define entrepreneurial or enterprise financial stability (EFS), it is pertinent to articulate some of the disruptions entrepreneurs/enterprises have been exposed to, due to COVID-19. The global COVID-19 pandemic has not only disrupted the lives and activities of billions of people, households, and of course, entrepreneurs, but it has also caused imbalances in the global economy. According to a report by OECD (2020), the financial crisis experienced globally during and after the COVID-19 pandemic exceeds the impact of the 2008 Global Financial Crisis by 60%. As forecasted by the International Monetary Fund (IMF), and the (World Bank, 2020) the global economic recession that followed is about the worst in the last since the 1950s (Congressional Research Service, 2021). As the lockdowns set in, economies and enterprises closed shops

(Belitski et al., 2021; Taghizadeh-hesary et al., 2021). The immediate effects were financial market volatility, rising insecurity, increase in unemployment, significant income disruptions for individuals, firms and governments, hike in prices, etc. (Belitski et al., 2021; OECD, 2020). As a result, enterprises (especially entrepreneurs), lost productivity, revenues, and financial liquidity (UNDP & NBS, 2021), especially in worst-hit countries (World Bank, 2020). On the part of entrepreneurs (and their enterprises), the immediate response for survival was to lay off employees to cut redundancy costs. This notwithstanding, more entrepreneurs lost their enterprises around the world. The impact of the COVID-19 pandemic severely undermined the development of sustainable enterprises. Besides, the disruptions created by the pandemic have also made some surviving entrepreneurial ventures scale down or suspend certain operations (Lambert et al., 2020; Slater, 2020).

Before the COVID-19 crisis, entrepreneurs around the world had grappled with varied challenges. A significant portion of these challenges revolved around access to, cost and utilisation of finance needed for sustaining entrepreneurial undertakings. It is no doubt that the shocks and disruptions arising from the COVID-19 crises would exacerbate financial challenges for entrepreneurs. This is because typically they have limited cash reserves, smaller client bases, and less capacity to manage commercial pressures than do larger companies (FSB, 2020).

4. CAMELS: A FRAMEWORK FOR UNDERSTANDING ENTERPRISE FINANCIAL STABILITY

Before we attempt framing a working definition of EFS for this chapter, it is imperative to consider a financial stability framework that can guide our thinking on EFS. In 2006, the International Monetary Fund (2006) published a guide on financial soundness indicators (FSIs). The guide explains the methodological tools that can be used to measure the soundness and weakness of a financial system. This financial soundness framework called CAMELS is built on the pillars of capital adequacy, asset quality, earnings, management soundness, earnings and profitability, liquidity, and sensitivity to market risk. A fundamental question is, how do these apply to the entrepreneur or the enterprise?

4.1. Capital Adequacy

Based on the CAMELS framework compiled by the International Monetary Fund (2006), we adopted capital adequacy to mean having sufficient capital to survive disruptive shocks arising from presumed order and disorder. As originally formulated in the Basel capital adequacy ratio, this measure of financial stability of an enterprise or entrepreneur is benchmarked against the weighted amount of risks associated with the enterprise or its operations. Specifically, capital adequacy is concerned with an enterprise's maintaining a minimum level of resources or at least, being able to access resources required to (a) quickly respond to financial shocks, (b) strength to endure the shocks for the time being until the firm/entrepreneur regains balance. Just as capital adequacy is not even across countries, so it varies amongst entrepreneurs/enterprises. This variability may arise from the differences in risk and assets valuation, size, and possibly, quality of assets.

4.2. Asset Quality

From the perspective of commercial banks, nonperforming loans are regarded as the best measures of asset quality concerning financial soundness estimation (International Monetary Fund, 2006). Generally, loans are assets to banks as they generate returns on them in form of interests charged. When borrowers fail to pay overdue amortisation for an extended period, the rules have it that such loans be declared nonperforming. Thus, reducing the total value of assets held as loans. While the International Monetary Fund (2006) framework estimates asset quality by comparing nonperforming loans with the total loans, we think of assets quality in terms of an entrepreneur's value-yielding investment moves, choices and strategies. That is, what is the estimation of yield on entrepreneurial decisions considered to be of good quality? How realistic is the expected yield from these decisions, and what proportion would be retained in case of exposure to unexpected shocks?

4.3. Management Soundness

A common phrase amongst financial experts is "the entrepreneur is responsible for the finance of their enterprise". This statement implies that the financial success or otherwise of an enterprise depends on the soundness of the entrepreneur's financial decisions – sourcing, allocating and utilising finances and other related issues. Therefore, the skills and competence to effectively drive financial management – accounts and finance – of an enterprise determines the level of success in "good times", but also its stability in both adverse situations.

4.4. Earnings and Profitability

More explicitly, we take earnings and profitability to mean how much revenue an entrepreneur or enterprise can generate over time, and what proportion of it – *minus* sales and operating expenses, including all short-term obligations – represents profit margin. Entrepreneur or enterprise's earnings and profitability could cushion the effects of financial shocks and disruptions, if well managed. However, being able to earn a profit margin or prevent loss of profit that could serve as internal resilience to withstand external shocks is of utmost importance when measuring enterprise financial stability.

4.5. Liquidity

Measurement of liquidity differs with firm types and markets. Nonetheless, liquidity essentially means the same thing irrespective of the firm type or situation – availability of cash to meet expected "order", and unexpected "disorder". The ability to withstand financial shocks is directly linked to the entrepreneur or enterprise's level of liquidity (International Monetary Fund, 2006). A critical point of interest here should, however, be how much imbalance an entrepreneur or enterprise could absorb ere being forced to liquidate other assets.

4.6. Sensitivity to Market Risk

More than often, systemic disorders trigger certain structural dynamics in markets, which in turn make some entrepreneurs/enterprises more susceptible, and less resilient, to external shocks. On the other hand, the changing dynamics make some other entrepreneurs/enterprises stronger. Sensitivity to market risks here intended to mean the ability of an entrepreneur/enterprise is absorb operational, financial, technical and/or economic risks arising from (a) sharp and unexpected fall in demand, (b) rising cost of doing business, (c) increasing cost of capital and associated elements such as ease to accessing funds, etc., (d) quick paradigm shift in regulatory framework forced by adverse circumstances, and (e) effects of the shocks from the financial/capital markets.

5. ENTREPRENEURSHIP (ENTERPRISE) FINANCIAL STABILITY

The CAMELS framework aptly provides a template to conceptualise entrepreneurship/entrepreneurial or enterprise financial stability. We consider this framework suitable in that it overcomes a major limitation of the z-score methodology of estimating an enterprise's financial stability. From the foregoing, therefore, we define *entrepreneurship (enterprise) financial stability as a set of conditions in which an entrepreneur/enterprise possesses the capacity to deploy some strategic internal resources, and/or leverage on external resources to maintain a fairly financial balance for a considerable time without external interventions, in the event of disruptive shocks arising from international, regional, national or industry disorders.* There are four facts we will like to articulate from this definition.

1. EFS is not limited to having enough cash (money) to meet necessary obligations when due, as some definitions insinuated. This is why we use the term "resources" to mean that financial stability goes way beyond having cash. So, by "resources", we mean, having both cash and flexible arrangements around an entrepreneur/enterprise's financial obligations. For instance, the ability to negotiate a longer credit period gives an entrepreneur/enterprise the flexibility to meet more pressing financial obligations, thereby relieving the pressures that exacerbate financial instability.
2. True estimation of an enterprise's financial stability can only be done from a 360 degrees perspective. That is why our definition, like others, acknowledges the impact of external and industrial environments, including some unexpected adverse situations like the COVID-19 pandemic, and the like.
3. The term "disorder" encompasses both systematic and unsystematic disruptions; adverse external situations and some internal situations that could impact the enterprise's stability. This means, our definition of EFS is not only relevant in adverse external situations but also when there are internal crises that could potentially induce financial instability.
4. Without relapsing into a form of "intellectual delusion", by our definition of EFS, we assert that an entrepreneur/enterprise's financial stability – without some "external" interventions – has an elastic limit. This means the ability to maintain financial stability is limited for a period, beyond which the enterprise/entrepreneur could be thrown into instability except for some "external interventions" are introduced. In this regard, external interventions, imply variables, policies, and intermediation, that do not account for the financial stability exhibited hitherto.

The absence of EFS exposes an entrepreneur or their fledgling enterprise to the risk of momentary business shrinkage, or outright failure. In the aggregate, this sort of situation, in turn, impacts the national economic stability (International Monetary Fund, 2006), because entrepreneurship (and/or SMEs) is critical to economic growth and development (citations).

Figure 1. Contextual framework for defining enterprise financial stability

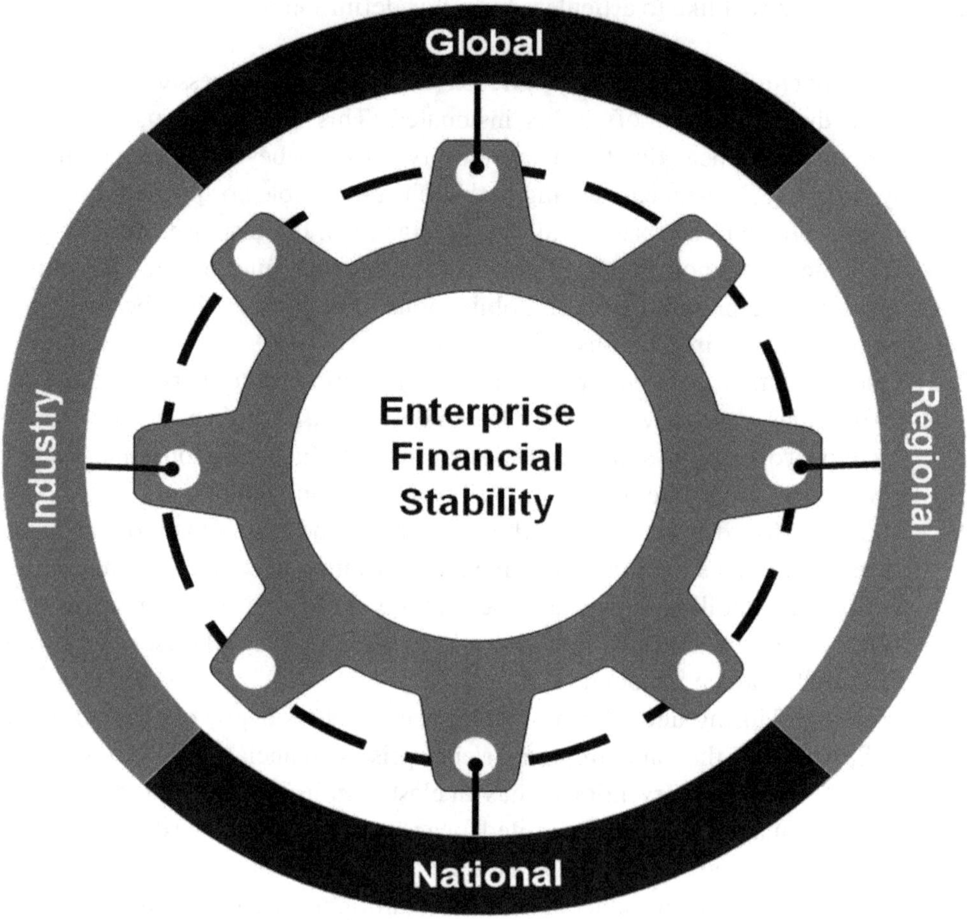

6. BUILDING AND MAINTAINING ENTERPRISE FINANCIAL STABILITY

A financially stable enterprise or entrepreneur can boast of having diverse resources readily available to ensure less or no disruptive impact on business, in the event of any disorders. In other words, EFS guarantees the ability to pay enterprise debt, operating expenses and other financial obligations to the government and its agencies, investors and other creditors. This is imperative for continued and smooth business operations, to assure business growth and profitability. This imperative, therefore, demands that available entrepreneurial or enterprise "resources" are strategically managed.

By standards, the cash flow statement, balance sheet and income statement are the financial documents that typically reflect the financial stability of an enterprise. However, there are other resources to help strengthen an enterprise's financial stability. An example is the goodwill/reputation of the entrepreneur or enterprise. For instance, the name Aliko Dangote (the wealthiest person in Africa and 73rd in the world, with an estimated net worth of US$14 billion as of March 2022) represents a strong brand. The reputation of the name Dangote, or any of his companies gives some sort of additional stability to the financial standing any business documents represent.

Building enterprise financial stability is essentially developing some financial capabilities which will require the following strategies.

6.1. Comprehensive Cash Flow Forecasting and Management Model

The fact that cash flow problems are a strong predictor of business distress, failure (Bertrand & Parnaudeau, 2019), and of course, financial instability, it, therefore, becomes critical for an entrepreneur or enterprise to identify future funding gaps and which aspects of the business process would be most impacted if not adequately addressed. Identifying funding gaps would require estimating income and expenses based on reliable, accurate and comprehensive data extracted both internally and externally. With this, a strategic entrepreneur would reliably forecast future cash needs. While setting up models for forecasting future cash needs, it is essential to incorporate all possible exogenous shocks that may arise from global financial crises, natural disasters, acts of terrorism, cybercrimes, conflicts (of all sorts – national, ethnoreligious, political, etc.), and pandemics (Isabelle et al., 2022). Incorporating these exogenous factors, which may be global, regional or national in scope, would enable the enterprise to reliably predict changes in consumption patterns, inflation rates, and government policies, and specifically determine how these could impact cash supply. All these would improve cash flow management which primarily aims at avoiding cash shortages while identifying strategically viable investment options for surplus funds.

6.2. Adaptive Billing Strategies

Maintaining financial stability for an enterprise is not the same in both "normal" and adverse times. One critical difference in this regard is customers' ability to pay bills when due, especially when exogenous shocks spread across the national, regional or global economic landscape. Customers' ability to pay bills is critical to financial stability. The business model, therefore, must that flexible enough to adapt efficient billing strategies that could assure EFS whether in normal or adverse times. For instance, as a result of the COVID-19 impact, a customer may not be able to pay overdue bills. This has a direct effect on the enterprise in terms of cash inflow. So, aligning invoicing timing and payment terms with the payment pattern of clients may be beneficial at such times.

6.3. Rewardable Customer Relationships

Customer relationships are not only important to business survival but also important for maintaining financial stability. Rewardable customer relationship entails maintaining customer relationships that deliver maximum value to both the clients and the enterprise. First, rewardable customer relationships enable the enterprise to drive maximum patronage which in turn delivers maximum sales revenue (Twum et al., 2022). Second, rewardable customer relationships enable the enterprise to build a unique brand that is more likely to easily survive adverse situations, than others. Third, rewardable customer relationships afford an enterprise to leverage such relationships to explore more valuable customers in their networks

To build rewardable customer relationships, an enterprise or entrepreneur should do the following. One, there must be a focus on customers' needs in two ways. By focusing on the customers, the enterprise must analyse current customers' needs to determine gaps in service or quality delivery. In addition, the focus must anticipate future needs. Two, the enterprise must maint close contact with customers through innovative ways to achieve the growing knowledge of customers' needs. Three, the enterprise must be transparent in data management, service delivery and in relating with customers. Rewardable customers relationships could increase value for an enterprise thereby, increasing its financial stability.

6.4. Effective Debt and Working Capital Management

Debts and working capital offer a strong basis for strategizing for financial stability. The loan is a source of finance that requires servicing. Sometimes debt servicing could impact available cash for operational purposes. When exogenous shocks cause some fluctuations in interest rates, enterprise/entrepreneur can leverage this for appropriate debt refinancing options that improve financial stability position.

In addition, enterprise/entrepreneur can (leveraging on goodwill) renegotiate some credit and payment terms with suppliers to allow for greater payment flexibility. The ease in repaying loans or credits will in turn improve the enterprise's available working capital to maintain financial stability. It should, however, be noted that overly focusing on working capital and debt management could lead an entrepreneur/enterprise to neglect market expansion opportunities. An enterprise should therefore strike to maintain a good balance between increasing market shares and focusing on debt and working capital management, as both are crucial to financial stability.

6.5. Simulate Enterprise Behaviour

One other way to strategise for financial stability ahead of presumed disorder is to simulate the enterprise behaviour in the event of firm-level, industry or national disorder. Simulation helps the enterprise to utilise appropriate management techniques such as cost optimization, inventory optimisation, and liquidity management. This will provide significant benefits to the enterprises in the long run, whether such presumed disorder occurred or not. To do this, enterprises could employ the services of professionals, where they can afford them. Otherwise, the onus lies on the entrepreneur to learn through self-development, and appropriately deploy these techniques in the most efficient manner possible.

6.6. Leverage "Unsystematic Opportunities"

In the event of unsystematic disorder, an enterprise can seek to take advantage of government grants/support, where such exist. In many counties, governments set up agencies that offer grants and intervention funds to entrepreneurs or enterprises for specific sets of objectives. This represents a unique unsystematic opportunity for an enterprise or entrepreneur to (a) find how their business aligns with these objectives; (b) maintain a linkage for exploiting these opportunities, and (c) effectively utilise the funds for stability and expansion when accessed.

6.7. Strategic Planning for Exploiting Growth Opportunities

Financial stability is not only tested under adverse situations but also when there exist market opportunities for growth, and an enterprise is unable to exploit them. With comprehensive cash forecasting and management, an entrepreneur or enterprise could readily access funds set aside. These funds can be utilised to exploit new growth/diversification opportunities without affecting the adequacy of working capital needed to fund existing business activities. With this, an entrepreneur can quickly scale up their enterprise's operation and ability to earn more, attract and retain highly valued customers and increase profitability. All these will, in turn, improve overall financial stability.

7. CONCLUSION

Finance is an important part of every enterprise. Accessing and allocating funds towards building and maintaining financial stability, and overall business success is a challenge both in "normal" and "adverse" situations. This is the crux of any enterprise's financial management with the business owner (entrepreneur) playing a crucial role. This role is not limited to just ensuring that the enterprise generates revenues, because unpredictable shocks that may occur at the firm, industry or economy level can potentially erode all the income. For instance, the unexpected outbreak of the COVID pandemic eroded many enterprises' revenues and subsequently forced a significant number out of business. Some surviving enterprises are yet to fully recover from the financial instability they had to grapple with. This, therefore, necessitates the pursuit of financial stability as a business goal. Periodically, the entrepreneur should assess the financial health of their enterprises by analysing the enterprise's cash flows and simulating enterprise stability to survive in the event of global, regional or national shocks. The adapted CAMELS framework explains how an enterprise can evolve strategies for building and maintaining sustainable finance. Through CAMELS-based strategies, an entrepreneur can reliably create a picture of potential shocks (financial liabilities) that could occur in a foreseeable future and effectively prepare to deal with them as they arise. Enterprise financial stability thus assures efficient use of available resources towards a longer and more profitable stay in business.

REFERENCES

Babajide, A., Lawal, A., Asaleye, A., Okafor, T., & Osuma, G. (2020). Financial stability and entrepreneurship development in sub-Sahara Africa: Implications for sustainable development goals. *Cogent Social Sciences*, *6*(1), 1798330. doi:10.1080/23311886.2020.1798330

Belitski, M., Guenther, C., Kritikos, A. S., & Thurik, R. (2021). *Economic effects of the COVID-19 pandemic on entrepreneurship and small businesses* (Issue 14630).

Bertrand, J. L., & Parnaudeau, M. (2019). Understanding the economic effects of abnormal weather to mitigate the risk of business failures. *Journal of Business Research*, *98*, 391–402. doi:10.1016/j.jbusres.2017.09.016

Congressional Research Service. (2021). *Global economic effects of COVID-19*. CRS.

FSB. (2020). *COVID-19 Pandemic: Financial stability implications and policy measures taken*. Issue July.

Gadanecz, B., & Jayaram, K. (2009). Measures of financial stability – a review. Irving Fisher Committee (IFC) - Bank for International Settlements.

International Monetary Fund. (2006). *Financial soundness indicators: Compilation guide*. International Monetary Fund.

Isabelle, D. A., Han, Y., & Westerlund, M. (2022). A machine-learning analysis on the impacts of the COVID-19 pandemic on small business owners and implications from Canadian government policy response. *Canadian Public Policy*, *48*(2), 1–50. doi:10.3138/cpp.2021-018 PMID:36039356

Korepanov, G., Yatskevych, I., Popova, O., Shevtsiv, L., Marych, M., & Purtskhvanidze, O. (2020). Managing the financial stability potential of crisis enterprises. *International Journal of Advanced Research in Engineering and Technology*, *11*(4), 359–371.

Lambert, D., Mccann, F., Mcquinn, J., Myers, S., Yao, F., Lambert, D., Mccann, F., Mcquinn, J., Myers, S., & Yao, F. (2020). *SME finances, the pandemic, and the design of enterprise support policies enterprise support policies*.

OECD. (2020). *The impact of the coronavirus (COVID-19) crisis on development finance*. Issue June.

Ozili, P. K. (2019). *Financial stability: Does social activism matter? 92192*.

Savchina, O., Bratanov, A., Savchina, O., & Shcherbachenko, P. (2019). Assessment of financial stability and business expansion of JSC Statoil in the context of economic instability. *Journal of Advanced Research in Law and Economics*, *10*(6), 1929–1938. doi:10.14505/jarle.v10.6(44).35

Schinasi, G. J. (2004). Defining Financial Stability. *IMF Working Paper*, *04*(187), 1. doi:10.5089/9781451859546.001

Slater, A. (2020). Coronavirus fallout threatens financial stability. *Economic Outlook*, *44*(2), 26–28. doi:10.1111/1468-0319.12481

Small Enterprise Development Agency (SEDA). (2016). *The small, medium and micro-enterprise sector of South Africa*. SEDA.

Taghizadeh-hesary, F., Phoumin, H., & Rasoulinezhad, E. (2021). *COVID-19 and regional solutions for mitigating the risk of small and medium-sized enterprise finance in ASEAN member states* (Issue 399).

Twum, K. K., Kosiba, J. P. B., Hinson, R. E., Gabrah, A. Y. B., & Assabil, E. N. (2022). Determining mobile money service customer satisfaction and continuance usage through service quality. *Journal of Financial Services Marketing, 945*(2021), 1–13. doi:10.1057/s41264-021-00138-5

UNDP, & NBS. (2021). *The Impact of COVID-19 on Business Enterprises in Nigeria*. UNDP & NBS.

Wennekers, S., & Thurik, R. (1999). Linking Entrepreneurship and Economic Growth. *Small Business Economics, 13*(1), 27–56. doi:10.1023/A:1008063200484

World Bank. (2020). *COVID-19 to Plunge Global Economy into Worst Recession since World War II*. The World Bank. https://www.worldbank.org/en/news/press-release/2020/06/08/covid-19-to-plunge-global-economy-into-worst-recession-since-world-war-ii

Yağcı, M. (2017). Institutional entrepreneurship and organisational learning: Financial stability policy design in Turkey. *Policy and Society, 36*(4), 539–555. doi:10.1080/14494035.2017.1369616

Chapter 2
Consumers' Perceptions of Innovation Capacity:
The Role of the Services at SMEs

Miguel Martins
ISAG – European Business School and Research Center in Business Sciences and Tourism (CICET-FCVC), Portugal

Ana Pinto Borges
https://orcid.org/0000-0002-4942-079X
ISAG – European Business School and Research Center in Business Sciences and Tourism (CICET-FCVC), Portugal

Elvira Vieira
https://orcid.org/0000-0002-9296-3896
ISAG – European Business School and Research Center in Business Sciences and Tourism (CICET-FCVC), Portugal

ABSTRACT

From the viewpoint of consumers, we assess how well Small and Medium-sized Businesses (SME) perceive their ability for innovation. This work seeks to close the gap in the literature caused by the lack of previous analysis of this topic. A questionnaire survey was utilized for the purposes of quantitative analysis. We performed principal component and confirmation analysis and a logistic regression. It was discovered that customers' perceptions of innovation in the services sectors vary depending on sociodemographic traits, the type of innovation, and the applicability of marketing innovation. Positive impacts were shown to be produced via organisational, marketing, cultural, and process innovation structures. The ability to innovate is influenced

DOI: 10.4018/978-1-6684-7140-1.ch002

by six factors: product, organisational, process, marketing, culture, and resources. Because customers and enterprises have a closer relationship, this strategy is appealing. The results will help some brands reflect on their positioning to show competitive advantages. Customers participated with their perception.

1. INTRODUCTION

Innovation has always existed in human thinking and these innovative thoughts have contributed to the development of the Earth. Currently the world is going through accelerated changes and for growth and sustainability it's increasingly important to invest in innovation.

For a long time, companies have worked with very closed systems in which there was a great deal of separation between the external environment and the internal environment. The focus was always on internal effectiveness and efficiency, leaving aside the interest in customer satisfaction. But at the end of the 20th century, these organizations began to be forced by society and the market to adopt a more open system that increases the number of processes, products and services that can be innovated.

According to Ramos and Zilber (2015), the market environment defines success for companies through the selective process, in which the companies that survive are those that can adapt to new market conditions.

Inevitably, technological evolution is associated with business innovation, but often a company's innovation is also directly linked to it's organizational structure and culture.

To support the challenge of continuous innovation, companies need to have a strategic posture directed toward investments in improving their ability to produce new knowledge. These investments can be in creating products, building new production processes, improving organizational structures and using new marketing designs (Ramos and Zilber, 2015).

According to Saunila (2020), research on innovation capabilities, generally ignores the situation of small businesses, so the need arises to redefine "innovation capacity" and identify their resources.

According to the European Commission (EC) (2015), Small and Medium Enterprises (SMEs) "represent the majority of businesses in the European Union and play an essential role in the economy, being crucial to foster competitiveness and employment." and in order to support and grow these companies EC try to help through financing programs.

The State should also intervene to help SMEs, since in Portugal the percentage of this type of company is around 99.9% and employ 78% of the active population, which is higher than the average in the European Union (respectively 99.8% and 64%).

Most SMEs in Portugal do not combine their innovation strategy with organizational strategy and some have no innovation plan at all. There are gaps in the strategy and resources of SMEs. With process strategy, the gap is relative to "the unevenness of direction between strategy formulation and implementation." (Schreiber, 2012). Regarding resources, according to McCartney (2020), the gap is that of funding, where only a small portion of capital investment can be used for innovation. This greatly affects and hinders the development of innovation capacity, which as a result demeans the competitive advantage and growth of the company.

In this sense, it's relevant and interesting to study from the consumers' perspective because consumers are increasingly making a major contribution to the success or failure of organizations.

It's the first time that this approch is presented directly to SME's innovation and this provides an opportunity for the consumers' participation, which could allow some enterprises and their brands to reflect on their positioning, in order to present competitive advantages. This study can be very useful for SMEs owner-managers, business managers and even state officials to acquire new concepts of innovation management as well as a sense of view of an external "entity".

In literature review the concept of innovation will be addressed in detail with approaches from different authors and the associated models, and studies. After that, the methodology and data collection process are described and the analysis of the results is presented. Finally, we finish the paper with the final conclusions and suggestions about future research.

2. THEORETICAL REFERENCE FRAMEWORK

Definition of Innovation

Innovation is a modification or creation of ideas, which result in useful applications with the objective of improving processes, operations and products or services. Therefore, innovation can originate from strategic alliance, R&D, internal/external development, or acquisition of new technologies (Cunha and Santos, 2005).

According to Schumpeter (2012), "Innovation is considered as a basic element for economic development". This economist and political scientist became known as the "father of innovation" because he introduced to the world a broader point of view, arguing that innovation also covers new production inputs, new management practices and new markets. This perspective goes beyond the concept of innovation that only involved processes and products.

There are several types of innovation, which have been identified by various authors. If an innovation has been introduced to the market (product innovation) or used in the production process (process innovation), the innovation is considered implemented (Ramos and Zilber, 2015).

The Organization for Economic Cooperation and Development (OECD) has also adopted two new innovation types which are marketing innovation and organizational innovation (OECD, 2012). Marketing innovation uses the marketing method by modifying products and processes (product packaging, pricing, and promotion). Organizational innovation includes the introduction of new organizational models in the organization's processes (example: external relationship or workplace).

According to Barbieri (2003) there are five factors related to innovation: creation of a new product; opening of a new market; implementation of a production method; acquisition of a new source of raw material; and establishment of a new organization for the business.

Organizational Innovation

Organizational Innovation can be divided into exploitation and exploration (Gupta et al., 2006; Jansen et al., 2006; Scandelari and Cunha, 2013).

Exploitation is an innovation related to the use of resources, processes, and strategies in incremental innovation, aiming to meet the needs and demands of customers in the current market (Benner and Tushman, 2003; Popadiuk et al., 2010). According to Jansen et al. (2006), the basis of exploitation Innovation is to be able to improve existing products and services and make frequent and small adjustments in the product portfolio to maintain and expand participation in current customers and markets.

Exploration in strategic functions, on the other hand, is related to the search for new ideas and solutions, including searching, discovery, experimentation, and adventurous organizational behavior (Ho and Lu, 2015; March, 1991). According to Jansen et al. (2006), innovation in exploration is supported by formulating strategies that will meet new demands for products and services, often reinvesting in portfolios, accepting challenges to serve new markets, developing new distribution channels and new production units and production lines to gain a competitive advantage. This innovation can develop the ability to frequently map the overall external environment to discover the factors that enhance the launch of new products and services, distinguish it from competitors, and become a leading company (Mintzberg et al., 2009; Porter, 1986).

Most Portuguese SMEs choose to follow the concept of exploitation, development, and betting on investment in new equipment and processes (such as artificial intelligence and industry 4.0), which may increase execution in the short term, but will bring certain challenges in the future.

There is useful strategies to promote organizational innovation, like the creation of internal communication tools, good working conditions, qualified human resources, self-learning environments, good organizational culture, and greater financial recognition. According to Bruhn et al. (2016) found evidence that small companies with resource constraints, are more likely in adopting organizational and strategic innovation.

Innovation Capacity

"Innovation capacity has been defined as the internal potential to generate new ideas, identify new market opportunities, and develop a marketable innovation through the firm's existing resources and skills" (Palma, 2004, p. 8). Furthermore, it reveals an important dynamic capacity to establish a competitive advantage.

According to the authors Zawislak et al. (2012) the innovative capacity can be divided by technology-driven capabilities and business-driven capabilities (Table 1).

Table 1. Model for analyzing the concept of innovation capacity

Capacity to develop Technology ↔	Operational capacity ↔ ↔	Management capacity ↔ ↔	Commercial capacity ↔
Technology-driven Capabilities		Business-driven Capabilities	

Source: Zawislak et al. (2012).

The business-driven capabilities are the "Management capacity" which is related to human resources, strategic planning, procedures, and rules and the "Commercial capacity", which involves the whole relationship with customers and suppliers including the management of contracts with these stakeholders.

Innovative companies are companies that succeed in competitive markets because they understand that innovation starts with ideas and use innovation as a source of promotion for differentiation and improved results. Their managers must overcome the tendency to administer routine to their companies and challenge solid and inflexible organizational structures (Ramos and Zilber, 2015).

Table 2 presents the various components of an innovative firm, addressing strategic, structural, personnel, the environment, and organizational learning.

Table 2. Innovative business components

Component	Key characteristics
Vision, leadership, and a willingness to innovate	- Clearly articulate, with a modern vision. - Leadership for innovation within the company. - Top management commitment leads to innovation success.
Appropriate structure	- The organization design allows for a high level of creativity. - Balance between organic and mechanistic management for particular contingencies.
Key individuals	- Promoters, champions, gatekeepers, and other roles that enhance or facilitate innovation.
Effective work teams	- Appropriate use of teams to solve problems. - Requires investment in building and selecting teams.
Continuous individual development	- Education and training to ensure high level of competence and skills to learn effectively.
Extensive communication	- Within and between the organization and external agents.
High involvement in innovation	- Participation in extensive continuous improvement activities within the organization.
Customer focus	- Internal and external customer orientation. Total quality culture.
Climate of creativity	- Positive approach to creating ideas, supported by a reward system and a culture of winners.
Organizational learning	- Processes, structure and cultures that help institutionalize individual learning.

Source: Tidd et al. (1997).

These key characteristics presented by the authors are relevant because they contemplate the domains of the organization that can influence the innovative capacity of the company.

The ability to innovate is central to small and medium-sized companies that aim to compete with competitors that have a larger organizational structure and in turn more available resources. Authors Zawislak et al. (2012) believe that managerial capabilities are related to strategic plans, human resources, rules, and procedures. On the other hand, commercial capabilities include customer relationships and contract management with customers and suppliers.

3 METHOD

3.1. Questionnaire

The questionnaire integrated three parts: first, the socio-demographic characteristics of the respondents (gender, age and education level); second, the questions about the consumer perception in relation to: i) which sector considers innovative (the response options were as follows: primary, secondary, tertiary, quaternary, none and I don't know), ii) the type of innovation that is considering most relevant in a company (the response options were as follows: product innovation, process innovation, organizational innovation, marketing Innovation, none and I don't know; iii) the perception if Portugal is a country that supports innovation SMEs (the response options were as follows: "yes", "no" and "I don't know"); third, to assess innovation capacity from the consumers' perspective, the authors Calik et al. (2017) scale was used, applying a 5-point Likert scale of agreement (1- Strongly disagree, 2- Disagree, 3- Neither agree nor disagree, 4- Agree, and 5- Strongly agree). Where they contemplate the following dimensions: product innovation capacity (5 statements), process innovation capacity (4 statements), organizational innovation capacity (4 statements), marketing innovation capacity (5 statements), innovation culture (5 statements), and innovation resources (4 statements). The aspect directed towards final consumers is something that had not yet been analyzed and studied both nationally and internationally.

Before applying the questionnaire, to ensure that respondents would easily understand the questions, it was disseminated by a group of 25 persons with different ages and literary abilities. To collect the data, the survey was dessiminate on social networks such as Facebook, Linkedin and WhatsApp. The researchers had no control over the participants who remained anonymous. The survey was available between May 1, 2021 and May 22, 2021 and 394 responses to the questionnaire were obtained.

3.2. Data Analysis

First, for the description of the variables, descriptive statistics were applied. Second, to evaluate the twenty-seven statements related to inovation capacity, we ran the principal component analysis with varimax rotation. The Kaiser-Meyer-Olkin (KMO) test of sampling adequacy and Bartlett's test of sphericity were contemplated to confirm the factorability and the adequacy of the analysis. After that, we applied the confirmation analysis, using the maximum likelihood estimation method and to assess if the model fit was evaluated the $\chi 2$, the root means square error of approximation (RMSEA), the comparative fit index (CFI), Tucker–Lewis index (TLI) and Incremental Fit Index (IFI). We also analysed the building reliability (CR) and average variance extracted (AVE) to assess the convergent validity. Third, for the econometric models to explain consumer perception of the sectors of activity. For the econometric model to explain the consumers' perception of the innovation capacity of the service sector, we performed a logistic regression. The dependent variable "consumers' perception of the innovation capacity of the sectors" was transformed into a binary choice, in which the option primary and secondary sectors took the value of zero, and the tertiary and quaternary sectors the value of one. In the model, the answers "none" "and I don't know" were not considered for the question "Which sector do you consider most innovative in Portugal?". As for the independent variables, the following were considered: gender, age, educational qualifications, people's perception of government support for SMEs, in relation to the most relevant type of innovation in the company, and the constructs of innovation capacity. For the analyses, we used the SPSS (version 21), AMOS (version 21), and STATA (version 14).

4. RESULTS AND DISCUSSION

4.1. Description of the Sample and Innovation From the Consumers' Perspective

The sample is composed of 45% male and 55% female individuals (see table 3). Regarding age groups, the sample was divided into three groups of people, group 1 which includes respondents 25 years old or younger (36%), group 2 composed of respondents over 25 years old and 35 years old or younger (37%), and group 3 composed of people over 35 years old (27%). As far as academic qualifications are concerned, it can be stated that the majority of respondents have a high school education or 12th grade, with a percentage of 35%, followed by the individuals who had obtained a degree, with about 34%. The remaining respondents have a master's or doctorate (16%), or a basic education (15%).

Table 3. Sample description and consumers perception about innovation

Variable	Percent %
Sociodemographic variables	
Gender	
Female	55%
Male	45%
Age	
[0-25]	36%
[26-35]	37%
More than 35 years old	27%
Education level	
High School	35%

continues on following page

Table 3. Continued

Variable	Percent %
Undergraduate/Baccalaureate	34%
Master's or Phd	16%
Basic	15%
Innovation from the Consumers' Perspective	
Which sector do you consider most innovative in Portugal?	
Quarterly Sector	47%
Tertiary Sector	23%
Secondary Sector	13%
Primary Sector	12%
I do not know	3%
None	2%
What type of innovation do you consider most relevant in the company?	
Marketing Innovation	47%
Product Innovation	21%
Organizational Innovation	18%
Process Innovation	9%
Don't Know	3%
None	2%
Do you consider Portugal a country that supports innovation in SMEs?	
Yes	40%
No	48%
I don't know	12%

Regarding the most innovative sector in Portugal, it was expected that the most chosen sector would be the quaternary sector (47%), because it's the sector usually connected with technology that is closely linked to innovation. Innovation is often automatically associated with the concept of technological innovation, and even in the remaining sectors, technology itself is the greatest contributor to their innovation. The second most selected was the tertiary sector with 23%, this reflects a perception of evolution in this sector much due to the recent digitalization of services, making them more convenient and more efficient.

About the consumer's perception on the type of innovation which is considered more relevant, we observe that the marketing Innovation left no room for doubt and was in fact the most chosen among the respondents with 47%, followed by product Innovation with 21%, organizational innovation with 18%, process innovation with

9% and the options "don't know" and "none" with 3% and 2% respectively. The question "Do you consider Portugal a country that supports innovation in small and medium enterprises?" had very balanced responses among the respondents of the different, but the general perception of final consumers is that Portugal is not a country that supports innovation in small and medium enterprises. About 48% of the respondents chose no, 40% chose yes, and the rest chose "don't know".

In scope of the scale that intends to evaluate the innovation capacity from the consumers' perspective, the authors Calik et al. (2017) classified each variable according to a theme, where "Prod" is the product innovation capacity, "Proc" is the process innovation capacity, "Org" is the organizational innovation capacity, "Mark" is the marketing innovation capacity, "Cult" is the innovation culture and "Res" are the innovation resources. Through the analysis of Table 2, it can be seen that the first variable "Provide customers with services that offer unique benefits superior to those of competitors" (Prod1) was the one with the highest degree of agreement with 65% of the answers as totally agree and a mean of 4.54, i.e., the mean of the answers was between the option "I agree" and "I totally agree". The variables corresponding to the topic of product innovation capacity (Prod) were the ones that obtained the highest percentage regarding the level 5 of agreement, always with values between 60.9% (Prod4) and 65% (Prod1). Regarding the capacity for process innovation, the variable with the highest level of agreement was "Work actively to constantly adjust business processes" (Proc4). In the organizational innovation capacity, the variable "Adopt innovative work projects" (Org1) was chosen by 57.9% of the respondents as the variable they totally agree with. On the topic of marketing innovation capacity, "Constantly look for new ways to deliver products to customers." (Mark2) was the variable with the highest degree of agreement (58.9%). Regarding Innovation culture, the variable "Encourage workers/employees to intelligently transform information from internal and external sources into valuable knowledge for the company" had 57.4% of the responses posited they were in total agreement concerning this topic. In the theme of innovation resources, it was found that the variables Res2 (Have a strong capacity in innovative design and manufacturing applications) and Res4 (Increase the budget in the item related to Research and Development), were those that obtained a higher degree of agreement on this topic, with 55.6%.

Table 4. Scale of innovation capacity, descriptive analysis

	Statements	CDIS (%)	DIS (%)	INDIF (%)	AGRE (%)	CAGR (%)	Mean	Standard Deviation
Prod1	Provide the clients with services that offer unique benefits superior to those of competitors	1,0	0,8	6,6	26,6	65,0	4,54	0,74
Prod2	The firms actively carry out their work on developing existing products and creating new products	0,5	1,0	6,9	28,4	63,2	4,53	0,71
Prod3	The firms enhance the range of their products and services with not previously released products and services	0,5	0,5	7,9	26,6	64,5	4,54	0,71
Prod4	We try to acquire new products by differing technical specifications and functionalities	0,5	0,5	7,1	31,0	60,9	4,51	0,70
Prod5	The companies see creating new products and services as critical tools to reach success	0,5	0,5	7,1	28,9	62,9	4,53	0,70
Proc1	The firms reduce the developing time of new products and services	0,8	0,5	7,6	32,0	59,1	4,48	0,72
Proc2	The firms are flexible to provide products and services according to the demands of the customers	0,5	0,8	7,4	32,2	59,1	4,49	0,71
Proc3	The firms develop in-house solutions to improve our manufacturing processes	0,5	0,8	7,9	34,5	56,3	4,45	0,72
Proc4	The firms actively work to constantly adjust its business processes	0,8	0,5	7,9	30,5	60,4	4,49	0,73
Org1	The firms adopt innovative work designs	0,5	0,8	7,1	33,8	57,9	4,48	0,71
Org2	The firms have good mechanisms for using technology from research to product development	0,8	0,5	7,6	35,8	55,3	4,44	0,72
Org3	The firms are better than our competitors in the manner of developing new managerial work, processes, and systems	0,5	1,0	7,6	34,0	56,9	4,46	0,72
Org4	The firms are successful in commercializing and institutionalizing of new products	0,5	0,8	8,1	34,8	55,8	4,44	0,72
Mark1	It's important for the companies to make changes in appearance, packaging, shape, and volume of the products	0,5	0,8	8,6	35,5	54,6	4,43	0,72
Mark2	The companies constantly look for new ways to deliver our products to the customers	0,5	0,5	8,1	32,0	58,9	4,48	0,71

continues on following page

Table 4. Continued

	Statements	CDIS (%)	DIS (%)	INDIF (%)	AGRE (%)	CAGR (%)	Mean	Standard Deviation
Mark3	The firms implement new marketing methods to promote the products	0,8	1,0	8,6	33,5	56,1	4,43	0,76
Mark4	The firms make improvements in the manner of customer relationships to obtain customer satisfaction	0,8	0,8	7,9	32,0	58,6	4,47	0,74
Mark5	New ideas that come from customers and suppliers are evaluated continuously, and the firms try to include them into product development activities	0,5	1,0	8,6	33,2	56,6	4,44	0,74
Cult1	The company see presenting new ideas and methods to improve business processes that are important for the success of the company	0,5	0,8	7,6	34,5	56,6	4,46	0,71
Cult2	The companies support employees to take initiatives in creating new ideas	0,5	0,8	7,6	35,3	55,8	4,45	0,71
Cult3	The employees cleverly transform information from internal and external sources into valuable knowledge for our company	0,8	0,8	7,9	33,2	57,4	4,46	0,74
Cult4	The companies encourage collaboration and exchange of ideas between the departments in order to produce new approaches	0,5	1,0	7,9	35,0	55,6	4,44	0,73
Cult5	The companies try out new ideas and methods to provide innovative solutions to our clients' problems	0,5	1,0	7,6	33,8	57,1	4,46	0,72
Res1	We constantly benefit from technology to enhance quality of products and services	0,5	0,8	8,9	36,3	53,6	4,42	0,73
Res2	The companies have strong capacities in innovative design and manufacturing applications	0,8	1,0	10,4	32,2	55,6	4,41	0,78
Res3	Importance is given to training R&D personnel	0,8	1,3	10,2	34,8	53,0	4,38	0,78
Res4	The companies constantly increase the allocated budget of R&D personnel	0,5	1,5	10,4	32,0	55,6	4,41	0,78

Notes: CDIS = Completely disagree; DIS = Disagree; INDIF = Neither agree or disagree; AGRE = Agree; CAGR = Completely agree.

4.2. Latent Constructs of the Innovation Capacity: Factorial and Confirmatory Analyses

Through the assessment of table 3, we verified that six constructs resulted from applying the factor analysis of the innovation capacity scale. The constructs resulting from the data analysis were: construct 1 - Product Innovation Capacity; construct 2 - Organizational Innovation Capacity; construct 3 – Process Innovation Capacity; 4 – Marketing Innovation Capacity; 5 - Innovation Culture and 6 - Innovation resource. Through the application of the 19-item innovation capacity scale, we found that the constructs are those proposed by the authors Calik et al. (2017), and express the important factors that they must assume in order to have competitive advantages over the competition.

Table 5. The identification of the latent constructs: factorial analysis

Statements	Product Inov. Cap.	Process Inov. Cap.	Organizational Inov. Cap.	Marketing Inov. Cap.	Culture Inov. Cap.	Resources Inov. Cap.
Prod1	0,910					
Prod2	0,945					
Prod3	0,930					
Prod4	0,933					
Prod5	0,910					
Proc1		0,907				
Proc2		0,920				
Proc3		0,930				
Proc4		0,901				
Org1			0,883			
Org2			0,932			
Org3			0,940			
Org4			0,916			
Mark1				0,902		
Mark2				0,915		
Mark3				0,927		
Mark4				0,936		
Mark5				0,915		
Cult1					0,910	
Cult2					0,938	
Cult3					0,925	

continues on following page

Table 5. Continued

Statements	Product Inov. Cap.	Process Inov. Cap.	Organizational Inov. Cap.	Marketing Inov. Cap.	Culture Inov. Cap.	Resources Inov. Cap.
Cult4					0,942	
Cult5					0,934	
Res1						0,928
Res2						0,937
Res3						0,947
Res4						0,941
Variance (%)	85,665	83,665	84,292	84,439	86,430	87,992
Bartlett's test (sig)	2209,140 (0,000)	1346,605 (0,000)	1407,637 (0,000)	2088,250 (0,000)	2352,409 (0,000)	1736,564 (0,000)
KMO test	0,886	0,847	0,862	0,881	0,848	0,838

Note: *Extraction Method: Principal Component Analysis. Rotation Method: Varimax with Kaiser Normalization; ** The results of KMO and Bartlett tests confirm the factorability and the adequacy of the analysis. Significant at $p < 0.01$.

Then, a confirmatory factor analysis was conducted. Table 4 shows the results of a confirmatory analysis, and we can see that the measurement model fits data well X^2/df /df = 6,221; RMSEA = 0,030; CFI = 0,933; TLI = 0,985; IFI = 0,967) (Hair et al., 2010). The following table shows the construct reliability (CR) and average variance extracted (AVE) to assess the convergent validity. Both the CR and AVE results are above the recommended threshold (Fornell and Larcker, 1981). The psychometric properties of measurement factors used in model estimation are satisfactory as indicated by composite reliability (CR) (> 0,7) and average variance extracted (AVE) (> 0,6) values (Bagozzi and Yi, 1988).

4.3. Econometric Model: Dependent Variable–Consumers' Perception of the Innovation Capacity of the Sectors

Table 7 presents the variables that have an impact on the consumers' perception of the innovation capacity of the service sectors (tertiary and quaternary). We observed that gender has a statistically significant impact on consumers' perception of the innovation capacity of the service sector. More specifically, being a woman reduces this perception by 12.4%, compared to being a man. Regarding age, it's observed that older respondents have a greater perception of the innovativeness of services compared to younger ones. Respondents with higher levels of education (undergraduate/baccalaureate), compared to those without academic qualifications (high school), have a greater perception of the innovation capacity of the service sector in relation to other sectors. As for the type of innovation, it appears that the perception of the innovation capacity of companies decreases in relation to the product, nationality and process when compared to the inovation of marketing. For example, the relevance of product innovation capacity in the services sector decreases by 33.9% when compared to marketing innovation capacity.

Regarding government support for innovation by SMEs, consumers who considered "no" caused the perception of innovation capacity to decrease by 7.5%. And, finally, the constructs of organizational, marketing, culture, and process innovation capacity increase consumers' perception of innovation capacity in service sectors.

Table 6. Measurement model: confirmatory factor analysis

Statements	Items	Factor Loading	CR	AVE	Cronbach's Alpha
Product Inov. Cap.	Prod1	0,833	0,953	0,802	0,958
	Prod2	0,939			
	Prod3	0,929			
	Prod4	0,933			
	Prod5	0,836			
Process Inov. Cap.	Proc1	0,899	0,950	0,825	0,935
	Proc2	0,918			
	Proc3	0,926			
	Proc4	0,889			
Organizational nov. Cap.	Org1	0,879	0,951	0,828	0,938
	Org2	0,924			
	Org3	0,935			
	Org4	0,901			
Marketing Inov. Cap.	Mark1	0,899	0,959	0,825	0,954
	Mark2	0,906			
	Mark3	0,911			
	Mark4	0,925			
	Mark5	0,901			
Innovation Culture	Cult1	0,878	0,963	0,837	0,961
	Cult2	0,922			
	Cult3	0,915			
	Cult4	0,933			
	Cult5	0,926			

continues on following page

Table 6. Continued

Statements	Items	Factor Loading	CR	AVE	Cronbach's Alpha
Innovation Resource	Res1	0,918	0,962	0,865	0,954
	Res2	0,929			
	Res3	0,937			
	Res4	0,936			
Goodness-of-Fit	Chi-square test: $X^2/df = 6{,}221$				
	Root Mean Square Error of Approximation (RMSEA) = 0,030				
	Comparative Fit Index (CFI) = 0,933				
	Tucker Lewis Index (TLI) = 0,985				
	Incremental Fit Index (IFI) = 0,967				

Note: Significant at *** $p < 0.01$. We also test the criterion for discriminant validity among latent variables.

Table 7. Econometric model to explain the consumers' perception of the innovation capacity of the sectors, logistic regression

Variable	Coefficient	Average marginal effects
Gender	-0.887 (0.308)***	-0.124
Age		
[0-25]	-	-
[26-35]	1.308 (0.405)***	0.182
More than 35 years old	0.993 (0.428)**	0.131
Education level		
High School	-	-
Undergraduate/Baccalaureate	0.702 (0.415)*	0.105
Master's or Phd	0.485 (0.449)	0.075
Basic	0.695 (0.501)	0.105
What type of innovation do you consider most relevant in the company?		
Marketing Innovation	-	-
Product Innovation	-2.106 (0.405)***	-0.339

continues on following page

Table 7. Continued

Variable	Coefficient	Average marginal effects
Organizational Innovation	-1.150 (0.411)***	-0.155
Process Innovation	-2.112 (0.473)***	-0.341
Don't Know	-1.785 (1.505)	-0.274
None	-0.575 (1.234)	-0.067
Do you consider Portugal a country that supports innovation in SMEs?		
Yes	-	-
No	-0.530 (0.306)*	- 0.075
I don't know	0.063 (0.540)	0.009
Product Inov. Cap.	0.216 (1.229)	0.030
Process Inov. Cap.	-0.088 (1.281)	-0.012
Organizational Inov. Cap.	0.329 (0.192)**	0.046
Marketing Inov. Cap.	0.249 (0.100)***	0.035
Innovation Culture	0.175 (0.027)***	0.025
Innovation Resource	0.359 (0.617)	0.056
Constant	2.767 (0.599)***	

Notes: Standard errors in parentheses. Significant at: * $p < 0.10$ level;** $p < 0.05$ level; *** $p < 0.01$.

5. DISCUSSION AND CONCLUSION

Entire sectors of our economy and fundamental forms of innovation have long been marginalized in the field of "innovation research". This innovation gap can be largely explained by the inertia of the conceptual tools we develop in the manufacturing economy. Desmarchelier et al. (2019) considered that services in general are gradually moving from a fringe position to a central position in the innovation network, at the same time as the shift from tangible to intangible innovation.

The term innovation network is often defined using two complementary functions and morphological perspectives (Desmarchelier et al., 2019). From a functional point of view, an innovation network is a mode of coordination between economic actors and is considered to be more efficient than markets and hierarchies, as it prevents the risks of innovation bureaucratization and leakage of strategies. In the morphological perspective, we can see innovation network as a structural arrangement that brings together multiple players with innovation as the main objective.

As studied by Gallouj et al. (2013), in the ServPPIN European project, collaboration and networking give an important contribution to services in general but they may focus on non-technological innovations as organizational innovation and marketing innovation, that aggregate the notion of product and process innovations (Pereira and Romero, 2013).

Services are evolving and are moving from simple passive adopters of innovations to services as active adopters and even producers of technological innovations (Djellal and Gallouj, 2015).

The latest development in service innovation reflects a dislocation of the analytical focus from visible to invisible (hidden or forgotten) innovation and it illustrates the conversion from a technologist, industrialist or assimilationist perspective to a non-technologist, servicebased or demarcation perspective (Djellal and Gallouj, 2015). Due to the relevance of the theme, and of the services in the economy, this article intends to study the the perception of innovation capacity from the perspective of consumers. For that, we used a scale proposed by the authors Calik et al. (2017). Theses authors conducted a study on the measurement of innovative capacity in a company, but the questionnaire that they applied was directed to owner-managers of several SMEs and applied a set of scales. This scale and its dimensions were adapted to the objective of this study, which aims to assess the perception of final consumers regarding innovation in SMEs in Portugal.

The results presented in the present study can support some strategic decisions to be implemented by companies and assume competitive advantages. Through the analysis of the studies it was possible to conclude that the service sectors (tertiary and quarterly) are the most innovative. The tertiary sector includes the service and trade sectors, and becomes quaternary (or higher tertiary) when it involves information technology or research and development. Marketing innovation, product innovation and organizational innovation were the types of innovation considered as the most relevant to companies, according to consumers. On the contrary, process innovation was the least relevant. Thus, for a company to present an innovative image to the consumer, it will have to invest in the area of marketing and assume a dynamic and innovative organization. It0s not enough to present new products or new services, marketing has to be bold and innovative.

The capacity to innovate is multidimensional and six factors have emerged: product innovation capacity; organizational innovation capacity; process innovation capacity; marketing innovation capacity; innovation culture and innovation resources. In general, factors such as marketing, communication, product, customer service and digitalization are part of the respondents' perception and with regard to innovation, these factors must be renewed and updated, thus allowing companies to become more innovative.

Additionally, the consumer's perception of innovation capacity is influenced by sociodemographic characteristics, namely gender and educational level. This result indicates that if a company intends to perform in relation to innovation, it has an indicative profile (men and respondents with a higher educational level) of those who are aware of the innovative drive. It was also found that the majority of consumers revealed that Portugal (Government support) does not support innovation in SMEs, and that this result negatively influences consumers' perception of innovation capacity of the companies. The Government is an essential element in reducing market failures and promoting economic development and social justice. The government's work must consider the best strategy to address the financing difficulties faced by small and medium enterprises through guaranteed loan schemes, direct loan schemes, microfinance and other guaranteed capital injections (Feranita et al., 2019). This is considered essential to support innovative SMEs as they have the ability to create workplaces, jobs, build and change the corporate environment for future generations and maintain a competitive environment through innovation. The reason why SMEs need to support Innovation is mainly based on the recognition that certain characteristics related to scale are of great importance to their support needs and the way they meet and give relevance to those needs. Due to the limited internal knowledge base and internal resources, it's much more difficult for these companies to obtain external funding and thus be able to support and benefit from innovation activities (North et al., 2001). The subsidy aims to encourage companies to improve their structure and performance, leading them to invest in high-tech products (Jin et al., 2018) and consequently providing better performances.

Regarding factors related to innovation capacity, it was found that organizational innovation capacity has a positive effect on consumer's perception in service sectors. Thus, companies' strategies to be innovative will involve adopting innovative work designs, they should have good mechanisms to use technologies from research to product development, trying to distinguish themselves from the competition as a way of developing new managerial work, processes, and systems and be successful in commercializing and institutionalizing new products.

Another factor that influences consumer's perception of innovation capacity in service sectors is marketing innovation capacity. Thus, it's important for companies to consider changes in appearance, packaging, shape, and volume of the products, constantly presenting and updating new ways to deliver the products to the customers, implement new marketing methods to promote the products, and make improvements as far as customer relationships are concerned, to finally obtain customer satisfaction. Furthermore, it's important to involve the different stakeholders (customers and suppliers) in the development and/or improvement of new products and services.

We also observe that innovative culture presents a positive and significant effect in the perception of the companies' innovation capacities in the service sector. Thus, the company's success should include in its strategy the presentation of new ideas and methods to improve business processes that are important for the success of the company, support employees to take initiatives in creating new ideas, and try out new ideas and methodologies to provide innovative solutions to the clients' problems. In addition, it should involve employees to collaborate and exchange ideas between the departments in order to produce new approaches.

Through the factors influencing innovation capacity, we conclude that if companies intend to maintain a continuous and sustainable growth in the long term, they must take into account the enormous value of innovation and, in addition to the need for greater investment through public funds, it's necessary to take into account the factors involved, such as human resources management, internal communication, financial management, internal and external business strategies and the constant updating of moves and updates in its area of activity.

Although we present an innovative analysis, since we analyze consumers' perception of innovation capacity, the article presents some limitations that may be the subject of future research. One of the limitations is that consumers gave their opinion in a generic way and did not consider any specific brand. Furthermore, it would be interesting to see if the results would be maintained with brands from different sectors. Also from a future research perspective, it was interesting to understand the results at an international level on consumer perception. More specifically, to assess whether the cultural level and consumption habits influence the consumers' perceptions of innovation capacity. This research could have interesting results, since countries, in terms of public investment, have different strategies and assume different initiatives to support innovation by SMEs. It would also be very interesting in future research to follow the innovation by complementing the measurement of the investment made in each dimension and in each action, as well as the variation in the business volume, the net result of the company's period and the return on assets. This financial data would further support the fact that investment in innovation is directly linked to the company's growth. These future studies could provide further evidence on other types of capabilities that small businesses should focus on, as well as address a more specific audience or delve deeper into a particular sector or activity.

REFERENCES

Barbieri, J. (2003). *Organizações inovadoras: estudos e casos brasileiros*. FGV Editora.

Benner, M. J., & Tushman, M. L. (2003). Exploitation, exploration, and process management: The productivity dilemma revisited. *Academy of Management Review*, *28*(2), 238–256. doi:10.2307/30040711

Bruhn, N. C. P., Alcântara, J. N. & Calegário, C. L. L. (2016). Multinational enterprises and spillover effects: A study on the factors associated with the innovation capacity of SMEs in Brazil. *Espacios*, *37*(10).

Calik, E., Calisir, F., & Centigue, B. (2017). A scale development for innovation capability measurement. *Journal of Advanced Management Science*, *5*(2), 69–76. doi:10.18178/joams.5.2.69-76

Cunha, N., & Santos, A. (2005). As práticas gerenciais e a inovação empresarial: Estudo de empresas líderes em inovação. *Revista Alcance*, *12*(3), 353–372.

Desmarchelier, B., Djellal, F., & Gallouj, F. (2019). *Towards a servitization of innovation networks: a mapping. Public Management Review, Taylor and Francis*. Routledge.

Djellal, F., & Gallouj, F. (2015). *The handbook of service business: management, marketing, innovation and internationalization*. Edward Elgar Publishers.

Drucker, P. (2004). *As fronteiras da administração: onde as decisões do amanhã estão sendo determinadas hoje*. Pioneira.

Feranita, N. V., Nugraha, A., & Sukoco, S. A. (2019). The Role of Government Support for Innovation and Performance of SMEs. *Politico (Pavia, Italy)*, *19*(2), 5–10.

Gallouj, F., Rubalcaba, L. & Windrum, P. (2013). Public–Private innovation networks in services. *Economics*.

Gupta, A. K., Smith, K. G., & Shalley, C. E. (2006). The interplay between exploration and exploitation. *Academy of Management Journal*, *49*(4), 693–706. doi:10.5465/amj.2006.22083026

Hair, J. F., Black, W. C., Babin, B. J., & Anderson, R. E. (2010). *Multivariate Data Analysis*. Pearson.

Ho, H., & Lu, R. (2015). Performance implications of marketing exploitation and exploration: Moderating role of supplier collaboration. *Journal of Business Research*, *68*(5), 1026–1034. doi:10.1016/j.jbusres.2014.10.004

Jansen, J. J. P., Van Den Bosch, F. A. J., & Volberda, H. W. (2006). Exploratory innovation, exploitative innovation, and performance: Effects of organizational antecedents and environmental moderators. *Management Science*, *52*(11), 1661–1674. doi:10.1287/mnsc.1060.0576

Jin, Z., Shang, Y., & Xu, J. (2018). he Impact of Government Subsidies on Private R&D and Firm Performance: Does Ownership Matter in China's Manufacturing Industry? *Sustainability (Basel)*, *10*(7), 2205. doi:10.3390u10072205

McCartney, S. (2020). Unlocking investment to scale innovation in fashion. *PR Newswire Association, LLC*, 1–4.

Mintzberg, H., Ahlstrand, B. W., & Lampel, J. (2009). *Strategy safari: The complete guide through the wilds of strategic management.* Financial Times Prentice Hall.

North, D., Smallbone, D., & Vickers, I. (2001). Public Sector Support for Innovating SMEs. *Small Business Economics*, *16*(4), 303–317. doi:10.1023/A:1011164801073

OECD. (2012). *Recomendação do conselho sobre política regulatória e governança.* OECD. / doi:10.1787/9789264209084-pt

Palma, M. A. M. (2004). *A capacidade de inovação como formadora de valor: análise dos vetores de valor em empresas brasileiras de biotecnologia* [Doctoral Thesis, São Paulo University].

Pereira, A. C., & Romero, F. (2013). A review of the meanings and the implications of the Industry 4.0 concept. *Procedia Manufacturing*, *13*, 1206–1214. doi:10.1016/j.promfg.2017.09.032

Popadiuk, S., Vidal, P., & Franklin, M. (2010). Measuring knowledge exploitation and exploration: An empirical application in a technological development center in Brazil. *Revista Espacios*, *31*(3), 36.

Porter, M. E. (1986). *Estratégia competitiva: técnicas para análise de indústrias e da concorrência*. Editora Campus.

Ramos, A. & Zilber, S. N. (2015). O Impacto do investimento na capacidade inovadora da empresa. *Review of Administration and Innovation - RAI*, *12*(1), 303. doi:10.11606/rai.v12i1.100326

Saunila, M. (2020). Innovation capability in SMEs: A systematic review of the literature. *Journal of Innovation and Knowledge*, *5*(4), 260–265. doi:10.1016/j.jik.2019.11.002

Scandelari, V. R. N., & Cunha, J. C. (2013). Ambidestralidade e desempenho socioambiental de empresas do setor eletroeletrônico. *RAE*, *53*(2), 183–198. doi:10.1590/S0034-75902013000200006

Schreiber, D. (2012). *Inovação e desenvolvimento organizacional*. Editora Feevale.

Schumpeter, J. (2012). *Teoria do desenvolvimento económico*. Fundação Calouste Gulbenkian.

Tidd, J., Bessant, J., & Pavitt, K. (1997). *Managing Innovation: integrating Technological, market and organizational change*. John Wiley and Sons Ltd.

Zawislak, P., Alves, C., Tello-Gamarra, J., Barbieux, D., & Reichert, F. (2012). Innovation capability: From technology development to transaction capability. *Journal of Technology Management & Innovation*, *7*(2), 14–27. doi:10.4067/S0718-27242012000200002

Chapter 3
Conditional Mediation of Entrepreneurial Self-Efficacy and Global Mindset in International Individual Entrepreneurial Intention of SME Entrepreneurs

Chérine Jneid
https://orcid.org/0000-0003-0287-3166
Azm University, Lebanon

ABSTRACT

The authors analyze the effect of conditional mediation of global mindset (GM) -entrepreneurial self-efficacy (ESE) in the international entrepreneurial intention (IEI) of small and medium enterprises (SMEs)' entrepreneurs in Brazil. They collected the data from 794 entrepreneurs and used the partial least square method to test the hypotheses and analyze the mediating and direct effects. The effect of the IEI on the international entrepreneurial orientation (IEO) of SMEs' entrepreneurs in Brazil improves with the mediation of the ESE and the moderation of the GM. The authors suggest more empirical and longitudinal analyses to extend the literature on IEI as well as future studies that lead to the generalizability of our results. Finally, they think that similar studies with different sample groups may be of interest. These findings may encourage would-be international entrepreneurs and vocational trainers on IE to consider the critical effect of ESE and GM on their future business activities.

DOI: 10.4018/978-1-6684-7140-1.ch003

1. INTRODUCTION

International entrepreneurship (IE) is a new research domain that is increasingly studied to understand the different international dimensions of entrepreneurship (Oviatt and McDougall, 1994, 2005; Krueger et al., 2000; Jones and Coviello, 2005; Kolvereid and Isaksen, 2006; Korsakienė and Tvaronavičienė, 2012; Olejnik and Swoboda, 2012; Felício et al., 2016). Coviello et al. (2011) and Oviatt and McDougall (2005) defined IE as the discovery, enactment, evaluation and exploitation of opportunities abroad the national borders to create and capture value. Previous IE research investigated different elements that have significant effect on IE behavior (Freeman and Cavusgil, 2007; Nummela et al.,2004) as situational factors, education and experience and demographic variables (Jafari Sadeghi et al., 2019; Jafari Sadeghi, 2020).

Hamelin (2013) argued that small and medium enterprises (SMEs) are different in international entrepreneurship growth. Sapienza et al. (2006) and Zahra et al. (2005) advised SMEs' entrepreneurs who intend to go international to understand the uncertain, risky, different and new market that is different from their domestic market. Siepel et al. (2019), Wright et al. (2007) and Cardoza and Fornes (2011) demonstrated that the performance of international entrepreneurship of SMEs is positively influenced by individuals' human capital and social capital as cross-cultural knowledge, attitude towards uncertainty, behavior towards diversity of culture and values. However, we believe that more IE studies are needed to understand the psychological and behavioral aspects of individuals in this process (Jones et al., 2011; Handrito et al., 2020). Authors confirmed that behaviors, motivations and perceptions of entrepreneurs in the international entrepreneurship process of SMEs are different than those demonstrated in others (Kiss et al., 2013). Thus, we put central the SMEs' entrepreneurs in Brazil for a better understanding of the international entrepreneurship of these firms.

Entrepreneurship is a complex process that includes entrepreneurial intention and entrepreneurial orientation. An individual demonstrates an entrepreneurial intention when assuming that he has a plan, intends and will try to take steps to start a business in the future (Kautonen et al., 2015). However, individuals with entrepreneurial orientation have a psychological and cognitive profile which includes proactive, risky and innovative behaviors to take an action in the entrepreneurial process (Kropp et al., 2006) even without the existence of an entrepreneurial intention. Our first research question is: Does the international individual entrepreneurial intention (IEI) influence the international individual entrepreneurial orientation (IEO) of entrepreneurs of SMEs in Brazil?

Rauch et al. (2009), Wales et al. (2011) and Covin and Miller (2014) confirmed the scarcity on the studies of entrepreneurial intention and entrepreneurial orientation on the individual level and advised to expand the research on investigating the factors that may mediate or moderate the entrepreneurial intention. We study here the influence of entrepreneurial self-efficacy ESE which many studies demonstrated its relevance for businesses on competitive environment (Khedhaouria et al., 2014).

Our second research question is: does entrepreneurial self-efficacy (ESE) mediate the influence of international IEO on the international IEI of entrepreneurs of SMEs in Brazil?

The fourth element that is included in this study is the global mindset. Previous studies showed the significant impact of global mindset on international entrepreneurship in general (Andresen and Bergdolt,2017; Nummela et al., 2004; Olejnik and Swoboda, 2012) including the international entrepreneurial and international IEO (Maitland and Sammartino, 2015). We pose our third research question: does the global mindset moderate the mediating effect of ESE on the influence of international IEI on the international IEO of entrepreneurs of SMEs in Brazil?

We empirically investigated these relationships through applying a PLS-SEM model of structural equations, using SmartPLS 3.2.7 software on a sample of 794 entrepreneurs in SMEs in Brazil. We are interested to explore the international entrepreneurship of SMEs in Brazil where firms are constantly increasing their international shares despite the attractiveness of the domestic market (Carneiro and Brenes, 2014).

After this introduction, we begin with a brief literature review on international IEI, ESE, global mindset and international IEO and we state our hypotheses. In the section of materials and methods, we describe the sample and the measurement of different variables used to test our hypotheses. We introduce our results in the next section. Finally, we discuss our findings, indicated our research limitations and propose some practical and research implications.

2. LITERATURE REVIEW

2.1. International Individual Entrepreneurial Intention

Entrepreneurial intention is theoretically determined by the expectancy-valence theory which involves the expected utility of an entrepreneurial behavior (Freeman and Cavusgil, 2007; Krueger and Brazeal,1994; Krueger et al., 2000; Steel and Koenig, 2006). This construct demonstrated to be significant and long-lasting in entrepreneurship studies (Bird, 1988; Carr and Sequeira, 2007; Krueger et al., 2000; Webster, 1977; Hmieleski and Corbett, 2006; Wilson et al. 2007; Lee and Wong, 2004; Zhao et al., 2005). It has been used as a dependent, an independent or a control variable in entrepreneurship research (Chen et al., 1998; Hmieleski and Corbett, 2006; Krueger et al.,2000; Lüthje and Franke, 2003). Researchers investigated abundantly the factors that affect the intentions to carry out entrepreneurial behaviors. They explored how cognitive, situational and cultural factors influence the entrepreneurial intentions of individuals to engage in entrepreneurial behaviors that may not be similar in different contexts (Ajzen, 1991; Ajzen, 1987; Boyd and Vozikis, 1994; Tubbs and Ekeberg, 1991; Krueger, 1993; Lee and Wong, 2004; Cooper, 1985, 1993; Hayton et al., 2002; Mitchell et al., 2000; Mueller and Thomas, 2001; George and Zahra, 2002).

Lee and Wong (2004) supposed that the entrepreneurial intention would be the initial step of the evolving process of entrepreneurship (Gartner et al., 1994). Other researchers assumed that this variable would be the strongest predictor of planned behavior, including entrepreneurial behavior (Ajzen, 1991; Bird, 1988; Webster, 1977; Krueger et al., 2000; Kolvereid and Isaksen, 2006, Kolvereid, L., 1996b).

Previous studies focused largely on the entrepreneurial intentions of individuals to launch a new business or to ensure its survival, growth and sustainability after its implementation (Wiklund and Shepherd, 2003; Davidsson et al., 2009; Knockaert et al., 2011). We are extending the previous research by applying the international IEI to the entrepreneurs of SMEs in Brazil. Knight (2001) provided evidence that the intention of some SMEs' entrepreneurs to expand internationally is challenged by the complexity of international business environment, the capabilities to overcome international threats that differ enormously from the challenges that they face in domestic markets.

Kiss et al. (2013) supposed that only entrepreneurs who demonstrated international entrepreneurial orientation, which involves innovative, proactive and risk taking behaviors, will be able to create a new value in international markets. Unfortunately, there is a scarcity on studies that investigate the individual factors that influence the relationship between international IEI and international IEO. We aim to address this research gap through understanding the mediating effect on entrepreneurial self-efficacy (ESE) between the International IEI and international IEO among SMEs' entrepreneurs in Brazil (Lin˜an et al., 2019; Paul et al., 2017).

2.2. International IEI and International IEO

Entrepreneurial orientation is a research area that focuses on the understanding of the proactive, risky and innovative behaviors of businesses in their international expansion (Kropp et al., 2006). Researchers assumed that the entrepreneurial orientation is a driver for entrepreneurial action which is modelled in processes (Bhave, 1994; Gartner, 1985). A large number of studies considered the entrepreneurial orientation as a firm-level construct which has a positive influence on the overall performance of the firms (Dada and Watson, 2013) including brand and market performance (Reijonen et al., 2015). They emphasized on the positive relationship between entrepreneurial orientation and financial, non-financial and social performance of firms (Miller, 1983; Covin and Slevin, 1989; Barringer and Bluedon, 1990; Zahra and Covin, 1995; Wiklund and Shepherd, 2005, Gupta and Batra, 2015). In addition, researchers supposed that the international entrepreneurial orientation is a powerful predictor of the process of international entrepreneurship (Jones and Coviello, 2005; Weerawardena et al., 2007; Joardar and Wu, 2011; Freeman and Cavusgil, 2007; Sundqvist et al., 2012). Lee and Peterson (2000) proved also the pertinence of entrepreneurial orientation construct on the societal level. Few years ago, researchers gave new insights to the entrepreneurial orientation as an individual-level construct (Chien, 2014; Ferreira et al., 2015). Herein, we intend to apply this construct on the individual level. We believe that our paper will extend the understanding of the relationships between the individual entrepreneurial intention, the individual behavior and the individual entrepreneurial orientation of SMEs' entrepreneurs in Brazil.

Miller (1983), Covin and Slevin (1989) and Covin and Miller (2014) considered a three-dimension model of entrepreneurial orientation to include innovativeness, risk-taking and proactiveness. Miller (1983) argued that businesses with entrepreneurial orientation succeed on different entrepreneurial actions of the entrepreneurial process: they are persistently searching for new opportunities, exploiting different opportunities, creating new values and leading the new markets. However, Gupta and Batra (2015) advised on the utility to expand the research on international entrepreneurial orientation from multinationals firms to study its influence on small and medium enterprises SMEs as well. We think that it is interesting to study the international entrepreneurial orientation construct for economies which are highly relying on SMEs to enhance their competitive advantage across the borders (Chetty et al., 2018).

The current study attempts to expand the international IEI and IEO studies by surveying SMEs' entrepreneurs in Brazil to investigate how some factors as entrepreneurial self-efficacy (ESE) and global mindset (GM) may mediate or moderate potential relationships between these constructs. One of the contributions of this paper is to analyze the influence of international IEI in international IEO. Therefore, we draw our first hypothesis:

H1: International IEI positively influence international IEO of SMEs' entrepreneurs in Brazil.

2.3. Entrepreneurial Self-Efficacy (ESE)

Entrepreneurial studies focused mainly on understanding the different factors that influence business performance. Some researchers investigated the role of corporate internal factors (Chirico et al.,2011; Hernández-Perlines et al., 2016a; Balabanis and Katsikea, 2004) while others explored the effect of external factors (Wiklund and Shepherd, 2005; Lumpkin and Dess, 2001; Stam and Elfring, 2008). Individual factors are gaining increasing attention to find out how the behaviors and characteristics of entrepreneurs have impact on the entrepreneurial process. In addition, more studies are oriented to study the relationships between the different levels of the entrepreneurial process from intention till sustainability of the business. Authors positively linked high levels of entrepreneurial self-efficacy to a variety of goal-oriented entrepreneurial behaviors (Krueger et al., 2000; Ardichvili et al.,2003). Our study focused on the mediating effect of entrepreneurial self-efficacy in the influence of international IEI on international IEO.

The concept of self-efficacy was originally conceived by Bandura (1977). The author defined this construct as the individual's perception of his own ability to perform specific behaviors in a certain context. Chen et al. (1998) studied the self-efficacy on entrepreneurial domain as the individual's own beliefs about his capacity to adopt entrepreneurial behaviors that enable them to successfully perform the different roles and actions of the entrepreneurial process. Chen et al. (1998) and Krueger et al. (2000) reported that entrepreneurial self-efficacy is positively associated with entrepreneurial intention. Zhao et al. (2005) explained how entrepreneurial self-efficacy shapes the perceptions of desirability and feasibility of entrepreneurs and mediates their entrepreneurial intentions.

Moreover, researchers postulated also positive association between the three determinants of entrepreneurial orientation and entrepreneurial self-efficacy. Bandura (1986) generated numerous studies to demonstrate that individuals with high levels of self-efficacy set challenging goals, deal better with uncertainty and behave better under uncertainty. Krueger and Brazeal (1994) asserted that entrepreneurs with high levels of ESE demonstrate more strategic risk-taking comparing to others with low level of self-efficacy. Ardichvili et al. (2003) suggested that high level of entrepreneurial self-efficacy is positively associated to high levels of innovative and proactive behaviors.

Ardichvili et al. (2003) gave evidence that a high level of self-efficacy reflects high confidence on attaining goals successfully which drives would-be entrepreneurs from entrepreneurial intention to entrepreneurial orientation. Therefore, we stated here our second hypothesis:

H2: The ESE positively mediates the relationship between international IEI and international IEO of SME's entrepreneurs in Brazil.

With alignment of Bandura (1977) assumption that a dynamic reciprocal relationship between the individual, his environment and his behavior determines the self-efficacy beliefs of an individual, international IEI becomes a background for ESE. Thus, we identified the following hypothesis:

H2a: International IEI positively influences the ESE of SME's entrepreneurs in Brazil.

Moreover, abundant studies reveal the positive relationship between ESE and IEO in SMEs (Poon et al. 2006; Shane and Nicolaou, 2015; Wiklund et al., 2009; Zahra and Covin, 1995; Lumpkin and Dess, 1996, Krueger and Brazeal, 1994; Rosenbusch et al., 2013). Then, we stated the next hypothesis:

H2b: ESE positively influences the international IEO of SME's entrepreneurs in Brazil.

2.4. Global Mindset (GM)

Crick (2009) demonstrated that international entrepreneurs are exposed to a diversity of cross-cultural issues that differ from the domestic challenges (Paul et al., 2017). Previous studies explored global mindset as a powerful instrument to overcome the different challenges that encounter firms' internationalization (Nummela et al., 2004) and an antecedent to competitive advantage in the process of international entrepreneurship (Nummela et al., 2004; Olejnik and Swoboda, 2012).

Andresen and Bergdolt (2017) considered that global mindset (GM) as a significant cross-cultural competence. Numerous studies highlighted that global mindset, characterized by the openness to cross-cultural learning, international know-how acquisition (Johnson et al., 2006; Felício et al., 2016, Nummela et al., 2004) and positive attitude towards international entrepreneurship (Paul, 2000; Nummela et al., 2004), as an important factor to boost international entrepreneurial intention (Levy et al., *2007)*. Entrepreneurs with global mindset are able to process effectively a diversity of contradictory information related to local and global factors which improves their international entrepreneurial orientation (Maitland and Sammartino, 2015). Global mindset is also positively associated to international networking that facilitates access to knowledge and resources which assist entrepreneurs in SMEs to develop better international entrepreneurial orientation because uncertainty and risk are reduced (Kedia and Mukherji, 1999; Bergman, 2009; Hoang and Antoncic, 2003; Pinho and Prange, 2016; Freixanet et al., 2018). Even more, Batjargal, 2010;

Arregle et al., 2015; Parida et al., 2017 demonstrated that entrepreneurs in SMEs succeed more in their international entrepreneurship experience when investing on their informal network system than the formal procedures because of the easy access to resources, knowledge and advice. However, Shi et al. (2019) argued that the SMEs' entrepreneurs can invest more effectively on these network resources in their international entrepreneurship process. We included GM in this study because individuals who have global mindset with international IEI demonstrate better international IEO.

Moreover, Javidan et al. (2016) tied the concept to global mindset to self-efficacy. They assumed that self-efficacy is a predictor of cross-cultural adjustments levels: high levels of self-efficacy predict higher levels of global mindset through more openness to navigate intercultural contexts, advanced motivation to acquire cross-cultural knowledge and skills and better capacity to interpret unfamiliar behaviors in an international context. We assumed that the success of entrepreneurs in SMEs, with global mindset, in international entrepreneurship is determined by entrepreneurial self-efficacy. However, there is little research on the relationships between GM, ESE, international IEI and international IEO. Hereafter, we identified our third hypothesis and its sub-hypotheses:

H3: GM moderates the mediation of ESE on international IEI of international IEO of SMES' entrepreneurs in Brazil.

H3a: GM moderates the relation between international IEI and ESE of SMES' entrepreneurs in Brazil.

H3b: GM moderates the relation between ESE and the international IEO of SMES' entrepreneurs in Brazil.

3. MATERIALS AND METHODS

3.1. Sample

Previous studied confirmed that the ownership, decision making and control in SMEs is typically centralized on the founders and their families who extremely influence the firms' strategies, allocation of its resources and management of its operations (Glancey, 1988; Gomez-Mejia et al., 2011; Hsu et al., 2013). The different firms' behaviors are consistent with the founders' behaviors (Kolvereid and Isaksen, 2006), including those related to international entrepreneurship. Thus, our sample consists of 1105 of founders and their families of SMEs located in Brazil. Only 794 people respond to our survey which represents 71.86%.

We analyzed the statistical power of our sample through Cohen's retrospective test (1992). Our result is 0.993 which exceeds the limit of 0.80 that is proposed by Cohen (1992).

We collected the data through a questionnaire that involves Likert-type questions. We did a pilot test before the distribution to the sample. We improved our questionnaire based on the feedbacks of the respondents.

3.2. Measurement of Variables

3.2.1. International IEI

To measure this variable, we considered the scale proposed by Kautonen et al. (2015) and adjusted it to the international level. International IEI was measured through three items (IEI 1- IEI 3) using the five point Likert scale ranged from 1= "strongly disagree" to 5 = "strongly agree".

3.2.2. Entrepreneurial Self-Efficacy

We adopted the entrepreneurial self-efficacy scale proposed by Chen et al. (1998) to test the perceived self-efficacy of entrepreneurs in SMEs in Brazil. The authors considered a self-assessment based on the individual's perception of their capabilities to perform five business domains: marketing, innovation, management, risk taking and financial control efficacy. It included 22 items which were gauged on a five-point Likert-scale (1 = "strongly disagree", 5 = "strongly agree").

3.2.3. International IEO

We measured this variable using the traditional scale recommended by Miller (1983), Covin and Slevin (1989) in an international context (Covin and Miller, 2014). International IEO was measured through three dimensions: innovativeness (3 items), risk-taking (3 items) and proactiveness (3 items) applied to a five-point Likert-scale (1 = "strongly disagree", 5 = "strongly agree").

3.2.4. Global Mindset

We measure the entrepreneurs' global mindset through the scale suggested by Felício et al. (2015). The authors used three items: capacity to see the world as a single vast market (glob1); internationalization as a means to achieve growth objectives (glob2); and lead their business into the international market (glob3) applied to a five-point Likert-scale (1 = "strongly disagree", 5 = "strongly agree").

3.2.5. Control Variables

In line with previous studies, we included three control variables: gender (Davidsson and Honig, 2003; Minniti and Nardone, 2007), age (Lamotte and Colovic, 2013; Levesque and Minniti, 2006; Stam and Elfring, 2008), and education abroad (Davidsson and Honig, 2003).

3.3. Data Analysis

We used the Partial Least Square (PLS) method to test the hypotheses and analyzed the mediating and direct effects. The software used is SmartPLS v.3.2.7. We are motivated to conduct PLS because it is a structural equation multivariate quantitative method which is less demanding on the sample size (Henseler et al., 2015), allows the investigation on different causal relationships (Astrachan et al., 2014) and has a predictive nature (Sarstedt et al.,2014).

4. FINDINGS

In order to ensure reliability and validity of the measurement scales, we followed two steps. We analyzed the measurement model as a first step. Then, we analyzed the structural model as a second step.

4.1. Analysis of the Measurement Model

The convergent reliability of the measurement scales in our study is supported as table I shows that the values of Cronbach's alpha and the Average Variance Extracted (AVE) exceed 0.7; 0.7 and 0.5 for composite reliability, Cronbach's alpha and AVE values, respectively (Fornell and Larcker, 1981).

The discriminant validity is confirmed in our study. First, AVE values shown in (Tables II-V) are higher than the related correlations in different cases after comparing the AVE square roots values for each compound with the correlations between constructs associated with the construct in question (Fornell and Larcker, 1981). In addition, the values of HTMT index for type A compounds (Table VI) are below 0.85 (Henseler et al., 2015), which supports the discriminant validity occurrence. Finally, we used the bootstrapping to calculate the HTMTinference. The interval result shows values that are lower than 1 which confirms also the discriminant validity in our study. (Table VII).

International individual entrepreneurial intention turned to be operational as a second order type B compound, calculated in two different steps based on the values of the latent variables (Wright et al., 2012). In this case, Diamantopoulos and Winklhofer (2001) advised that the different items should not show any collinearity problem unless the Inflation Variance Factor (IVF) reaches or exceeds the value 5 (Kleinbaum et al., 1988). Based on this, our study does not show any collinearity problem (Table VIII).

The confirmation of the discriminant validity and the convergent validity of the model allows us to test the relationships between the variables.

4.2. Analysis of Structural Model

First, the international IEI explains 32.6% of the international IEO of the entrepreneurs in SMEs in Brazil. We concluded this result after checking the value and the significance of the path coefficient ($\beta = 0.419$; $p < 0.001$) as shown in table X.

Second, we included the mediating effect of the entrepreneurial self-efficacy ESE. Table X shows a positive and significant indirect effect between international IEI and ESE ($\beta = 0.698$; $p < 0.001$) and between ESE and international IEO ($\beta = 0.439$; $p < 0.001$). However, $\beta = -0.094$ (Table X) explains the non-significance of the direct effect between international IEI and international IEO. This direct effect is completely eliminated by the mediating effect.

International IEI explains 38.1% of the ESE, which in turn explains 40.7% of the international IEO in entrepreneurs of SMEs in Brazil (Table X). Therefore, we proved the mediation between ESE in relation to international IEI and international IEO of entrepreneurs in SMEs in Brazil. Following Baron and Kenny (1986) and Cepeda et al., (2016), this mediating effect removes the direct effect and represents consequently a total effect.

Third, we introduced the moderating effect of global mindset. Table X shows that global mindset has a moderator effect in the relation between international IEI and ESE ($\beta = 0.240$; $p< 0.001$) and between ESE and international IEO ($\beta = 0.258$; $p< 0.001$). Our results show also an increase on the variance of international IEO from 40.7% to 46.4% which confirms the double moderator effect of global mindset. The magnitude of moderator effect of international IEI is average since the value of first moderator effect of global mindset is $f^2 = 0.20$ (global mindset moderates the relation between international IEI and ESE) and is 0.25 for the second moderator of global mindset (global mindset moderates the relation between ESE and international IEO).

The control variables have an influence that may be considered relevant and are significant ($p < 0.001$) (Table IX).

Our results show an adequate goodness of fit (Henseler et al., 2015) as the Standardized Root Mean Square Residual (SRMR) is enhanced. (Table X) indicates also that the mediating role is more improved than the direct effect: the mediating role has a 0.062 SRMR while the direct role obtains a 0.074 SRMR. Both SRMR values are below 0.08 set by Henseler et al. (2015).

5. CONCLUSION

5.1. Summary of Findings

The variables of this study and their dimensions are reliable and valid (Fornell and Larcker, 1981; Henseler et al., 2015).

Our study demonstrated that international IEO can be largely explained by international IEI. This result is consistent with previous research (Kiss et al., 2013; Wiklund and Shepherd, 2003; Davidsson et al., 2009; Knockaert et al., 2011). International IEI explains 32.6% of international IEO of entrepreneurs in SMEs in Brazil. Our first hypothesis is confirmed, so international IEI positively influence international IEO of SMEs' entrepreneurs in Brazil. The positive relationship between international IEI and international IEO answers our first research question.

Our second hypothesis is also confirmed. Previous studies showed the direct role of the entrepreneurial self-efficacy (ESE), its moderating role as well as its mediating role (Krueger et al., 2000; Ardichvili et al.,200; Chen et al., (1998); Zhao et al., 2005; Krueger and Brazeal (1994). In our study, ESE mediates the relationship between international IEI and international IEO of entrepreneurs in SMEs in Brazil. Our results showed that the ESE maximizes the potential of the model as the variation of international IEO increases to 40.7%. This study extends the investigation of the mediating role of ESE and answers our second research question.

Finally, the global mindset positively moderates the mediation model of ESE between the international IEI and international IEO of entrepreneurs of SMEs in Brazil. This study confirms the moderating effect of the global mindset, and it also confirms that with global mindset in international marketplace, ESE becomes critical to improve international IEI (Javidan et al., 2016). This conclusion confirms our third hypothesis and answers our third research question.

6. LIMITATIONS OF THIS STUDY

Our limitation is the use of single-informant in Likert-type scales. We followed the recommendations of Rong and Wilkinson (2011), Woodside (2013), and Woodside et al. (2015) of carefully selecting our sample to overcome this limitation. We addressed our questionnaire to the SME's founders and their families (Glancey, 1988; Gomez-Mejia et al., 2011; Hsu et al., 2013; Kolvereid and Isaksen, 2006).

This study is also limited to SMEs' entrepreneurs in Brazil only. So that, our findings cannot be generalized.

7. RESEARCH CONTRIBUTIONS AND PRACTICAL IMPLICATIONS

This research is contributing to the extension of the entrepreneurial intention literature where studies demonstrated the power of intention on entrepreneurial behavior (Krueger et al., 2000; Liñán, and Chen, 2009).

We think that our sample of founders and their families of SMEs is also contributing to the entrepreneurship research where the majority of the previous studies focused on university student samples as "potential entrepreneurs" (Kickul et al., 2009; Krueger et al., 2000; Liñán, and Chen, 2009).

Our results offered interesting ESE and GM insights. Thus, we suggest the following practical implications.

Our results may orient would-be international entrepreneurs to take further entrepreneurial actions to empower their international ESE and develop their GM. Many activities are recommended as observing others' success stories (Cooper and Park, 2008) or being involved in international experience abroad the national borders (Krueger, 2000; Doll and Ajzen, 1992).

In addition, our findings may encourage vocational trainers to develop training contents that enhance ESE and GM within would-be international entrepreneurs to decrease their perception of barriers that may encounter across the borders (Lüthje and Franke, 2003).

Besides the practical implications, this paper has also some research implications.

Being an international entrepreneur is considered an intentional behavior (Bird, 1988). Thus, we believe that it is critical to conduct more empirical analyses to test the mediating or moderating effects of additional variables in the development of international IEI and investigate the factors that may inhibit it to move forward to the international IEO (Zhao et al., 2005) as a next level in the international entrepreneurship process.

In addition, future research may develop new measures for international IEI or test the existing measures already used in previous IEI on different contexts (Freeman et al., 2007), and combine with other constructs as international IEO, ESE and GM to guarantee the generalizability.

Another scope of research may be directed to conduct longitudinal analyses that check intention-behavior relation by examining who are the would-be international entrepreneurs in SMEs, who are initially surveyed, will actually become international entrepreneurs (Carr et al., 2007).

We think also that further studies should be encouraged to understand the international entrepreneurship in emerging markets, including Brazil. Even more, comparative studies between different contexts may extend the international entrepreneurship research area.

Finally, similar studies that are oriented to entrepreneurs or executives of large companies may be interesting to test the results for different sample groups.

REFERENCES

Ajzen, I. (1987). Attitudes, traits, and actions—Dispositional prediction of behavior in personality and social-psychology. *Advances in Experimental Social Psychology*, *20*, 1–63. doi:10.1016/S0065-2601(08)60411-6

Ajzen, I. (1991). The theory of planned behavior. *Organizational Behavior and Human Decision Processes*, *50*(2), 179–211. doi:10.1016/0749-5978(91)90020-T

Andresen, M., & Bergdolt, F. (2017). A systematic literature review on the definitions of global mindset and cultural intelligence merging two different research streams. *International Journal of Human Resource Management*, *28*(1), 170–195. doi:10.1080/09585192.2016.1243568

Ardichvili, A., Cardozo, R., & Ray, S. (2003). A theory of entrepreneurial opportunity identification and development. *Journal of Business Venturing*, *18*(1), 105–123. doi:10.1016/S0883-9026(01)00068-4

Arregle, J. L., Batjargal, B., Hitt, M. A., Webb, J. W., Miller, T., & Tsui, A. S. (2015). Family ties in entrepreneurs' social networks and new venture growth. *Entrepreneurship Theory and Practice*, *39*(2), 313–344. doi:10.1111/etap.12044

Astrachan, C. B., Patel, V. K., & Wanzenried, G. (2014). A comparative study of CB-SEM and PLS-SEM for theory development in family firm research. *Journal of Family Business Strategy*, *5*(1), 116–128. doi:10.1016/j.jfbs.2013.12.002

Balabanis, G., & Katsikea, E. (2004). Being an entrepreneurial exporter: Does it pay? *International Business Review*, *12*(2), 233–252. doi:10.1016/S0969-5931(02)00098-7

Bandura, A. (1977). Self-efficacy: Toward a unifying theory of behavioral change. *Psychological Review*, *84*(2), 191–215. doi:10.1037/0033-295X.84.2.191 PMID:847061

Bandura, A. (1986). *The Social Foundations of Thought and Action*. Prentice-Hall.

Baron, R. M., & Kenny, D. A. (1986). The moderator–mediator variable distinction in social psychological research: Conceptual, strategic, and statistical considerations. *Journal of Personality and Social Psychology*, *51*(6), 1173–1182. doi:10.1037/0022-3514.51.6.1173 PMID:3806354

Barringer, R. B., & Bluedon, A. C. (1990). The relationship between corporate entrepreneurship and strategic management. *Strategic Management Journal*, *20*(5), 421–444. doi:10.1002/(SICI)1097-0266(199905)20:5<421::AID-SMJ30>3.0.CO;2-O

Batjargal, B. (2010). Network dynamics and new ventures in China: A longitudinal study. *Entrepreneurship and Regional Development*, *22*(2), 139–153. doi:10.1080/08985620802628864

Bergman, E. M. (2009). Embedding network analysis in spatial studies of innovation. *The Annals of Regional Science*, *43*(3), 559–565. doi:10.100700168-008-0250-y

Bhave, M. P. (1994). A process model of entrepreneurial venture creation. *Journal of Business Venturing*, *9*(3), 233–242. doi:10.1016/0883-9026(94)90031-0

Bird, B. (1988). Implementing entrepreneurial ideas—The case for intention. *Academy of Management Review*, *13*(3), 442–453. doi:10.2307/258091

Boyd, N. G., & Vozikis, G. S. (1994). The influence of self-efficacy on the development of entrepreneurial intentions and actions. *Entrepreneurship Theory and Practice*, *18*(4), 63–77. doi:10.1177/104225879401800404

Cardoza, G., & Fornes, G. (2011). The internationalisation of SMEs from China: The case of Ningxia Hui autonomous region. *Asia Pacific Journal of Management*, *28*(4), 737–759. doi:10.100710490-009-9174-z

Carneiro, J., & Brenes, E. R. (2014). Latin American firms competing in the global economy. *Journal of Business Research*, *67*(5), 831–836. doi:10.1016/j.jbusres.2013.07.001

Carr, J. C., & Sequeira, J. M. (2007). Prior family business exposure as intergenerational influence and entrepreneurial intent: A theory of planned behavior approach. *Journal of Business Research*, *60*(10), 1090–1098. doi:10.1016/j.jbusres.2006.12.016

Cepeda, G., Henseler, J., Ringle, C., & Roldán, J. L. (2016). Prediction-oriented modeling in business research by means of partial least squares path modeling. *Journal of Business Research*, *69*, 4545–4551. doi:10.1016/j.jbusres.2016.03.048

Chen, C. C., Greene, P. G., & Crick, A. (1998). Does entrepreneurial self-efficacy distinguish entrepreneurs from managers? *Journal of Business Venturing*, *13*(4), 295–316. doi:10.1016/S0883-9026(97)00029-3

Chetty, S., Karami, M., & Martín, O. M. (2018). Opportunity discovery and creation as duality: Evidence from small firms' foreign market entries. *Journal of International Marketing*, *26*(3), 70–93. doi:10.1509/jim.17.0005

Chien, S. Y. (2014). Franchisor resources, spousal resources, entrepreneurial orientation, and performance in a couple-owned franchise outlet. *Management Decision*, *52*(5), 916–933. doi:10.1108/MD-07-2013-0368

Chirico, F., Sirmon, D. G., Sciascia, S., & Mazzola, P. (2011). Resource orchestration in family firms: Investigating how entrepreneurial orientation, generational involvement, and participative strategy affect performance. *Strategic Entrepreneurship Journal*, *5*(4), 307–326. doi:10.1002ej.121

Cohen, J. (1992). A power primer. *Psychological Bulletin*, *112*(1), 155–159. doi:10.1037/0033-2909.112.1.155 PMID:19565683

Cooper, A. C. (1985). The role of incubator organizations in the founding of growth-oriented firms. *Journal of Business Venturing*, *1*(1), 75–86. doi:10.1016/0883-9026(85)90008-4

Cooper, A. C. (1993). Challenges in predicting new firm performance. *Journal of Business Venturing*, *8*(3), 241–253. doi:10.1016/0883-9026(93)90030-9

Cooper, S. Y., & Park, J. S. (2008). The impact of incubator' organizations on opportunity recognition and technology innovation in new, entrepreneurial high-technology ventures. *International Small Business Journal*, *26*(1), 27–56. doi:10.1177/0266242607084658

Coviello, N. E., McDougall, P. P., & Oviatt, B. M. (2011). The emergence, advance and future of international entrepreneurship research: An introduction to the special forum. *Journal of Business Venturing*, *26*(6), 625–631. doi:10.1016/j.jbusvent.2011.07.002

Covin, J. G., & Miller, D. (2014). International entrepreneurial orientation: Conceptual considerations, research themes, measurement issues, and future research directions. *Entrepreneurship Theory and Practice*, *38*(1), 11–44. doi:10.1111/etap.12027

Covin, J. G., & Slevin, D. P. (1989). Strategic management of small firms in hostile and benign environments. *Strategic Management Journal*, *10*(1), 75–87. doi:10.1002mj.4250100107

Crick, D. (2009). The internationalisation of born global and international new venture SMEs. *International Marketing Review*, *26*(4), 453–476. doi:10.1108/02651330910971986

Dada, O., & Watson, A. (2013). Entrepreneurial orientation and the franchise system: Organizational antecedents and performance outcomes. *European Journal of Marketing*, *47*(6), 790–812. doi:10.1108/03090561311306877

Davidsson, P., & Honig, B. L. (2003). The role of social and human capital among nascent entrepreneurs. *Journal of Business Venturing*, *18*(3), 301–331. doi:10.1016/S0883-9026(02)00097-6

Davidsson, P., Steffens, P., & Fitzsimmons, J. (2009). Growing profitable or growing from profits: Putting the horse in front of the cart? *Journal of Business Venturing*, *24*(4), 388–406. doi:10.1016/j.jbusvent.2008.04.003

Diamantopoulos, A., & Winklhofer, H. M. (2001). Index construction with formative indicators: An alternative to scale development. *JMR, Journal of Marketing Research*, *38*(2), 269–277. doi:10.1509/jmkr.38.2.269.18845

Doll, J., & Ajzen, I. (1992). Accessibility and stability of predictors in the theory of planned behavior. *Journal of Personality and Social Psychology*, *63*(5), 754–765. doi:10.1037/0022-3514.63.5.754

Felício, J., Meidutė, I., & Kyvik, Ø. (2016). Global mindset, cultural context, and the internationalization of SMEs. *Journal of Business Research*, *69*(11), 4924–4932. doi:10.1016/j.jbusres.2016.04.054

Felício, J. A., Caldeirinha, V. R., and Ribeiro-Navarrete, B. (2015). Corporate and individual global mindset and internationalization of European SMEs. *Journal of Business Research*, *68*(4), 797–802. doi:10.1016/j.jbusres.2014.11.031

Ferreira, F. A. F., Marques, C. S. E., Bento, P., Ferreira, J. J. M., & Jalali, M. S. (2015). Operationalizing and measuring individual entrepreneurial orientation using cognitive mapping and MCDA techniques. *Journal of Business Research*, *68*(12), 2691–2702. doi:10.1016/j.jbusres.2015.04.002

Fornell, C., & Larcker, D. F. (1981). Evaluating Structural Equation Models with Unobservable Variables and Measurement Error. *JMR, Journal of Marketing Research*, *18*(1), 39–50. doi:10.1177/002224378101800104

Freeman, S., & Cavusgil, S. T. (2007). Toward a typology of commitment states among managers of born-global firms: A study of accelerated internationalization. *Journal of International Marketing*, *15*(4), 1–40. doi:10.1509/jimk.15.4.1

Freixanet, J., Renart, G., & Rialp-Criado, A. (2018). The Impact of Managers' Global Orientation on SME Export and Economic Performance. *MIR. Management International Review*, *58*(4), 571–604. doi:10.100711575-018-0358-y

Gartner, W. B. (1985). A conceptual framework for describing the phenomenon of new venture Creation. *Academy of Management Review*, *10*(4), 696–706. doi:10.2307/258039

Gartner, W. B., Shaver, K. G., Gatewood, E. J., & Katz, J. (1994). Finding the entrepreneur in entrepreneurship. *Entrepreneurship Theory and Practice*, *18*(3), 5–10. doi:10.1177/104225879401800301

George, G., & Zahra, S. (2002). Culture and its consequences for entrepreneurship. *Entrepreneurship Theory and Practice*, *26*(4), 5–8. doi:10.1177/104225870202600401

Glancey, K. (1998). Determinants of growth and profitability in small entrepreneurial firms. *International Journal of Entrepreneurial Behaviour & Research*, *4*(1), 18–27. doi:10.1108/13552559810203948

Gomez-Mejia, L. R., Cruz, C., Berrone, P., & De Castro, J. (2011). The bind that ties: Socioemotional wealth preservation in family firms. *The Academy of Management Annals*, *5*(1), 653–707. doi:10.5465/19416520.2011.593320

Gupta, V. K., & Batra, S. (2015). Entrepreneurial orientation and firm performance in Indian SMEs: Universal and contingency perspectives. *International Small Business Journal*, 1–23. doi:10.1177/0266242615577708

Hamelin, A. (2013). Influence of family ownership on small business growth. Evidence from French SMEs. *Small Business Economics*, *41*(3), 563–579. doi:10.100711187-012-9452-x

Handrito, R. P., Slabbinck, H., & Vanderstraeten, J. (2020). Enjoying or Refraining from Risk? The Impact of Implicit Need for Achievement and Risk Perception on SME Internationalization. *Cross Cultural & Strategic Management*, *27*(3), 317–342. doi:10.1108/CCSM-03-2019-0068

Hayton, J. C., George, G., & Zahra, S. A. (2002). National culture and entrepreneurship: A review of behavioral research. *Entrepreneurship Theory and Practice*, *26*(4), 33–52. doi:10.1177/104225870202600403

Henseler, J., Ringle, C. M., & Sarstedt, M. (2015). A new criterion for assessing discriminant validity in variance-based structural equation modeling. *Journal of the Academy of Marketing Science*, *43*(1), 115–135. doi:10.100711747-014-0403-8

Hernández-Perlines, F., Moreno-García, J., & Yañez-Araque, B. (2016a). The mediating role of competitive strategy in international entrepreneurial orientation. *Journal of Business Research*, *69*(11), 5383–5389. doi:10.1016/j.jbusres.2016.04.142

Hmieleski, K. M., & Corbett, A. C. (2006). Proclivity for improvisation as a predictor of entrepreneurial intentions. *Journal of Small Business Management*, *44*(1), 45–63. doi:10.1111/j.1540-627X.2006.00153.x

Hoang, H., & Antoncic, B. (2003). Network-based research in entrepreneurship: A critical review. *Journal of Business Venturing*, *18*(2), 165–187. doi:10.1016/S0883-9026(02)00081-2

Hsu, W. T., Chen, H. L., & Cheng, C. Y. (2013). Internationalization and firm performance of SMEs: The moderating effects of CEO attributes. *Journal of World Business*, *48*(1), 1–1. doi:10.1016/j.jwb.2012.06.001

Jafari-Sadeghi, V. (2020). The motivational factors of business venturing: Opportunity versus necessity? A gendered perspective on European countries. *Journal of Business Research*, *113*, 279–289. doi:10.1016/j.jbusres.2019.09.058

Jafari Sadeghi, V., Kimiagari, S., & Biancone, P. (2019). Level of Education and Knowledge, Foresight Competency, and International Entrepreneurship: A Study of Human Capital Determinants in the European Countries. *European Business Review*, *32*(2), 46–68. doi:10.1108/EBR-05-2018-0098

Jafari Sadeghi, V., Nkongolo-Bakenda, J.-M., Anderson, B., & Dana, L.-P. (2019). An institution-based view of international entrepreneurship: A comparison of context-based and universal determinants in developing and economically advanced countries. *International Business Review*, *28*(6), 1–1. doi:10.1016/j.ibusrev.2019.101588

Javidan, M., Bullough, A., & Dibble, R. (2016). Mind the gap: Gender differences in global leadership self-efficacies. *The Academy of Management Perspectives*, *30*(1), 59–73. doi:10.5465/amp.2015.0035

Joardar, A., & Wu, S. (2011). Examining the dual forces of individual entrepreneurial orientation and liability of foreignness on international entrepreneurs. *Canadian Journal of Administrative Sciences*, *28*(3), 328–340. doi:10.1002/cjas.203

Johnson, J., Lenartowicz, T., & Apud, S. (2006). Cross-cultural competence in international business: Toward a definition and a model. *Journal of International Business Studies*, *37*(4), 525–543. doi:10.1057/palgrave.jibs.8400205

Jones, M. V., Coviello, N., & Tang, Y. K. (2011). International Entrepreneurship research (1989-2009): A domain ontology and thematic analysis. *Journal of Business Venturing*, *26*(6), 632–659. doi:10.1016/j.jbusvent.2011.04.001

Jones, M. V., & Coviello, N. E. (2005). Internationalisation: Conceptualising an entrepreneurial process of behaviour in time. *Journal of International Business Studies*, *36*(3), 284–303. doi:10.1057/palgrave.jibs.8400138

Kautonen, T., van Gelderen, M., & Fink, M. (2015). Robustness of the Theory of Planned Behavior in Predicting Entrepreneurial Intentions and Actions. *Entrepreneurship Theory and Practice*, *39*(3), 655–674. doi:10.1111/etap.12056

Kedia, B., & Mukherji, A. (1999). Global managers: Developing a mindset for global competitiveness. *Journal of World Business*, *34*(3), 230–251. doi:10.1016/S1090-9516(99)00017-6

Khedhaouria, A., Gurău, C., & Torrès, O. (2014). Creativity, self-efficacy, and small-firm performance: The mediating role of entrepreneurial orientation. *Small Business Economics*, *44*(3), 485–504. doi:10.100711187-014-9608-y

Kickul, J., Gundry, L. K., Barbosa, S. D., & Whitcanack, L. (2009). Intuition versus analysis? Testing differential models of cognitive style on entrepreneurial self-efficacy and the new venture creation process. *Entrepreneurship Theory and Practice*, *33*(2), 439–453. doi:10.1111/j.1540-6520.2009.00298.x

Kiss, A., Williams, D., & Houghton, S. (2013). Risk bias and the link between motivation and new venture post-entry international growth. *International Business Review*, *22*(6), 1068–1078. doi:10.1016/j.ibusrev.2013.02.007

Kleinbaum, D. G., Kupper, L. L., Muller, K. E., & Nizam, A. (1988). *One-Way Analysis of Variance. Applied Regression Analysis and Other Multivariable Methods*. PWS-Kent Publishing.

Knight, G. (2001). Entrepreneurship and strategy in the international SME. *Journal of International Management*, *7*(3), 155–171. doi:10.1016/S1075-4253(01)00042-4

Knockaert, M., Ucbasaran, D., Wright, M., & Clarysse, B. (2011). The relationship between knowledge transfer, top management team composition, and performance: The case of science-based entrepreneurial firms. *Entrepreneurship Theory and Practice*, *35*(4), 777–803. doi:10.1111/j.1540-6520.2010.00405.x

Kolvereid, L. (1996b). Prediction of employment status choice intentions. *Entrepreneurship Theory and Practice*, *21*(1), 47–57. doi:10.1177/104225879602100104

Kolvereid, L., & Isaksen, E. (2006). New business start-up and subsequent entry into self-employment. *Journal of Business Venturing, 21*(6), 866–885. doi:10.1016/j.jbusvent.2005.06.008

Korsakienė, R., & Tvaronavičienė, M. (2012). The internationalization of SMEs: An integrative approach. *Journal of Business Economics and Management, 13*(2), 294–307. doi:10.3846/16111699.2011.620138

Kropp, F., Lindsay, N. J., & Shoham, A. (2006). Entrepreneurial, market, and learning orientations and international entrepreneurial business venture performance in South African firms. *International Marketing Review, 23*(5), 504–523. doi:10.1108/02651330610703427

Krueger, N. F. (1993). The impact of prior entrepreneurial exposure on perceptions of new venture feasibility and desirability. *Entrepreneurship Theory and Practice, 18*(1), 5–21. doi:10.1177/104225879301800101

Krueger, N. F. Jr. (2000). The cognitive infrastructure of opportunity emergence. *Entrepreneurship Theory and Practice, 24*(3), 5–22. doi:10.1177/104225870002400301

Krueger, N. F. Jr, & Brazeal, D. V. (1994). Entrepreneurial potential and potential entrepreneurs. *Entrepreneurship Theory and Practice, 18*(3), 91–104. doi:10.1177/104225879401800307

Krueger, N. F., & Carsrud, A. L. (1993). Entrepreneurial intentions: Applying the theory of planned behavior. *Entrepreneurship and Regional Development, 5*(4), 315–330. doi:10.1080/08985629300000020

Krueger, N. F. Jr, Reilly, M. D., & Carsrud, A. L. (2000). Competing models of entrepreneurial intentions. *Journal of Business Venturing, 15*(5-6), 411–432. doi:10.1016/S0883-9026(98)00033-0

Lamotte, O., & Colovic, A. (2013). Innovation and Internationalization of Young Entrepreneurial Firms. *Management International Review, 18*(1), 87–103.

Lee, S., & Peterson, S. (2000). Culture, entrepreneurial orientation, and global competitiveness. *Journal of World Business, 35*(4), 401–416. doi:10.1016/S1090-9516(00)00045-6

Lee, S. H., & Wong, P. K. (2004). An exploratory study of technopreneurial intentions: A career anchor Perspective. *Journal of Business Venturing, 19*(1), 7–28. doi:10.1016/S0883-9026(02)00112-X

Levesque, Moren and Minniti, M. (2006). The Effect of Aging on Entrepreneurial Behavior. *Journal of Business Venturing, 21* (2), 177-194.

Levy, O., Beechler, S., Taylor, S., & Boyacigiller, N. A. (2007). What we talk about when we talk about 'global mindset': Managerial cognition in multinational corporations. *Journal of International Business Studies*, *38*(2), 231–258. doi:10.1057/palgrave.jibs.8400265

Liñán, F., & Chen, Y. W. (2009). Development and cross-cultural application of a specific instrument to measure entrepreneurial intentions. *Entrepreneurship Theory and Practice*, *33*(3), 593–617. doi:10.1111/j.1540-6520.2009.00318.x

Lin˜an, F., Paul, J., & Fayolle, A. (2019). SMES and entrepreneurship in the era of globalization. *Small Business Economics*, *55*(3), 695–703. doi:10.100711187-019-00180-7

Lumpkin, G. T., & Dess, G. G. (1996). The entrepreneurial clarifying it construct and linking orientation. *Academy of Management Review*, *21*(1), 135–172. doi:10.2307/258632

Lumpkin, G. T., & Dess, G. G. (2001). Linking two dimensions of entrepreneurial orientation to firm performance: The moderating role of environment and industry life cycle. *Journal of Business Venturing*, *16*(5), 429–451. doi:10.1016/S0883-9026(00)00048-3

Lüthje, C., & Franke, N. (2003). The 'making' of an entrepreneur: Testing a model of entrepreneurial intent among engineering students at MIT. *R & D Management*, *33*(2), 135–147. doi:10.1111/1467-9310.00288

Maitland, E., & Sammartino, A. (2015). Managerial cognition and internationalization. *Journal of International Business Studies*, *46*(7), 733–760. doi:10.1057/jibs.2015.9

Miller, D. (1983). The correlates of entrepreneurship in three types of firms. *Management Science*, *29*(7), 770–791. doi:10.1287/mnsc.29.7.770

Minniti, M., & Nardone, C. (2007). Being in Someone Else's Shoes: The Role of Gender in Nascent Entrepreneurship. *Small Business Economics*, *28*(3), 223–238. doi:10.100711187-006-9017-y

Mitchell, R. K., Smith, B., Seawright, K. W., & Morse, E. A. (2000). Cross cultural cognition and venture creation decision. *Academy of Management Review*, *43*(5), 974–993.

Mueller, S. L., & Thomas, A. S. (2001). Culture and entrepreneurial potential: A nine country study of locus of control and innovativeness. *Journal of Business Venturing*, *16*(1), 51–75. doi:10.1016/S0883-9026(99)00039-7

Nummela, N., Saarenketo, S., and Puumalainen, K. (2004). A global mindset – a prerequisite for successful internationalization? *Canadian Journal of Administrative Sciences/Revue Canadienne des Sciences de l'Administration, 21*(1), 51–64. https://doi.org/ doi:10.1111/j.1936-4490.2004.tb00322.x

Olejnik, E., & Swoboda, B. (2012). SMEs' internationalisation patterns: Descriptives, dynamics and Determinants. *International Marketing Review, 29*(5), 466–495. doi:10.1108/02651331211260340

Oviatt, B., & McDougall, P. (1994). Toward a Theory of International New ventures. *Journal of International Business Studies, 25*(1), 45–64. doi:10.1057/palgrave.jibs.8490193

Oviatt, B., & McDougall, P. (2005). Defining international entrepreneurship and modeling the speed of internationalization. *Entrepreneurship Theory and Practice, 29*(5), 537–553. doi:10.1111/j.1540-6520.2005.00097.x

Parida, V., Pesämaa, O., Wincent, J., & Westerberg, M. (2017). Network capability, innovativeness, and performance: A multidimensional extension for entrepreneurship. *Entrepreneurship and Regional Development, 29*(2), 94–115. doi:10.1080/08985626.2016.1255434

Paul, H. (2000). Creating a global mindset. *Thunderbird International Business Review, 42*(2), 187–200. doi:10.1002/1520-6874(200003/04)42:2<187::AID-TIE4>3.0.CO;2-7

Paul, J., Parthasarathy, S., & Gupta, P. (2017). Exporting challenges of SMEs: A review and future research agenda. *Journal of World Business, 52*(3), 327–342. doi:10.1016/j.jwb.2017.01.003

Pinho, J., & Prange, C. (2016). The effect of social networks and dynamic internationalization capabilities on international performance. *Journal of World Business, 51*(3), 391–403. doi:10.1016/j.jwb.2015.08.001

Poon, J. M. L., Ainuddin, R. H., & Junit, S. A. (2006). Effects of self-concept traits and entrepreneurial orientation on firm performance. *International Small Business Journal, 24*(1), 61–82. doi:10.1177/0266242606059779

Rauch, A., Wiklund, J., Lumpkin, G. T., & Frese, M. (2009). Entrepreneurial orientation and business performance: an assessment of past research and suggestions for the future. *Entrepreneurship Theory and Practice, 33,* 761–787. doi:. 00308.x doi:10.1111/j.1540-6520.2009

Reijonen, H., Hirvonen, S., Nagy, G., Laukkanen, T., & Gabrielsson, M. (2015). The impact of entrepreneurial orientation on B2B branding and business growth in emerging markets. *Industrial Marketing Management*, *51*, 35–46. doi:10.1016/j.indmarman.2015.04.016

Rong, B., & Wilkinson, I. F. (2011). What do managers' survey responses mean and what affects them? The case of market orientation and firm performance. *Australasian Marketing Journal*, *19*(3), 137–147. doi:10.1016/j.ausmj.2011.04.001

Rosenbusch, N., Rauch, A., & Bausch, A. (2013). The mediating role of entrepreneurial orientation in the task environment—Performance relationship: A meta-analysis. *Journal of Management*, *39*(3), 633–659. doi:10.1177/0149206311425612

Sapienza, H. J., Autio, E., George, G., & Zahra, S. A. (2006). A capabilities perspective on the effects of early internationalization on firm survival and growth. *Academy of Management Review*, *31*(4), 914–933. doi:10.5465/amr.2006.22527465

Sarstedt, M., Ringle, C. M., Smith, D., Reams, R., & Hair, J. F. Jr. (2014). Partial least squares structural equation modeling (PLS-SEM): A useful tool for family business researchers. *Journal of Family Business Strategy*, *5*(1), 105–115. doi:10.1016/j.jfbs.2014.01.002

Shane, S., & Nicolaou, N. (2015). Creative personality, opportunity recognition and the tendency to start businesses: A study of their genetic predispositions. *Journal of Business Venturing*, *30*(3), 407–419. doi:10.1016/j.jbusvent.2014.04.001

Shi, H. X., Graves, C., & Barbera, F. (2019). Intergenerational succession and internationalization strategy of family SMEs: Evidence from China. *Long Range Planning*, *52*(4), 101838. doi:10.1016/j.lrp.2018.05.004

Siepel, J., Camerani, R., & Masucci, M. (2019). Skills combinations and firm performance. *Small Business Economics*, *5*, 1–23.

Stam, W., & Elfring, T. (2008). Entrepreneurial orientation and new venture performance: The moderating role of intra-and extraindustry social capital. *Academy of Management Journal*, *51*(1), 97–111. doi:10.5465/amj.2008.30744031

Steel, P., & Koenig, C. J. (2006). Integrating theories of motivation. *Academy of Management Review*, *31*(4), 889–913. doi:10.5465/amr.2006.22527462

Sundqvist, S., Kyläheiko, K., Kuivalainen, O., & Cadogan, J. W. (2012). Kirznerian and Schumpeterian entrepreneurial– oriented behavior in turbulent export markets. *International Marketing Review*, *29*(2), 203–219. doi:10.1108/02651331211216989

Tubbs, M. E., & Ekeberg, S. E. (1991). The role of intentions in work motivation: Implications for goal-setting theory and research. *Academy of Management Review*, *16*(1), 180–199. doi:10.2307/258611

Wales, W., Monsen, E., & McKelvie, A. (2011). The organizational pervasiveness of entrepreneurial orientation. *Entrepreneurship Theory and Practice, 5,* 895–923. doi:. 00451.x doi:10.1111/j.1540-6520.2011

Webster, F. A. (1977). Entrepreneurs and ventures: An attempt at classification and clarification. *Academy of Management Review*, *2*(1), 54–61. doi:10.2307/257605

Weerawardena, J., Mort, G. S., Liesch, P. W., & Knight, G. (2007). Conceptualizing accelerated internationalization in the born global firm: A dynamic capabilities perspective. *Journal of World Business*, *42*(3), 294–306. doi:10.1016/j.jwb.2007.04.004

Wiklund, J., Patzelt, H., & Shepherd, D. A. (2009). Building an integrative model of small business growth. *Small Business Economics*, *32*(4), 351–374. doi:10.100711187-007-9084-8

Wiklund, J., & Shepherd, D. (2003). Knowledge-based resources, entrepreneurial orientation, and the performance of small and medium-sized businesses. *Strategic Management Journal*, *24*(13), 1307–1314. doi:10.1002mj.360

Wiklund, J., & Shepherd, D. (2005). Entrepreneurial orientation and small business performance: A configurational approach. *Journal of Business Venturing*, *20*(1), 71–91. doi:10.1016/j.jbusvent.2004.01.001

Wilson, F., Kickul, J., & Marlino, D. (2007). Gender, entrepreneurial self-efficacy, and entrepreneurial career intentions: Implications for entrepreneurship education. *Entrepreneurship Theory and Practice*, *31*(3), 387–406. doi:10.1111/j.1540-6520.2007.00179.x

Woodside, A. G. (2013). Moving beyond multiple regression analysis to algorithms: Calling for adoption of a paradigm shift from symmetric to asymmetric thinking in data analysis and crafting theory. *Journal of Business Research*, *66*(4), 463–472. doi:10.1016/j.jbusres.2012.12.021

Woodside, A. G., Prentice, C., & Larsen, A. (2015). Revisiting problem gamblers' harsh gaze on casino services: Applying complexity theory to identify exceptional customers. *Psychology and Marketing*, *32*(1), 65–77. doi:10.1002/mar.20763

Wright, M., Westhead, P., & Ucbasaran, D. (2007). Internationalization of small and medium-sized enterprises (SMEs) and international entrepreneurship: A critique and policy implications. *Regional Studies, 41*(7), 1013–1030. doi:10.1080/00343400601120288

Wright, R. T., Campbell, D. E., Thatcher, J. B., & Roberts, N. (2012). Operationalizing multidimensional constructs in structural equation modeling: Recommendations for IS research. *Communications of the Association for Information Systems, 30*, 367–412. doi:10.17705/1CAIS.03023

Zahra, S. A., & Covin, J. G. (1995). Contextual influences on the corporate entrepreneurship performance relationship: A longitudinal analysis. *Journal of Business Venturing, 10*(1), 43–58. doi:10.1016/0883-9026(94)00004-E

Zahra, S. A., Korri, J. S., & Yu, J. (2005). Cognition and international entrepreneurship: Implications for research on international opportunity recognition and exploitation. *International Business Review, 14*(2), 129–146. doi:10.1016/j.ibusrev.2004.04.005

Zhao, H., Hills, G. E., & Siebert, S. E. (2005). The mediating role of self-efficacy in the development of entrepreneurial intentions. *The Journal of Applied Psychology, 90*(6), 1265–1272. doi:10.1037/0021-9010.90.6.1265 PMID:16316279

Chapter 4
Examining Technical Undergraduates' Entrepreneurial Attitudes as Mediators Between Entrepreneurial Characteristics and Self-Employment Intention

Pushkar Dubey
Pandit Sundarlal Sharma (Open) University, Chhattisgarh, India

Kailash Kumar Sahu
Pandit Sundarlal Sharma (Open) University, Chhattisgarh, India

Parul Dubey
https://orcid.org/0000-0001-8903-6664
G.H. Raisoni College of Engineering and Technology, Nagpur, India

ABSTRACT

Entrepreneurial ventures are the only way through which unemployment can be handled effectively. Emerging economies such as India knows their strength, but its searching ways to effectively cash it out. The present helps in finding the mediating effect of entrepreneurial attitude (i.e., achievement, innovation, personal control, and self-esteem) in the link between entrepreneurial characteristics and self-employment intention among technical undergraduates of different government

DOI: 10.4018/978-1-6684-7140-1.ch004

and private technical institutions of Chhattisgarh. Stratified random sampling was used to collect 1000 responses from technical undergraduates. Regression and confirmatory factor analysis were applied to analyse the data. The findings explained that entrepreneurial attitude dimensions were found partially mediated between entrepreneurial characteristics and self-employment intention among engineering undergraduates.

1. INTRODUCTION

Unemployment is one of the most difficult issues that every economy has to cope with. Unemployment is not only among uneducated people, but also the educated with high degree are searching for employment in the job market. India, being a young country, has a large proportion of its people who are under the age of 30, and in order for them to reach their full potential, it becomes imperative to provide the appropriate combination of skills and opportunities to students. According to Pandey (2019), based on the State of India's Environment (SoE) 2019 figures, India's unemployment rate has climbed almost 1.9 times to 7.6 percent in April 2019, the highest in the last two years. Rural unemployment has also hit an all-time high of 7.61 percent. The report also shows a 15% rise in the young unemployment rate (20-24 years) during the last two years.

Western nations have been able to leverage the potential of human creativity in science and technology to establish a pool between business and academics, but India has fallen far behind in this area. For years, India has followed the current scenario by ignoring the need of partnership between business and academics in addressing India's most pressing challenges.

The influence of the entrepreneurial factor and its significance in current engineering school programmes or determining career pathways for latent entrepreneurs is mostly unknown. However, more engineering students are becoming acquainted with entrepreneurial programmes, and relatively few research are being undertaken to discover entrepreneurial attitudes, affect their learning, or assess professional competency. It is not surprising that the integration of entrepreneurship in the engineering discipline is a relatively recent endeavour by concentrating on becoming entrepreneurs inside their engineering curriculum (Standish-Kuon and Rice, 2002).

According to Bhagchandani (2017), the young and skilled youth and graduates are the ever-growing challenges since they are always looking for work rather than beginning a new firm. The need to provide assistance and mentoring to young and mature entrepreneurs continues unacknowledged, and self-financing is highly fragmented, concentrated in a few locations, and notably low in quantity throughout the country. However, according to Rodrigues *et al.* (2021), individuals with a strong entrepreneurial mindset and intention are required for development, expansion, and innovation in the business sector. These activities may inspire pupils to become future entrepreneurs, so boosting company success and overall economic progress.

Former President of India Dr. A.P.J. Abdul Kalam has firm belief that science and technology has the capability to pave the country towards growth and development. Also, in order to address the unemployment issue effectively, inclination of technical students towards entrepreneurship must be assessed. Thus, the present study examines the mediating effect of entrepreneurial attitude dimensions (i.e., achievement, innovation, personal control, and self-esteem) in the link between entrepreneurial characteristics and self-employment intention among technical undergraduates of different government and private engineering institutions of Chhattisgarh state.

2. LITERATURE REVIEW

2.1 Entrepreneurial Characteristics (EC)

Researchers have identified the significance of several personality qualities in relation to entrepreneurial activity at various stages. Several research on various personality qualities looked at the distinctions between entrepreneurs and non-entrepreneurs. Individual qualities or personality characteristics have remained important subjects of study for scholars in the past and now (Robinson *et al.,* 1991; Ho and Koh, 1992; Koh, 1996; Bakotic and Kruzic, 2010). Entrepreneurs are defined by a collection of qualities or attributes. An person is defined by a characteristic. Characteristics are different characteristics of an individual that aid in the formation of the personality. A trait approach to entrepreneurship defines and emphasizes a person's personality/ psychological variables and features (McClelland, 1961; Brockhaus, 1980). An individual's entrepreneurial qualities or characteristics may include demonstrating certain psychological characteristics such as a devotion to their profession, a demand for ultimate control, and the capacity to manage with uncertainty and problems (Mitton, 1989).

An individual's entrepreneurial goals are significantly influenced by his or her ability to take risks and hold firm in the time of adversity. A number of other relevant studies have shown that persons with a greater risk tolerance have better and more severe intents of becoming entrepreneurs (Luthje and Franke, 2003; Segal *et al.,* 2005; Nabi *et al.,* 2011; Luthje and Franke, 2003). The socio-cultural characteristics and experience of individual entrepreneurs, according to Morrison (2000), impact their choice to pursue entrepreneurship as a profession. Perceptions and actions are influenced by personal attributes such as technical knowledge, management experience, entrepreneurial experience, and other such traits Cooper *et al.,* 1988; Ronstadt, 1988).

2.2 Entrepreneurial Attitude (EA)

Entrepreneurship may be properly understood by examining the significance of attitude as outlined by numerous theorists and researchers (Drucker, 1970; Olson and Bosserman, 1984; Gasse, 1985; Greenberger and Sexton, 1987). There are two basic or fundamental techniques to understanding a person's attitude. The former defines attitude as a unidimensional construct, while the latter defines it as a multidimensional approach. The depiction of the unidimensional approach consists only of affective response (Fishbein and Ajzen, 1975). According to the multidimensional component, individual responses are based on three sorts of reactions: affect, cognition, and conation. This is also known as the tripartite model, where attitude is a mixture of all three components (Carlson, 1985; Chaiken and Stangor, 1987; Shaver, 1987).

Entrepreneurial attitude may be defined as a personal drive to become an entrepreneur (Kolvereid, 1996). According to the theory of planned behaviour, a positive attitude toward an activity increases one's intention to engage in the behaviour (Armitage and Conner, 2001). The benefit derived from developing entrepreneurial abilities is the outcome of a good mental attitude. It may considerably increase a person's inclination to start a business (Krueger *et al.,* 2000). Several research have shown a link between attitude and behavioural intention (Krueger *et al.,* 2000; Autio *et al.,* 2001; Van Gelderen *et al.,* 2008; Tegtmeier, 2012; Yang, 2013). Previous study has shown that personality characteristics, beliefs, attitudes, and (early) learning experiences all have a direct impact on entrepreneurial aspirations (Zhao *et al.,* 2005). Hatten and Ruhland (1995) investigated the entrepreneurial traits and attitudinal change of college students after participation in a small business institute (SBI) programme. According to the findings, young individuals and those with a stronger locus of control are more likely to have a major positive attitude shift regarding entrepreneurship.

2.3 Self-Employment Intention (SEI)

Self-employment intention may be described as an individual's preparation, engagement, or desire to start a company (Krueger and Carsrud, 1993; Luthje and Franke, 2003; Drennan *et al.,* 2005; Souitaris *et al.,* 2007). Individual intention is a person's mental state in which they seek towards a goal (Bird and West, 1998). As a result, the greater the purpose, the more realistic the behaviour implementation. For start-ups, entrepreneurship is a deliberate process that requires decision-making

(Krueger *et al.,* 2000; Kautonen *et al.,* 2011). Thus, entrepreneurial intention is critical in the development of being an entrepreneur (Sharaf *et al.,* 2018). The notion of graduate entrepreneurship has been extensively researched at the university level (Wang and Wong, 2004; Van Gelderen *et al.,* 2008; Nabi *et al.,* 2011). Several variables influence entrepreneurial intent. According to the literature, a positive entrepreneurial mindset is conducive to increasing entrepreneurial intention (Robinson *et al.,* 1991; Phan *et al.,* 2002; Luthje and Franke, 2003; Rodrigues *et al.,* 2021) Furthermore, entrepreneurial qualities are thought to be a predictor of entrepreneurial intent (Rasheed and Rasheed, 2003).

3. METHODOLOGY

3.1 Theoretical Framework

Since the present study attempts to answer the following question: -

- Whether the EA dimensions (i.e., achievement, innovation, personal control, and self-esteem) play as positive mediator in the link between EC and SEI among technical undergraduates of Chhattisgarh state.

Hence, the authors propose the following theoretical model for the study: -

Figure 1. Theoretical model of the present study

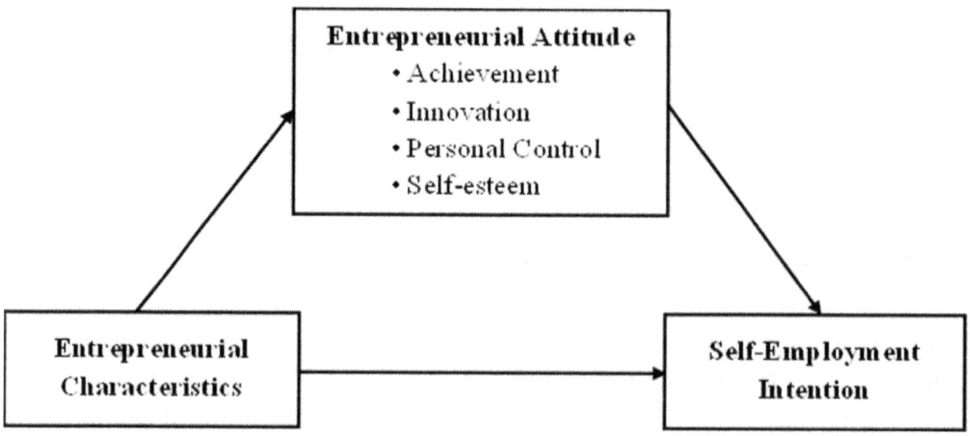

3.2 Hypotheses

Based on the above theoretical model, the following hypotheses have been formulated for the further analysis: -

H1. Achievement would emerge as positive mediator between EC and SEI.
H2. Innovation would emerge as positive mediator between EC and SEI.
H3. Personal control would emerge as positive mediator between EC and SEI.
H4. Self-esteem would emerge as positive mediator between EC and SEI.
H5. EA would emerge as positive mediator between EC and SEI.

3.3 Operational Definition

3.3.1 Entrepreneurial Characteristics (EC)

EC are the set of features or skills that a person has or acquires through time and various experiences. Entrepreneurial characteristics consists of ambiguity tolerance, self-sufficiency, locus of control, risk-taking propensity, planning and organising ability, and social networking.

3.3.2 Self-Employment Intention (SEI)/Entrepreneurial Intention

SEI has been described in a variety of ways, including the desire to start a new venture (Zhao et al., 2005), the intention to own a firm (Crant, 1996), and the ambition to work for oneself (Douglas and Shepherd, 2002).

3.3.3 Entrepreneurial Attitude (EA)

Ajzen (1987) defined attitude as a learned predisposition of an individual to behave favorably or unfavorably towards an action; its formation can occur either through past or prior experiences or perceptions accumulated over an individual's life span (Kuehn, 2008). Mitchell *et al.* (2003) explained entrepreneurial attitude as their opinion about the abilities, adaptability and actions in the entrepreneurial process.

3.3.4 Achievement

Achievement refers to the feeling to achieve the desired outcome in the entrepreneurial process. McClelland argued that a person's desire to succeed is the driving force behind entrepreneurialism (Chell, 2008).

3.3.5 Innovation

The term "innovation" refers to the process of coming up with something new, whether it's a new product, technique, market, or organisation altogether. The term innovation refers to the ability to see and act on business operations in a fresh and novel manner (Kirton, 1978; Drucker, 1985).

3.3.6 Personal Control

A person's sense of power and influence over the course of his or her business is referred to as "perceived personal control." Positivity in entrepreneurship is a result of self-control on the part of the entrepreneur (Robinson et al., 1991).

3.3.7 Self-Esteem

Self-esteem refers to the belief that one's abilities and skills are sufficient for a new venture's success, which motivates one to put out the required effort (Douglas and Shepherd, 2000).

3.4 Research Design and Sampling

The study's primary respondents were engineering undergraduates belonging to any technical college/university/institution offering engineering programmes in Chhattisgarh state. The correlational research design was applied in this study. For collecting the data, stratified random sampling method was incorporated. A sample of 1000 respondents was considered for the study as shown in the Table 1.

3.5 Research Instrument

The present study adapted or modified the items/constructs as per the current research needs. The required constructs and measurement items along with its supporting literatures in which EC (i.e., ambiguity tolerance, self-sufficiency, locus of control, risk-taking propensity, planning and organising ability, and social networking), EA dimensions (i.e., achievement, innovation, personal control, and self-esteem), and SEI are taken. After the identification and development of the measurement items, the researcher sent the questionnaire to the three subject experts to examine its content validity. A few items were modified as per the expert suggestions. After that, a pilot study was administered to check its content validity whether the questionnaire is prepared to take participants' responses. No major changes were needed after the pilot study. Hence, the final 47-item questionnaire were prepared to collect primary

Table 1. Demographic description

Demographic Characteristics	Variable	Frequency	Percent	Total Sample Size
Age	19-22 Years	813	81.3	1000
	23-25 Years	111	11.1	
	26-29 Years	30	3	
	30 Years and Above	46	4.6	
Gender	Female	571	57.1	1000
	Male	429	42.9	
Father's Occupation	Government Service	306	30.6	1000
	Private Service	138	13.8	
	Business	168	16.8	
	Cultivation	221	22.1	
	Others	167	16.7	
Locality	Rural	434	43.4	1000
	Urban	566	56.6	
Family Monthly Income	<Rs. 30,000	320	32	1000
	Rs. 30,001-Rs. 50,000	330	33	
	Rs. 50,001-Rs. 70,000	210	21	
	>Rs. 70,000	140	14	

responses. The final constructs are achievement (6 items from Ismail *et al.,* 2013), Innovation (6 items from Ismail *et al.* (2013)), Personal control (5 items from Ismail *et al.* (2013)), self-esteem (6 items from Ismail *et al.* (2013)), self-employment intention (6 items from Ismail *et al.* (2013)), ambiguity tolerance (3 items from Bezzina (2010)), self-sufficiency (3 items from Bezzina (2010)), locus of control (3 items from Bezzina (2010)), risk-taking propensity (3 items from Bezzina (2010)), planning and organising ability (3 items from Rocha and Freitas (2014), Schmidt and Bohnenberger (2009), Moraes *et al.* (2018)), social networking (3 items from Schmidt and Bohnenberger (2009)).

3.6 Scale Validation

The scale was validated using a partial least squares confirmatory factor analysis in the study. In Table 3, Cronbach's alpha (Nunnally, 1978) and Rho A value is indicated more than 0.7 for the all variables which explains a fair measure of reliability of the scale. For validity measure, convergent validity's value must be more than 0.7 (Hair *et al.,* 2010; Bagozzi and Yi, 1988) and average variance extracted (AVE) value must be greater than 0.5 for all the variables as indicated in the Table 3. Thus, the results produce fair measures for reliability and validity of scale.

Table 2. Measurement results

Factors	Cronbach's Alpha	Rho A	CR	AVE
Achievement	0.857	0.887	0.861	0.52
Innovation	0.882	0.884	0.881	0.554
Personal Control	0.844	0.846	0.844	0.52
Self Esteem	0.716	0.733	0.715	0.503
Overall EA	0.944	0.951	0.946	0.539
SEI	0.812	0.827	0.817	0.531
Overall EC	0.893	0.897	0.894	0.521

Table 3. Discriminant validity (Fornell-Larcker Criterion)

	Achievement	Innovation	Personal Control	SEI	Self Esteem
Achievement	**0.988**				
Innovation	0.846	**0.917**			
Personal Control	0.759	0.841	**0.925**		
SEI	0.491	0.59	0.621	**0.877**	
Self Esteem	0.635	0.613	0.656	0.738	**0.742**

3.7 Data Analysis

Regression and confirmatory factor analysis (CFA) were run to analyse the data.

4. ANALYSIS AND INTERPRETATION

4.1 Mediation of Achievement

It can be observed from Table 4 and Figure 2 that path (Z) [I.D., (total effect)] from EC to SEI ($\beta = .725$, $p < 0.01$) is significant, suggesting that higher EC can result in higher SEI.

Path (X) IM, indicated that those who had higher EC can result in higher achievement ($\beta = .603$, $p < 0.01$). Path (Y) MD.I, indicated that higher achievement motive can result in higher SEI ($\beta = .175$, $p < 0.01$).

Since the estimates of paths (X), (Y) and (Z) are significant, it is worthy of introducing self-achievement as a mediator between EC and SEI.

Path (Z') ID.M (direct effect) indicated that the total effect of EC on SEI was reduced ($\beta = .620$, $p < 0.01$) when achievement was integrated into the model.

Table 4 further suggested that the indirect effect ($\beta = .105$, $p < 0.01$) of EC and SEI through achievement [path (X) * (Y)] was statistically significant and is a case of partial mediation.

Figure 2. Direct, total and indirect effects of achievement as a mediator between EC and SEI

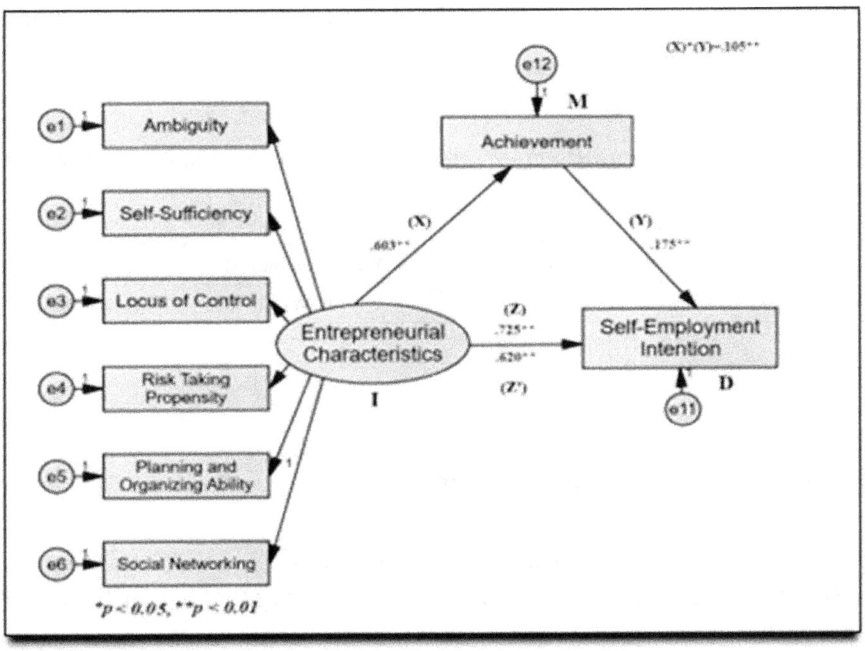

Table 4. Direct, total and indirect effects of achievement as a mediator between EC and SEI

β (Standardized Regression Weight Estimates)				
ID (Z)	IM (X)	MD. I (Y)	ID.M (Z')	IM (X)*MD.I (Y)
.725**	.603**	.175**	.620**	.105**

*p = 0.05, **p = 0.01

4.2. Mediation of Innovation

It can be observed from Table 5 and Figure 3 that path (Z) [I.D., (total effect)] from EC to SEI (β = .725**, $p < 0.01$) is significant, suggesting that higher EC can result in higher SEI.

Path (X) IM, indicated that those who had higher EC can result in higher innovation (β = .627**, $p < 0.01$). Path (Y) MD.I, indicated that higher innovative behaviour can result in higher SEI (β = .106**, $p < 0.01$).

Since the estimates of paths (X), (Y) and (Z) are significant, it is worthy of introducing innovation as a mediator between EC and SEI.

Path (Z') ID.M (direct effect) indicated that the total effect of EC on SEI was reduced (β = .572**, $p < 0.01$) when innovation was integrated into the model.

Table 5 further suggested that the indirect effect (β = .025, $p > 0.05$) of EC on SEI through innovation [path (X) * (Y)] was statistically insignificant and is a condition of no mediation.

Table 5. Direct, total and indirect effects of innovation as a mediator between EC and SEI

β (Standardized Regression Weight Estimates)				
ID (Z)	IM (X)	MD. I (Y)	ID.M (Z')	IM (X)*MD.I (Y)
.725**	.627**	.106**	.572**	.025

*p = 0.05, **p = 0.01

4.3 Mediation of Personal Control

It can be observed from Table 6 and Figure 4 that path (Z) [I.D., (total effect)] from EC to SEI (β = .725, $p < 0.01$) is significant, suggesting that higher EC can result in higher SEI.

Figure 3. Direct, total and indirect effects of innovation as a mediator between EC and SEI

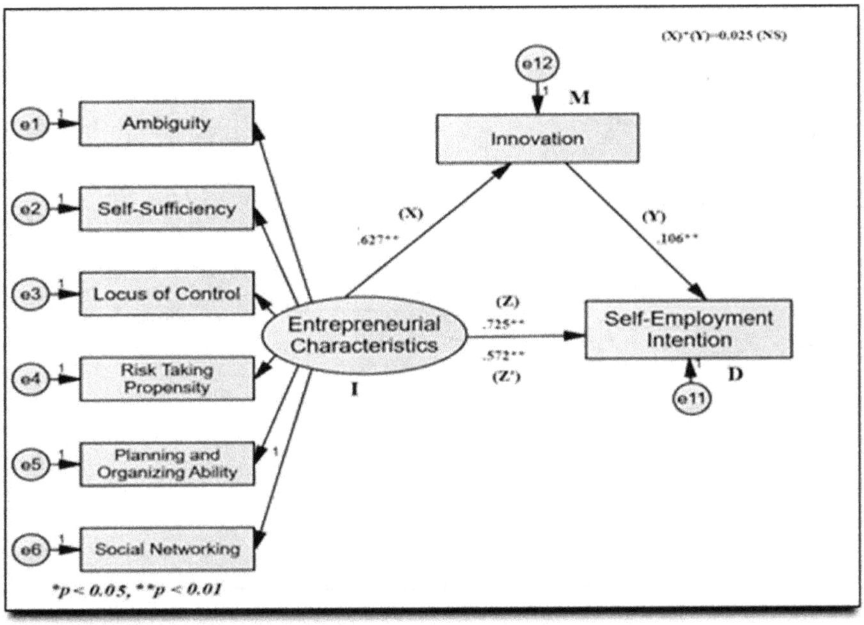

Path (X) IM, indicated that those who had higher EC can result in higher personal control (β = .654**, $p < 0.01$). Path (Y) MD.I, indicated that higher personal control can result in higher SEI (β = .067*, $p < 0.05$).

Since the estimates of paths (X), (Y) and (Z) are significant, it is worthy of introducing personal control as a mediator between EC and SEI.

Path (Z') ID.M (direct effect) indicated that the total effect of EC on SEI was reduced (β = .681**, $p < 0.01$) when personal control was integrated into the model.

Table 6 further suggested that the indirect effect (β = .44**, $p < 0.01$) of EC on SEI through personal control [path (X) * (Y)] was statistically significant and is a case of partial mediation.

Table 6. Direct, total and indirect effects of personal control as a mediator between EC and SEI

β (Standardized Regression Weight Estimates)				
ID (Z)	**IM (X)**	**MD. I (Y)**	**ID.M (Z')**	**IM (X)*MD.I (Y)**
.725**	.654**	.067*	.681**	.44**

*p = 0.05, **p = 0.01

Figure 4. Direct, total and indirect effects of personal control as a mediator between EC and SEI

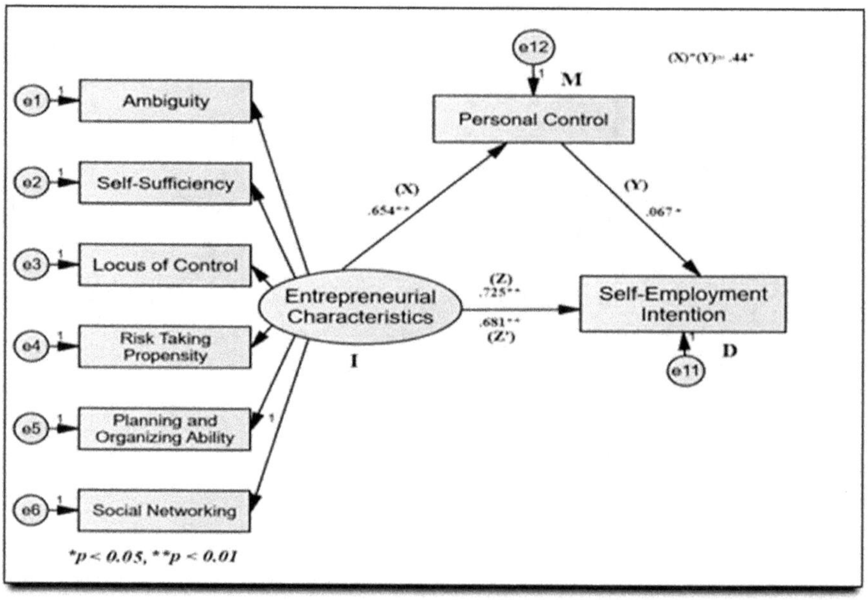

4.4 Mediation of Self Esteem

It can be observed from Table 7 and Figure 5 that path (Z) [I.D., (total effect)] from EC and SEI (β = .725, $p < 0.01$) is significant, suggesting that higher EC can result in higher SEI.

Path (X) IM, indicated that those who had higher EC can result in higher self-esteem (β = .596**, $p < 0.01$). Path (Y) MD.I, indicated that higher self-esteem can result in higher SEI (β = .20**, $p < 0.01$).

Since the estimates of paths (X), (Y) and (Z) are significant, it is worthy of introducing self-esteem as a mediator between EC and SEI.

Path (Z') ID.M (direct effect) indicated that the total effect of EC on SEI was reduced (β = .602**, $p < 0.01$) when self-esteem was integrated into the model.

Table 7 further suggested that the indirect effect (β = .119**, $p < 0.01$) of EC on SEI through self-esteem [path (X) * (Y)] was statistically significant and is a case of partial mediation.

Table 7. Direct, total and indirect effects of self-esteem as a mediator between EC and SEI

β (Standardized Regression Weight Estimates)				
ID (Z)	IM (X)	MD. I (Y)	ID.M (Z')	IM (X)*MD.I (Y)
.725**	.596**	.20**	.602**	.119**

*p = 0.05, **p = 0.01

Figure 5. Direct, total, and indirect effects of self-esteem as a mediator between EC and SEI

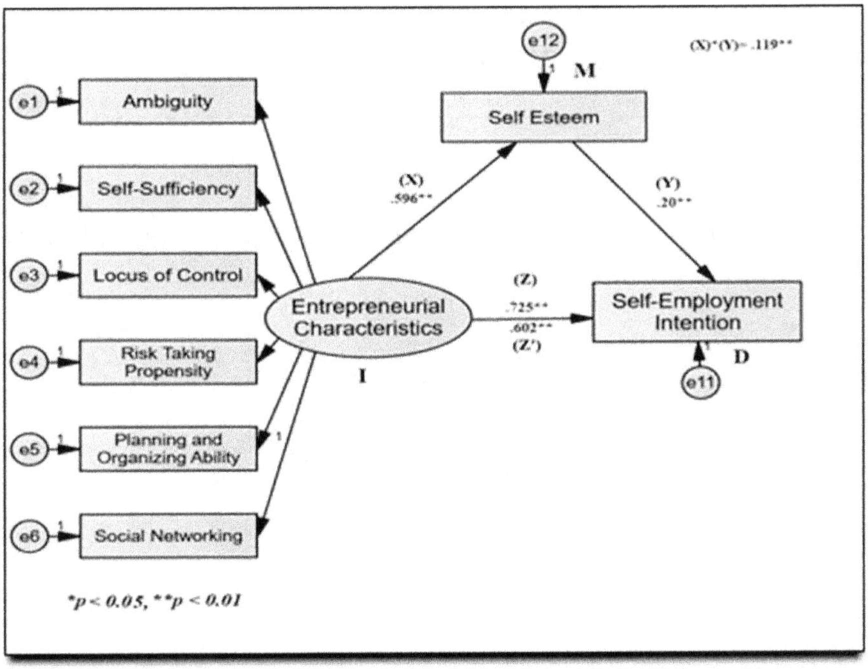

4.5 Mediation of Overall Entrepreneurial Attitude

It can be observed from Table 8 and Figure 6 that path (Z) [I.D., (total effect)] from EC to SEI (β = .725, $p < 0.01$) is significant, suggesting that higher EC can result in higher SEI.

Path (X) IM, indicated that those who had higher EC can result in higher EA (β = .702**, $p < 0.01$). Path (Y) MD.I, indicated that higher EA can result in higher SEI (β = .178**, $p < 0.01$).

Since the estimates of paths (X), (Y) and (Z) are significant, it is worthy of introducing EA as a mediator between EC and SEI.

Path (Z') ID.M (direct effect) indicated that the total effect of EC on SEI was reduced (β = .601**, $p < 0.01$) when the EA was integrated into the model.

Table 8 further suggested that the indirect effect (β = .125**, $p < 0.01$) of EC on SEI through EA [path (X) * (Y)] was statistically significant and is a case of partial mediation.

Table 8. Direct, total and indirect effects of EA as a mediator between EC and SEI

B (Standardized Regression Weight Estimates)				
ID (Z)	**IM (X)**	**MD. I (Y)**	**ID.M (Z')**	**IM (X)*MD.I (Y)**
.725**	.702**	.178**	.601**	.125**

**p = 0.05, **p = 0.01*

Figure 6. Direct, total and indirect effects of EA as a mediator between EC and SEI

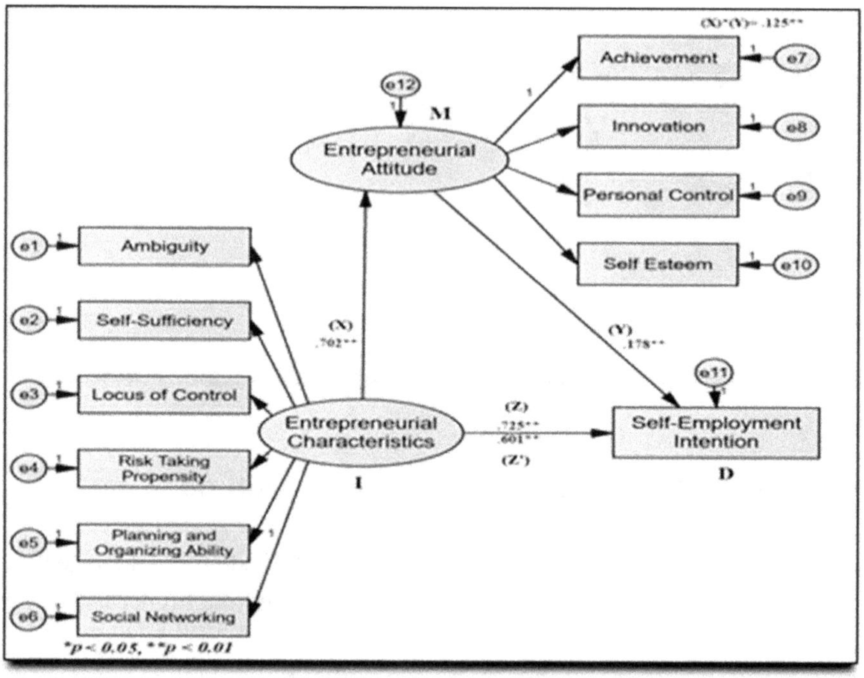

5. DISCUSSION AND FINDINGS

Achievement component of EA partially mediated the relationship between EC and SEI. All the direct paths between EC, achievement and SEI were statistically significant (Table 4 and Figure 2). The indirect effect of EC on SEI through achievement component of attitude was found to be statistically significant. Thus, EC of undergraduates can explain their SEI through achievement dimension of EA (need for accomplishment, meaningful work etc.).

Innovation component of EA didn't mediate the relationship between EC and SEI. All the direct paths between EC, innovation and SEI were statistically significant (Table 5 and Figure 3). The indirect effect of EC on SEI through innovation component of EA was found to be statistically insignificant. Thus, EC of undergraduates cannot elucidate their SEI through innovation dimension of EA.

Personal control component of EA partially mediated the relationship between EC and SEI. All the direct paths between EC, personal control and SEI were statistically significant (Table 6 and Figure 4). The indirect effect of EC on SEI through personal control component of EA was found to be statistically significant. Thus, EC of undergraduates can explain their SEI through personal control dimension of EA (need for accomplishment, meaningful work etc).

Self-esteem component of EA partially mediated the relationship between EC and SEI. All the direct paths between EC, self-esteem and SEI were statistically significant (Table 7 and Figure 5). The indirect effect of EC on SEI through self-esteem component of EA was found to be statistically significant. Thus, EC of undergraduates can explain their SEI through self-esteem dimension of EA (need for accomplishment, meaningful work etc).

The overall EA construct also partially mediated the link between EC and SEI of engineering undergraduate students. The direct paths between EC, overall EA and SEI were statistically significant (Table 8 and Figure 6). The indirect effect of EC on SEI through overall EA was found to be statistically significant. Thus, EC of undergraduates can explain their SEI through their EA.

Potential student entrepreneurs are likely to have strong characteristics which helps them to identify their own business opportunities which guides them to have positive mindset for creation of their own new venture. This idea of self-sustaining themselves and idea of becoming employed by their own is guided through their positive attitude. Motive to have high sense of accomplishment and achievement, personal control in the form of planning, responsibility seeking, skills to handle business and people etc. and self-esteem in the form of performance involvement, effective dealing capability, ability to get along with others and specialisation etc., are some of the essential factors which can enhance the self-employment intention motive among technical graduates in the state.

6. CONTRIBUTION OF THE STUDY

Entrepreneurs are the savior of the society as well as the country. It is the entrepreneurs who generate employments by offering a required product/services and significantly contribute towards the nation building. Thus, it wouldn't be wrong to say that in order to eradicate or effectively handle the unemployment and poverty in the any country, especially in the developing/ emerging countries like India, young nascent entrepreneurs needs to be nourished so that a transformed society with no social evils such as unemployment, poverty, hunger etc. can be seen. Previous studies suggested that technical students have the ability to operate business venture effectively as they know the technical know-how better than any other discipline students. The present study investigated the mediating effect of EA dimensions (i.e., achievement, innovation, personal control, and self-esteem) in the link between EC and SEI among technical undergraduates of different technical institutions of Chhattisgarh. The findings indicated that all the EA dimensions, except innovation factor, were found to be partially mediated between EC and SEI. It predicts that the entrepreneurial intention will be higher if the technical students' personal characteristics are directed with their attitude, which ultimately creates entrepreneurial behaviour among them.

Effective tackling of rising unemployment situation in the countries like India, they should be more focused on developing congenial environments for the technical undergraduates to effective nourishment of their mindset for choosing entrepreneurship as a career. The nourishment will help the students to realize their strength and potential, which will eventually transform into entrepreneurial desire. The present study's findings helps to understand the technical undergraduates' personal characteristics along with attitude that how it effectively affects their self-employment intention which gives insights for the concern authorities such as government to take concrete steps towards achieve such opportunity in order to encounter unemployment issue.

Also, due to Covid-19 situation, the unemployment issue has become worsen. The only solution is there is to produce more and more employment through harnessing entrepreneurial desire of nascent entrepreneurs. So, it is not wrong to say that "Young generation are the future", so the government should be working to harness their entrepreneurial desire to serve the whole society. The findings of the present study will not only help to governmental agencies to understand the available opportunities to tackle unemployment, but it will also provide insights to educational institutes to provide a congenial environment for the effective nourishment of the technical students.

7. CONCLUSION

Entrepreneurs are the pillars of the growth and development of any country. The more the entrepreneurial venture in the country, the higher their prosperity would be. This the reason behind encouragement for starting up new entrepreneurial venture in their country/state. Also due to the sudden impact of Covid-19 on the economy in every country, there is a need to accelerate the rate of entrepreneurial venture in the country, and it has been seen in the previous studies that technical students possess the technical know-how to starting up new entrepreneurial venture. The present study examined the EA dimensions (i.e., self-esteem, personal control, achievement, and innovation) as mediator in the link between EC and SEI among technical students of different technical institutions of Chhattisgarh state. The analysis explained that the all the dimensions of EA, except innovation factor, were partially mediated in the link between EC and SEI, which indicates that technical students possess EC, and in the presence of their EA, it shows higher level of SEI toward entrepreneurship. Thus, the government and other concerned authorities (such as educational institutes) should look into providing adequate nourishment and a congenial environment for the effective development and encouragement towards entrepreneurship.

ACKNOWLEDGMENT

This study is a piece of a comprehensive research project financed by the Indian Council of Social Sciences Research (ICSSR), New Delhi, under the IMPRESS scheme (File no.: IMPRESS/ P42/ 85/ 18-19/ ICSSR dated 20.03.2019). The author sincerely acknowledges ICSSR, New Delhi, for providing resources for accomplishing the research work.

REFERENCES

Ajzen, I. (1987). Attitudes, traits, and actions: Dispositional prediction of behavior in personality and social psychology. In Advances in experimental social psychology, 20, 1-63. doi:10.1016/S0065-2601(08)60411-6

Armitage, C. J., & Conner, M. (2001). Efficacy of the theory of planned behaviour: A meta-analytic review. *British Journal of Social Psychology*, *40*(4), 471–499. doi:10.1348/014466601164939 PMID:11795063

Autio, E., Keeley, R. H., Klofsten, M., Parker, G. G. C., & Hay, M. (2001). Entrepreneurial Intent Among Students in Scandinavia and in the USA. *Enterprise and Innovation Management Studies*, *2*(2), 145–160. doi:10.1080/14632440110094632

Bagozzi, R. P., & Yi, Y. (1988). On the evaluation of structural equation models. *Journal of the Academy of Marketing Science*, *16*(1), 74–94. doi:10.1007/BF02723327

Bakotic, D., & Kruzic, D. (2010). Students' perceptions and intentions towards entrepreneurship: The empirical findings from Croatia. *The Business Review, Cambridge*, *14*(2), 209.

Bezzina, F. (2010). Characteristics of the Maltese entrepreneur. *The International Journal of the Arts in Society*, *3*(7), 292–312.

Bhagchandani, R. (2017). How India can up its startup game by bolstering student entrepreneurship. *Your Story*. https://yourstory.com/2017/01/india-startup-game-bolstering-student-entrepreneurship

Bird, B. J., & West, G. P. III. (1998). *Time and Entrepreneurship*. Entrepreneurship. doi:10.1177/104225879802200201

Brockhaus, R. H. Sr. (1980). Risk taking propensity of entrepreneurs. *Academy of Management Journal*, *23*(3), 509–520. doi:10.2307/255515

Chell, E. (2008). *The Entrepreneurial Personality: A Social Construction* (2nd ed.). Routledge. doi:10.4324/9780203938638

Cooper, A. C., Dunkelberg, W. C. & Woo, C. Y. (1988). Survival and failure: A longitudinal study. *Frontiers of entrepreneurship research*, *1*, 225-237.

Douglas, E. J., & Shepherd, D. A. (2000). Entrepreneurship as a utility maximizing response. *Journal of Business Venturing*, *15*(3), 231–251. doi:10.1016/S0883-9026(98)00008-1

Drennan, J., Kennedy, J., & Renfrow, P. (2005). Impact of childhood experiences on the development of entrepreneurial intentions. *International Journal of Entrepreneurship and Innovation*, *6*(4), 231–238. doi:10.5367/000000005775179801

Drucker, P. F. (1985). Principles of successful innovation. *Research Management*, *28*(5), 10–12. doi:10.1080/00345334.1985.11756915

Drucker, P. F. (1985). Principles of successful innovation. *Research Management*, *28*(5), 10–12. doi:10.1080/00345334.1985.11756915

Hair, J. F., Black, W. C., Babin, B. J., & Anderson, R. E. (2010). *Multivariate data analysis: International version*. Pearson.

Hatten, T. S., & Ruhland, S. K. (1995). Student attitude toward entrepreneurship as affected by participation in an SBI program. *Journal of Education for Business, 70*(4), 224–227. doi:10.1080/08832323.1995.10117754

Ho, T. S. and Koh, H. C. (1992). Differences in psychological characteristics between entrepreneurially inclined and non-entrepreneurially inclined accounting graduates in Singapore. *Entrepreneurship, Innovation and Change: an international journal, 1*(2), 243-254.

Ismail, N., Jaffar, N., & Hooi, T. S. (2013). Using EAO model to predict the self-employment intentions among the Universities' Undergraduates in Malaysia. *International Journal of Trade, Economics and Finance, 4*(5), 282–287. doi:10.7763/IJTEF.2013.V4.302

Katz, D. and Stotland, E. (1959). A preliminary statement to a theory of attitude structure and change. *Psychology: A study of a science, 3*, 423-475.

Kautonen, T., Tornikoski, E. T., & Kibler, E. (2011). Entrepreneurial intentions in the third age: The impact of perceived age norms. *Small Business Economics, 37*(2), 219–234. doi:10.100711187-009-9238-y

Kirton, M. (1978). Field dependence and adaption-innovation theories. *Perceptual and Motor Skills, 47*(3), 1239–1245. doi:10.2466/pms.1978.47.3f.1239 PMID:745906

Koh, H. C. (1996). Testing hypotheses of entrepreneurial characteristics. a study of Hong Kong MBA students. *Journal of Managerial Psychology, 11*(3), 12–25. doi:10.1108/02683949610113566

Kolvereid, L. (1996). Prediction of employment status choice intentions. *Entrepreneurship Theory and Practice, 21*(1), 47–58. doi:10.1177/104225879602100104

Krueger, N. F., & Carsrud, A. L. (1993). Entrepreneurial intentions: Applying the theory of planned behaviour. *Entrepreneurship and Regional Development, 5*(4), 315–330. doi:10.1080/08985629300000020

Krueger, N. F. Jr, Reilly, M. D., & Carsrud, A. L. (2000). Competing models of entrepreneurial intentions. *Journal of Business Venturing, 15*(5-6), 411–432. doi:10.1016/S0883-9026(98)00033-0

Kuehn, K. W. (2008). Entrepreneurial intentions research: Implications for entrepreneurship education. *Journal of Entrepreneurship Education, 11*, 87.

Luthje, C., & Franke, N. (2003). The 'making' of an entrepreneur: Testing a model of entrepreneurial intent among engineering students at MIT. *Research Management, 33*(2), 135–147.

McClelland, D. C. (1961). *The Achieving Society*. D. Van Norstrand Co Inc. doi:10.1037/14359-000

Mitton, D. G. (1989). The compleat entrepreneur. *Entrepreneurship Theory and Practice, 13*(3), 9–20. doi:10.1177/104225878901300303

Moraes, G. H. S. M. D., Iizuka, E. S., & Pedro, M. (2018). Effects of entrepreneurial characteristics and university environment on entrepreneurial intention. *RAC. Revista de Administração Contemporânea, 22*(2), 226–248. doi:10.1590/1982-7849rac2018170133

Morrison, A. (2000). Entrepreneurship: What triggers it? *International Journal of Entrepreneurial Behaviour & Research, 6*(2), 59–71. doi:10.1108/13552550010335976

Nabi, G., Liñán, F., Ertuna, Z. İ., & Gurel, E. (2011). The moderating role of higher education on entrepreneurship. *Education + Training, 53*(5), 387–402. doi:10.1108/00400911111147703

Nabi, G., Liñán, F., Ertuna, Z. İ., & Gurel, E. (2011). The moderating role of higher education on entrepreneurship. *Education + Training, 53*(5), 387–402. doi:10.1108/00400911111147703

Nunnally, J. C. (1978). An overview of psychological measurement, Clinical diagnosis of mental disorders, pp. 97-146. Springer. doi:10.1007/978-1-4684-2490-4_4

Olson, P. D., & Bosserman, D. A. (1984). Attributes of the entrepreneurial type. *Business Horizons, 27*(3), 53–56. doi:10.1016/0007-6813(84)90027-2

Pandey, K. (2019). India's Unemployment Rate Doubled in Two Years: SoE in Figures. https://www.downtoearth.org.in/news/economy/india-s-unemployment-ratedoubled-in -two-years-soe-in-figures-64953

Phan, P. H., Wong, P. K., & Wang, C. K. (2002). Antecedents to entrepreneurship among university students in Singapore: Beliefs, attitudes and background. *Journal of Enterprising Culture, 10*(2), 151–174. doi:10.1142/S0218495802000189

Rasheed, H. S., & Rasheed, B. Y. (2003). Developing entrepreneurial characteristics in minority youth: The effects of education and enterprise experience. In *Ethnic entrepreneurship: Structure and process*. Emerald Group Publishing Limited. doi:10.1016/S1074-7877(03)04012-1

Robinson, P. B., Stimpson, D. V., Huefner, J. C., & Hunt, H. K. (1991). An attitude approach to the prediction of entrepreneurship. *Entrepreneurship Theory and Practice, 15*(4), 13–32. doi:10.1177/104225879101500405

Robinson, P. B., Stimpson, D. V., Huefner, J. C., & Hunt, H. K. (1991). An attitude approach to the prediction of entrepreneurship. *Entrepreneurship Theory and Practice, 15*(4), 13–32. doi:10.1177/104225879101500405

Rocha, E. L. C., & Freitas, A. A. F. (2014). Evaluation of entrepreneurship teaching among university students through the entrepreneurial profile. *Contemporary Administration Magazine, 18*(4), 465–486.

Rodrigues, M., Silva, R., & Franco, M. (2021). Entrepreneurial Attitude and Intention in Higher Education Students: What Factors Matter? *Entrepreneurship Research Journal*. doi:10.1515/erj-2020-0107

Rodrigues, M., Silva, R., & Franco, M. (2021). Entrepreneurial Attitude and Intention in Higher Education Students: What Factors Matter? *Entrepreneurship Research Journal*. doi:10.1515/erj-2020-0107

Schmidt, S., & Bohnenberger, M. C. (2009). Entrepreneurial profile and organizational performance. *Contemporary Administration Magazine, 13*(3), 450–467.

Segal, G., Borgia, D., & Schoenfeld, J. (2005). The motivation to become an entrepreneur. *International Journal of Entrepreneurial Behaviour & Research, 11*(1), 42–57. doi:10.1108/13552550510580834

Sharaf, A., El-Gharbawy, A., & Ragheb, M. A. (2018). Factors That Influence Entrepreneurial Intention within University Students in Egypt. *OAlib, 5*(10), 1–14. doi:10.4236/oalib.1104881

Souitaris, V., Zerbinati, S., & Al-Laham, A. (2007). Do entrepreneurship programmes raise entrepreneurial intention of science and engineering students? The effect of learning, inspiration and resources. *Journal of Business Venturing, 22*(4), 566–591. doi:10.1016/j.jbusvent.2006.05.002

Standish-Kuon, T., & Rice, M. P. (2002). Introducing engineering and science students to entrepreneurship: Models and influential factors at six American universities. *Journal of Engineering Education, 91*(1), 33–39. doi:10.1002/j.2168-9830.2002.tb00670.x

Tegtmeier. (2012). Empirical implications for promoting students' entrepreneurial intentions. *Journal of Enterprising Culture, 20*(2), 151–169.

Van Gelderen, M., Brand, M., Van Praag, M., Bodewes, W., Poutsma, E., & Van Gils, A. (2008). Explaining entrepreneurial intentions by means of the theory of planned behaviour. *Career Development International, 13*(6), 538–559. doi:10.1108/13620430810901688

Wang, C. K., & Wong, P. K. (2004). Entrepreneurial interest of university students in Singapore. *Technovation, 24*(2), 163–172. doi:10.1016/S0166-4972(02)00016-0

Yang. (2013). The theory of planned behavior and prediction of entrepreneurial intention among Chinese undergraduates. *Social Behavior and Personality,* 41(3), 367–376.

Zhao, H., Seibert, S. E., & Hills, G. E. (2005). The mediating role of self-efficacy in the development of entrepreneurial intentions. *The Journal of Applied Psychology, 90*(6), 1265–1272. doi:10.1037/0021-9010.90.6.1265 PMID:16316279

Zhao, H., Seibert, S. E., & Hills, G. E. (2005). The mediating role of self-efficacy in the development of entrepreneurial intentions. *The Journal of Applied Psychology, 90*(6), 1265–1272. doi:10.1037/0021-9010.90.6.1265 PMID:16316279

Chapter 5
The Impact of Geographical and Cultural Factors on Ethical Issues and Dilemmas:
An Investigation From Social Enterprises

Shajara Ul-Durar
https://orcid.org/0000-0001-6574-026X
University of Sunderland, UK

Khuram Shahzad
https://orcid.org/0000-0002-1074-8683
University of Lahore, Pakistan

Paula Danby
University of Sunderland, UK

ABSTRACT

Social enterprises are oriented towards reversing an imbalance in the social system by creating a positive social change. Ethical issues and dilemmas are, therefore, of prime importance to achieve social objectives. This theoretical chapter's core purpose was to identify the ethical issues and dilemmas faced by social enterprises. Variances in the ethical issues concerning geographical and cultural factors have also been highlighted. This study will discuss the organizational theory and its concept. Secondly, this study evaluates the functions of social enterprises and their aims and objectives; and, thirdly, it identifies the shift of social enterprises towards hybrid organizations to achieve both social and economic objectives. The study concludes with a discussion on how ethical challenges impact organizations' performance and sustainability. The results have implications for future research on social entrepreneurship and hybrid organizations.

DOI: 10.4018/978-1-6684-7140-1.ch005

1. INTRODUCTION

Social enterprises (SEs) are explicitly distinguished from all other enterprises based on bringing social change (Pareja-Cano et al., 2020; Pelizza Vier Machado et al., 2021). Social enterprises focus more on developing and creating social, cultural, and natural value (Seymour, 2012). Most social enterprises operate in environments where resources are inhibited. Therefore, they actively look for ways to improve their performance to acquire critical resources to sustain their activities (Di Domenico et al., 2010; Ketprapakorn and Kantabutra, 2019).

Social enterprises often experience complex situations and aim to satisfy different community expectations, creating conflicts (Żur, 2020). Social enterprises hire people with various skill sets, cultural backgrounds, and competencies (Roumpi et al., 2020). Influenced by their national cultures, employees of a firm may have different values and perceptions which may cause conflict such as the allocation of resources (Battilana et al., 2014). These differing perceptions can impact the decision-making process such as acquiring financial resources, utilizing human resources, and overall all management practices of the social enterprises (Doherty et al., 2014).

A systematic review of the literature regarding social enterprises and related concepts indicates a gap in research regarding social enterprise ethical issues to geographical and cultural context. Therefore, this study aims to address this gap by exploring ethical issues and dilemmas faced by social enterprises and how they vary with geographical and cultural factors. It is a theoretical paper that uses organizational theory in identifying ethical issues and dilemmas faced by social enterprises. Furthermore, it aims to find out their variance in terms of geographical and cultural factors. The main focus will be on social enterprises and the ethical issues to achieve their social and economic organizational objectives. It is believed that social enterprises hold their importance because they want to meet the social needs of the community they operate in. Hence, it is essential to identify and solve social enterprises' ethical issues regarding geographical and cultural factors because sometimes the cultural aspects can promote social enterprises functioning. At the same time, on some occasions, it can hinder their sustainability.

Firstly, the study will discuss the organizational theory and its concept. Secondly, it evaluates the functions of SEs and their aims and objectives and, thirdly, this study identifies the shift of SEs towards hybrid organizations to achieve both social and economic objectives. Along the way, it also identifies the ethical challenges faced by SEs or hybrid organizations that may affect the organization's performance and sustainability.

2. LITERATURE REVIEW

Social enterprises should focus on the long-term aims and objectives of the firm. The focus should be on the degree of formalization, specialization, centralization, and relevant control and coordination (Ouchi, 1980; Child, 1984; Taylor, 1914 Scott, 1991; Gentile-Lüdecke et al., 2020). In regard to SE literature, many studies advocate the correlation between organizational design and organizational achievements, for instance social entrepreneur leadership advocated by Dees (1998) and Oberoi et al. (2021), internal commitment advocated by Post and Waddock (1991), continuous training advocated by Choi et al. (2020) and Smallbone et al. (2001), and volunteer support advocated by Akingbola et al. (2021) and Thompson (2002). However, very few studies offer a comprehensive approach to the organizational design that fits with current ethical challenges for social enterprises (Battilana and Lee, 2014; Ko and Liu, 2021).

2.1 Organizational Configuration Approach for Social Entrepreneurship

The organizational configuration approach is being advocated among social enterprises. It is appropriate as it helps the organization align its business processes with the organization's social and economic missions (Akhmedova et al., 2022; Imperatori and Ruta, 2015). It helps to find a solution by finding a correlation between various organizational dimensions and performance indicators. It is of great significance that one single organizational configuration may not be considered adequate to achieve one firm's single objective. However, it may be deemed effective when used along with other organizational configurations to achieve multiple objectives and to meet multi-faceted stakeholder expectations (Imperatori and Ruta, 2015; Short et al., 2008). However, not every configuration can be applied to any organization (Krug and Weinberg, 2004).Social Enterprises face extreme difficulty finding distinctiveness and face many ethical issues (Bull and Crompton, 2006; Ghalwash et al., 2017). According to McGregor et al. (2003) and Littlewood and Holt, (2018)., obtaining funds has become a challenge for social enterprises since grant funding is diminishing. Therefore, SEs concentrate more on generating funds and can sometimes blur the line between commercial enterprise and social enterprise. SEs are perceived as quality providers of products or services with a customer-focused approach but they struggle to do so due to immense pressure within similar industries. Becoming commercial brings more problems for social enterprise as the demand for transparency and accountability has increased in the recent past (Honeyman and Jana, 2019; Krug and Weinberg, 2004). Hence, SEs often behave like and become commercial enterprises (CEs) to sustain the business.

Standard business models are different from SE models hence conflicts arise in their application. According to Siegner et al. (2018), it is not always possible for a SE to replicate standard business strategies and models because, at times, goals and objectives do not align and, in SEs, not all its goals and objectives can be measurable. Organizational configuration helps a SE to achieve this alignment.

SEs require dynamic business processes to run. It is about finding a balance between the business's analysis and strategic direction and its key stakeholders to sustain the business for a more extended period and achieve goals and objectives (Bull and Crompton, 2006; Fitriasari, 2020). Hence, it is essential to identify ethical issues and dilemmas faced by SEs and their impact based on geographical and cultural factors.

2.2 Organizational Theory

According to organizational theory, the structure of a SE and its practices are significant in facing various unforeseen situations and enhancing performance (Cheah et al., 2019; Pache and Santos, 2010). Therefore, an effective organizational design is critical for the success of a SE (Parrish, 2010; Santos et al., 2015). The theory advocates that organizational performance is increased when the culture and organizational strategies are related to the environment (Pelizza Vier Machado et al., 2021). Literature supports the fact that SEs looking to enhance their performance need to acquire certain aspects, for instance, generating revenue, effective communication, building relationships, and acquiring and retaining skilled staff that meet the business' and the market's needs (Bloom and Chatterji, 2009; Iskandar and Kaltum, 2021). Initially, Taylor (1911) introduced a classic organization theory, i.e. the scientific management. Taylor proposed that organizations may enhance the efficiency of production and productivity by enhancing the workforce's skills. He argued that it is critical for a business to know what the workforce is required to do for the business and then find out the cheapest and the most appropriate way to do it. It also advocates training existing employees to do their jobs effectively and efficiently, enhancing productivity instead of hiring new employees. On the other hand, Henry Fayol's (1937) administrative theory offers a top-down approach to the management as it aims to enhance the firm's efficiency by focusing on the management and its practices. Fayol advocates critical elements, forecasting, and planning to train and develop management and enhance the firm's productivity.

Fayol (1937) was more concerned about the human and behavioral aspects of management. Fayol believed that organizations could diminish conflicts and enhance their efficiency by focusing on management and its practices. Fayol developed fourteen principles of management to help managers to conduct their work effectively and enhance efficiency. These fourteen principles are still used today but sometimes interpreted in a different manner. These principles are division of work, delegation of authority, discipline, chain of commands, friendly workplace, alignment of individual interests and organizational objectives, compensation package, centralization, scalar chains, order, equity, job guarantee, initiatives, and team spirit (Shafritz et al.2015).

Measuring the performance of a SE is essential, however it is challenging. A SEs' mission is social and it aims to adopt a market position that aids in responding to the challenging and ambiguous environment (Austin et al., 2006; Ghafar et al., 2023). Hence, a SE has three primary objectives: a social mission, the firm's sustainability, and exploiting the business environment to gain competitive advantage (Muñoz, and Kimmitt, 2019; Sullivan et al., 2006). Therefore, a SE's performance can be measured based on its strategies aligned with a social mission, enhancing its survival competence, and producing development resources from within the business market (Lerner and Sharir, 2006; Mamabolo and Myres, 2020).

SEs continuously face complex situations and influences of the community and aim to satisfy different expectations that may create conflicts (Dionisio, 2019; Greenwood et al., 2010). To achieve its social mission, a SE may hire people with various skill sets, cultural backgrounds, and competencies (Pache and Santos, 2012; Roumpi et al., 2020). Influenced by their national cultures, employees of a firm may have different values and perceptions which may cause conflict such as the allocation of resources (Battilana et al., 2014). These differing perceptions can impact the decision-making process such as acquiring financial resources, utilizing human resources, and overall all management practices of the SE (Doherty et al., 2014). SEs may face organizational challenges such as uncertainty or ambiguity (Ashforth et al., 2014). According to Adler (2012), uncertain expectations of beliefs, behaviors, and attitudes may result in conflict in objectives and roles. SEs should adopt an organizational configuration that can include all these conflicting elements to be effective and efficient.

2.3 The Multidimensional Nature of Social Enterprises

The nature of a SE is multidimensional and it also has to satisfy multi-focused stakeholder expectations which means it must devise relevant organizational resolutions (Bunduchi et al., 2023; Di Domenico et al., 2009). The aspects of social typical nonprofit enterprises and profit companies are combined in SEs to deliver social values. They combine orientation for social values and objectives to achieve economic value (Costa and Andreaus, 2020).

According to stakeholder theory, giving proper attention to the organization's stakeholders and engaging them can benefit a SE (Freeman, 1994; Parmar et al., 2010; Ramus and Vaccaro, 2017). Engaging stakeholders also aids in developing environmental policies which help reduce or diminish the organization's risk

(Monteduro et al., 2021; Polonsky, 1995). Organizations that give importance to their stakeholders and maintain sustainable relationships achieve a higher level of success (Imperatori and Ruta, 2015; Tencati and Zsolani, 2009). Literature shows that stakeholder identification is carried similarly as another process of the firm, however, some identify different stakeholders (Mitchell et al., 1997), for instance, internal and external stakeholders, primary stakeholders, and the firm's secondary stakeholders (Freeman et al., 2007; Ramus et al., 2018). Meeting stakeholder expectations is critical for any type of organization to achieve its goals and objectives.

Expectations of SE leaders and social stakeholders should be aligned. In the context of SEs, social stakeholders are those stakeholder groups that may affect or may get affected by the goal achievement of the firm in regard to their social objectives whereas economic stakeholders are those which may have an impact on the aim or purpose of the organizational performance (Savitz, 2013). In SEs social leaders and social stakeholders both have similar expectations, for instance, social stakeholders expect to receive social benefits whereas social leaders expect that social stakeholders are active and cooperative. SEs can achieve sustainable social goals only when social leaders and social stakeholders have mutual expectations (Bissola and Imperatori, 2012).Leaders of the SE often face conflicting demands which result in a shift in boundaries. For instance, if a SE wants to hire disadvantaged people such as people with physical disabilities or mental health concerns, this strategy directly conflicts with a profit-maximizing strategy that can be best achieved by hiring skilled and fit people (Ahmed et al., 2023; Tian and Smith 2014). Hence, the boundaries often shift due to varying demands' dynamic nature (Lewis and Smith, 2011). For instance, if the human resource department finds a way to hire the most disadvantaged people with relevant skills to perform the required tasks effectively and efficiently and helps the organization stay competitive, it may cause a shift in the boundaries. Later, the focus will be to hire more skilled but disadvantaged workers to balance the difference in performance and achieve the SE's social and economic mission. Other factors that may cause a shift in the boundaries are technological advancements, competitive forces, and business cycles (Tian and Smith, 2014).

2.4 Shift Towards Hybrid Organizations

Hybrid Organizational SEs sometimes evolves into hybrid organizations to find that balance essential to achieving social and economic goals. The hybrid organization does not have a specific type thus it can be any organization, for instance government, non-government, social, and commercial organizations (Karré, 2023; Kickert, 2001). The difference between hybrid organizations is mainly associated with its organizational and financial structure (Bauwens et al., 2020; Koppell, 2003). Moreover, hybrid organizations may set social and environmental missions and economic missions to generate profit, helping the organization achieve its social or environmental missions (Haigh and Hoffman, 2012; Gamble et al., 2020). Hybrid organizations, which are part SEs and part CEs, are social mission-driven organizations that are financially self-sufficient (Haigh et al., 2015).

Moreover, a Hybrid organization may lose its focus and drift away from the mission (O' Toole and Vogel, 2011; Wolf and Mair, 2019) and sacrifice its social mission to pursue financial sustainability (Brandsen and Karré, 2011; de Mon et al., 2022). The pursuit of enhancing social and financial performance may give birth to managerial tensions because managers will most likely prioritize financial performance which conflicts with the organizational aim to achieve social mission (Battilana and Dorado, 2010). This shift also impacts the firm's stakeholders, hence its legitimacy (Nicholls, 2010c). Based on organizational theory, these issues arise due to its social and cultural environment (Pache and Santos, 2010). The major challenge for hybrid firms is to satisfy their stakeholders because, sometimes, stakeholders may agree on the goals but do not agree on the means of achieving those goals and sometimes they may not agree on the goals at all (Mocsary, 2016; Pache and Santos, 2013).

From another perspective, it is common among hybrid organizations to adopt a new legal structure that aligns their financial and social goals. Haigh et al. (2015) studied 48 hybrid organizations and found out that half of these organizations adopted a new legal structure to achieve social and economic goals. Literature shows that hybrid organizations help achieve social and economic missions, however, some argue that they may have a negative impact (Kaufman, 2012). The major challenge for hybrid organizations is to measure performance (Ormiston and Seymour, 2011; Sargiacomo and Walker, 2022) and then analyze the results to interpret success or failure (Jay, 2013). Vakkuri, et al. (2021)states that hybrid organizations are often criticized for lack of transparency.

Hybrid organizations have the characteristics of adopting an activity to generate revenue and to achieve a social mission (Haigh et al., 2014; Peattie and Morley, 2008). Hence, hybrid organizations are distinct from other organizations as they enhance their revenue to accomplish social objectives such as reducing poverty, unemployment, CO2 emissions, and inequality (Powell et al., 2019) and these organizations are motivated to enhance community development which is a SE trait (Lumpkin et al., 2013).

Hence, Hybrid organizations seek both social and economic missions but to do so they have more stakeholders which they must satisfy (Jannsson, 2005). Financial and social objectives often create conflict. Therefore, paradoxical strategies are adapted which primarily contradict each dimension but meets the needs of the SEs mission (Smith, 2014). It is crucial to identify the critical challenges that social enterprises face to enhance performance and meet key stakeholders' expectations. A SE often faces many challenging and ambiguous situations hence it must identify and address these ambiguous issues to achieve its mission and satisfy various stakeholders (Battilana and Lee, 2014; Molecke and Pinkse, 2017).

SEs face more complex relationships compared to CEs. Molecke and Pinkse, (2017) argue that leaders of SEs must actively engage a larger group of stakeholders with diverse, challenging priorities. However, if the consultative approach is adopted to engage multiple stakeholders, it can slow down the decision-making process and hinder the SE's competitiveness (Franks and Mayer, 1995). Hence, advocating legitimacy, leaders of the SE must bridge the gap between SE and its key stakeholders (Zander, 1993).

2.5 Ethical Issues and Dilemmas

Addressing complex relationships between social objectives and business objectives may cause complex and challenging identity issues (Davis et al., 2021; Tracey and Philips, 2007). Internal conflicts arise when SE leaders face identification issues regarding different organizational aims and objectives and norms. In such a situation, the SE leaders need to position themselves as divergent stakeholders by adopting a hybrid identity approach. (Tian and Smith, 2014).

Table 1. Ethical issues and dilemmas: Themes from literature

Religion	
Lambooy et al. (2020)	Religion is part of the goals that social enterprise aims to achieve.
Alarifi and Alrubaishi (2018)	Islamic teachings in Saudia Arabia influence the activities of social enterprises.
Chandra and Shang (2017)	Spiritualism is one of the eight biographical antecedents in the emergence of social enterprises.
Tlaiss (2015)	Values and ethics in Islamic practices are embedded in social entrepreneurship activities in Arab countries.
Hattab (2011)	Women, according to Islamic values, are appreciated for pursuing entrepreneurship in Middle Eastern countries.
Mimouni (2010)	Muslims generally hold a balance between two extremes in their business dealings.
Farid (2007)	Religion is a significant force that shapes the value system in the business.
Youness (2007)	The successful Islamic female entrepreneurs suggest that success and honesty in business stems from their religion.
Variance in aims and objectives	
Bradač Hojnik et al. (2020)	The definition of social enterprises lacks clarity due to the diverse nature of aims and objectives associated.

continues on following page

Table 1. Continued

Smith (2014)	Financial and social objectives often create conflicts for social entrepreneurship.
Besharov and Smith (2013)	Multiple unpredictable goals, values, and norms are embedded within one firm.
Battalina et al. (2012)	SEs combine the resources, innovation, and resources of a profit-generating firm with the mission, values, and passion of a not-for-profit firm.
Dees (2012)	The social enterprises are based upon the interplay of different clusters which are sometimes conflicting.
Tracey et al. (2011)	Integrating into aims is achieved by offering skill training to employees.
Alter (2008)	SEs adopt many strategies to address the conflicts in the aims and objectives of social enterprises.
Establishing a sustainable supply chain	
Mani et al. (2020)	Social Sustainability in supply chain management continues to receive less attention. Most sustainability research addresses the economic and environmental aspects of sustainability.
Gimenez and Tachizawa (2012)	Most studies regarding SEs focus on environmental issues instead of social issues which need to be addressed.
Carter and Easton (2011)	Sustainability is one of the environmental attributes of supply chain management.
Sarkis et al. (2011)	Organizational theory does not contain lenses required to study sustainable supply chain management.
Liu et al. (2009)	Institutional theory, which is one of the organizational theories, has been used in previous literature regarding sustainable supply chain management.
Ketchen and Hult (2007)	Organizational theory can be used to study supply chain management further.
Organizational culture	
Roumpi et al.(2020)	Organizational culture is significantly related to the performance outcome in social enterprises.
Dauber et al. (2012)	Organizational theory analyses and explores the vibrant correlation among an organization's internal environment (culture, strategy, structure, business operations) and external environments.
Tsui et al. (2007)	The dimensions approach focuses on measuring a firm's culture based on scales correlated with other interest variables.
Cameron and Quinn (2005)	Success is not only determined by the external factors of the firm but also internal factors.
Meyer et al. (1993)	The organizational configuration is multidimensional, including various environments, cultures, strategies, structures, people, and industries
Marcoulides and Heck (1993)	Organizational culture is one of the significant factors that influences organizational performance in social enterprises.
The imbalance between commercial and social objectives	
Pfeilstetter et al. (2020)	The social and economic values are inaccurately placed in social organizations, creating false hybridity.

continues on following page

Table 1. Continued

Ramus et al. (2018)	Creating a balance between social and commercial objectives in social enterprise is exceptionally challenging.
Smith et al. (2013)	Most of the social enterprises are either commercially or socially centric.
Poor coordination	
Hazenberg et al. (2016)	Poor coordination among social enterprises leads to resource scarcity.
Beer and Eisenstat (2000)	Poor vertical communication and poor coordination of business functions are the significant barriers to learning in an organization.
Scott (2008)	SEs are required to justify the activities of the firm to diverse stakeholders.
Freeman (1984).	A firm's legitimacy refers to a comprehensive assumption that a firm's actions are appropriate in terms of social constructs based on norms, values, and other various beliefs.
Child (1972)	Firms often do not incorporate the goals of their members.

2.5.1 Religion

Religion is a critical factor that can affect the SEs behavior in a country with solid religious norms, such as in Middle Eastern countries. It is an essential aspect because many international SEs have their subsidiaries or branches in these Middle Eastern countries. Most of the Middle East's religious studies are based on barriers and problems (Chandra and Shang, 2017; Hattab, 2011). Gender equality is a primary concern for social enterprises in Arab countries. It is their culture that does not treat women equally whereas Islam does not stop women from trading or working (Lambooy et al., 2020; Tliass, 2015) Islam is considered a comprehensive religion that covers all crucial aspects of life such as social and political aspects (Alarifi and Alrubaishi, 2018) hence it is a strong force that shapes its followers' personal and business value systems (Farid, 2007; Tliass, 2015). Therefore, any SE operating in such a religious environment must understand its impact on the businesses. The number of female entrepreneurs is increasing in the Middle East, contributing to the local economies by generating revenue, creating jobs, and successfully establishing new organizations (Bastian et al., 2018; Youness, 2007). Tliass (2015) interviewed several Arab entrepreneurs and found that their work quality, business ethics, and overall business function are influenced by their religion and its teachings. This was also advocated by Mimouni (2010) and Tlaiss and McAdam, (2021). Therefore, SEs operating in such countries must find ways to manage this cultural difference, which is sacred to Arabs, to establish SEs successfully.

2.5.2 Varied Aims and Objectives

SEs face various ethical dilemmas due to varied aims and objectives. According to Battalina et al. (2012) and Madajova et al. (2017), SEs combine the resources, innovation, and resources of a profit-generating firm with the mission, values, and passion of a not-for-profit firm. Consequently, multiple unpredictable goals, values, and norms are embedded within one firm which creates opposing treatments for action (Besharov and Smith, 2013) and ends up creating ethical dilemmas for their leaders (Dees, 2012). To understand SEs effectively, it is vital to get an insight into the nature and management of these tensions. Literature suggests less about these social business tensions, their types, linked challenges, and nature of actions to manage these challenges. Hence, current literature cannot portray the SE phenomenon's full complexity (Smith, Gonin, and Besharov, 2013; Żur, 2021).

SE adopts many strategies to address the problems and opportunities in a society (Alter, 2008; Bacq et al., 2018). Digital divide data SEs aim to achieve social welfare through employment. These work integration firms pursue social enhancement by offering skill training, development, and salaries to help employable individuals achieve employment (Lysaght et al., 2018; Tracey et al., 2011). Other firms enhance human and environmental welfare through their products or services and business processes. Fair trade organizations help to shift power and resources to enhance the market conditions of production in developing countries (Nayak et al., 2019; Nicholls and Opal, 2004). Now manufacturing organizations are finding ways to meet people's needs by manufacturing products that are affordable for people with less buying power (Prahalad, 2006).

2.5.3 Establishing Sustainable Supply Chain

Establishing a sustainable supply chain management (SCM) is another major challenge faced by SEs. Sustainability is one of the environmental attributes of supply chain management (Ansari and Qureshi, 2015; Carter and Easton, 2011). According to Bubicz et al., (2019) and Gimenez and Tachizawa (2012), most studies focus on environmental issues instead of social issues. Ketchen and Hult (2007) believe that organizational theory can further study supply chain management. Similarly, according to Sarkis et al. (2011), organizational theories present considerable opportunities to study supply chain management but Carter and Easton (2011) believe that organizational theory does not contain the lenses required to study sustainable supply chain management. The institutional theory, which is one of the organizational theories, has been used in previous literature regarding sustainable supply chain management (Barratt and Choi, 2007; Dhillon et al., 2023; Liu et al., 2009).

2.5.4 Organizational Culture

Organizational culture is an essential factor that allows the analysis of a firm in various settings. According to Campos-Blázquez et al. (2023) and Cameron and Quinn (2005), it is a means of measuring a firm's competitive advantage and, according to Marcoulides and Heck (1993) and Shamsudin and Velmurugan, (2023), it has an impact on organizational performance. Cameron and Quinn (2005) and Strielkowski, (2012) argue that success is determined by the firm's external factors and internal factors that can help the firm achieve success. Many studies explained the importance of organizational cultures, such as Abdul-Halim et al. (2019), Hall (1976), Schein (1985), Hofstede et al. (1990), and Sagiv and Schwartz (2007). Tsui et al. (2007) reviewed extensive literature and proposed that a configuration model should be developed, enhancing the importance of culture in a firm. According to Meyer et al. (1993), the organizational configuration is multidimensional including various environments, cultures, strategies, structures, people, and industries hence the configuration model of culture should be multidimensional as well.Organizational culture has been researched for many decades now and various models have been proposed. These are classified into three categories: dimensions approach, interrelated structure approach, and typology approaches The significant studies which fall under the category of dimensions approach are Chatterjee et al. (1992), Hofstede et al. (1990), Sagiv and Schwartz (2007), and Siemiński, et al. (2022). According to Tsui et al. (2007) the dimensions approach focuses on measuring a firm's culture based on scales that are correlated with other variables of interest. The studies which outline the interrelated structure approach are Allaire and Firsirotu (1984), Schein (1985), Hatch (1993), and Homburg and Pflesser (2000). The interrelated structure approach links organizational culture with other major characteristics or concepts of the firm instead of particular variables, hence offering a theory for empirical research design (Meyer et al., 1993). Studies that comprise typology approaches are Cartwright and Cooper (1993), and Handy (1993). Typology approaches are based on those characteristics of the firm that help firms define categories, however, it does not define the firm's relationship with these characteristics.

The dimensions approach is highly prominent regarding cultural paradigms, especially in quantitative research. Five cultural dimensions of Hofstede (2001) ruled out the conventional research designs and gave way to the new research settings. According to Fink and Mayrohofer (2009), Hofstede et al.'s cultural dimensions have simplified the cultural approach because Hofstede et al. (1990) highlighted a noticeable difference among various national cultures and organizational cultures. They argued that organizational cultures are distinct and different and cannot be the same as national cultures.

Grosskopf and Barmeyer (2021) and Sagiv and Schwartz (2007) used the theoretical considerations to define the organizations' cultural paradigms. They argued that an organization's culture is highly influenced by the society that surrounds them, the personal values of the employees which they prioritize, and the aim of the organization. Gallego-Álvarez and Ortas, (2017) and Sagiv and Schwartz (2007) advocate that firms constantly face pressure from societies because firms embed them into the societies defined through national cultures and their values. Hence, firms need to satisfy and accommodate the norms and values of society members to achieve social and financial goals. These members of society try to influence organizational culture with their norms, beliefs, and values and they therefore shape and influence organizational culture at some level. Similar to Hofstede et al. (1990), Sagiv and Schwartz (2007) believe that the organization's business nature also influences the organizational culture because different goals and the nature of the business require a different set of business processes, strategies, and structures.

Akpa et al. (2021) and Dauber et al. (2012) also proposed an organizational culture model based on organizational theory. The model's primary purpose was to analyze and explore the vibrant correlation among the internal environment of an organization which is culture, strategy, structure, and business operations, and external environments. This model has a well-defined process and offers a wide range of systems allowing internal and external environmental factors to correlate.

The organizational theory states various organizational structures to achieve the firm's social and economic goals (Lunenberg, 2012). These organizational structures are coupled with business strategies and business operations to achieve the aim of the business. According to Ahmed and Streimikiene (2021) and Whittington (2001), organizational strategies are the chosen methods to achieve social and economic organizational goals and objectives. According to Schein (1985), strategies affect and influence the way structures and business operations interact with each other. Many researchers, such as Chandler (1962), Ansoff (1965), Andrews (1971), Hamilton and Shergill (1993), Islami et al. (2020) and Donaldson (1996), propose that every strategy needs a new structure to be successful. Chandler (1962) and Islami et al. (2020) observed that as soon as a firm adopts a new strategy the firm's performance declines, however, once the changes are made to the structure of the firm it results in enhanced performance. Therefore, according to Verhoef et al. (2021) and Wolf and Egelhoff (2002), every distinct strategy requires a distinct structure for it to be successful. Structures of the firm facilitate information processing and aid in strategic decision-making hence structure impacts when devising future strategies of the firm (Wolf and Egelhoff, 2002). According to Harris and Ruefli (2000), research proposes a correlation based on organizational structure and strategy feedback.

2.5.5 Imbalance Between Commercial and Social Objectives

Ko et al. (2020) describe business ethics in social enterprise. They found that social enterprises often overemphasize efficacy, business revenue, and specialization diverting their attention from social objectives. Therefore social enterprises are at risk of paying less attention to the beneficiaries. Moreover, the study suggests that organizations fail to balance commercial and social aspects (Pfeilstetter et al., 2020). Moving from traditional nonprofit organizations to social enterprises is a complex issue that requires individual practices to incorporate commercial practices with social aims. (Ramus et al., 2018)

2.5.6 Poor Coordination

According to Dodgson (1993) aand Haile and Tüzüner, (2022)., firms deliberately construct structures and devise strategies to enhance organizational learning. According to Beer (2021) and Beer and Eisenstat (2000), poor vertical communication and poor coordination of business functions are the significant barriers to learning in an organization. Conversely, open and fluent communication structures allow organizations to maximize learning. Learning in SEs is limited based on internal environments. However, it extends to the firm's external environment because it helps an organization identify and analyze forces that may offer opportunities, threats, or create barriers in achieving social and economic goals. According to Distanont and Khongmalai (2020) and Daft (2009), a firm's external environment comprises every driving force outside the organization's boundary. Organizations learn the environment and adapt accordingly, however, they may affect the environment in some cases. According to Dauber et al. (2012) and Donnelly-Cox and O' Regan (1999), every organization is essentially linked to two external environments: legitimization environment and task environment.

Legitimization environment refers to the external stakeholders of the firm as explained by Freeman (1984) and Li, et al. (2018). It means that any SE organization is required to justify the firm's activities to the diverse stakeholders (Sparviero, 2019; Scott, 2008). Suchman (1995) states that a firm's legitimacy refers to a comprehensive assumption that the actions of a firm are appropriate in terms of social constructs based on norms, values, and other various beliefs. According to Anh et al. (2022) and Child (1972), firms often do not incorporate their members' goals such as employees; they may depend on the goals, needs, and expectations of the stakeholders in the external environment. Hence, it is correct to believe that organizations may face pressure from society external to the organization and comprise a group of stakeholders. This notion is also advocated by Gandhi and Raina (2018) and Sagiv and Schwartz (2007) who argue that firms are always under ethical influence due to societal pressures. Therefore, it is critical to align organizational culture to society's values and beliefs because organizational culture is based on values, norms, and beliefs of its people and, therefore, aids in legitimizing strategies, structures, and business operations.

Task environment is associated with the business aims of which there can be more than one in a firm. Typically, firms develop specific strategies to achieve various tasks. According to Child (1972) and Abualoush et al. (2018), organizational structures need to ensure that certain performance levels are achieved. Social enterprises aim to meet the business's expense in regard to the revenues or donations whereas profit firms aim to enhance profitability to exceed the firm's expense. Structures sometimes do not meet the firm's goals, however, they facilitate business operations to do so.

Organizational structures are not changed due to the firm's external environment but the internal environment influences structural change. Instead, it is the internal environment assessment that helps identify that change is required to initiate the change process. New structures are defined by the firm and are aligned to the task achievement in the task environment. It can be argued that, to some extent, change in the structure of the organization is triggered by the external environment (Hanelt et al., 2021; Thompson, 2003).

2.6 Organizational Configuration

The organizational configuration has an integral part in both organization theory and organizational research (Doty and Glick, 1994; Bensaou and Venkatraman, 1995). The configuration approach proposes that organizations can be studied in a better way as constellations of interrelated structures. The organizational configuration is multidimensional so it is related to strategic management (Amburgey and Dacin, 1994; Inkpen and Choudhury, 1995; Küng, 2016; Miller, 1996). One of the key aspects of an effective strategy is finding a strategy relevant to organizational structures, environment, and business activities which means that organizational configuration covers every aspect of a business strategy (Miller, 1996).

The configuration approach's perspective is very attractive. As a result, many researchers have tested various configuration settings to identify effects such as performance. However, the correlation between configuration and performance has been unclear and some studies even doubt that this relationship does not exist (Ajagbe et al., (2016); Barney and Hoskisson, 1990). On the other hand, Ketchen et al. (1997) found that configuration affects performance through a meta-analysis. According to Ferguson and Ketchen (1999), previous studies fail to find a correlation mainly due to insufficient statistical power. Similarly, Khan et al. (2018) propose a further study of these results to authenticate the configuration view's effectiveness.

Fiss (2007) suggests that issues found in previous research regarding the organizational configuration are due to disparity among methods and theory. Configuration analysis advocates the notion of equifinality which, in turn, advocates that multiple configurations can be correspondingly effective in achieving high performance (Delmas and Pekovic, 2018; Katz and Kahn, 1978). These ideas are theoretical and have not translated well because the notion of multiple approaches to achieve one goal is against conventional methods of analysis which usually opt for one approach to achieve an outcome (Whitington et al., 1999).

Set-theoretic methods conceptualize various situations as combinations of characteristics, giving them a unique nature, making set-theoretic methods very suitable for configurational theory (Nagy et al., 2022; Ragin, 1987). The set-theoretic approach takes each configuration as a different case type which is against the conventional approach. It is a better fit as it also allows assessment of various causes which in combination affect the outcome of the firm such as performance (Fiss, 2007).

According to Imperatori and Ruta (2015), adopting an organizational design that offers the best structure to achieve social and economic missions is vital for hybrid SEs. According to Nyarko et al., (2016)the organizational structure is a configuration among individuals and groups regarding defining responsibilities and authority and allocating goals. According to Armanious and Padgett, (2021) an organization's structure helps to achieve its purpose in the business environment. According to Eze et al. (2017) and Oliveira and Takahashi (2012), earlier structures of the firm were arranged regarding the product or the firm's service. Some researchers went beyond and analyzed the correlation between the firm's strategy and structure (Brickley et al. 2002). Chandler (2003) and Parthasarth and Sethi, (2018) proposed that the strategy of a firm influences the structure of the firm. He further stated that strategy helps determine variables for instance, aims, technology, and the firm's environment which influences the organizational structure. Amplifying the concept proposed by Chandler (2003), Hall and Tolbert (2009), Miles et al. (2011), and Parthasarth and Sethi (2018) stated that the strategy of the firm regulates tasks, environment, and technology. These variables affect organizational structure when combined with growth rates and power distribution.

An organization with poor structure or design faces many issues such as confusion among job roles, lack of coordination between business functions, ideas not being shared, decision making becoming a slow, stressful, and complex process and resulting in conflicts (Corkindale, 2011). According to Henry Mintzberg, there are three dimensions to the organizational differentiation, i.e. one key part of the firm which plays a vital role in the success or failure of the firm, the prime coordinating system which helps to coordinate activities of the firm, and decentralization used by the firm which refers to the level at which an organization involves employees in the decision-making process (Kumar, 2015; Lampel and Mintzberg, 1996). The first-dimension mechanism, the critical parts of an organization, includes the strategic apex which is the top management and support staff, the operative core employees who complete the task of the firm. This middle line is middle or low-level management; the technostructure is analysts in a firm such as planners, researchers, accountants, and the support staff which are the employees who offer indirect services (Mintzberg, 2007).

The mechanism of the second dimension, which is the prime coordinating mechanism, includes direct supervision (which means that one person is responsible for the work of a group of people), standardization of work process (meaning that the work is programmed), standardization of skills (meaning that training which is essential to perform the job-related tasks is specified), standardization of output (results of the tasks are specified), and mutual adjustments (meaning that informal communication is used to coordinate work) (Schmidt, 2006; Mintzberg, 2007).

The mechanism of the third dimension, which is the type of decentralization, includes vertical decentralization (referring to the dissemination of power within the chain of command and authority), horizontal decentralization (the level at which non-administrators makes decisions), and selective decentralization (the level of decision-making power which is delegated to various departments of the firm) (Schmidt, 2006).

Mintzberg (2009) suggests five key organizational structures based on five basic dimensions that can help an organization achieve its social and economic missions: entrepreneurial, machine, professional, diversified, and innovative organizations.

The entrepreneurial organization has a simple structure. It employs direct supervision and both horizontal and vertical centralization (Kumar, 2015; Mintzberg, 1991, 2009). This type of organization is relatively new, small in size, and is unstructured. It is a flexible and rapid model that offers much control to the leaders and can make necessary shifts based on the environmental changes (Anning-Dorson, 2021; Schmidt, 2006). It also offers innovation and long-term survival, however, it does not offer space for innovation (Lunenberg, 2012).

Machine organization is distinctively similar to Weber's (1947) organizational theory based on bureaucracy and Hage's (1965) mechanism organization. It is a formal organization and advocates work specialization. Management is in the hands of a small number of powerful people who control the firm and make necessary decisions. These types of organizations are automobile manufacturing companies and large government firms. The environment is stable in machine organizations and it advocates enhanced internal efficiency (Lunenberg, 2012). It follows a well-structured planning process tailored to budgets and audits. Jobs are clearly defined, and specific policies and procedures are reviewed in a timely manner to maintain efficiency (Daft, 2009).

A professional organization is also known as professional bureaucracy, as advocated by Mintzberg (2009). They are distinct from machine organizations in that they highly rely upon skilled, trained, and efficient employees and let them control their work. As a result, decision making in professional organizations is decentralized. It is a complex organization and encompasses several rules, policies, and procedures. Highly trained employees hold more power in professional organizations and therefore offer less control and power to senior managers (Brickley et al., 2002). This attribute results in making the change process very difficult in such organizations. Innovation is highly advocated to enhance productivity (Chandler, 2003). The immediate environment of such organizations is complex, however stable. They are medium to large organizations such as universities and hospitals (Lunenberg, 2012).

The divisional or diversified organization usually has multiple products and business units. This type of structure is mainly found in large and mature firms that may operate in various geographical locations with multiple products or services (Oliveria and Takahashi, 2012). The organization has a central headquarters which has its organizational structure. It offers more control and accountability to the line managers of the firm. The central team in headquarters focuses on the firm's broader mission whereas day-to-day decision-making is left to the line managers (Nelson and Quick, 2011). One of the significant weaknesses of this type is that it may duplicate resources and tasks. Different business divisions often arise in conflict to acquire more headquarter resources (Burton and Obel, 2004). These organizations are inflexible and therefore thrive in a stable environment that is not too complex (Mintzberg, 1992, 2009; Schmidt, 2006; Lunenberg, 2012).

An innovative organization, or an adhocracy, is primarily found in new organizations that require innovation and these firms limit complexity and bureaucracy (Miller, 1990). They have a pool of talent in which people with various expertise are brought together to achieve a task. People can be assigned to any task they need to offer workforce flexibility (Roscigno and Hodson, 2004). It is also flexible towards a change since experts work together to meet new challenges. Power and authority are transferred to whoever is required for the task resulting in ambiguity and conflicts (Alvesson, 2002). Adapting to rapid change can be challenging for the workforce, however, organizations require flexibility to adapt to this organizational structure (Mintzberg, 1991, 2009; Schmidt, 2006; Lunenberg, 2012).

3. TYPOLOGY

Strategic management and organizational theory scholars have emphasized typology as a critical theory explaining (building) approach to understanding the complex and holistic phenomenon (Doty and Glick, 1994; Fiss, 2011). Researchers prefer typologies and they have also been used to guide strategic analysis and map out the competitive landscape. (Porter, 2011). Doty and Glick (1994) defined typologies as 'conceptually derived interrelated sets of ideal types that identify multiple ideal types, each of which represents a unique combination of the organizational attributes that are believed to determine the relevant outcome(s)'. Thus, typology is an essential tool for theory development (Wang et al., 2015).

The typology emphasizes the ideal inter-relationship among the organization process and outcomes. The classification does not identify a unique and distinct set of a perfect type of inter-organization relationship. For example, McKelvey (1982) presents a classification system for organization, emphasizing discovering and incorporating governing behavior laws and compromising many divisions. The conceptual study of Doty and Glick (1994) suggests that the typology theory approach does not establish the hypothesis. Typologies can better explain theoretical assumptions associated with each construct used to describe the ideal type. (Doty and Glick, 1994). However, for all of their theoretical attractiveness, the logic of typology is based on consistency; that is, there is a fit among the different configuration approaches that makes up the overall ideal type (Fiss, 2011). On the other hand, typology predominantly directs attention to the focal object creating a situation where the typology boundary between the focused object and the context tends to be parsimony and can be reflected in the form or organizational outcomes.

Despite the application of typology in recent studies, typologies also present some considerable challenges, thus limiting understanding as to what causal mechanism is at work and what is driving and dependence on an effect (Putnam and Jablin, 2001). On the other hand, typologies are helpful as heuristic tools for researchers and practitioners alike (Mintzberg, 1993). Moreover, classification typology (focusing on structural and functional features and the configurational approach focus assume complex relationships among variables) and variables may be causally related to another (Meyer et al., 1993).

Recently, Fan et al. (2016) demonstrated the concept empirically. Studies respond to calls that shift focus toward configurational core based on causal relations with an outcome (Fiss, 2011); in this study, an equifinality approach has been used based on the configurational core by using two perspectives. The typology theory approach's application has necessary implications for understanding the relationship among organization structure, design, strategy, and different contextual factors. In order words, typologies need to be assessed in the context of organizational structure and outcomes. The equifinality approach, which assumed two or more organizational configurations could effectively achieve the same goals even if they are faced with some contingencies (Gresov and Drazin, 1997; Fiss, 2011), was used. In sum, typologies tend to be interdependent and tend to focus on others because the dependent variable is better explained than the classification theory. This study develops four ideal types of social entrepreneurship by theorizing about a set of dimensions: first-order constructs that form the blocks used to characterize each ideal-typical role relate to specific sets of behaviors and actions.

4. CONCLUSION

Every organization has specific goals and objectives. Social Enterprises focus on developing and creating social value by setting social objectives whereas CEs focus on financial performance to enhance the firm's profitability. To ensure a SE achieves its social goals, performance is measured, however, it is not as straightforward a task as it is in CEs because SEs may have numerous stakeholders and therefore measuring social impact becomes immensely complex. Organizations like SEs face many issues today, mainly because the focus now is not only on social goals but also on economic goals to ensure the firm's sustainability. In the pursuit of sustainability, SEs sometimes lose focus over their social mission and concentrate more on an economic mission.

SEs are adopting commercial strategies to meet the financial objectives of the firm. That is why the distinctiveness of SEs is now fading away and sometimes it is not easy to identify an organization as either a SE or a CE. Therefore, they are now being called hybrid organizations. Increased competition among SEs and reduction in funds is another reason why SEs are adopting conventional business models and strategies, however, these strategies may not serve the SE's aim. SEs require a balanced strategy that can satisfy its mission, its stakeholders, and its financial viability.

Hybrid organizations adopt a unique organizational structure that helps the organization to satisfy both social and economic missions. Their goal remains the same: to enhance social value. However, they also try to focus on economic missions. Organizational culture is another important aspect for SEs because the culture of the organization may be different from the culture of the community. National cultures are distinct hence people will be influenced by the national culture and influence the firm's culture however, in some cases, the organization may influence the national culture. In any case, organizational culture has a distinct relationship with the organization's performance. Organizations must analyze their internal and external environment to make changes to their strategies, structures, and business processes so that the social and economic missions of the SEs can be achieved.

SEs primarily aim to achieve three primary goals: the social mission, the firm's sustainability, and identifying threats and opportunities in the business environment to gain competitive advantage. SEs may face resistance from the local community which may create a conflict thus hindering the social mission. SEs may also face uncertainty and ambiguity due to their uncertain beliefs, behaviors, attitudes, and the people in the business environment. Due to this fact, the demand for each social stakeholder may be different and result in conflicts. SEs need to find a way to meet the demands and expectations of each stakeholder to ensure sustainability.

Organization theory is often associated with organizations that are looking to enhance their performance. It advocates that the organization adopt a suitable organizational structure that is most appropriate based on the SE's aim. Taylor (2019 as cited by King and Lawley) introduced this concept. However, its focus was more on enhancing the skills of the workforce to improve organizational performance. However, Fayol (2019 as cited by King and Lawley) proposed that higher performance can be achieved if management practices and functions are improved.

The organizational configuration is advocated among SEs to achieve both social and economic missions. It helps the firm to find one or more configurations which are most appropriately aligned to the needs of the business, its goals, and to satisfy its multiple stakeholders. There has been a debate on which configuration is most appropriate for an organization but it is not fair to pick one ultimate configuration because each SE has its own unique needs that require one or more configurations to succeed. Authors advocate various configurations, however, some of the most significant configurations were proposed by Henry Mintzberg (2019 as cited by King and Lawley), which were entrepreneurial organization, machine organization, professional organization, divisional or diversified organization, and innovative or adhocracy organization. Each configuration has some limitations but SEs should adopt a suitable configuration and structure their organization in a way that facilitates its strategy, business mission, processes, and environment.

This study offers a theoretical perspective that can be further studied. The validity of suggested configurations or structures can be tested based on various organizational goals and objectives or settings to find which configuration is more hybrid as SEs today are rapidly becoming hybrid organizations.

5. PRACTICAL IMPLICATIONS

The ethical argument in this study negates inappropriate actions in a cross-cultural context that leads to unlawful practices such as bribery (Jackson, 2001), which eventually jeopardizes the survival of the business in the global marketplace. While relying on organizational theory, this research indicates a strong need to adopt ethical management practices and ethical decision-making processes both in the UK and Pakistani business sectors. Understanding ethical issues from the perspectives of business professionals is also recommended for future research.

The study highlights the ethical issues and dilemmas faced by social enterprises (SEs) in their pursuit of both social and economic objectives. By identifying these challenges, the study equips researchers and practitioners with a deeper understanding of the complex ethical landscape within which SEs operate. This understanding is important to craft effective strategies to navigate these challenges while upholding the organization's mission. Next, the impact of geographical and cultural factors on ethical issues highlights the need for SEs to be culturally sensitive and context aware. Practitioners can use this insight to tailor their approaches and strategies to align with local values, customs, and expectations. This awareness can foster stronger relationships with communities and stakeholders thereby enhancing the social impact and credibility of SEs. The concept of hybrid organizations is a significant implication of the paper. As SEs increasingly adopt commercial strategies to ensure financial sustainability they transform into hybrid entities. This realization prompts researchers and practitioners to delve deeper into the evolving nature of such organizations and explore innovative ways to harmonize social and economic missions. This study highlights the complexity of measuring social impact due to the diverse stakeholder landscape of SEs. This calls for the development of robust measurement and evaluation frameworks that capture both quantitative and qualitative dimensions of social value. The implications here extend to researchers who can explore novel methodologies for assessing impact and practitioners who can refine their impact measurement practices to effectively communicate their organizations' outcomes. Practitioners can also cultivate an inclusive and value-driven culture that enhances performance and societal impact. The study's introduction of organizational configurations, inspired by Mintzberg's work, suggests practical implications for SEs looking to structure their organizations effectively. Practitioners can use these configurations as frameworks for organizing their teams, processes, and resources to achieve a harmonious balance between social and economic objectives.

REFERENCES

Abdul-Halim, H., Ahmad, N. H., Geare, A., & Thurasamy, R. (2019). Innovation culture in SMEs: The importance of organizational culture, organizational learning and market orientation. *Entrepreneurship Research Journal*, *9*(3), 20170014. doi:10.1515/erj-2017-0014

Abualoush, S., Bataineh, K., & Alrowwad, A. A. (2018). The role of knowledge management process and intellectual capital as intermediary variables between knowledge management infrastructure and organization performance. *Interdisciplinary Journal of Information, Knowledge, and Management, 13*, 279–309. doi:10.28945/4088

Adler, P. S. (2012). Perspective – the sociological ambivalence of bureaucracy: From Weber via Gouldner to Marx. *Organization Science, 23*(1), 244–266. doi:10.1287/orsc.1100.0615

Ahmed, J. U., Talukdar, A., & Ahmed, A. (2023). *Dignity Kitchen: Social Enterprise for Differently Abled People in the Labor Market*. SAGE Publications: SAGE Business Cases Originals.

Ahmed, R. R., and Streimikiene, D. (2021). Environmental issues and strategic corporate social responsibility for organizational competitiveness. *Journal of Competitiveness*, (2).

Ajagbe, M. A., Peter, O. F., Ekanem, E. U. U., Uduimoh, A. A., & Akpan, E. S. (2016). Business strategy as a contributor to organizational performance. *International Journal of Advanced Academic Research, 2*(3), 1–19.

Akingbola, K., & Phaetthayanan, S. (2021). The paradox of employee–volunteer interchangeability in a supported social enterprise. *Journal of Public and Nonprofit Affairs, 7*(1), 89–107. doi:10.20899/jpna.7.1.89-107

Akpa, V. O., Asikhia, O. U., & Nneji, N. E. (2021). Organizational culture and organizational performance: A review of literature. *International Journal of Advances in Engineering and Management, 3*(1), 361–372.

Alarifi, G., & Alrubaishi, D. (2018). The Social Entrepreneurship Landscape in Saudi Arabia. *Academy of Entrepreneurship Journal, 24*(4), 1–8.

Allaire, Y., & Firsirotu, M. E. (1984). Theories of organizational culture. *Organization Studies, 5*(3), 193–226. doi:10.1177/017084068400500301

Alter, S. K. (2008). Social enterprise models and their mission and money relationship. In A. Nicholls (Ed.), *Social entrepreneurship: New models of sustainable social change* (pp. 205–232). Oxford University Press.

Amburgey, T. L., & Dacin, T. M. (1994). As the left foot follows the right? The dynamics of strategic and structural change. *Academy of Management Journal, 37*(6), 1427–1452. doi:10.2307/256794

Andrews, K. (1971). *The concept of corporate strategy*. Dow Jones-Irwin.

Anh, D. B. H., Duc, L. D. M., Yen, N. T. H., Hung, N. T., & Tien, N. H. (2022). Sustainable development of social entrepreneurship: Evidence from Vietnam. *International Journal of Entrepreneurship and Small Business*, *45*(1), 62–76. doi:10.1504/IJESB.2022.120553

Anheier, H. K. (2000). *Managing nonprofit organizations: Towards a new approach*. Civil Society.

Anning-Dorson, T. (2021). Organizational culture and leadership as antecedents to organizational flexibility: Implications for SME competitiveness. *Journal of Entrepreneurship in Emerging Economies*, *13*(5), 1309–1325. doi:10.1108/JEEE-08-2020-0288

Ansari, Z. N., and Qureshi, M. N. (). Sustainability in supply chain management: An overview. *IUP Journal of Supply Chain Management, 12*(2)," 2015.

Ansoff, H. I. (1965). *Corporate strategy: An analytic approach to business policy for growth and expansion*. McGraw-Hill.

Armanious, M., & Padgett, J. D. (2021). Agile learning strategies to compete in an uncertain business environment. *Journal of Workplace Learning*, *33*(8), 635–647. doi:10.1108/JWL-11-2020-0181

Ashforth, B. E., Rogers, K. M., Pratt, M. G., & Pradies, C. (2014). Ambivalence in organizations: A multilevel approach. *Organization Science*, *25*(5), 1453–1478. doi:10.1287/orsc.2014.0909

Austin, J., Stevenson, H., & Wei-Skillern, J. (2006). Social and commercial entrepreneurship: Same, different, or both? *Entrepreneurship Theory and Practice*, *30*(1), 1–22. doi:10.1111/j.1540-6520.2006.00107.x

Bacq, S., & Eddleston, K. A. (2018). A resource-based view of social entrepreneurship: How stewardship culture benefits scale of social impact. *Journal of Business Ethics*, *152*(3), 589–611. doi:10.100710551-016-3317-1

Bageac, D., Furrer, O., & Reynaud, E. (2011). Management students' attitudes toward business ethics: A comparison between France and Romania. *Journal of Business Ethics*, *98*(3), 391–406. doi:10.100710551-010-0555-5

Barney, J. B., & Hoskisson, R. E. (1990). Strategic groups: Untested assertions and research proposals. *MDE. Managerial and Decision Economics*, *11*(3), 187–198. doi:10.1002/mde.4090110306

Barratt, M., & Choi, T. (2007). Mandated RFID and institutional responses: Cases of decentralised business units. *Production and Operations Management*, *16*(5), 569–585. doi:10.1111/j.1937-5956.2007.tb00281.x

Bastian, B. L., Sidani, Y. M., & El Amine, Y. (2018). Women entrepreneurship in the Middle East and North Africa: A review of knowledge areas and research gaps. *Gender in Management*, *33*(1), 14–29. doi:10.1108/GM-07-2016-0141

Battilana, J., & Dorado, S. (2010). Building sustainable hybrid organizations: The case of commercial microfinance organizations. *Academy of Management Journal*, *53*(6), 1419–1440. doi:10.5465/amj.2010.57318391

Battilana, J., & Lee, M. (2014). Advancing research on hybrid organizing – Insights from the study of social enterprises. *The Academy of Management Annals*, *8*(1), 397–441. doi:10.5465/19416520.2014.893615

Battilana, J., Sengul, M., Pache, A. C., & Model, J. (2014). Harnessing productive tensions in hybrid organizations: The case of work integration social enterprises. *Academy of Management Journal*.

Bauwens, T., Huybrechts, B., & Dufays, F. (2020). Understanding the diverse scaling strategies of social enterprises as hybrid organizations: The case of renewable energy cooperatives. *Organization & Environment*, *33*(2), 195–219. doi:10.1177/1086026619837126

Beer, M. (2021). Reflections: Towards a normative and actionable theory of planned organizational change and development. *Journal of Change Management*, *21*(1), 14–29. doi:10.1080/14697017.2021.1861699

Beer, M., & Eisenstat, R. A. (2000). The silent killers of strategy implementation and learning. *Sloan Management Review*, *41*, 29–40.

Bensaou, M., & Venkatraman, N. (1995). Configurations of inter-organizational relationships: A comparison between the US and Japanese automakers. *Management Science*, *41*(9), 1471–1492. doi:10.1287/mnsc.41.9.1471

Besharov, M. L., & Smith, W. K. (2013). *Multiple logics within organizations: An integrative framework and model of organizational hybridity*. Cornell University.

Bissola, R., & Imperatori, B. (2012). Sustaining the stakeholder engagement in the social enterprise: the human resource architecture. *Patterns in Social Entrepreneurship Research*, 137-160.

Bloom, P. N., & Chatterji, A. K. (2009). Scaling social entrepreneurial impact. *California Management Review*, *51*(3), 114–133. doi:10.2307/41166496

Bradač Hojnik, B., & Crnogaj, K. (2020). Social impact, innovations, and market activity of social enterprises: Comparison of European countries. *Sustainability (Basel)*, *12*(5), 1915. doi:10.3390u12051915

Brandsen, T., & Karré, P. M. (2011). Hybrid organizations: No cause for concern. *International Journal of Public Administration*, *34*(13), 827–836. doi:10.1080/01900692.2011.605090

Brickley, J., Smith, C., Zimmerman, J. L., & Willett, J. (2002). *Designing organizations to create value: From strategy to structure*. McGraw-Hill.

Bubicz, M. E., Barbosa-Póvoa, A. P. F. D., & Carvalho, A. (2019). Incorporating social aspects in sustainable supply chains: Trends and future directions. *Journal of Cleaner Production*, *237*, 117500. doi:10.1016/j.jclepro.2019.06.331

Bull, M., & Crompton, H. (2006). () "Business practices in social enterprises. *Social Enterprise Journal*, *2*(1), 42–60. doi:10.1108/17508610680000712

Bunduchi, R., Smart, A. U., Crisan-Mitra, C., & Cooper, S. (2023). Legitimacy and innovation in social enterprises. *International Small Business Journal*, *41*(4), 371–400. doi:10.1177/02662426221102860

Cameron, K. S., & Quinn, R. E. (2005). Diagnosing and changing organizational culture: Based on the competing values framework. Jossey-Bass.

Campos-Blázquez, J. R., Rubio-Andrada, L., & Celemín-Pedroche, M. S. (2023). Voices from within. To what extent can internal crowdsourcing drive a change in organizational culture? *Journal of Business Research*, *157*, 113618. doi:10.1016/j.jbusres.2022.113618

Carter, C., & Easton, P. L. (2011). Sustainable supply chain management: Evolution and future directions. *International Journal of Physical Distribution & Logistics Management*, *41*(1), 46–62. doi:10.1108/09600031111101420

Cartwright, S., & Cooper, C. L. (1993). The role of culture compatibility in successful organizational marriage. *The Academy of Management Perspectives*, *7*(2), 57–70. doi:10.5465/ame.1993.9411302324

Chandler, A. D. (2003) Strategy and structure: Chapters in the history of the American industrial enterprise. Beard Books.

Chandra, Y., & Shang, L. (2017). Unpacking the biographical antecedents of the emergence of social enterprises: A narrative perspective. *Voluntas*, *28*(6), 2498–2529. doi:10.100711266-017-9860-2

Chatterjee, S., Lubatkin, M. H., Schweiger, D. M., & Weber, Y. (1992). Cultural differences and shareholder value in related mergers: Linking equity and human capital. *Strategic Management Journal*, *13*(5), 319–334. doi:10.1002mj.4250130502

Cheah, J., Amran, A., & Yahya, S. (2019). Internal oriented resources and social enterprises' performance: How can social enterprises help themselves before helping others? *Journal of Cleaner Production*, *211*, 607–619. doi:10.1016/j.jclepro.2018.11.203

Child, J. (1984). *Organization: A Guide to Problems and Practice*. SAGE. doi:10.4135/9781446280348

Choi, D., Lee, K. H., & Hur, H. (2020). Social enterprises' social orientation: The impact on the organizational commitment of employees. *Journal of Public and Nonprofit Affairs*, *6*(1), 44–62. doi:10.20899/jpna.6.1.44-62

Conti, T. (2002). Human and Social Implications of Excellence Models: Are They Really Accepted by the Business Community. *Managing Service Quality*, *12*(3), 151–158. doi:10.1108/09604520210429213

Corkindale, G. (2011). *The Importance of Organizational Design and Structure*. HBR. https://hbr.org/2011/02/the-importance-of-organization

Costa, E., & Andreaus, M. (2020). Social impact and performance measurement systems in an Italian social enterprise: A participatory action research project. *Journal of Public Budgeting, Accounting & Financial Management*.

Dacin, P. A., Dacin, M. T., & Matear, M. (2010). Social entrepreneurship: Why we don't need a new theory and how we move forward from here. *The Academy of Management Perspectives*, *24*(3), 37–57.

Daft, R.L. (2009). Organization theory and design. *South-Western Publication*, *17*.

Dauber, D., Fink, G., & Yolles, M. (2012). A configuration model of organizational culture. *SAGE Open*, *2*(1). doi:10.1177/2158244012441482

Davis, P. E., Bendickson, J. S., Muldoon, J., & McDowell, W. C. (2021). Agency theory utility and social entrepreneurship: Issues of identity and role conflict. *Review of Managerial Science*, *15*(8), 2299–2318. doi:10.100711846-020-00423-y

De Mon, I. A., Gabaldón, P., & Nuñez, M. (2022). Social entrepreneurs: Making sense of tensions through the application of alternative strategies of hybrid organizations. *The International Entrepreneurship and Management Journal*, *18*(2), 975–997. doi:10.100711365-020-00731-5

Dees, J. G. (2012). A tale of two cultures: Charity, problem-solving, and the future of Social Entrepreneurship. *Journal of Business Ethics, 111*(3), 321–334. doi:10.100710551-012-1412-5

Dees, J. G., Battle Anderson, B., & Wei-Skillem, J. (2004). Scaling social entrepreneurship: Strategies for spreading social innovations. *Stanford Social Innovation Review, 1*(4), 24–32.

Delery, J. E., & Doty, D. H. (1996). Modes of theorising in strategic human resource management: Tests of universalistic, contingency, and configurational performance predictions. *Academy of Management Journal, 39*(4), 802–835. doi:10.2307/256713

Delmas, M. A., & Pekovic, S. (2018). Organizational configurations for sustainability and employee productivity: A qualitative comparative analysis approach. *Business & Society, 57*(1), 216–251. doi:10.1177/0007650317703648

Dhillon, M. K., Rafi-Ul-Shan, P. M., Amar, H., Sher, F., & Ahmed, S. (2023). Flexible Green Supply Chain Management in Emerging Economies: A Systematic Literature Review. *Global Journal of Flexible Systems Managment, 24*(1), 1–28. doi:10.100740171-022-00321-0 PMID:37519431

Di Domenico, M., Haugh, H., & Tracey, P. (2010). Social bricolage: Theorising social value creation in social enterprises. *Entrepreneurship Theory and Practice, 34*(4), 681–703. doi:10.1111/j.1540-6520.2010.00370.x

Dionisio, M. (2019). The evolution of social entrepreneurship research: A bibliometric analysis. *Social Enterprise Journal, 15*(1), 22–45. doi:10.1108/SEJ-05-2018-0042

Distanont, A., & Khongmalai, O. (2020). The role of innovation in creating a competitive advantage. *Kasetsart Journal of Social Sciences, 41*(1), 15–21.

Dodgson, M. (1993). () “Organizational learning: A review of some literature. *Organization Studies, 14*(3), 375–394. doi:10.1177/017084069301400303

Doherty, B., Haugh, H., & Lyon, F. (2014). Social enterprises as hybrid organizations: A review and research agenda. *International Journal of Management Reviews, 16*(4), 417–436. doi:10.1111/ijmr.12028

Donaldson, L. (1996). *For positive organization theory: Proving the hardcore. London*. SAGE. doi:10.4135/9781446280331

Donnelly-Cox, G., & O’ Regan, A. (1999). *Resourcing organizational growth and development: A typology of third sector service delivery organizations*. IRSPMIII: Aston.

Doty, D. H., & Glick, W. H. (1994). Typologies as a unique form of theory building: Toward improved understanding and modelling. *Academy of Management Review*, *19*(2), 230–251. doi:10.2307/258704

Eze, S. C., Bello, A. O., & Adekola, T. A. (2017). The effects of organizational structure on the performance of organizations. *European Journal of Business and Innovation Research*, *5*(6), 46–62. doi:10.37745/ejbir.vol5.no6.p46-62.2017

Farid, M. (2007). Entrepreneurship in Egypt and the US compared: Directions for further research suggested. *Journal of Management Development*, *26*(5), 428–440. doi:10.1108/02621710710748266

Fayol, H. (1937). The administrative theory in the state. *Papers on the Science of Administration*. 99-114.

Ferguson, T. D., & Ketchen, D. J. Jr. (1999). Organizational configurations and performance: The role of statistical power in extant research. *Strategic Management Journal*, *20*(4), 385–395. doi:10.1002/(SICI)1097-0266(199904)20:4<385::AID-SMJ24>3.0.CO;2-X

Ferrell, O. C., Fraedrich, J., & Ferrell, L. (2013). *Business Ethics: Ethical Decision Making and Cases* (10th ed.). Cengage Learning.

Fink, G., & Mayrhofer, W. (2009). Cross-cultural competence and management–setting the stage. *European Journal of Cross-Cultural Competence and Management*, *1*(1), 42–65. doi:10.1504/EJCCM.2009.026733

Fiss, P. C. (2007). A Set-Theoretic Approach to Organizational Configurations. *Academy of Management Review*, *32*(4), 1180–1198. doi:10.5465/amr.2007.26586092

Fitriasari, F. (2020). How do Small and Medium Enterprise (SME) survive the COVID-19 outbreak? *Journal Inovasi Ekonomi*, *5*(02). doi:10.22219/jiko.v5i3.11838

Franks, J., & Mayer, C. (1995). Ownership and control. In H. Siebert (Ed.), *Trends in business organization: Do participation and cooperation increase cometitiveness?* Mohr.

Freeman, R. E. (1994). The politics of stakeholder theory: Some future directions. *Business Ethics Quarterly*, *4*(4), 409–421. doi:10.2307/3857340

Freeman, R. E., Harrison, J. S., & Wicks, A. C. (2007). *Managing for Stakeholders: Survival, Reputation, and Success*. Yale University Press.

Gallego-Álvarez, I., & Ortas, E. (2017). Corporate environmental sustainability reporting in the context of national cultures: A quantile regression approach. *International Business Review*, *26*(2), 337–353. doi:10.1016/j.ibusrev.2016.09.003

Gamble, E. N., Parker, S. C., & Moroz, P. W. (2020). Measuring the integration of social and environmental missions in hybrid organizations. *Journal of Business Ethics*, *167*(2), 271–284. doi:10.100710551-019-04146-3

Gandhi, T., & Raina, R. (2018). Social entrepreneurship: The need, relevance, facets and constraints. *Journal of Global Entrepreneurship Research*, *8*(1), 1–13. doi:10.118640497-018-0094-6

Gentile-Lüdecke, S., R.T. de Oliveira, & Paul, J. (2020). Does organizational structure facilitate inbound and outbound open innovation in SMEs? *Small Business Economics, 55*(4), 091-1112.

Ghafar, A., Nair, M., Elalfy, S., & Fenech, R. (2023). The Pursuit of Gaining Legitimacy through Marketing Strategy: A Case of Social Enterprises in UAE. *Journal of Social Entrepreneurship*, 1–23. doi:10.1080/19420676.2023.2205865

Ghalwash, S., Tolba, A., & Ismail, A. (2017). What motivates social entrepreneurs to start social ventures? An exploratory study in the context of a developing economy. *Social Enterprise Journal*, *13*(3), 268–298. doi:10.1108/SEJ-05-2016-0014

Gimenez, C., & Tachizawa, E. (2012). Extending sustainability to suppliers: A systematic literature review. *Supply Chain Management*, *17*(5), 531–543. doi:10.1108/13598541211258591

Greenberg, J. (2011). *Behaviour in organizations* (10th ed.). Prentice-Hall.

Greenwood, R., Magán Díaz, A., Li, S. X., & Céspedes Lorente, J. (2010). The multiplicity of institutional logics and the heterogeneity of organizational responses. *Organization Science*, *21*(2), 521–539. doi:10.1287/orsc.1090.0453

Gresov, C., & Drazin, R. (1997). Equifinality: Functional equivalence in organization design. *Academy of Management Review*, *22*(2), 403–428. doi:10.2307/259328

Grosskopf, S., & Barmeyer, C. (2021). Learning from multi-paradigmatic sensitivity in cross-cultural management? Empirical and theoretical considerations. *International Journal of Cross Cultural Management*, *21*(2), 181–202. doi:10.1177/14705958211019437

Hage, J. (1965). An axiomatic theory of organizations. *Administrative Science Quarterly*, *10*(3), 289–320. doi:10.2307/2391470

Haigh, N., & Hoffman, A. J. (2012). Hybrid organizations: The next chapter of sustainable business. *Organizational Dynamics, 41*(2), 126–134. doi:10.1016/j.orgdyn.2012.01.006

Haigh, N., Kennedy, E. D., & Walker, J. (2015). E.D., Kennedy, and J. Walker, "Hybrid Organizations as Shape-Shifters: Altering Legal Structure for Strategic Gain.". *California Management Review, 57*(3), 59–82. doi:10.1525/cmr.2015.57.3.59

Haigh, N., Walker, J., Bacq, S., & Kickul, J. (2015). Hybrid Organizations: Origins, Strategies, Impacts, and Implications. *California Management Review, 57*(3), 5–12. doi:10.1525/cmr.2015.57.3.5

Haile, E. A., & Tüzüner, V. L. (2022). Organizational learning capability and its impact on organizational innovation. *Asia Pacific Journal of Innovation and Entrepreneurship, 16*(1), 69–85. doi:10.1108/APJIE-03-2022-0015

Hall, E. T. (1976). *Beyond culture*. Anchor Books.

Hall, R. H., & Tolbert, P. S. (2009). *Organizations: structures, processes, and outcome* (9th ed.). Prentice-Hall.

Hamilton, R. T., & Shergill, G. S. (1993). *The logic of New Zealand business: Strategy, structure, and performance*. Oxford University Press.

Handy, C. B. (1993). *Understanding organizations*. Oxford University Press.

Hanelt, A., Bohnsack, R., Marz, D., & Antunes Marante, C. (2000). A systematic review of the literature on digital transformation: Insights and implications for strategy and organizational change. *Journal of Management Studies, 58*(5), 1159-1197

Hatch, M. J. (1993). The dynamics of organizational culture. *Academy of Management Review, 18*(4), 657–693. doi:10.2307/258594

Hattab, H. (2011). *Towards understanding women entrepreneurship in MENA countries. 56th ICSB World Conference*, Stockholm, Sweden.

Hazenberg, R., Bajwa-Patel, M., Mazzei, M., Roy, M. J., & Baglioni, S. (2016). The role of institutional and stakeholder networks in shaping social enterprise ecosystems in Europe. *Social Enterprise Journal, 12*(3), 302–321. doi:10.1108/SEJ-10-2016-0044

Hoffman, A. J., Badiane, K. K., & Haigh, N. (2010). Hybrid organizations as agents of positive social change: Bridging the for-profit and nonprofit divide. Ross School of Business.

Hofstede, G. (2001). *Culture's consequences: Comparing values, behaviours, institutions and organizations across nations*. SAGE.

Hofstede, G., Neuijen, B., Ohayv, D. D., & Sanders, G. (1990). Measuring organizational cultures: A qualitative and quantitative study across twenty cases. *Administrative Science Quarterly*, *35*(2), 286–316. doi:10.2307/2393392

Homburg, C., & Pflesser, C. (2000). A multiple-layer model of market-oriented organizational culture: Measurement issues and performance outcomes. *JMR, Journal of Marketing Research*, *37*(4), 449–462. doi:10.1509/jmkr.37.4.449.18786

Honeyman, R., & Jana, T. (2019). *The B Corp handbook: How you can use business as a force for good*. Berrett-Koehler Publishers.

Hsieh, C.-M. (2003). Counting importance: The case of life satisfaction and relative domain importance. *Social Indicators Research*, *61*(2), 227–240. doi:10.1023/A:1021354132664

Imperatori, B., & Ruta, D. D. (2015). Designing a social enterprise: Organization configuration and social stakeholders' work involvement. *Social Enterprise Journal*, *11*(3), 321–346. doi:10.1108/SEJ-08-2014-0034

Inkpen, A., & Choudhury, N. (1995). The seeking of strategy is not: Towards a theory of strategy absence. *Strategic Management Journal*, *16*(4), 313–323. doi:10.1002mj.4250160405

Iskandar, Y., & Kaltum, U. (2021). The Relationship Between Intellectual Capital and Performance of Social Enterprises: A Literature Review. *Academic Journal of Interdisciplinary Studies*, *10*(5), 309–330. doi:10.36941/ajis-2021-0141

Islami, X., Mustafa, N., & Topuzovska Latkovikj, M. (2020). Linking Porter's generic strategies to firm performance. *Future Business Journal*, *6*(1), 1–15. doi:10.118643093-020-0009-1

Jay, J. (2013). Navigating Paradox as a Mechanism of Change and Innovation in Hybrid Organizations. *Academy of Management Journal*, *56*(1), 137–159. doi:10.5465/amj.2010.0772

Karré, P. M. (2023). The Thumbprint of a Hybrid Organization—A Multidimensional Model for Analysing Public/Private Hybrid Organizations. *Public Organization Review*, *23*(2), 777–791. doi:10.100711115-021-00598-2

Katz, D., & Kahn, R. L. (1978). *The social psychology of organizations* (2nd ed.). Wiley.

Kaufman, Z. (2012). Social Entrepreneurship in the Age of Atrocities: Changing Our World. Cheltenham: Edward Elgar, 01-19.

Ketchen, D. J. Jr, Combs, J. G., Russell, C. J., Shook, C., Dean, M. A., Runge, J., Lohrke, F. T., Naumann, S. E., Haptonstahl, D. E., Baker, R., Beckstein, B. A., Handler, C., Honig, H., & Lamoureux, S. (1997). Organizational configurations and performance: A meta-analysis. *Academy of Management Journal*, *40*(1), 223–240. doi:10.2307/257028

Ketchen, D. J. Jr, & Hult, G. T. (2007). Bridging organizational theory and supply chain management: The case of best value supply chains. *Journal of Operations Management*, *25*(2), 573–580. doi:10.1016/j.jom.2006.05.010

Ketprapakorn, N., & Kantabutra, S. (2019). Sustainable social enterprise model: Relationships and consequences. *Sustainability (Basel)*, *11*(14), 3772. doi:10.3390u11143772

Khan, H. U. R., Ali, M., Olya, H. G., Zulqarnain, M., & Khan, Z. R. (2018). Transformational leadership, corporate social responsibility, organizational innovation, and organizational performance: Symmetrical and asymmetrical analytical approaches. *Corporate Social Responsibility and Environmental Management*, *25*(6), 1270–1283. doi:10.1002/csr.1637

Kickert, W. J. M. (2001). Public Management of Hybrid Organizations: Governance of Quasi-Autonomous Executive Agencies. *International Public Management Journal*, *4*(2), 35–150. doi:10.1016/S1096-7494(01)00049-6

Ko, W. W., & Liu, G. (2020). The transformation from traditional nonprofit organizations to social enterprises: An institutional entrepreneurship perspective. *Journal of Business Ethics*, 1–18.

Ko, W. W., & Liu, G. (2021). The transformation from traditional nonprofit organizations to social enterprises: An institutional entrepreneurship perspective. *Journal of Business Ethics*, *171*(1), 15–32. doi:10.100710551-020-04446-z

Koppell, J. G. S. (2003). *The Politics of Quasi-Government: Hybrid Organizations and the Dynamics of Bureaucratic Control*. University Press.

Krug, K., & Weinberg, C. B. (2004). Mission, Money and Merit: Strategic Decision Making by Nonprofit Managers. *Nonprofit Management & Leadership*, *14*(3), 325–342. doi:10.1002/nml.37

Kumar, P. (2015). An analytical study on mintzberg's framework: Managerial roles. *International Journal of Research in Management and Business Studies*, *2*(3), 12–19.

Küng, L. (2016). Strategic management in the media: Theory to practice. *Strategic Management in the Media*, 1-256.

Lambooy, T., Anthoni, P., & Argyrou, A. (2020). Aren't we all pursuing societal goals in our businesses? Defining "societal purpose" as pursued by social enterprises. *Sustainable Development (Bradford), 28*(3), 485–494. doi:10.1002d.2039

Lampel, J., & Mintzberg, H. (1996). Customising customisation. *Sloan Management Review, 38*(1), 21.

Lerner, M., & Sharir, M. (2006). Gauging the success of social ventures initiated by individual social entrepreneurs. *Journal of World Business, 41*(1), 6–20. doi:10.1016/j.jwb.2005.09.004

Lewis, M. W., & Smith, W. K. (2011). Toward a theory of paradox: A dynamic equilibrium model of organising. *Academy of Management Review, 36*(2), 381–403.

Li, D., Huang, M., Ren, S., Chen, X., & Ning, L. (2018). Environmental legitimacy, green innovation, and corporate carbon disclosure: Evidence from CDP China 100. *Journal of Business Ethics, 150*(4), 1089–1104. doi:10.100710551-016-3187-6

Littlewood, D., & Holt, D. (2018). Social entrepreneurship in South Africa: Exploring the influence of environment. *Business & Society, 57*(3), 525–561. doi:10.1177/0007650315613293

Liu, H., Ke, W., Wei, K. K., Gu, J., & Chen, H. (2009). The role of institutional pressures and organizational culture in the firm's intention to adopt Internet-enabled supply chain management systems. *Journal of Operations Management, 28*(5), 372–384. doi:10.1016/j.jom.2009.11.010

Low, W., & Davenport, E. (2006). Mainstreaming fair trade: Adoption, assimilation, appropriation. *Journal of Strategic Marketing, 14*(4), 315–327. doi:10.1080/09652540600947912

Lumpkin, G. T., Moss, T. W., Gras, D. M., Kato, S., & Amezcua, A. S. (2013). Entrepreneurial processes in social contexts: How are they different, if at all? *Small Business Economics, 40*(3), 61–783. doi:10.100711187-011-9399-3

Lunenberg, F.C. (2012). Organizational Structure: Mintzberg's Framework. *International Journal of Scholarly, Academic, Intellectual Diversity 14*, 01-08.

Lysaght, R., Krupa, T., & Bouchard, M. (2018). The Role of Social Enterprise in Creating Work Options for People With Intellectual and Developmental Disabilities. *Journal on Developmental Disabilities, 23*(3).

Madajova, M., Pallabi, P., & Mpumwire, S. (2017). *Social entrepreneurship: The dual role of Bricolage on Innovation*. Semantic Scholar.

Mamabolo, A., & Myres, K. (2020). Performance measurement in emerging market social enterprises using a balanced scorecard. *Journal of Social Entrepreneurship, 11*(1), 65–87. doi:10.1080/19420676.2018.1561499

Mani, V., Jabbour, C. J. C., & Mani, K. T. (2020). Supply chain social sustainability in small and medium manufacturing enterprises and firms' performance: Empirical evidence from an emerging Asian economy. *International Journal of Production Economics, 227*, 227. doi:10.1016/j.ijpe.2020.107656

Marcoulides, G. A., & Heck, R. H. (1993). Organizational culture and performance: Proposing and testing a model. *Organization Science, 4*(2), 209–225. doi:10.1287/orsc.4.2.209

Mati, A., Machuki, V., Ogutu, M., & Njihia, J. M. (2020). The Joint Effect Of Organizational Strategy, Organizational Culture And External Environment On Organizational Performance Of Large Private Health Facilities In Kenya. *Dba Africa Management Review, 10*(1), 11–27.

McGregor, A., Glass, A., & Clark, S. (2003). *Revaluing the Social Economy, Training and Employment Research Unit*. The University of Glasgow.

Meyer, A.D., Tsui, A.S., and Hinings, C.R. (1993) Configurational approaches to organizational analysis. *Academy of Management Journal, 36*, 1175-1195.

Miles, R. E., Snow, C. C., Meyer, A. D., & Coleman, H. J. (2011). *Organizational strategy, structure, and process*. Stanford University Press.

Miller, D. (1996). Configurations revisited. *Strategic Management Journal, 17*(7), 505–512. doi:10.1002/(SICI)1097-0266(199607)17:7<505::AID-SMJ852>3.0.CO;2-I

Mimouni, F. (2010). *Implications of Islam on management theory and practice: A case study of two organizations in the Middle East*. Lambert Academic Publishing.

Mintzberg, H. (2009). *Tracking strategies: Toward a general theory of strategy formation*. Oxford University Press.

Mitchell, R., Agle, B., & Wood, D. (1997). Toward a theory of stakeholder identification and salience: Defining the principle of who and what really counts. *Academy of Management Review, 22*(4), 853–886. doi:10.2307/259247

Mocsary, G. A. (2016). Freedom of corporate purpose. *BYU L. Rev.*, 1319.

Molecke, G., & Pinkse, J. (2017). Accountability for social impact: A bricolage perspective on impact measurement in social enterprises. *Journal of Business Venturing*, *32*(5), 550–568. doi:10.1016/j.jbusvent.2017.05.003

Monteduro, F., Cecchetti, I., Lai, Y., & Allegrini, V. (2021). Does stakeholder engagement affect corruption risk management? *The Journal of Management and Governance*, *25*(3), 759–785. doi:10.100710997-020-09527-9

Muñoz, P., & Kimmitt, J. (2019). Social mission as competitive advantage: A configurational analysis of the strategic conditions of social entrepreneurship. *Journal of Business Research*, *101*, 854–861. doi:10.1016/j.jbusres.2018.11.044

Murphy, P. J., & Coombes, S. M. (2009). A model of social entrepreneurial discovery. *Journal of Business Ethics*, *87*(3), 325–336. doi:10.100710551-008-9921-y

Nagy, G., Bilgin-Wührer, Z., Akrout, H., Lioliou, E., Hofer, K. M., & Beracs, J. (2022). Achieving high international market performance via simple vs complex configuration of international managerial network ties: A set theoretic approach across two countries. *Journal of Small Business Management*, 1–48. doi:10.1080/00472778.2022.2046014

Nayak, R., Akbari, M., & Far, S. M. (2019). Recent sustainable trends in Vietnam's fashion supply chain. *Journal of Cleaner Production*, *225*, 291–303. doi:10.1016/j.jclepro.2019.03.239

Nelson, D. B., & Quick, J. C. (2011). *Understanding organizational behaviour*. South-Western Cengage Learning.

Nicholls, A. (2010). The legitimacy of social entrepreneurship: Reflexive isomorphism in a pre-paradigmatic field. *Entrepreneurship Theory and Practice*, *34*(4), 611–633. doi:10.1111/j.1540-6520.2010.00397.x

Nicholls, Alex., and C. Opal, Fairtrade: Market-driven ethical consumption. (2004). Sage Publications.

Nyarko, I. K., Dorkenoo, C. B., Semordey, E. Y., & Agbanu, P. (2016). Organizational Structure as a Logical Tool for Determining the Flow of Responsibility and Authority. *International Journal of Management and Administrative Sciences*, *3*(3), 1–19.

O' Toole, J., & Vogel, D. (2011). Two and a Half Cheers for Conscious Capitalism. *California Management Review*, *53*(3), 60–76. doi:10.1525/cmr.2011.53.3.60

Oberoi, R., Halsall, J. P., & Snowden, M. (2021). Reinventing social entrepreneurship leadership in the COVID-19 era: Engaging with the new normal. *Entrepreneurship Education*, *4*(2), 117–136. doi:10.100741959-021-00051-x

Oliveira, N., & Takahashi, N. (2012). *Automated organizations: Development and structure of the modern business firm*. Springer. doi:10.1007/978-3-7908-2759-0

Ormiston, J., & Seymour, R. (2011). Understanding Value Creation in Social Entrepreneurship: The Importance of Aligning Mission, Strategy and Impact Measurement. *Journal of Social Entrepreneurship*, *2*(2), 125–150. doi:10.1080/19420676.2011.606331

Ouchi, W. G. (1980). Markets, bureaucracies, and clans. *Administrative Science Quarterly*, *25*(1), 129–141. doi:10.2307/2392231

Pache, A. C., & Santos, F. (2013). Embedded in hybrid contexts: How individuals in organizations respond to competing institutional logics. *Research in the Sociology of Organizations*, *39*, 3–35. doi:10.1108/S0733-558X(2013)0039b014

Pareja-Cano, B., Valor, C., & Benito, A. (2020). How Social Enterprises Nurture Empowerment: A Grounded Theoretical Model of Social Change. *Journal of Social Entrepreneurship*, 1–21.

Parmar, B. L., Freeman, R. E., Harrison, J. S., Wicks, A. C., Purnell, L., & De Colle, S. (2010). Stakeholder theory: The state of the art. *The Academy of Management Annals*, *4*(1), 403–445. doi:10.5465/19416520.2010.495581

Parrish, B. D. (2010). Sustainability-driven entrepreneurship: Principles of organization design. *Journal of Business Venturing*, *25*(5), 510–523. doi:10.1016/j.jbusvent.2009.05.005

Parthasarthy, R., & Sethi, S. P. (2018). The impact of flexible automation on business strategy and organizational structure. In *Organizational Innovation* (pp. 319–344). Routledge.

Peattie, K., & Morley, A. (2008). Eight paradoxes of the social enterprise research agenda. *Social Enterprise Journal*, *4*(2), 91–107. doi:10.1108/17508610810901995

Pelizza Vier Machado, H., Gaiotto, S. A. V., & Rovaris Machado, M. C. (2021). *Growth and social entrepreneurs: the challenge of conciliating economic and social values*. Revista de Gestão.

Pfeilstetter, R., & Gómez Carrasco, I. (2020). Local meanings of social enterprise. A historical-particularist view on hybridity of organizations. *Revista de Estudios Cooperativos 134*.

Polonsky, M. J. (1995). A stakeholder theory approach to designing an environmental marketing strategy. *Journal of Business and Industrial Marketing*, *10*(3), 29–46. doi:10.1108/08858629510096201

Post, J. E., & Waddock, S. (1991). Social entrepreneurs and catalytic change. *Public Administration Review, 51*(5), 393–401. doi:10.2307/976408

Powell, M., Gillett, A., & Doherty, B. (2019). Sustainability in social enterprise: Hybrid organizing in public services. *Public Management Review, 21*(2), 159–186. doi:10.1080/14719037.2018.1438504

Prahalad, C. K. (2006). *The fortune at the bottom of the pyramid*. Pearson Education, India.

Ragin, C. C. (1987). *The comparative method: Moving beyond qualitative and quantitative strategies*. University of California Press.

Ramus, T., La Cara, B., Vaccaro, A., & Brusoni, S. (2018). Social or commercial? Innovation strategies in social enterprises at times of turbulence. *Business Ethics Quarterly, 28*(4), 463–492. doi:10.1017/beq.2017.55

Ramus, T., & Vaccaro, A. (2017). Stakeholders matter: How social enterprises address mission drift. *Journal of Business Ethics, 143*(2), 307–322. doi:10.100710551-014-2353-y

Roumpi, D., Magrizos, S., & Nicolopoulou, K. (2020). Virtuous circle: Human capital and human resource management in social enterprises. *Human Resource Management, 59*(5), 401–421. doi:10.1002/hrm.22002

Sagiv, L., & Schwartz, S. H. (2007). Cultural values in organizations: Insights for Europe. *European Journal of International Management, 1*(3), 176–190. doi:10.1504/EJIM.2007.014692

Santos, F., Pache, A. C., & Birkholz, C. (2015). Making hybrids work: Aligning business models and organizational design for social enterprises. *California Management Review, 57*(3), 36–58. doi:10.1525/cmr.2015.57.3.36

Sargiacomo, M., & Walker, S. P. (2022). Disaster governance and hybrid organizations: Accounting, performance challenges and evacuee housing. *Accounting. Accounting, Auditing & Accountability Journal, 35*(3), 887–916. doi:10.1108/AAAJ-12-2019-4323

Sarkis, J., Zhu, Q., & Lai, K. H. (2011). An organizational theoretic review of green supply chain management literature. *International Journal of Production Economics, 130*(1), 1–15. doi:10.1016/j.ijpe.2010.11.010

Savitz, A. (2013). *The triple bottom line: how today's best-run companies are achieving economic, social and environmental success and how you can too*. John Wiley and Sons.

Schein, E. H. (1985). *Organizational culture and leadership*. Jossey-Bass.

Schmidt, T. (2006). *A review of Structure in Fives; Designing Effective Organizations* [Thesis, MSC]. http://www.thesis.msc-cse.com/pdf/article_mintzberg.pdf

Scott, J. (1991). *Social Network Analysis*. Sage Publications.

Scott, W. R. (2008). *Institutions and organizations: Ideas and interests*. SAGE.

Shafritz, J. M., Ott, J. S., & Jang, Y. S. (2015). *Classics of organization theory*. Cengage Learning.

Shamsudin, S., & Velmurugan, V. P. (2023). A study on the drivers of corporate culture impacting employee performance in IT industry. *International Journal of Professional Business Review: Int. J. Prof. Bus. Rev.*, *8*(2), 13. doi:10.26668/businessreview/2023.v8i2.1023

Short, J. C., Tyge Payne, G., & Jr Ketchen, D. J. (2008). Research on organizational configurations: Past accomplishment and future challenges. *Journal of Management*, *34*(6), 1053–1079. doi:10.1177/0149206308324324

Siegner, M., Pinkse, J., & Panwar, R. (2018). Managing tensions in a social enterprise: The complex balancing act to deliver a multi-faceted but coherent social mission. *Journal of Cleaner Production*, *174*, 1314–1324. doi:10.1016/j.jclepro.2017.11.076

Siemiński, M., Andruszkiewicz, K., & Pinho, T. (2022). Application of the 6D Hofstede Model in an Analysis of the Polish and Portuguese Business Culture. *Olsztyn Economic Journal*, *17*(1), 59–69. doi:10.31648/oej.8651

Smallbone, D., Evans, M., Ekanem, I., & Butters, S. (2001). *Researching Social Enterprise*. Small Business Service.

Smith, P., McVilly, K. R., McGillivray, J., & Chan, J. (2018). Developing open employment outcomes for people with an intellectual disability utilising a Social Enterprise Framework. *Journal of Vocational Rehabilitation*, *48*(1), 59–77. doi:10.3233/JVR-170916

Smith, S. (2010). For love or money? Fairtrade business models in the UK supermarket sector. *Journal of Business Ethics*, *92*(S2, no. S2), 257–266. doi:10.100710551-010-0582-2

Smith, W.K., Leonard, H. & Epstein, M. (2007). Digital divide data: A social enterprise in action. *Harvard Business School Case Study*.

Smith, W. K., & Lewis, M. W. (2011). Toward a theory of paradox: A dynamic equilibrium model of organising. *Academy of Management Review*, *36*(2), 381–403.

Sparviero, S. (2019). The case for a socially oriented business model canvas: The social enterprise model canvas. *Journal of Social Entrepreneurship, 10*(2), 232–251. doi:10.1080/19420676.2018.1541011

Stephan, U., & Folmer, E. (2017). Context and social enterprises: which environments enable social entrepreneurship? *European Policy Brief*, 1-5.

Strielkowski, W. (2012). Factors that determine success of small and medium enterprises: The role of internal and external factors. *Journal of Applied Economic Sciences, 7*(21), 326–333.

Suchman, M. C. (1995). Managing legitimacy: Strategic and institutional approaches. *Academy of Management Review, 20*(3), 571–610. doi:10.2307/258788

Sullivan Mort, G., & Weerawardena, J. (2006). Investing social entrepreneurship: A multidimensional model. *Journal of World Business, 41*(1), 21–35. doi:10.1016/j.jwb.2005.09.001

Taylor, F. W. (1914). *The Principles of Scientific Management*. Harper.

Tencati, A., & Zsolnai, L. (2009). The collaborative enterprise.. *Journal of Business Ethics, 85*(43), 367–376. doi:10.100710551-008-9775-3

Thompson, J. D. (2003). *Organizations in action: Social science bases of administrative theory*. Transaction Publishers.

Thompson, J. L. (2002). The world of the social entrepreneur. *International Journal of Public Sector Management, 15*(5), 412–431. doi:10.1108/09513550210435746

Tian, Y., & Smith, W. K. (2014). Entrepreneurial Leadership of Social Enterprises: Challenges and Skills for Embracing Paradoxes. *Journal of Leadership Studies, 8*(3), 42–45. doi:10.1002/jls.21339

Tlaiss, H. A. (2015). How Islamic business ethics impact women entrepreneurs: Insights from four Arab Middle Eastern countries. *Journal of Business Ethics, 129*(4), 859–877. doi:10.100710551-014-2138-3

Tlaiss, H. A., & McAdam, M. (2021). Unexpected lives: The intersection of Islam and Arab women's entrepreneurship. *Journal of Business Ethics, 171*(2), 253–272. doi:10.100710551-020-04437-0

Tracey, P., & Phillips, N. (2007). The distinctive challenge of educating social entrepreneurs: A postscript and rejoinder to the special issue on entrepreneurship education. *Academy of Management Learning & Education, 6*(2), 264–271. doi:10.5465/amle.2007.25223465

Tracey, P., Phillips, N., & Jarvis, O. (2011). Bridging institutional entrepreneurship and the creation of new organizational forms: A multilevel model. *Organization Science*, *22*(1), 60–80. doi:10.1287/orsc.1090.0522

Tsui, A. S., Nifadkar, S. S., & Ou, A. Y. (2007). Cross-national, cross-cultural organizational behaviour research: Advances, gaps, and recommendations. *Journal of Management*, *33*(3), 26–478. doi:10.1177/0149206307300818

Vakkuri, J., Johanson, J. E., Feng, N. C., & Giordano, F. (2021). Governance and accountability in hybrid organizations–past, present and future. *Journal of Public Budgeting, Accounting & Financial Management*, *33*(3), 245–260. doi:10.1108/JPBAFM-02-2021-0033

Verhoef, P. C., Broekhuizen, T., Bart, Y., Bhattacharya, A., Dong, J. Q., Fabian, N., & Haenlein, M. (2021). Digital transformation: A multidisciplinary reflection and research agenda. *Journal of Business Research*, *122*, 889–901. doi:10.1016/j.jbusres.2019.09.022

Weber, M. (1947). *The theory of social and economic organization*. Oxford University Press.

Whittington, R. (2001). *What is a strategy—And does it matter?* Routledge.

Whittington, R., Pettigrew, A., Peck, S., Fenton, E., & Conyon, M. (1999). M. "Change and complementarities in the new competitive landscape: A European panel study, 1992–1996.". *Organization Science*, *10*(5), 583–600. doi:10.1287/orsc.10.5.583

Wolf, J., & Egelhoff, W. G. (2002). A reexamination and extension of the international strategy-structure theory. *Strategic Management Journal*, *23*(2), 181–189. doi:10.1002mj.210

Wolf, M., & Mair, J. (2019). Purpose, commitment and coordination around small wins: A proactive approach to governance in integrated hybrid organizations. *Voluntas*, *30*(3), 535–548. doi:10.100711266-019-00116-5

Zander, A. (1993). *Making boards effective: The dynamics of nonprofit governing boards*. Jossey-Bass.

Żur, A. (2021). Entrepreneurial identity and social-business tensions–the experience of social entrepreneurs. *Journal of Social Entrepreneurship*, *12*(3), 438–461. doi:10.1080/19420676.2020.1740297

Section 2
Case Studies

Chapter 6
Policy Implications From Selected Countries for a Sustainable Future of the Society Through Green Entrepreneurship and Economic Development

Ajay Kumar Singh
https://orcid.org/0000-0003-0429-0925
Department of Economics, DIT University, Dehradun, India

Bhim Jyoti
College of Forestry, Veer Chandra Singh Garhwali, India

Vikash Kumar Mishra
Department of Economics, DIT University, Dehradun, India

ABSTRACT

Green entrepreneurship (GE) seems optimistic to increase sustainable future of the society. Though, it is difficult to measure GE due to its multiple interaction with green activities and practices in the production sectors. This chapter, therefore, creates a green entrepreneurship index (GEI) as an integration of 43 variables which help to increase GE. Composite Z-score method is applied to develop GEI for selected 34 countries during 2000 - 2019. Accordingly, it describes the relative progress of these countries in GE in different time periods. It also observes a causal

DOI: 10.4018/978-1-6684-7140-1.ch006

relationship between GE and ED using a Cobb-Douglas production approach. This chapter provides several policy proposals to increase ED, GE, green growth, and green GDP. It also claimed that GE will be favorable to increase green development and sustainable future of society in global countries.

1. INTRODUCTION

The prime objective of global countries is to achieve high economic growth to meet the social-economic needs of people (Singh et al., 2019a; Singh et al., 2020b). While, high economic development (ED) is main cause to increase environmental degradation. Primarily environment meets the requirements of raw materials of the production sectors and it plays a significant role to increase social-economic development. Sustainable future of society, therefore, may be in alarming position due to overutilization of environmental resources in the production sector (Singh et al., 2021). Also, most countries wish to be competitive in the global market. Thus, these countries are implementing their policies in diversified areas such as science & technological development (S&TD), intellectual property rights (IPRs), entrepreneurship ecosystem (EE), startup ecosystem, digitalization, ICTs infrastructure and foreign trade to achieve high economic growth (Jyoti & Singh, 2023). For instance, in the last two decades, India has been implemented various policies such as 'Make in India', 'Startup India', and 'Digital India' to increase EE, startup ecosystem, digitalization, financial inclusion, S&TD, technology transfer and commercialization (Singh et al., 2019b; Jyoti & Singh, 2020; Singh & Kumar, 2022a). The Chinese government also taken significant steps to increase entrepreneurial intention of students to be entrepreneurs in higher educational institutions (HEIs) (Guo et al., 2020; Gao & Qin, 2022). Nowadays, the entrepreneurship ecosystem (EE) has been emerged as a key focus area for the global countries for economic development (ED) in multiple ways (Singh & Ashraf, 2020; Sharma et al., 2023). Most emerging countries are also increasing their attention to make people entrepreneurs and job creators instead of job seekers. Entrepreneurs make significant changes through producing goods and services in the market. Entrepreneurs also take crucial initiatives to use labour, capital, skills, technology and raw materials to create innovative products for the consumers, and create jobs, reduce monopoly in the markets and enhance entrepreneurship. Entrepreneurship is a system of economic agents who take positive initiatives to start new business to meet the needs of consumers in the market (Dhahri & Omri, 2018; Singh et al., 2023d). Entrepreneurship is also a process in which entrepreneurial skills of people absorb labour, finance, capital, technology, raw materials and natural resources to produce innovative goods to satisfy the need of people (Zahedi & Otterpohl, 2015) EE, therefore, nurtures an appropriate business platform and it increases inspiration of the entrepreneurs to start new businesses or start-ups (Iversen et al., 2008; Singh & Jyoti, 2021; Gao & Qin, 2022; Sharma et al., 2023). Thus, EE helps to increases the intention of economic agents to be self-employed (Singh & Kumar, 2022b), creates jobs and innovation, and makes social-economic change (Omoruyi et al., 2017; Sharma et al., 2023). EE also creates a conducive ecosystem for industrial development (ID) that is a prime goal of global countries (Singh & Kumar, 2022b). Most studies have been highlighted a positive impact of EE on ED and ID (Baumol, 1990; Acs et al., 2008). ID is essential to increase jobs (Chen et al., 2023), while, it produces several negative impacts on environment (Vasilescu et al., 2023). ID is also caused to increase air population, water pollution, global warming and climate change (Kumar et al., 2017; Sharma & Singh, 2017; Neumann, 2022; Chen et al., 2023; Kumar & Singh, 2023; Mondal, 2023; Singh et al., 2023f). Thus, process of ID creates numerous impediments for sustainable development (SD) (Singh & Kumar, 2022c; Chen et al., 2023).

Environmental development and its components are diminishing due to industrial development (ID) (Singh & Kumar, 2022c; Mondal, 2023; Singh et al., 2023a). The global countries, therefore, should renew their developmental policies to give more protection of ecosystem services and natural resources to make a sustainable future of society (Zahedi & Otterpohl, 2015; Singh et al., 2020b). Sustainable future of society is positively associated with all components of sustainable development (SD). Whereas, SD meet the social, economic and environmental objectives of people (Hall et al., 2010; Singh et al., 2021). Above-mentioned targets can be achieved through increasing green entrepreneurial activities in the production activities (Saari & Joensuu-Salo, 2019; Singh et al., 2022a; Chen et al., 2023). Green entrepreneurship (GE) creates high possibilities for SD (Alwakid, et al., 2021; Chandel, 2022; Vasilescu et al., 2023; Chen et al., 2023; Mondal, 2023). GE is potential to solve environmental issues through adopting environmental and green practices in the production sectors (Li et al., 2023). GE is a green business or venture that work for betterment of environment (Navarathinam & Amutha, 2022), and contribute towards sustainable future of the society. Sustainable future helps to maintain the bridge among all components of SD and make humanity more productive. SD also brings several alternatives to minimize the negative consequences of social and economic development and human driven activities on environmental and ecosystem services (Li et al., 2023). The conception of SD suggests that renewable resources should be used in the production activities at large scale (Hall et al., 2010). Accordingly, a group of scholars, researchers and development organizations have proposed the global countries should adopt GE in production activities for ensuring a sustainable future of society (Navarathinam & Amutha, 2022; Santika et al., 2022).

Most researchers believe that green entrepreneurship (GE) will be helpful to increase the sustainability of all inputs in different sectors (Domańska et al., 2018; Santika et al., 2022; Singh et al., 2023d). GE also create green markets, and increases green growth and improvement in environmental resources (Gupta & Dharwal, 2022). Thus, GE is beneficial to create a new paradigm for social-economic development and environmental sustainability (ES) (Mia et al., 2022). Subsequently, GE will be highly helpful for global economies to attain the SDGs by 2030s (Söderholm, 2020). Several studies investigated the implications of GE on developmental related indicators across countries (Karimi & Chashmi, 2019; Alwakid, et al., 2021; Singh et al., 2022a; Neumann, 2022; Chandel, 2022; Gupta & Dharwal, 2022; Mondal, 2023; Singh et al., 2023e). Singh et al. (2023d), for instance, investigated the interconnection of GE with economic and social development, environmental sustainability (ES), and SD. Previous evidence explained that green entrepreneurship (GE) and green entrepreneurial opportunities help to improve economic, social and environmental development (Neumann, 2022; Vasilescu et al., 2023; Mondal, 2023). Thus, GE create a conducive stage for sustainable future of society. Existing researchers also developed the theoretical foundation to perceive the implication of GE on economic development (ED) and other activities (Alwakid, et al., 2021). Though, it is difficult to determine the progress of GE due to its multiple interconnections with various variables in the production sectors. GE is a fruit of all initiatives which helps for a country to be green economy (Ahmad et al., 2015) that has a minimal adverse impact on natural resources and ecosystem services (Farinelli et al., 2011). Green economy, therefore, prepares a foundation for the sustainable future of people. It is advisable that green entrepreneurial activities at micro level are helpful to increase GE (Vasilescu et al., 2023). Several studies described the role of GE in firm's growth and sustainability using firm level information (Alwakid, et al., 2021; Skordoulis et al., 2022; Neumann, 2022). Also, previous studies investigated that factor affecting GE in manufacturing firms (Vasilescu et al., 2023). While, existing researchers could not suggest the uniform indicators of GE to examine its overall progress across countries. Furthermore, earlier studies have an insignificant focus on how GE and ED can be integrated to ensure a sustainable future of the society? Hence, this chapter makes a remarkable contribution in the existing literature and seeks the answers for following research questions:

- How can existing researchers realize the relative progress of GE across countries?
- What is the causal association of GE with ED?
- How changes in social-economic development produce a negative impact on GE?

- Why is it essential for global countries to adopt green entrepreneurial practices in the production activities?
- How can GE and ED create a sustainable future of the society?

The present chapter achieved following objectives:

- To develop green entrepreneurship index (*GEI*) for selected 34 countries.
- To described the relative performance of GE in selected countries.
- To observe the causal relationship between GE and ED.
- To provide the possibilities of a sustainable future of the society through GE and ED.

2. REVIEW OF LITERATURE

Past economic studies have been observed a positive and significant impact of the entrepreneurship ecosystem (EE) on economic development (ED) (Iversen et al., 2008; Acs et al., 2008; Adusei, 2016). Most studies used diversified indicators such as business density rate, startup rate, number of firms, employed rate and employment rate to examine the empirical association of EE with ED. Previous studies reported a uniform and positive relationship between EE and ED (Audretsch et al., 2015). Earlier studies also used entrepreneurship ecosystem index, entrepreneurship ecosystem development index, global innovation index, etc. as a representative variable for EE to explore its association with ED (Sharma et al., 2023; Singh et al., 2023c). EE is most essential to meet the requirements of ED and growth (Audretsch et al., 2015; Singh et al., 2023c). Further, per capita income, foreign direct investment, foreign trade, technology transfer, entrepreneurial skills, entrepreneurial intention, entrepreneurial education, population growth, science and technology, knowledge transfer, innovation, intellectual property rights, exchange rate, exports of goods and services, savings and investment, industrial development, financial development, infrastructural development, money supply, price stability, and government support and policies have a significant impact on EE (Dhahri & Omri, 2028; Singh, 2020; Singh & Kumar, 2022b; Singh & Kumar, 2022a). Although, high income and low-income group countries are not getting similar benefits from EE due to diversity in technological upgradation, entrepreneurial skills and attitudes of people, technology transfer, technology commercialization and digitalization (Singh et al., 2023c; Singh & Jyoti, 2023a,c). Also, most developing countries have ineffective market mechanisms, high unemployment, poor R&D ecosystem, low R&D expenditure, unproductive infrastructure in research institutions and low entrepreneurial skills (Singh et al., 2019b; Singh et al., 2020a). Also, higher educational institutions

(HEIs) could not create a conducive start-ups ecosystem for nurturing an effective EE in most low-income group countries. HEIs are also unable to create ample entrepreneurial skills among the students and entrepreneurs in most developing countries. For instance, the success rate of startups is very low in India due to low entrepreneurial and technical skills, and low financial accessibility of startups or business creators (Jyoti & Singh, 2020; Singh & Jyoti, 2021).

Past literature also emphasized that economic development (ED) is noteworthy to increase entrepreneurship ecosystem (EE) (Acs et al., 2008; Galindo & Méndez, 2013; Doran et al., 2018; Sharma et al., 2023). Hence, ED depend on EE, and EE depend on ED, thus, both have a positive causality (Singh & Kumar, 2022b). EE is also supportive to create business opportunities, thus, it also enhances industrial development (ID). While, extensive ID contribute GHGs and CO_2 emissions in the atmosphere (Singh et al., 2019a; Neumann, 2022; Singh et al., 2023a). Extensive quantities of GHGs and CO_2 emissions in the atmosphere are harmful for ecosystem services and biodiversity. Research community also claimed that climatic factors are fluctuating due to rising GHGs emissions in the atmosphere (Sharma & Singh, 2017; Singh & Sharma, 2018). Furthermore, climate change is producing negative impact on all sectors especially for agriculture and its sustainability (Kumar et al., 2016; Singh et al., 2022b; Kumar and Singh, 2023; Singh & Jyoti, 2023b). Hence, ID is extremely detrimental for environmental and human development (Singh et al., 2023a). Environment is also adversely affecting due to rising population growth, urbanization, globalization, foreign trade, infrastructural development and competition across countries (Neumann, 2022; Singh et al., 2023a). Environmental degradation is also increasing due to modernization of the agricultural sector (Kumar et al., 2016; Singh et al., 2023f). Low technology transfer and high inflexibility in IPRs regime are also responsible for environmental degradation in most developing countries (Singh & Kumar, 2022a). Moreover, environmental, green and appropriate technologies are not being transfer from developed countries to developing countries. Accordingly, most countries could not adopt green entrepreneurial practices in the production sectors.

The most countries especially from low and lower-income groups, therefore, should apply advanced and green technologies in the production sector to increase environmental sustainability (ES) and GE (Chen et al., 2023). The production sectors should also use those technologies which reduce GHGs and CO_2 emissions. Appropriate technology may be a best option to increase ES (Mia et al., 2022; Jyoti et al., 2023). Green entrepreneurial intention of entrepreneurs also works as effective driver to increase GE (Santika et al., 2022; Navarathinam & Amutha, 2022; Mia et al., 2022). Appropriate technologies are also highly supportive to create GE in the developing countries. At present, appropriate technology is working as a boon to meet all requirements of the sustainable future of the society (Singh et al., 2023b).

Application of appropriate technologies are also seemed as crucial supporters to increase SD (Singh et al., 2022a,b; Jyoti et al., 2023). The researchers and scientists are suggesting that global countries should work for green economy and GE to increase sustainable future of the humanity (Singh et al., 2023d,e). Therefore, green entrepreneurship (GE) is a new study area in the academic research and it attracts the attention of most countries to pursue green activities in the production sectors. Practices of green activities in business and industrial sectors help to create GE (Mia et al., 2022; Navarathinam & Amutha, 2022). GE is the practice of green activities in the production sector which reduce GHGs (Haldar, 2019; Santika et al., 2022; Jyoti et al., 2023). GE also creates a scientific process to increase minimum utilization of natural resources in the production activities (Singh et al., 2023d). The global countries, therefore, should pay widespread attention to abate GHGs emissions using green entrepreneurial practices in all sectors and create green entrepreneurship (GE) (Singh et al., 2023d). GE produce positive return in terms of green GDP, green growth, green jobs and green markets (Vasilescu et al., 2023). GE would help to increase SD and sustainable future of the society (Karimi & Chashmi, 2019; Navarathinam & Amutha, 2022). Accordingly, the existing researchers have been provided a theoretical and empirical framework to observe implications of GE on social-economic development and SD (Gupta & Dharwal, 2022; Singh et al., 2023g). Navarathinam and Amutha (2022), for instance, provided the conceptual framework to determine the opportunities of SD through GE. Past studies also estimated the implications of GE on SD across countries using different factors (Moya-Clemente et al., 2020; Mia et al., 2022; Mondal, 2023). Haldar (2019), for instance, assessed the role of GE in energy sector in Gujarat. Alwakid et al. (2020) considered share of environmentally friendly small medium enterprises (SMEs) as proxy variable for GE to assess its association with cultural characteristics in Saudi Arabia. Environmental actions and environmental consciousness are also key players of GE (Alwakid et al., 2020). Alwakid et al. (2021) considered waste management, recycling rate, agriculture trend index and assistance to conserve biodiversity as proxy variables for GE in regression analysis. Moreover, any practice in the production sector that reduces GHGs emissions can be considered as green entrepreneurial activity (Nuringsih et al., 2020; Tawiah et al., 2021).

CO_2 emissions, sulphur dioxide and nitrogen oxide can be used to explain the green performance of industries. Zeng and Ren (2022), for instance, considered sulphur dioxide and nitrogen oxide emissions from industries to perceive their performance in GE. Few scholars and scientists investigated the impact of different variables related to economic, social and development on GE (Singh et al., 2022a). Neumann (2022) investigated that impact of green entrepreneurial activity on all pillars of SD in 53 countries. Zeng and Ren (2022) examined the association of GE with environmental regulation using the primary data of 293 enterprises in China. It noticed that GE helps to nurture technological innovation and increase environmental regulation. Gupta and Dharwal (2022) highlighted the role of green markets to increase ES. Singh et al. (2022a) developed green entrepreneurship ecosystem index to measure the impact of GE on SD. Skordoulis et al. (2022) reported that GE produce positive impact on product innovation and green process. Chen et al. (2023) verified that interconnection between background of entrepreneurs, green entrepreneurial practices and corporate financial performance in 173 Chinese companies. Vasilescu et al. (2023) observed significant implications of company's age, financial performance and country's development on GE in 36 European countries. Mondal (2023) detected the association of GE with credit policy, financial development, SDGs and trade openness in 114 countries. Li et al. (2023) identified the impact of green entrepreneurial intention on green entrepreneurial action in Pakistan.

3. METHODOLOGY

3.1. Study Area and Source of Data

The main purpose of this chapter is to create GEI across countries. The GEI is the integration of 43 variables that are related to environmental sustainability (ES), entrepreneurship ecosystem (EE) and green entrepreneurship (GE). Thus, we could include only those countries which have the data for related variables during 2000 – 2019. Accordingly, 34 countries are found reliable to be included in this chapter. The name of these countries is listed here: Norway, Canada, Finland, Estonia, Netherlands, Denmark, Sweden, USA, Switzerland, Portugal, Lithuania, Luxembourg, Austria, Australia, Spain, Germany, Belgium, Latvia, Tunisia, France, Mexico, Japan, United Kingdom, Argentina, China, Poland, Brazil, Greece, India, Romania, Russia, Hungary, Croatia and South Africa.

The statistics of variables related to the entrepreneurship ecosystem is derived from the website of Global Entrepreneurship Monitor (GEM). Statistics of remaining variables are taken from world development indicators (World Bank). Few data are taken from the website of Organisation for Economic Co-operation and Development (OECD). Interpolation and extrapolation techniques are also applied to examine the middle values for those variables which have missing terms.

3.2. Statistical and Empirical Analysis of Data

3.2.1. Consistency of Indicators Included for Estimation of GEI

Existing review of literature infer that green entrepreneurship (GE) is reflected by multiple initiatives in the area of green activities. Hence, GE cannot be measured by a single variable (Singh et al., 2022a). Previous literature signifies that GE helps to increase green economy (Ahmad et al., 2015). While, the prime aim of the green economy is to increase ES and reduce GHGs and CO_2 emissions (Santika et al., 2022; Singh et al., 2023d). The main focus of ES is to produce green products (Gupta & Dharwal, 2022), and increase green growth and GDP (Onsay, 2021). Therefore, extensive green entrepreneurial practices and initiatives in production sectors especially in industrial and agricultural sectors are favourable to increase GE (Singh et al., 2022a). Use of green technologies, appropriate technologies, environmental technologies, green innovation in social-economic activities, and creation of green products are highly supportive to create GE (Farinelli et al., 2011; Ebrahimi & Mirbargkar, 2017; Alwakid et al., 2021; Söderholm, 2020; Vasilescu et al., 2023). Thus, GE is essential to promote SD and its drivers (Singh et al., 2022a). Singh et al. (2023e) also recognized that GE has a positive impact on ED. While, ED does not promote GE due to its negative association of ED with ES (Singh et al. 2023a). Hence, in this chapter we include 15 variables related to ES to create GEI. These 15 variables are adopted from the study of Singh et al. (2023e).

Existing researchers also found that the entrepreneurship ecosystem (EE) produces a positive impact on economic development (ED). A group of researchers assessed the cause-and-effect relationship between EE and ED (Singh & Kumar, 2022b). Singh and Jyoti (2023a) also analysed the causal relationship between EE and digitalization. Earlier researchers also included 12 variables of EE suggested by GEM to create GEI (Singh et al., 2022a). In this chapter, we also include these 12 variables that are used by Singh et al. (2023e) to create GEI. Singh and Ashraf (2020), Singh and Jyoti (2023a) also used these 12 variables to create representative index for EE. For said investigation, it assumes that EE helps to increase ED, and ED is caused to increase environment degradation. Accordingly, EE produce a negative impact on ES. In this chapter, we also assume that less CO_2 and GHGs emitter countries are using more green entrepreneurial practices in the production activities (Ahmad et al., 2015; Kumar et al., 2015). Discovery of alternative ways to reduce dependency on natural resources also reflect the green practices and green entrepreneurship (GE) (Singh et al., 2022a). Use of electricity and sources of electricity helpful to nurture appropriate GE (Demirel et al., 2017; Singh et al., 2021). GE is also positively influenced by energy intensity, water saving, energy saving and minimize wastage materials (Vasilescu et al., 2023). Greater values of energy intensity also show the progress of a country towards green GE. Water productivity improve as use of green entrepreneurial practices and green technologies increase. Water productivity, therefore, may have positive reflection on GE. Sources of renewable energy for sun and air, sources of renewable water and wasted materials also measure the green initiatives (Mrkajic et al., 2017; Singh et al., 2021). Therefore, we identified 16 most reliable variables to create GEI in this chapter. These 16 variables are adopted from the study of Singh et al. (2023e). *Composite Z-score* technique is applied to develop GEI in this chapter (Singh & Jyoti, 2023a).

3.2.2. Reliability of Dependent Variables (*DV*s) and Independent Variables (*IV*s)

This chapter is intended to measure the impact of GE on ED and vice-versa. We, therefore, developed two simultaneous equations to define the functional relationship between ED and GE. In the 1st functional relationship, we assume that ED depends on GE (Singh et al., 2022a). In the 2nd functional relationship, we accept that GE depends on ED. For empirical analysis, per capita gross domestic product and GEI are used as representative indicators for ED and GE, respectively in this chapter. Dhahri and Omri (2018); Galindo-Martín et al. (2020) also used estimated indexes as dependent and independent variables in empirical analysis. Education expenditure (Singh et al., 2023e), unemployment rate (Singh et al., 2023c), labour force participation rate (Singh et al., 2023e), inflation GDP deflator (Ashraf & Singh, 2019; Singh et al., 2023c), wage and salaried workers (Sharma et al., 2023), population growth (Sharma et al., 2023), manufacturing value added per capita (Singh et al., 2023e), foreign direct investment net inflows (Singh et al., 2023c) and vulnerable employment (Jyoti & Singh, 2023) are also effective determinants of ED and GE (Nguyen, 2021; Singh et al., 2023d). Therefore, above-mentioned variables are used as control variables in the both the models. The functional relationship of ED and GE with explanatory variables are applied as:

$$gdppc = f(gei, eepgni, utptlf, lfprtptp, igdpdap, wswtpte, pgap, mvapc, mvapc, vetpte) \quad (1)$$

$$gei = f(gdppc, eepgni, utptlf, lfprtptp, igdpdap, wswtpte, pgap, mvapc, mvapc, vetpte) \quad (2)$$

Here, *gdppc* is GDP per capita that is used a proxy variable for ED; *gei* is green entrepreneurship index that is consider as proxy variable for GE in equation (1) and (2). While, the clarification of remaining variables is given in Table: 1.

Table 1. Brief summary of DVs and IVs

Description	Code	Unit
Green entrepreneurship index	*gei*	Number
GDP per capita (constant 2015 US$)	*gdppc*	US$
Education expenditure (% of GNI)	*eepgni*	%
Unemployment rate total (% of total labour force)	*utptlf*	%
Labour force participation rate total (% of total population ages 15-64)	*lfprtptp*	%
Inflation GDP deflator (annual %)	*igdpdap*	%
Wage and salaried workers total (% of total employment)	*wswtpte*	%
Population growth (annual %)	*pgap*	%
Manufacturing value added per capita (constant 2015 US$)	*mvapc*	US$
Foreign direct investment net inflows (% of GDP)	*fdinipgdp*	%
Vulnerable employment total (% of total employment)	*vetpte*	%

3.2.3. Empirical Analysis

The Cobb-Douglas production model produces rational coefficient of explanatory variables with *DV*s (Singh et al., 2023d). Also, the estimated coefficients of associated *IV*s measure their elasticities with *DV*s. Accordingly, elasticities of respective *IV*s explain the percentage variation in *DV*s due to 1 unit or 1% change in values of *IV*s. Previous studies also employed similar model to investigate the empirical relationship between GEI and ED (Singh et al., 2022a; Singh et al., 2023d); digitalization and ED (Jyoti & Singh, 2023; Singh & Jyoti, 2023c); environmental degradation and ED (Singh et al., 2023a); GE and SD (Singh et al., 2022a); ES and ED (Singh et al., 2019a); EE with ED (Ashraf & Singh, 2019; Singh et al., 2022a); EE and financial inclusion (Sharma et al., 2023); and EE and digitalization (Singh & Jyoti, 2023a) across countries. Therefore, Cobb-Douglas production functions models are used in following forms to explore the empirical association between GE and ED:

$$ln(gdppc)_{ct} = \beta_0 + \beta_1 ln(gei)_{ct} + \beta_2 ln(eepgni)_{ct} + \beta_3 ln(utptlf)_{ct} + \beta_4 ln(lfprtptp)_{ct} + \beta_5 ln(igdpdap)_{ct} + \beta_6 ln(wswtpte)_{ct} + \beta_7 ln(pgap)_{ct} + \beta_8 ln(mvapc)_{ct} + \beta_9 ln(mvapc)_{ct} + \beta_{10} ln(vetpte)_{ct} + \epsilon_{ct} \quad (3)$$

$$ln(gei)_{ct} = \xi_0 + \xi_1 ln(gdppc)_{ct} + \xi_2 ln(eepgni)_{ct} + \xi_3 ln(utptlf)_{ct} + \xi_4 ln(lfprtptp)_{ct} + \xi_5 ln(igdpdap)_{ct} + \xi_6 ln(wswtpte)_{ct} + \xi_7 ln(pgap)_{ct} + \xi_8 ln(mvapc)_{ct} + \xi_9 ln(mvapc)_{ct} + \xi_{10} ln(vetpte)_{ct} + \lambda_{ct} \quad (4)$$

Here, *ln* is the natural logarithm of associated variables; β_0 and ξ_0 are the constant coefficients; $\beta_1, ..., \beta_{10}$ are elasticities of explanatory variables with respect to *gdppc*; $\xi_1, ... \xi_{10}$ are also the elasticities of explanatory variables with respect to *gei*; ϵ_{ct} and λ_{ct} are error terms; *t* is time; and *c* is specific country in equation (3) and (4).

3.2.4. Existence of Casualty of GE and ED with Explanatory Variables

The causality deals the cause-and-effect relationship between two different variables in a time series. There may be a positive and negative causal association between two variables. One specific variable may be caused for existence of another phenomenon that may be caused for existence of first phenomenon. In this study, therefore, we applied the Granger causality co-integration test to observe the causal association of GE and with ED and explanatory variables (Singh et al., 2023d). For said investigation, following regression equation is used:

$$(gei)_{ct} = \alpha_0 + \alpha_1 (gei)_{c,t-1} + \beta_1 (gdppc)_{c,t-1} + ¥_{ct} \quad (5)$$

Here, α_0 is constant coefficient; α_1 is coefficient of 1st lag of *gei*; β_1 is the coefficient of 1st lag of *gdppc*; *t* is time period; *c* is cross-sectional country; $¥_{ct}$ is error-term in equation (5). The statistically significant values of α_1 and β_1 infer the causation between GE and ED. The causation of GE and ED with other control variables are also estimated as using the similar equation.

3.2.5. Finalization of Appropriate Models and Application of Statistical Software

This chapter include the panel data of specific dependent variables (*DV*s) and independent variables (*IV*s) for 34 countries during 2000–2019. These countries have a high diversity in *DV*s and *IV*s, also social-economic development related variables of a country have a dependency on other countries. It is, therefore, obvious that panel data of this chapter have auto-correlation, serial correlation and heteroskedasticity. Since, panels corrected standard errors (PCEs) estimation technique is helpful to avoid the existence of auto-correlation, serial correlation and heteroskedasticity in panel data analysis (Singh & Ashraf, 2020; Singh and Jyoti, 2023a). Thus, the coefficients of *IV*s with *DV*s are estimated using the mentioned technique in this chapter. SPSS and STATA software are used to analysis the data.

4. RESULTS AND DISCUSSION

4.1. Relative Performance of Across Countries in Green Entrepreneurship

The relative progress of green entrepreneurship (GE) across countries in different time periods (i.e., 2000 – 2004, 2005 – 2009, 2010 – 2014 and 2015 – 2019) is presented in Figure: 1. The estimated values of *GEI* is used to explain the progress of 34 countries in GE. While, GEI is the composition of different variables that are related to entrepreneurship ecosystem (EE), environmental sustainability (ES), and green entrepreneurship (GE). Norway, Canada, Finland and Estonia have a best performance in GE as per mean values of *GEI* during said time periods. Further, the GEI's values varies during 2000 – 2004, 2005 – 2009, 2010 – 2014 and 2015 – 2019 within a specific country and across countries. Accordingly, the positions of most countries have changed in different time periods (Table: 2). For instance, the GEI's values of for Norway are reported 0.580, 0.630, 0.590 and 0.611 during 2000 – 2004, 2005 – 2009, 2010 – 2014 and 2015 – 2019, respectively. Similarly, GEI's values varies for most countries in different time periods.

The progress of GE for few countries like Netherland, Denmark and Sweden are improved during 2015 – 2019. While, the evolution of GE in USA is declined after 2010. It could be happened due to that other countries are also giving more attention to increase green entrepreneurial activities in the industrial sector. Switzerland, Portugal, Lithuania and Luxembourg could also improve their position in GE during 2015 – 2019. The performance of Austria, Australia, Spain, Germany, Belgium, Latvia, Tunisia, France, Mexico, Japan and United Kingdom in GE are reported sustainable in different time periods. While, Argentina, China, Poland, Brazil, Greece, India, Romania, Russia, Hungry, Croatia and South Africa have relative low position in GE. Hence, these countries should focus to increase their positions in GE through adopting green entrepreneurial practices in the production sector.

Figure 1. Relative progress of GE across countries in different time periods
Source: *Author's estimation.*

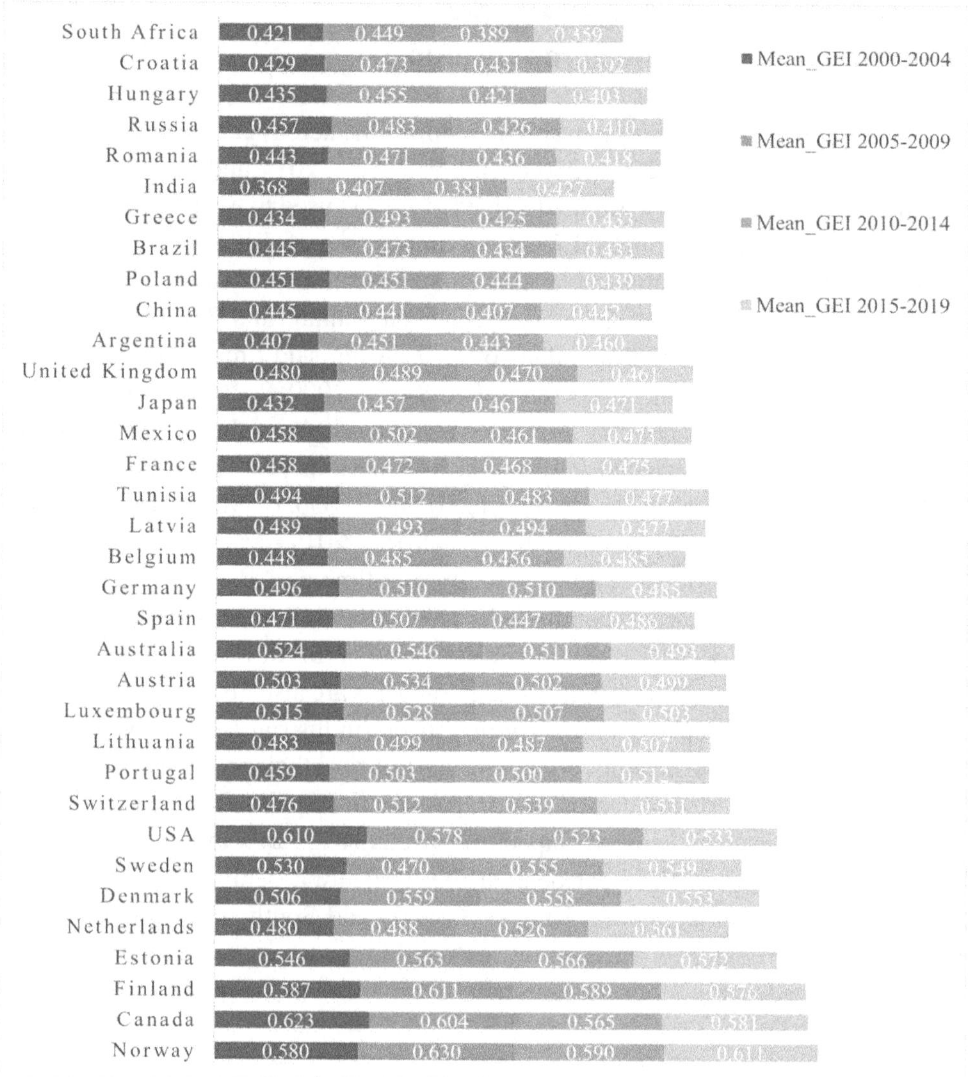

Table 2. Ranking of countries as per the GEI's values

Country	GEI_2000-2004		GEI_2005-2009		GEI_2010-2014		GEI_2015-2019	
	Value	Rank	Value	Rank	Value	Rank	Value	Rank
Norway	0.580	4	0.630	1	0.590	1	0.611	1
Canada	0.623	1	0.604	3	0.565	4	0.581	2
Finland	0.587	3	0.611	2	0.589	2	0.576	3
Estonia	0.546	5	0.563	5	0.566	3	0.572	4
Netherlands	0.480	15	0.488	20	0.526	8	0.561	5
Denmark	0.506	9	0.559	6	0.558	5	0.553	6
Sweden	0.530	6	0.470	27	0.555	6	0.549	7
USA	0.610	2	0.578	4	0.523	9	0.533	8
Switzerland	0.476	17	0.512	10	0.539	7	0.531	9
Portugal	0.459	19	0.503	14	0.500	14	0.512	10
Lithuania	0.483	14	0.499	16	0.487	16	0.507	11
Luxembourg	0.515	8	0.528	9	0.507	12	0.503	12
Austria	0.503	10	0.534	8	0.502	13	0.499	13
Australia	0.524	7	0.546	7	0.511	10	0.493	14
Spain	0.471	18	0.507	13	0.447	23	0.486	15
Germany	0.496	11	0.510	12	0.510	11	0.485	16
Belgium	0.448	24	0.485	21	0.456	22	0.485	17
Latvia	0.489	13	0.493	18	0.494	15	0.477	18
Tunisia	0.494	12	0.512	11	0.483	17	0.477	19
France	0.458	20	0.472	25	0.468	19	0.475	20
Mexico	0.458	21	0.502	15	0.461	21	0.473	21
Japan	0.432	30	0.457	28	0.461	20	0.471	22
United Kingdom	0.480	16	0.489	19	0.470	18	0.461	23
Argentina	0.407	33	0.451	31	0.443	25	0.460	24
China	0.445	25	0.441	33	0.407	32	0.442	25
Poland	0.451	23	0.451	30	0.444	24	0.439	26
Brazil	0.445	26	0.473	23	0.434	27	0.433	27
Greece	0.434	29	0.493	17	0.425	30	0.433	28
India	0.368	34	0.407	34	0.381	34	0.427	29
Romania	0.443	27	0.471	26	0.436	26	0.418	30
Russia	0.457	22	0.483	22	0.426	29	0.410	31
Hungary	0.435	28	0.455	29	0.421	31	0.403	32
Croatia	0.429	31	0.473	24	0.431	28	0.392	33
South Africa	0.421	32	0.449	32	0.389	33	0.359	34

Source: Author's estimation.

4.2. Correlation Coefficients of GEI and ED With Explanatory Variables

The correlation coefficients of *GEI* and *gdppc* with explanatory variables are provided in Table: 3. The estimates indicate that education expenditure as a % of gross national income (*eepgni*), fixed telephone subscriptions per 100 people (*ftsphp*), GDP per person employed (*gdpppe*), labour force participation rate (*lfprtptp*), exports of goods and services as a % of GDP (*egspgdp*), foreign direct investment net inflows as a % of GDP (*fdinipgdp*), wage and salaried workers (*wswtpte*), manufacturing value added per capita (*mvapc*), compulsory education duration (*ced*), employment to population ratio (*epr*), individuals using the internet as a % of population (*iui*), mobile cellular subscriptions per 100 people (*mcs*), and women business and the law index score (*wblis*) are positively correlated with GE and ED.

Table 3. Pearson correlation coefficients of GEI with explanatory variables

Variables	*GEI*	*eepgni*	*ftsphp*	*utptlf*	*gdpppe*	*lfprtptp*	*igdpdap*	*egspgdp*	*fdinipgdp*
GEI	1	0.452[a]	0.343[a]	-0.300[a]	0.450[a]	0.512[a]	-0.201[a]	0.188[a]	0.083[b]
eepgni	0.452[a]	1	0.092[a]	0.067[b]	0.305[a]	0.101[a]	-0.125[a]	0.188[a]	0.058
ftsphp	0.343[a]	0.092[a]	1	-0.243[a]	0.580[a]	0.514[a]	-0.331[a]	0.162[a]	0.148[a]
utptlf	-0.300[a]	0.067[b]	-0.243[a]	1	-0.258[a]	-0.442[a]	0.036	-0.136[a]	-0.168[a]
gdpppe	0.450[a]	0.305[a]	0.580[a]	-0.258[a]	1	0.355[a]	-0.300[a]	0.662[a]	0.411[a]
lfprtptp	0.512[a]	0.101[a]	0.514[a]	-0.442[a]	0.355[a]	1	-0.225[a]	0.040	0.025
igdpdap	-0.201[a]	-0.125[a]	-0.331[a]	0.036	-0.300[a]	-0.225[a]	1	-0.173[a]	-0.065[b]
egspgdp	0.188[a]	0.188[a]	0.162[a]	-0.136[a]	0.662[a]	0.040	-0.173[a]	1	0.577[a]
fdinipgdp	0.083[b]	0.058	0.148[a]	-0.168[a]	0.411[a]	0.025	-0.065[b]	0.577[a]	1
gdppc	0.576[a]	0.354[a]	0.603[a]	-0.415[a]	0.902[a]	0.559[a]	-0.312[a]	0.472[a]	0.296[a]
vetpte	-0.470[a]	-0.486[a]	-0.511[a]	-0.025	-0.559[a]	-0.424[a]	0.186[a]	-0.319[a]	-0.162[a]
wswtpte	0.479[a]	0.473[a]	0.494[a]	-0.020	0.565[a]	0.444[a]	-0.168[a]	0.330[a]	0.166[a]
mvapc	0.489[a]	0.245[a]	0.619[a]	-0.415[a]	0.638[a]	0.616[a]	-0.337[a]	0.237[a]	0.154[a]
ced	0.082[b]	0.130[a]	0.229[a]	-0.211[a]	0.317[a]	0.155[a]	0.033	0.273[a]	0.311[a]
epr	0.407[a]	-0.008	0.263[a]	-0.688[a]	0.187[a]	0.792[a]	-0.027	-0.048	0.037
iui	0.474[a]	0.375[a]	0.364[a]	-0.270[a]	0.587[a]	0.615[a]	-0.328[a]	0.325[a]	0.156[a]
mcs	0.166[a]	0.241[a]	0.065[b]	-0.066[b]	0.376[a]	0.262[a]	-0.129[a]	0.318[a]	0.114[a]
wbli	0.402[a]	0.319[a]	0.389[a]	-0.098[a]	0.538[a]	0.553[a]	-0.338[a]	0.318[a]	0.139[a]

Table 3. Continued

Variables	*gdppc*	*vetpte*	*wswtpte*	*mvapc*	*ced*	*epr*	*iui*	*mcs*	*wbli*
GEI	0.576[a]	-0.470[a]	0.479[a]	0.489[a]	0.082*	0.407[a]	0.474[a]	0.166[a]	0.402[a]
eepgni	0.354[a]	-0.486[a]	0.473[a]	0.245[a]	0.130[a]	-0.008	0.375[a]	0.241[a]	0.319[a]
ftsphp	0.603[a]	-0.511[a]	0.494[a]	0.619[a]	0.229[a]	0.263[a]	0.364[a]	0.065*	0.389[a]
utptlf	-0.415 [a]	-0.025	-0.02	-0.415[a]	-0.211[a]	-0.688[a]	-0.270[a]	-0.066*	-0.098[a]
gdpppe	0.902[a]	-0.559[a]	0.565[a]	0.638[a]	0.317[a]	0.187[a]	0.587[a]	0.376[a]	0.538[a]
lfprtptp	0.559[a]	-0.424[a]	0.444[a]	0.616[a]	0.155[a]	0.792[a]	0.615[a]	0.262[a]	0.553[a]
igdpdap	-0.312[a]	0.186[a]	-0.168[a]	-0.337[a]	0.033	-0.027	-0.328[a]	-0.129[a]	-0.338[a]
egspgdp	0.472[a]	-0.319[a]	0.330[a]	0.237[a]	0.273[a]	-0.048	0.325[a]	0.318[a]	0.318[a]
fdinipgdp	0.296[a]	-0.162[a]	0.166[a]	0.154[a]	0.311[a]	0.037	0.156[a]	0.114[a]	0.139[a]
gdppc	1	-0.501[a]	0.509[a]	0.806[a]	0.249[a]	0.464[a]	0.629[a]	0.289[a]	0.489[a]
vetpte	-0.501[a]	1	-0.994[a]	-0.458[a]	-0.306[a]	-0.102[a]	-0.587[a]	-0.443[a]	-0.519[a]
wswtpte	0.509[a]	-0.994[a]	1	0.455[a]	0.302[a]	0.135[a]	0.597[a]	0.447[a]	0.521[a]
mvapc	0.806[a]	-0.458[a]	0.455[a]	1	0.228[a]	0.474[a]	0.557[a]	0.256[a]	0.370[a]
ced	0.249[a]	-0.306[a]	0.302[a]	0.228[a]	1	0.143[a]	0.326[a]	0.246	0.269[a]
epr	0.464[a]	-0.102[a]	0.135[a]	0.474[a]	0.143[a]	1	0.330[a]	0.023	0.206[a]
iui	0.629[a]	-0.587[a]	0.597[a]	0.557[a]	0.326[a]	0.330[a]	1	0.726[a]	0.730[a]
mcs	0.289[a]	-0.443[a]	0.447[a]	0.256[a]	0.246[a]	0.023	0.726[a]	1	0.507[a]
wbli	0.489[a]	-0.519[a]	0.521[a]	0.370[a]	0.269[a]	0.206[a]	0.730[a]	0.507[a]	1

Source: Author's calculation. [a] refer that correlation is significant at the 0.01 level; [b] refers that correlation is significant at the 0.05 level.

Hence, these variables are seemed beneficial to increase GE and ED. Further, the estimates claimed that ED and GE are positively correlated with each other. While, unemployment rate, vulnerable employment and inflation GDP deflator are negatively correlated with GE and ED. Fixed telephone subscriptions, individuals using the internet, and mobile cellular subscriptions are most representative variables of digitalization (Jyoti & Singh, 2023; Singh & Jyoti, 2023c). The results suggested that digitalization may be supportive to increase GE and ED. Ashraf and Singh (2019)'s study also reported a positive association between digitalization and entrepreneurship ecosystem (EE). Labour force participation rate, wage and salaried workers and employment to population ratio reflect the level of employment in a country. The results also proposed the extensive employment opportunities play a key role to increase GE and ED. GDP per person employed measures the contribution of per worker in GDP. Thus, GDP per person employed will be imperative to increase GE and ED. Exports of goods and services, and foreign direct investment net inflows also help to increase the trade relationship between two or more than two countries. These variables are also found as significant drivers to increase technology and knowledge transfer, business opportunities, money flow, infrastructural development, and per capita income. Hence, GE and ED are likely to be improved as exports of goods and services, and foreign direct investment net inflows increase. Education is an effective determinant to increase technological skills, knowledge and entrepreneurial skills of people. Henceforth, GE and ED to be improved as education expenditure and compulsory education duration increase. Industrial development (ID) increases as share of manufacturing sector in GDP increases. Our results also showed that manufacturing value added may be effective to increase GE and ED.

4.3. Regression Results

Table 4 provide the statistical summary of the variables. The statistical values of standard deviation (SD) for all variables varies between and within countries. Hence, undertaken 34 countries have a significant diversity in these variables. The statistical values of skewness indicate that education expenditure as a % of GNI, labour force participation rate, wage and salaried workers, and population growth are not in normal form. While, statistical values of Cronbach's α test suggested that all variables have scale reliability. The regression results which demonstrate the impact of explanatory variables on *gei* and *gdppc* is given in Table: 5. The coefficient of *gei* with *gdppc* are appeared positive and vice-versa. The estimate indicates that GE has a positive impact on ED, and ED is also produced a positive impact on GE. Singh et al. (2022a); Singh et al. (2023d,e) also reported a positive association between GE and ED. Knowledge and technical skills of the people increases as education level increases. Subsequently, education is a key determinant to create innovation, S&TD and social development. Education is also effective to increase the ability of people to be engaged in economic and social activities. Also, educated people have better job opportunities and make significant contribution in social-economic development. Moreover, people are also motivated to be involved in green entrepreneurial activities as their education level increases. Thus, education is an essential determinant to create entrepreneurial skills and EE. Educated people have more consciousness towards ES as compared to illiterate people. Hence, education play a positive role to increase GE and ED. The regression coefficients of *eepgni* with *gei* and *pcgdp* are reported positive and statistically significant. Thus, GE and ED increase due to increase in education expenditure. The estimates infer that GE and ED are expected to increase by 0.12% and 0.26% due to 1% increase in education expenditure.

The impact of labour force participation rate, and wage and salaried workers on GE and ED are found positive and statistically significant. GE and ED may increase by 0.26% and 0.65% respectively as labour force participation increases by 1%. GE and ED also increase by 0.01% and 0.07% as wage and salaried workers increases by 1%. Hence, employment opportunities are seemed supportive to increase GE and ED. Population growth helps to create human resources, demand of goods and services, new market and new business opportunities. Hence, population growth may be positive to increase ED. However, population growth may produce negative impact on ED in highly populated countries like India, China, Indonesia and Bangladesh (Singh et al., 2023a). Further, environmental degradation may also increase due to increase in annual population growth (Singh et al., 2019a). Our empirical results also found a positive impact of annual population growth on ED and GE. GE and ED may be increased by 0.01% and 0.06% respectively as annual population growth increases by 1%. Similar relationship between annual population growth and EE is also confirmed by Sharma et al. (2023). Singh et al. (2023e) also reported a positive implication of annual population growth on ED in developed and developing countries.

Table 4. Statistical summary of DVs and IVs

Variables		Mean	Std. Dev.	Min	Max	Obs.	Skewness	Cronbach's α test
gei	Overall	-0.724	0.119	-1.109	-0.431	*N*=680	0.041	0.798
	Between		0.107	-0.930	-0.507	*n*=34		
	Within		0.055	-0.903	-0.550	*T*=20		
gdppc	Overall	9.910	1.008	6.630	11.566	*N*=680	-0.689	0.772
	Between		1.011	7.094	11.492	*n*=34		
	Within		0.155	9.076	10.616	*T*=20		
eepgni	Overall	1.513	0.276	0.582	2.088	*N*=680	-1.101	0.823
	Between		0.268	0.582	2.006	*n*=34		
	Within		0.080	1.200	1.810	*T*=20		
utptlf	Overall	1.978	0.526	0.593	3.505	*N*=680	0.553	0.831
	Between		0.457	1.282	3.296	*n*=34		
	Within		0.271	0.878	2.681	*T*=20		
lfprtptp	Overall	4.257	0.108	3.888	4.433	*N*=680	-1.154	0.796
	Between		0.106	3.923	4.409	*n*=34		
	Within		0.029	4.152	4.386	*T*=20		
igdpdap	Overall	0.864	1.126	-3.912	3.930	*N*=677	-0.591	0.825
	Between		0.779	-0.729	2.823	*n*=34		
	Within		0.825	-2.957	2.644	*T*=20		

continues on following page

Table 4. Continued

Variables		Mean	Std. Dev.	Min	Max	Obs.	Skewness	Cronbach's α test
wswtpte	Overall	4.352	0.294	2.725	4.542	*N*=680	-3.891	0.793
	Between		0.295	2.890	4.533	*n*=34		
	Within		0.044	4.138	4.646	*T*=20		
pgap	Overall	-0.632	1.006	-4.605	1.348	*N*=680	-1.403	0.846
	Between		0.831	-2.907	0.570	*n*=34		
	Within		0.596	-3.632	2.321	*T*=20		
mvapc	Overall	7.896	0.925	4.645	9.734	*N*=680	-0.720	0.773
	Between		0.919	5.194	9.577	*n*=34		
	Within		0.183	6.984	8.607	*T*=20		
fdinipgdp	Overall	1.040	1.193	-4.605	4.461	*N*=680	-0.640	0.840
	Between		0.899	-1.736	3.119	*n*=34		
	Within		0.801	-3.015	3.471	*T*=20		
vetpte	Overall	2.487	0.693	1.358	4.427	*N*=680	0.820	0.786
	Between		0.690	1.458	4.385	*n*=34		
	Within		0.130	1.843	2.953	*T*=20		

Source: Author's estimation.

Manufacturing sector create jobs for skilled and unskilled labours, produce goods and services to meet the need of people, and develop various ICTs tools. This sector also plays a significant role to increase foreign trade and foreign direct investment. It is also supportive to increase industrial development (ID) (Singh & Kumar, 2021). Therefore, manufacturing sector is considered an engine of economic growth (Singh et al., 2019c). The regression coefficients of manufacturing value added per capita with GE and ED are observed positive and statistically significant. Thus, manufacturing sector have a positive impact on GE and ED. GE and ED are likely to be improved by 0.01% and 0.025%, respectively as manufacturing value added per capita increases by 1%. Moreover, foreign direct investment net inflows also have a positive impact on ED and GE. Singh and Kumar (2022a) also noted a significant association between EE and foreign direct investment net inflows.

Inflation is caused to reduce per capita income, investment, saving, real income, consumption, new business opportunities and level of employment (Ashraf & Singh, 2019; Sharma et al., 2023; Singh et al., 2023c). Cost of production in manufacturing sector may also increase due to increase in inflation. Subsequently, inflation is responsible to increase unemployment and vulnerable employment (Singh & Jyoti, 2023c). Henceforth, inflation GDP deflator, unemployment rate and vulnerable employment have a negative impact on GE and ED. Ashraf & Singh (2019) also detected a negative impact of inflation on ED. The negative relationship of EE with inflation GDP deflator is also comparable with the findings of Sharma et al. (2023).

Table 5. Impact of explanatory variables on GE and ED

DVs	*ln(gei)*			*ln(gdppc)*		
Number of obs.	674			674		
R-squared	0.4812			0.9225		
*Wald Chi*²(10)	1729.86*			178213.74*		
Mean *VIF*	4.35			2.5		
IVs	***Reg. Coef.***	***Std. Err.***	***P>lzl***	***Reg. Coef.***	***Std. Err.***	***P>lzl***
ln(gdppc)	0.0181	0.0074	0.015	-	-	-
ln(gei)	-	-	-	0.1932	0.0744	0.009
ln(eepgni)	0.1265	0.0146	0.000	0.2670	0.0369	0.000
ln(utptlf)	-0.0133	0.0078	0.091	-0.0109	0.0189	0.564
ln(lfprtptp)	0.2670	0.0333	0.000	0.6511	0.1058	0.000
ln(igdpdap)	- 0.0014	0.0043	0.751	-0.0315	0.0137	0.022
ln(wswtpte)	0.0126	0.0218	0.564	0.0720	0.0321	0.025
ln(pgap)	0.0111	0.0029	0.000	0.0691	0.0111	0.000
ln(mvapc)	0.0181	0.0105	0.085	0.8340	0.0252	0.000
ln(fdinipgdp)	0.0054	0.0021	0.010	0.0179	0.0084	0.032
ln(vetpte)	-0.0132	0.0043	0.002	-0.1576	0.0100	0.000
Con. Coef.	-2.2601	0.1150	0.000	0.4429	0.4560	0.331

Source: Author's calculation.

4.4. Results of Granger Casualty Test

The casual association of GE with explanatory variables is provided in Table: 6. For the mentioned investigation, we tested a null hypothesis that individual variable does not cause GE and ED. For most variables, we rejected the null hypothesis due to presence of statistically significant values of Z-bar and Z-bar. The estimates indicate that economic development, unemployment, labour force participation rate, wage and salaried workers, manufacturing value added, foreign direct investment net inflows, and vulnerable employment have a causal relationship with GE. Inflation GDP deflator and population growth do not have causal relationship with GE.

Table 6. Casual association of GE with explanatory variables

DV	Green entrepreneurship index (*GEI*)			
Null Hypothesis (H_0): Individual variable does not Granger-cause *GEI* Alternate Hypothesis (H_1): Individual variable does Granger-cause *GEI*				
IVs	***W-bar***	***Z-bar***	***Z-bar tilde***	***Conclusion***
gdppc	2.0414	4.2938*	2.8995*	Not supported H_0
utptlf	2.0139	4.1806*	2.8108*	Not supported H_0
lfprtptp	1.8417	3.4704*	2.2550*	Not supported H_0
igdpdap	1.5141	2.1198**	1.1981	Supported H_0
wswtpte	1.8081	3.3320*	2.1467**	Not supported H_0
pgap	1.2045	0.8433	0.1990	Supported H_0
mvapc	2.2359	5.0957*	3.5270*	Not supported H_0
fdinipgdp	1.8504	3.5063*	2.2831*	Not supported H_0
vetpte	1.7739	3.1910*	2.0364**	Not supported H_0

Source: Author's estimation. **Note:** * and ** indicate that coefficients are statistically significant at 1% and 5% significance level, respectively.

Table: 7 show the causal relationship of ED with *IV*s. The results also showed that unemployment rate, labour force participation rate, inflation GDP deflator, wage and salaried workers, population growth, manufacturing value added, foreign direct investment net inflows, and vulnerable employment have a causal relationship with economic development (ED). While, GE does not have a causal association with ED.

Table 7. Casual association of ED with explanatory variables

DV	Economic development (ED)			
Null Hypothesis (H_0): Individual variable does not Granger-cause *ED* Alternate Hypothesis (H_1): Individual variable does Granger-cause *ED*				
IVs	***W-bar***	***Z-bar***	***Z-bar tilde***	***Conclusion***
gei	0.8943	-0.4356	-0.8019	Supported H_0
utptlf	2.9055	7.8564*	5.6876*	Not supported H_0
lfprtptp	3.5525	10.5242*	7.7755*	Not supported H_0
igdpdap	2.3535	5.5805*	3.9064*	Not supported H_0
wswtpte	3.0346	8.3888*	6.1043*	Not supported H_0
pgap	1.8301	3.4225*	2.2176*	Not supported H_0
mvapc	2.4596	6.0181*	4.2489*	Not supported H_0
fdinipgdp	1.8099	3.3395*	2.1526**	Not supported H_0
vetpte	2.4644	6.0378*	4.2644*	Not supported H_0

Source: Author's estimation. **Note:** * and ** indicate that coefficients are statistically significant at 1% and 5% significance level, respectively.

5. CONCLUSION

This chapter provides the relative progress of green entrepreneurship (GE) for selected 34 countries. It, therefore, creates green entrepreneurship index (GEI) which is the composition of 43 diverse variables. Thereupon, it examines the impact of GE on ED and vice-versa using Cobb-Douglas production function approach. Finally, causal association of independent variables with GE and ED are detected through Granger casualty co-integration test. The GEI's values indicate that there is a noteworthy diversity in the progress of GE among the 34 countries in different time periods i.e., 2000 – 2004, 2005 – 2009, 2010 – 2014 and 2015 – 2019. Norway, Canada, Finland, Estonia and Netherland have 1st, 2nd 3rd 4th and 5th position, respectively in GE. Thus, these countries have best performance in GE among the 34 countries. The performance of Denmark in GE increased after 2004. While, the performance of USA in GE is consistently declined after 2014. Switzerland, Portugal, Lithuania, Luxembourg, Austria, Australia, Spain, Germany, Belgium, Latvia, Tunisia, France, Mexico, Japan, United Kingdom and Argentina have a better performance in GE during 2015 – 2019. China, Poland, Brazil, Greece, India, Romania, Russia and Hungry have average performance in GE during 2015 – 2019. While, Croatia and South Africa have 33rd and 34th rank in GE during 2015 – 2019. Hence, both the countries are in poor position in GE. The results infer that low-ranking countries should focus those activities which are helpful to increase their position in GE.

The correlation coefficients results reveal that GE and ED are positively associated with education expenditure, fixed telephone subscriptions, GDP per person employed, exports of goods and services, wage and salaried workers, manufacturing value added per capita, compulsory education duration, employment to population ratio, individuals using the internet, mobile cellular subscriptions and women business and the law index score. Hence, above-mentioned variables will be supportive to increase GE and ED.

The empirical findings suggest that economic development, education expenditure, labour force participation rate, wage and salaried workers, population growth, manufacturing value added and FDI net inflows have a positive impact on GE and ED. Also, GE showed a positive impact on ED, and ED also showed a positive impact on GE. The results based on Granger casualty test infer that ED, unemployment, labour force participation rate, wage and salaried workers, manufacturing value added, FDI net inflows, and vulnerable employment have a causal relationship with GE. Unemployment rate, inflation GDP deflator, population growth, manufacturing value added, foreign direct investment net inflows and vulnerable employment have a causal relationship with ED.

6. IMPLICATIONS

This chapter has following contribution in the theoretical and empirical literature: It develops GEI for selected 34 countries using composite Z-score method. It includes 43 variables which are supportive to increase appropriate green entrepreneurship (GE). The estimated values of GEI are also used to describe the relative progress of these countries in GE. Log linear regression models are also applied to assess the impact of GE on ED and vice-versa as compiling a country-wise panel data during 2000 – 2019. Granger Causality cointegration test is employed to check the existence of causal association of GE and ED with *IV*s. It also provides scope for further research in different aspects.

Scientific research community should develop green and environmental technologies and appropriate technologies for all sectors to reduce GHGs emissions in the atmosphere. For instance, largely agricultural intensive countries should develop and invent appropriate technologies for this sector (Ashraf & Singh, 2022; Singh et al., 2022b). While, highly industrialized countries should discover appropriate technologies and ICTs for manufacturing and industrial sectors (Yin et al., 2022; Singh & Kumar, 2021; Singh et al., 2023d). Appropriate R&D grants for the research institutions and universities will be helpful to develop green technologies, environmental technologies, green innovation, green product, recycling wings and ICTs tools for the manufacturing and industrial sectors (Singh & Jyoti, 2020; Singh & Kumar, 2021). Green innovation, green technologies and eco-friendly technologies will also increase GE. The manufacturing sector also increase green practices in production activities to increase GE and ED. Application of appropriate technologies in the production sectors may be best option to maintain the sustainability of all inputs (Jyoti et al., 2023). Production of eco-friendly products, reuse of resources and reducing waste materials may also increase GE (Navarathinam & Amutha, 2022). Higher educational institutions (HEIs) should create green infrastructure to increase the intention of students and entrepreneurs towards green entrepreneurial activities (Li et al., 2023). HEIs should create green start-ups to increase GE. Creation of more ICTs infrastructure and digital technologies will also promote digitalization and green economy (Singh & Jyoti, 2023c). The global should also promote digitalization to reduce the dependency of people and industrial sector on natural resources. This initiative will be crucial option to cultivate GE. The developing countries should also apply ICTs tools to increase GE (Jyoti & Singh, 2023). The government should also provide green fund to new entrepreneurs to start green ventures in different sectors. Green funding and green investment may be supportive to increase GE and SD (Singh & Jyoti, 2021; Mondal, 2023). Transfer of green and environmental technologies from developed countries to developing countries may be positive to increase the GE. Research institutions and universities should also provide regular trainings to the entrepreneurs and students to increase their awareness towards green ventures and green entrepreneurial activities. The government should also implement green taxation policies to increase GE. Above-mentioned proposals may be integrated to increase ED and GE, and ensure a sustainable future of society in near future.

7. SCOPE FOR FUTURE RESEARCH

This study develops country-wise GEI as an integration of 43 variables which helps to increase green entrepreneurship (GE), entrepreneurship ecosystem (EE) and environmental sustainability (ES). Accordingly, it could explain the relative performance of selected countries in GE. However, statistical values of GEI for undertaken countries may be varied due to inclusion or dropping of one or set of variables in GEI estimation. Also, ranking and performance of a specific country in GE may not be remain same due to inclusion or dropping of single or group of countries in GEI estimation. Thus, the findings based on estimated values of GEI may not be generalized for global countries. In this chapter, we also include limited control variables in regression analysis. Although, GE and ED depend on other variables like foreign trade, S&TD, IPRs regime, technology transfer, infrastructural development, government policies and environmental tax in short and long terms. While, these variables are not included in regression analysis. Furthermore, GE has multiple impacts on most social-economic and technological activities and vice-versa. Thus, existing researchers can check the validity of empirical findings of this chapter as including more countries in further study. Existing researchers can also examine the impact of GE on social, environmental and SD in further study. Further research can be considered to assess the impact of GE on green growth and green GDP. Existing researchers can also estimate the impact of green technologies, environmental technologies, appropriate technologies, digitalization, IPRs, technology transfer and green entrepreneurial activities on GE in further research.

REFERENCES

Acs, Z., Desaid, S., & Hessels, J. (2008). Entrepreneurship, economic development, and institutions. *Small Business Economics*, *31*(1), 219–234. doi:10.100711187-008-9135-9

Adusei, M. (2016). Does entrepreneurship promote economic growth in Africa? *African Development Review*, *28*(2), 201–214. doi:10.1111/1467-8268.12190

Ahmad, N. H., Halim, H. A., Ramayah, T., & Rahman, S. A. (2015). Green entrepreneurship inclination among generation Y: The road towards a green economy. *Problems and Perspectives in Management, 13*(2), 211–218. https://www.businessperspectives.org/images/pdf/applications/publishing/templates/article/assets/6626/PPM_2015_02cont_Ahmad.pdf

Alwakid, W., Aparicio, S., & Urbano, D. (2021). The influence of green entrepreneurship on sustainable development in Saudi Arabia: The role of formal institutions. *International Journal of Environmental Research and Public Health, 18*(10), 1–23. doi:10.3390/ijerph18105433 PMID:34069588

Alwakid, W., Sebastian, A., & David, U. (2020). Cultural antecedents of green entrepreneurship in Saudi Arabia: An institutional approach. *Sustainability (Basel), 12*(9), 36–73. doi:10.3390u12093673

Ashraf, S. N., & Singh, A. K. (2019). Does entrepreneurship ecosystem have a long-term relationship with economic Growth in selected economies? A statistical investigation. In Misra S., Shukla S. and Batthini G. (Eds.), *Proceedings of the 13th Biennial Conference on Entrepreneurship, EDII Ahmedabad,* (pp. 176-187). Bookwell Publishing House, New Delhi.

Ashraf, S. N., & Singh, A. K. (2022). Implications of appropriate technology and farm inputs in the agricultural sector of Gujarat: Empirical analysis based on primary data. *Agricultural Economics Research Review, 35*(2), 59–77. doi:10.5958/0974-0279.2022.00031.3

Audretsch, D. B., Belitski, M., & Desai, S. (2015). Entrepreneurship and economic development in cities. *The Annals of Regional Science, 55*(1), 33–60. doi:10.100700168-015-0685-x

Baumol, W. J. (1990). Entrepreneurship: Productive, unproductive and destructive. *Journal of Political Economy, 80*(5), 893–921. doi:10.1086/261712

Chandel, T. A. (2022). Green entrepreneurship and sustainable development. In M. Magd, D. Singh, D. Spicer, & R. T. Syed (Eds.), *International Perspectives on Value Creation and Sustainability Through Social Entrepreneurship*. IGI Global. doi:10.4018/978-1-6684-4666-9.ch009

Chen, S., Shen, W., Qiu, Z., Liu, R., & Mardani, A. (2023). Who are the green entrepreneurs in China? The relationship between entrepreneurs' characteristics, green entrepreneurship orientation, and corporate financial performance. *Journal of Business Research, 165*, 113960. doi:10.1016/j.jbusres.2023.113960

Demirel, P., Li, Q. C., Rentocchini, F., & Tamvada, J. P. (2017). Born to be green: New insights into the economics and management of green entrepreneurship. *Small Business Economics*, *52*(1), 759–771. doi:10.100711187-017-9933-z

Dhahri, S., & Omri, A. (2018). Entrepreneurship contribution to the three pillars of sustainable development: What does the evidence really say? *World Development*, *106*(1), 64–77. doi:10.1016/j.worlddev.2018.01.008

Domańska, A., Żukowska, B., & Zajkowski, R. (2018). Green entrepreneurship as a connector among social, environmental and economic pillars of sustainable development. Why some countries are more agile? *Problemy Ekorozwoju*, *13*(2), 67-76. https://ekorozwoj.pollub.pl/no26/i.pdf

Doran, J., McCarthy, N., & O'Connor, M. (2018). The role of entrepreneurship in stimulating economic growth in developed and developing countries. *Cogent Economics & Finance*, *6*(1), 1442093. doi:10.1080/23322039.2018.1442093

Ebrahimi, P., & Mirbargkar, S. M. (2017). Green entrepreneurship and green innovation for SME development in market turbulence. *Eurasian Business Review*, *7*(2), 203–228. doi:10.100740821-017-0073-9

Farinelli, F., Bottini, M., Akkoyunlu, S., & Aerni, P. (2011). Green entrepreneurship: The mission link towards a greener economy. *ATDF Journal*, *8*(3/4), 42–48.

Galindo, M. Á., & Méndez, M. T. (2013). Entrepreneurship, economic growth, and innovation: Are feedback effects at work? *Journal of Business Research*, *67*(5), 825–829. Advance online publication. doi:10.1016/j.jbusres.2013.11.052

Galindo-Martín, M. A., Castaño-Martínez, M. S., & Méndez-Picazo, M. T. (2020). The relationship between green innovation, social entrepreneurship, and sustainable development. *Sustainability (Basel)*, *12*(11), 1–19. doi:10.3390u12114467

Gao, Y., & Qin, X. (2022). Entrepreneurship education and entrepreneurial intention of Chinese college students: Evidence from a moderated multi-mediation model. *Frontiers in Psychology*, *13*(1), 1–12. doi:10.3389/fpsyg.2022.1049232 PMID:36524159

Guo, Y., Wang, L., & Chen, Y. (2020). Green entrepreneurial orientation and green innovation: The mediating effect of supply chain learning. *SAGE Open*, *10*(1), 1–24. doi:10.1177/2158244019898798

Gupta, M., & Dharwal, M. (2022). Green entrepreneurship and sustainable development: A conceptual framework. *Materials Today: Proceedings*, *49*(8), 3603–3606. doi:10.1016/j.matpr.2021.08.148

Haldar, S. (2019). Green entrepreneurship in the renewable energy sector – a case study of Gujarat. *Journal of Science and Technology Policy Management, 10*(1), 234–250. doi:10.1108/JSTPM-12-2017-0070

Hall, J., Daneke, G. A., & Lenox, M. (2010). Sustainable development and entrepreneurship: Past contributions and future directions. *Journal of Business Venturing, 25*(1), 439–448. doi:10.1016/j.jbusvent.2010.01.002

Iversen, J., Jørgensen, R., $ Malchow-Møller, N. (2008). Defining and measuring entrepreneurship. *Foundations and Trends R in Entrepreneurship, 4*(1), 1 – 63.

Jyoti, B., & Singh, A. K. (2020). Characteristics and determinants of new start-ups in Gujarat, India. *Entrepreneurship Review, 1*(2), 1–25. doi:10.38157/entrepreneurship-review.v1i2.154

Jyoti, B., & Singh, A. K. (2023). Does digitalization have a causal relationship with economic development? an experience from a country-wise panel data statistical analysis. In R. Sine Nazlı & G. Sari (Eds.), Handbook of Research on Perspectives on Society and Technology Addiction (pp. 34-61). IGI Global. doi:10.4018/978-1-6684-8397-8.ch003

Jyoti, B., Singh, A. K., & Ashraf, S. N. (2023). Appropriate technologies and their implications in the agricultural sector. In P. H. Alex Khang (Ed.), *Advanced Technologies and AI-Equipped IoT Applications in High-Tech Agriculture* (pp. 65–87). IGI Global. doi:10.4018/978-1-6684-9231-4.ch004

Karimi, R. F., & Chashmi, S. A. N. (2019). Designing green entrepreneurship model in sustainable development consistent with the performance of Tehran industrial towns. *Journal of Business-To-Business Marketing, 26*(1), 95–102. doi:10.1080/1051712X.2019.1565143

Kumar, A., Ahmad, M. M., & Sharma, P. (2015). Carbon emission and global food security: A cross country analysis. *PENCIL Publication of Agricultural Sciences, 2*(1), 7–24.

Kumar, A., Ahmad, M. M., & Sharma, P. (2017). Influence of climatic and non-climatic factors on sustainable food security in India: A statistical investigation. *International Journal of Sustainable Agricultural Management and Informatics, 3*(1), 1–30. doi:10.1504/IJSAMI.2017.082917

Kumar, A., Sharma, P., & Joshi, S. (2016). Assessing the impacts of climate change on land productivity in Indian crop agriculture: An evidence from panel data analysis. *Journal of Agricultural Science and Technology, 18*(1), 1–13. https://jast.modares.ac.ir/article-23-4491-en.pdf

Kumar, S., & Singh, A. K. (2023). Modeling the effects of climate change on agricultural productivity: Evidence from Himachal Pradesh, India. *Asia-Pacific Journal of Regional Science*, *7*(2), 1–28. doi:10.100741685-023-00291-w

Li, C., Murad, M., & Ashraf, S. F. (2023). The influence of women's green entrepreneurial intention on green entrepreneurial behaviour through university and social support. *Sustainability (Basel)*, *15*(3), 1–17. doi:10.3390u151310123

Mia, M. M., Rizwan, S., Zayed, N. M., Nitesenko, V., Miroshnyk, O., Kryshtal, H., & Ostapenko, R. (2022). The impact of green entrepreneurship on social change and factors influencing AMO theory. *System*, *10*(5), 1–19. doi:10.3390ystems10050132

Mondal, S. (2023). The nexus between green entrepreneurship and sustainable development: An econometric study. *Global Business Review*, 09721509231157009. doi:10.1177/09721509231157009

Moya-Clemente, I., Ribes-Giner, G., & Pantoja-Dıaz, O. (2020). Identifying environmental and economic development factors in sustainable entrepreneurship over time by partial least squares (PLS). *PLoS One*, *15*(9), 1–17. doi:10.1371/journal.pone.0238462 PMID:32886680

Mrkajic, B., Murtinu, S., & Scalera, V. G. (2017). Is green the new gold? Venture capital and green entrepreneurship. *Small Business Economics*, *52*(4), 929–950. doi:10.100711187-017-9943-x

Navarathinam, K., & Amutha, V. (2022). Green entrepreneurship: A sustainable development initiative with special reference to selected districts. *Journal of Positive School Psychology*, *6*(3), 7517–7526.

Neumann, T. (2022). Impact of green entrepreneurship on sustainable development: An ex-post empirical analysis. *Journal of Cleaner Production*, *377*, 134317. doi:10.1016/j.jclepro.2022.134317

Nguyen, V. B. (2021). The digitalization – economic growth relationship in developing countries and the role of governance. *Scientific Annals of Economics and Business*, *68*(4), 481–493. doi:10.47743aeb-2021-0028

Nuringsih, K., & Nuryasman, M. N. (2020). Role of green entrepreneurship in raising the effect of green toward sustainable development. *International Journal of Economics, Business, and Entrepreneurship*, *3*(2), 29–46. doi:10.23960/ijebe.v3i2.69

Omoruyi, E. M. M., Olamide, K. S., Gomolemo, G., & Donath, O. A. (2017). Entrepreneurship and economic growth: Does entrepreneurship bolster economic expansion in Africa? *Journal of Socialomics*, *6*(4), 1–11.

Onsay, E. A. (2021). The analysis of green growth indicators in predicting the economic development of southeast Asian countries. *Review of Socio -. Economic Perspectives*, *6*(3), 1–15. https://reviewsep.com/wp-content/uploads/2021/09/1_ONSAY-1.pdf

Saari, U. A., & Joensuu-Salo, S. (2019). Green entrepreneurship. In W. Leal Filho, A. Azul, L. Brandli, P. Özuyar, & T. Wall (Eds.), *Responsible Consumption and Production. Encyclopedia of the UN Sustainable Development Goals*. Springer. doi:10.1007/978-3-319-71062-4_6-1

Santika, I. W., Wardana, I. M., Setiawan, P. Y., & Widagda, I. G. N. J. A. (2022). Entrepreneurship education and green entrepreneurial intention: A conceptual framework. *Linguistics and Culture Review*, *6*(S1), 797–810. doi:10.21744/lingcure.v6nS1.2159

Sharma, A., Das, N., & Singh, S. P. (2023). Causal association of entrepreneurship ecosystem and financial inclusion. *Heliyon*, *9*(3), 1–13. doi:10.1016/j.heliyon.2023.e14596 PMID:36950562

Sharma, P., & Singh, A. K. (2017). Association of state-wise food security index with climatic factors in India: Evidence from state-wise panel data. *Journal of Global Agriculture and Ecology*, *6*(3), 196–205.

Singh, A. K. (2020). Technology transfer and commercialization models and policies in India, USA, China and Malaysia: A conceptual review. *Asian Journal of Sociological Research*, *3*(1), 19–45. https://globalpresshub.com/index.php/AJSR/article/view/916

Singh, A. K., Arya, A., & Jyoti, B. (2019b). A conceptual review on economic, business, intellectual property rights and science & technology related activities in Asian economies. *JNNCE Journal of Engineering & Management*, *3*(2), 1–22.

Singh, A. K., & Ashraf, S. N. (2020). Association of entrepreneurship ecosystem with economic growth in selected countries: An empirical exploration. *Journal of Entrepreneurship. Business Economics (Cleveland, Ohio)*, *8*(2), 36–92.

Singh, A. K., Ashraf, S. N., & Arya, A. (2019c). Estimating factors affecting technical efficiency in Indian manufacturing sector. *Eurasian Journal of Business and Economics*, *12*(24), 65–86. doi:10.17015/ejbe.2019.024.04

Singh, A. K., Ashraf, S. N., & Sharma, S. K. (2023f). Farmer's perception on climatic factors and social-economic characteristics in the agricultural sector of Gujarat. *Research on World Agricultural Economy*, *4*(1), 36–53. doi:10.36956/rwae.v4i1.788

Singh, A. K., Ashraf, S. N., Sharma, S. K., & Kumar, S. (2023b). Factors affecting farm income and climate adaptation strategies in the farming sector of Gujarat state of India. In B. J. Sadhik, J. Adewole, A. Yeneneh, & L. Abidoye (Eds.), *Opportunities and Challenges in Climate-Friendly Clean Water and Energy Technologies* (pp. 122–147). IGI Global. doi:10.4018/978-1-6684-7303-0.ch006

Singh, A. K., Issac, J., & Narayanan, K. G. S. (2019a). Measurement of environmental sustainability index and its association with socio-economic indicators in selected Asian economies: An empirical investigation. *International Journal of Environment and Sustainable Development, 18*(1), 57–100. doi:10.1504/IJESD.2019.098641

Singh, A. K., & Jyoti, B. (2020). Factors affecting firm's annual turnover in selected manufacturing industries of India: An empirical study. *Business Perspectives and Research, 2*(3), 33–59. doi:10.38157/business-perspective-review.v2i3.206

Singh, A. K., & Jyoti, B. (2021). Further research direction for indicators of technology entrepreneurship ecosystem, technology start-ups ecosystem and technology-business incubators: A conceptual review. *Dimensions International Journal of Management ICFAI Business School (IBS) Mumbai, 7*(1), 14-33.

Singh, A. K., & Jyoti, B. (2023a). Does digitalization have a bi-directional causal relationship with the entrepreneurship ecosystem? evidence from a country-wise panel data analysis. In *Ramakrishna Yanamandra and Logaiswari Indiran (Edt.), Handbook of Research on Designing Sustainable Strategies to Develop Entrepreneurial Intention*. IGI Global. doi:10.4018/978-1-6684-8781-5.ch007

Singh, A. K., & Jyoti, B. (2023b). Appropriate technology and adaptation strategies mitigate the adverse impact of climate change on the agricultural sector: A case study in Gujarat, India. In P. H. Alex Khang (Ed.), *Advanced Technologies and AI-Equipped IoT Applications in High-Tech Agriculture* (pp. 389–416). IGI Global. doi:10.4018/978-1-6684-9231-4.ch023

Singh, A. K., & Jyoti, B. (2023c). Empirical evidence from a different income group countries on the interdependency between digitalization and economic development. In Patricia Ordóñez de Pablos and Xi Zhang (Eds.), 5G, Artificial Intelligence, and Next Generation Internet of Things: Digital Innovation for Green and Sustainable Economies, (pp. 44-85). IGI Global. doi:10.4018/978-1-6684-8634-4.ch003

Singh, A. K., Jyoti, B., Kumar, S., & Lenka, S. K. (2021). Assessment of global sustainable development, environmental sustainability, economic development and social development index in selected economies. *International Journal of Sustainable Development and Planning, 16*(1), 123–138. doi:10.18280/ijsdp.160113

Singh, A. K., & Kumar, S. (2021). Assessing the performance and factors affecting industrial development in Indian states: An empirical analysis. *Journal of Social Economics Research, 8*(2), 135–154. doi:10.18488/journal.35.2021.82.135.154

Singh, A. K., & Kumar, S. (2022a). Expert's perception on technology transfer and commercialization, and intellectual property rights in India: Evidence from selected research organizations. *Journal of Management, Economics, and Industrial Organization, 6*(1), 1–33. doi:10.31039/jomeino.2022.6.1.1

Singh, A. K., & Kumar, S. (2022b). Factors influencing entrepreneurship ecosystem and economic development: Evidence from cross-sectional country-wise imbalanced panel data analysis. *The IUP Journal of Entrepreneurship Development, 19*(3), 24–47.

Singh, A. K., & Kumar, S. (2022c). Exploring the impact of sustainable development on social-economic, and science and technological development in selected countries: A panel data analysis. *Society & Sustainability, 4*(1), 55–83. doi:10.38157s.v4i1.405

Singh, A. K., Kumar, S., Ashraf, S. N., & Jyoti, B. (2022b). Implications of farmer's adaptation strategies to climate change in agricultural sector of Gujarat: Evidence from farm level data. *Research on World Agricultural Economy, 3*(1), 42–57. doi:10.36956/rwae.v3i1.498

Singh, A. K., Kumar, S., & Jyoti, B. (2023c). Does entrepreneurship ecosystem have a causal relationship with economic development? A country-wise imbalanced panel data investigation. In H. Magd, S. A. Khan, N. D. Nte, & M. Sarim (Eds.), *Entrepreneurship and Economic Sustainability* (pp. 1–15). Prestige Publishers.

Singh, A. K., Kumar, S., & Sharma, A. K. (2023e). Does green entrepreneurship ecosystem have causal association with economic development? Evidence from country-wise panel data investigation. *Journal of International Business Research, 22*(2), 1–18. https://www.abacademies.org/articles/Does-Green-Entrepreneurship-Ecosystem-have-1544-0230-22-2-191.pdf

Singh, A. K., Kumar, S., Sharma, A. K., & Sinha, S. (2022a). Does green entrepreneurship have an association with sustainable development and its components? Evidence from a country-wise panel data investigation. In M. Magd, D. Singh, D. Spicer, & R. T. Syed (Eds.), *International Perspectives on Value Creation and Sustainability Through Social Entrepreneurship* (pp. 132–172). IGI Global. doi:10.4018/978-1-6684-4666-9.ch008

Singh, A. K., Sharma, A. K., & Jyoti, B. (2023a). Does economic development have a causal relationship with environmental degradation? Experience from different income group countries. In G. Sart (Ed.), *Considerations on Education for Economic, Social, and Environmental Sustainability* (pp. 300–333). IGI Global. doi:10.4018/978-1-6684-8356-5.ch015

Singh, A. K., & Sharma, P. (2018). Implications of climatic and non-climatic variables on food security in developing economies: A conceptual review. *MOJ Food Processing & Technology*, *6*(1), 1–12. doi:10.15406/mojfpt.2018.06.00138

Singh, A. K., Sharma, S. K., & Lenka, S. K. (2023d). Causality between green entrepreneurship and sustainable development: A cross-country analysis using ARDL model. *The IUP Journal of Applied Economics*, *22*(1), 5–38.

Singh, A. K., Singh, B., & Ashraf, S. N. (2020a). Implications of intellectual property protection, and science and technological development in the manufacturing sector in selected economies. *Journal of Advocacy. Research in Education*, *7*(1), 16–35.

Singh, A. K., Singh, B. J., & Negi, V. (2020b). Does sustainable development have a causal relationship with environmental development? Evidence from a country-wise panel data analysis. *International Journal of Technology Management & Sustainable Development*, *19*(2), 147–171. doi:10.1386/tmsd_00020_1

Skordoulis, M., Kyriakopoulos, G., Ntanos, S., Galatsidas, S., Arabatzis, G., Chalikias, M., & Kalantonis, P. (2022). The mediating role of firm strategy in the relationship between green entrepreneurship, green innovation, and competitive advantage: The case of medium and large-sized firms in Greece. *Sustainability (Basel)*, *14*(6), 1–18. doi:10.3390u14063286

Söderholm, P. (2020). The green economy transition: The challenges of technology change for sustainability. *Sustainable Earth*, *3*(6), 1–11. doi:10.118642055-020-00029-y

Tawiah, V., Zakari, A., & Adedoyin, F. F. (2021). Determinants of green growth in developed and developing countries. *Environmental Science and Pollution Research International*, *28*(1), 39227–39242. doi:10.100711356-021-13429-0 PMID:33751350

Vasilescu, M. D., Dimian, G. C., & Gradinaru, G. I. (2023). Green entrepreneurship in challenging times: A quantitative approach for European countries. *Ekonomska Istrazivanja*, *36*(1), 1828–1947. doi:10.1080/1331677X.2022.2093767

Yin, C., Salmador, M. P., Li, D., & Lloria, M. B. (2022). Green entrepreneurship and SME performance: The moderating effect of firm age. *The International Entrepreneurship and Management Journal*, *18*(1), 255–275. doi:10.100711365-021-00757-3

Zahedi, A., & Otterpohl, R. (2015). Towards sustainable development by creation of green social entrepreneur's communities. *Procedia CIRP*, *26*, 196–201. doi:10.1016/j.procir.2014.07.037

Zeng, J., & Ren, J. (2022). How does green entrepreneurship affect environmental improvement? Empirical findings from 293 enterprises. *The International Entrepreneurship and Management Journal*, *18*(1), 409–434. doi:10.100711365-021-00780-4

Chapter 7
Entrepreneurial Alertness in the Perusal of New Venture Creation:
Serial Mediation Raid of Opportunities Creation, Discovery and Entrepreneurial Recognition

Farhan Mirza
https://orcid.org/0000-0001-9472-8905
Universiti Teknologi PETRONAS, Malaysia

Shabeeb Ahmad Gill
Government College University, Faislabad, Pakistan

Ding Hooi Ting
Universiti Teknologi PETRONAS, Malaysia

Ahsan Riaz
Government College University, Faislabad, Pakistan

Ali Hasan
Beijing Institute of Technology, China

ABSTRACT

This chapter propelled a transparent model or road map to start a new business venture that addresses literature and practices. The study aimed to investigate the serial mediation of opportunity creation, opportunity discovery, and entrepreneurial recognition between the relationship of entrepreneurial Alertness and new venture

DOI: 10.4018/978-1-6684-7140-1.ch007

creation through the authority of entrepreneurship theory. The post-positivist school of thought has followed to unfold the current phenomenon. The study used the online survey forum of Google Forms and sent the link to the respondents through e-mail. The quantitative research method was implemented, and data were collected through stratified random sampling—the sample of 575 responses was collected from 54 Universities in South Asia and South Europe. The one-shot serial mediation model has run through user-defined in AMOS version 26. A partial serial mediation has been reported in the results of the study. All six hypotheses resulted in significant relationships.

1. INTRODUCTION

Entrepreneurship has become an integral sector of research and development since the last century; directly or indirectly, many subfields emerged during this journey. The end terminal was the new venture creation or the new business development (Kirzner, 1999). Professor Schumpeter presented the entrepreneurship theory revolutionising the economic and industrial sectors (Mehmood et al., 2019; Sweezy, 1943). The current study is constructed on the bedrock of Schumpeterian entrepreneurship theory. Many of those got substantial theoretical and practical importance, but unfortunately, we still struggle to find a sustainable business process model or framework. Slow but incremental growth has been determined during the last three decades in theoretical context about the possible impact of entrepreneurial Alertness on the entrepreneurial opportunity and new venture creation process (Begley & Boyd, 1987; Kaish & Gilad, 1991; Sternberg & Wennekers, 2005; Z. Tang & Tang, 2012).

In antecedents, Ekelund and Kirzner (1974) emphasized entrepreneurial opportunity research and identified entrepreneurial Alertness as an 'ability to notice' based on observation without any search and data collection. Before other people (Gaglio and Katz, 2001), the entrepreneur`s ability to recognize the entrepreneurial opportunity is referred to as entrepreneurial Alertness. Entrepreneurial Alertness led the entrepreneurial process faster than others towards new business ventures (Adomako et al., 2018).

Kaish and Gilad (1991) and Gozukara and Colakoglu (2016) mentioned that this field has a vast and developed theoretical background that is impossible for one to conclude and find a new research passage to answer the current questions from the authors and practitioners just based on three and four studies. So, I have adopted the bibliometric analysis approach to explore the possible theoretical connections and determine the path for future research. Figure 1 shows the adopted bibliometric journey step by step and clarifies the scholar's approach to forming the current research paper`s topic.

Figure 1. Bibliometric analysis process

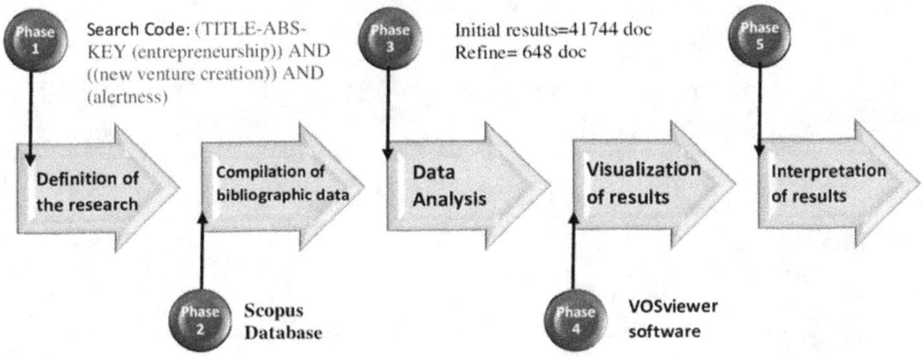

(Burnham, 2006) has refined the entrepreneurial theoretical knowledge and gotten the bibl Data from the 'Scopus index published research for the last five years. In the first step, this study got 41,744

Figure 2. First literature mapping of 41,744 documents

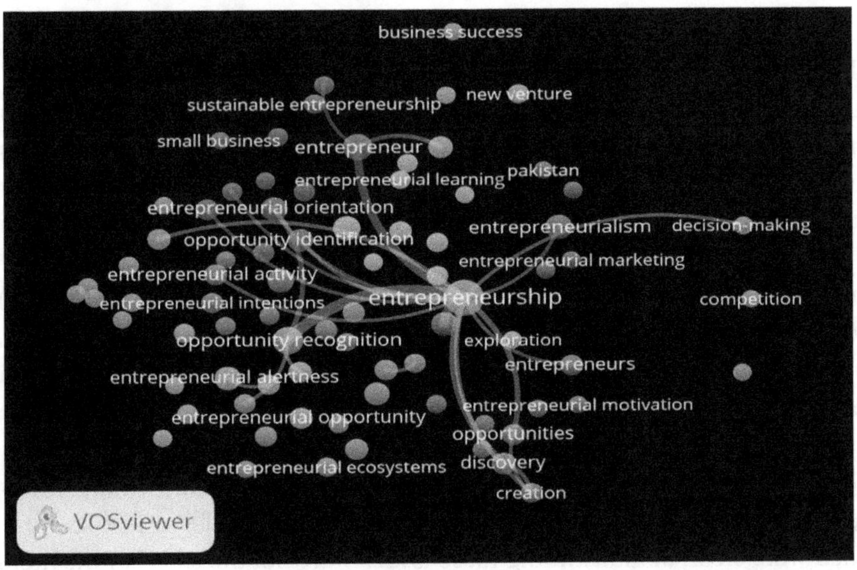

The results show a considerable scholarly effort to enhance the theoretical body of knowledge about entrepreneurial Alertness, but a vast gap exists. Knowledge specification that how entrepreneurial Alertness affects new venture creation.

Figure 3. Second literature mapping of 648 documents

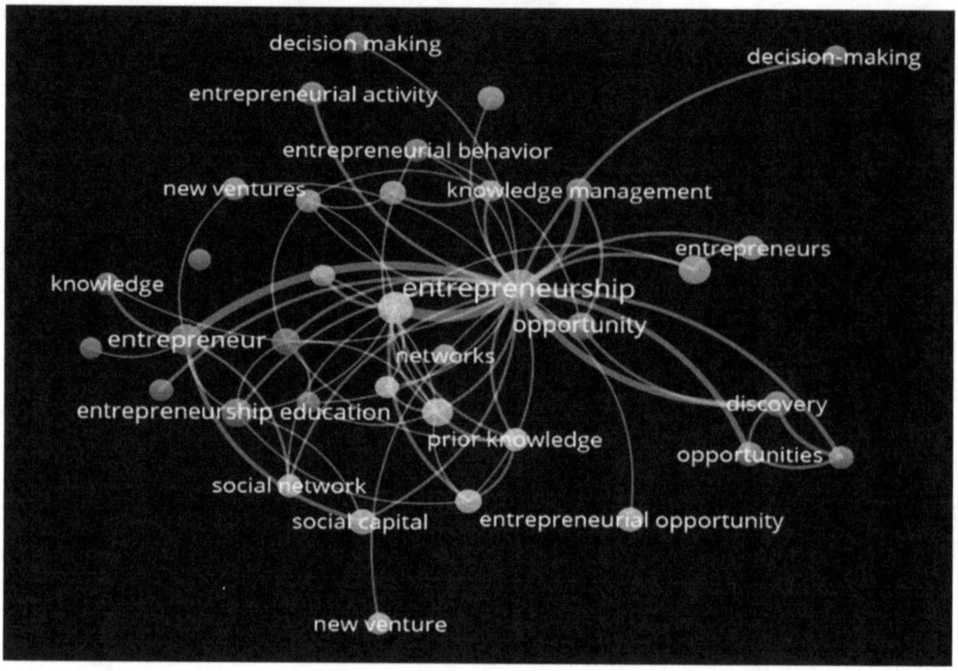

Although conceptual limitations among opportunity, discovery, creation, and recognition have been identified, the theoretical connection of entrepreneurial Alertness to new venture creation has not yet been conceptualized with the relationships of entrepreneurial opportunity exploitation (Dimov, 2011). In addition, although the distinctions between opportunity recognition and entrepreneurial opportunities have been well defined, comprehensive literature is available about the role and importance of opportunity discovery and creation (Alvarez and Barney, 2007).

Hence, the unique connection of opportunity recognition with discovery and creation is unavailable in the literature. Here the extension in entrepreneurial opportunity is required by adding the recognition as the third factor. While the discussion stopped there on the content domain and limitation of the factors, but the problem was unanswered. Even the measurement scales (Seerat, 2016; McDonald et al., 2015) have been developed of all the opportunity-related factors, research designed were clear, demonstrating these issues were not the cause of the literature gap. Nevertheless, the unexplored side was their combined impact on new venture creation to strengthen the entrepreneurial process or model development.

Figure 4. Gap analysis tree

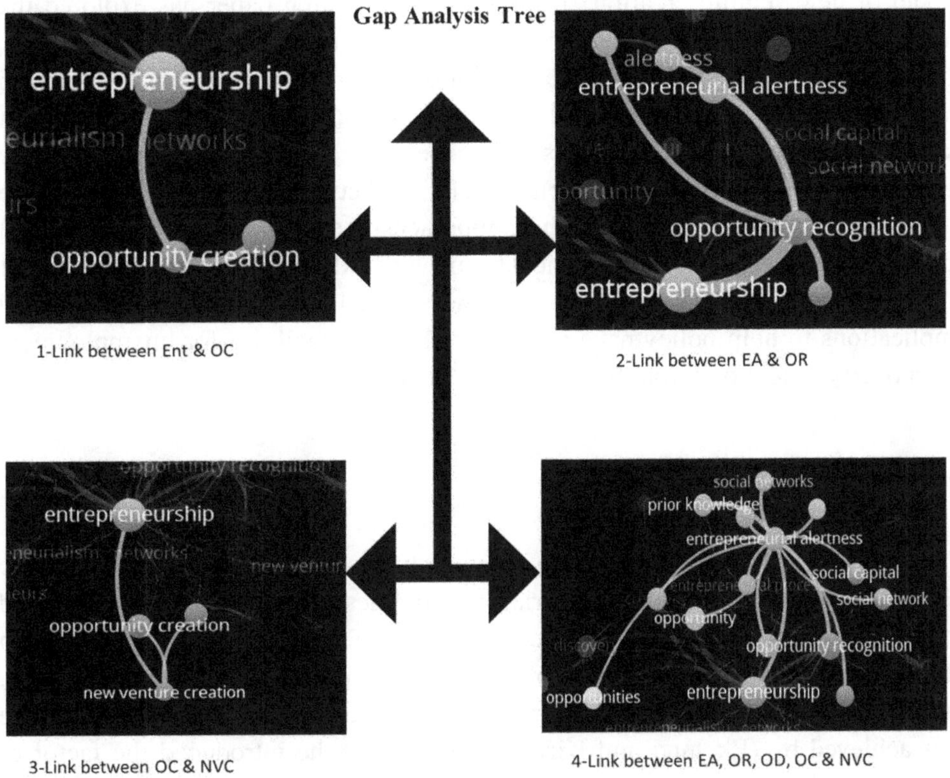

The entrepreneurial opportunities creation played a vital role in starting a new business venture, but unfortunately, minor theoretical importance was given to this crucial process. The complete process of new venture creation has several stages and steps. However, available entrepreneurial literature does not provide a transparent model and process to enable the investors, educationists, unemployed people, Universities, business incubators, and Governments to start and provide suitable facilities for new venture creation.

It has been well established that literature-based resources emphasized the positive relationship of entrepreneurial opportunities on new business development (Lumpkin & Dess, 1996; Wiklund & Shepherd, 2003). However, the body of knowledge has given little space from this development to the relationship between entrepreneurial opportunities and new business creation (Shambare and Shambare, 2019). Consequently, this study raised unanswered questions: 1) How to extend the entrepreneurship theory of opportunities? 2) What is the role of entrepreneurial opportunity factors on new venture creation? 3) How the entrepreneurial Alertness accelerates the process of new venture creation? 4) What should be the simplified model of new venture creation? Moreover, this research paper has explored the empirical knowledge-based answers to these questions.

Based on the traditional format from the introduction to the discussion, this research paper propelled a transparent model or road map to start a new business venture that addresses the literature and practices. This paper provided plinth literature for future research to explore the possible empirical relations between the study variables. The practitioners have been provided with a comprehensive entrepreneurial process model to create a new venture. The theoretical framework did help for the establishment of a new business framework and future business models. We suggested the practical implications to help policymakers enhance the state facilities for unemployment and poverty reduction through new venture creation.

2. LITERATURE REVIEW

The core subject of entrepreneurship in many studies has investigated how specific people feel about the new entrepreneurial opportunities and why they become engaged in new venture creation (Shane & Venkataraman, 2000; Scheaf et al., 2020). Such ability and sense trigger the process of entrepreneurship and new venture formation, but these types of drivers and enablers are still unexplored. Then a milestone was achieved by (Ekelund and Kirzner, 1974) when he introduced the factor of entrepreneurial Alertness to accelerate the process. He elaborated entrepreneurial Alertness as a fundamental driver of the entrepreneurial process that is dynamic and competitive by default.

Hattwick (1979) also urged about entrepreneurial Alertness and defined it gradually "the ability to notice without search opportunities that have hitherto been overlooked," "a motivated propensity of man to formulate an image of the future" (Barreto and Kirzner, 1986). An attitude of receptiveness to available but hitherto overlooked opportunities (Kirzner, 2000). Or "a sense of what might be 'around the corner,' i.e., the sense to notice that which has hitherto not been suspected of existing at all."

Unfortunately, all of the definitions mentioned above are ambiguous and unable to provide a clear theoretical foundation (Busenitz and Lau, 1996). From entrepreneurial actions to opportunity realization, the concept of entrepreneurial Alertness is a unique approach to capture opportunity progress. It is undoubtedly controlled by behaviors of information collected from the existing markets and business environment even though entrepreneurial Alertness is widely well-known as a psychological factor or a state of individual mind that always welcome new venture opportunities (Adomako et al., 2018).

Z. Tang and Tang (2012) have suggested a positive relationship between innovation and entrepreneurial Alertness. Individuals could seek entrepreneurial opportunities through entrepreneurial Alertness even with fewer data, information, and experience (Gaglio and Katz, 2001). Innovation leads to realizing new opportunities that ultimately start the new venture creation process.

Ozgen and Baron (2007), and Scheaf et al. (2020) antecedences studies have discussed that entrepreneurial Alertness developed the cognitive domain of people to utilize their experience, prior knowledge, market patterns, environment capabilities, business information, and utilization of social capital. Cox and Castrogiovanni (2016) Elaborated that competitive readiness, complete preparation to discover and create entrepreneurial opportunities before competitors referred to entrepreneurial Alertness. Many researchers have investigated the term entrepreneurial alertness and emphasized its implied influence in previously published work (Gozukara and Colakoglu, 2016).

Jiao et al. (2014), and Z. Tang and Tang (2012) discussed, Later on, conceptualized the entrepreneurial Alertness formally in the domain of entrepreneurship, he discussed the three dimensions of Alertness: a) inclination to explore new information, b) a skill to link disparate information, c) a proclivity to examine whether a new set of information demonstrates an opportunity. Gaglio and Katz (2001) explained that people with a higher level of entrepreneurial Alertness tend to explore the changes in entrepreneurial environment targeting to fetch a business opportunity. Entrepreneurial Alertness has the ability to enable entrepreneurs about opportunities recognition (Kirzner, 1999).

Entrepreneurial Alertness can create and explain knowledge-based information to start the process of new venture creation (Kaish & Gilad, 1991; Gozukara & Colakoglu, 2016). Although scholars have made a great effort to expand the body of knowledge related to new venture creation due to entrepreneurial Alertness, the gap is still vast. The insight analyses of new venture creation could tell the story of this advanced feature of entrepreneurial Alertness., All these studies presented different conceptualizations about the process of entrepreneurial opportunities and its journey towards new venture creation (Gozukara & Colakoglu, 2016; Kuckertz et al., 2017; Cox & Castrogiovanni, 2016).

S.A. Alvarez and Barney (2007), Sharon A. Alvarez and Barney (2010), and Sharon A. Alvarez et al. (2015) have elaborated that opportunity discovery has objectives to find new opportunities, and opportunity creation is the process of exploration (Gozukara & Colakoglu, 2016; Kuckertz et al., 2017). Shane and Venkataraman (2000) stated about the discovery perspective that entrepreneurs could recognize an opportunity in a business environment to start a new venture, but it could be assumed to capture the opportunity before their peers.

The theoretical perspective also played a fundamental role in opportunity identification, emphasizing entrepreneurial Alertness as a behavioral trait (McMullen & Shepherd, 2006). Kirzner et al. (1983) suggested that entrepreneurial Alertness is supposed to have a practical impact on new venture creation. Recently conceptualized entrepreneurial Alertness as a behavioral component to enable the people before their competitors to start a new venture creation (Helfat & Peteraf, 2015; Messersmith & Wales, 2013).

H1: There is a direct positive link between Entrepreneurial Alertness and Opportunity Creation

Adomako et al. (2018) argued that entrepreneurial opportunity recognition deals in exploring a new venture creation. The published literature Forbes (1999) presented two dimensions to understand this opportunity recognition. The first one is how the internal capabilities of entrepreneurs like knowledge, experience, creativity, and behavioral confidence govern opportunity recognition. The second one is how external connections like market information, business knowledge from the capital market, competitors' actions, and social capital trigger opportunity recognition (Kuckertz et al., 2017; Khin & Lim, 2018).

In this way, two types of approaches exist to address this issue: opportunity discovery and opportunity creation (Bhave, 1994). The entrepreneurial discovery is based on the pre-defined objectives about the opportunity, and on the other hand, the opportunity is not the subject of availability, but it is the process of creation on its own. The entrepreneurial recognition could further explain the distinctions between opportunity discovery and creation through empirical investigation to answer the ambiguous literature framework (Cox & Castrogiovanni, 2016; Bergner et al., 2019).

So, in previous literature Gielnik et al. (2014) opportunity recognition and opportunity discovery overlap by default. On some occasions, these measured the same construct while, on the other hand, opportunity creation Is the result of the interaction between the business environment and entrepreneurs (Carland and Carland, 2000). So, it seems that the opportunity is a matter of entrepreneurs' preferences and what kind of opportunity they need to explore or use for venture creation or business development. Here the literature has depicted the multiple roles of these opportunities, so; it needs to study these again in a well-determined pattern (Hayton et al., 2011; Ozgen & Baron, 2007; Gozukara & Colakoglu, 2016).

Recognizing entrepreneurial opportunities is a fundamental step toward establishing a new venture creation (Siegel and Renko, 2012). The entrepreneurial opportunity is fortuitous to meet a market-based need and interest or desire through a unique arrangement of available resources to deliver the products and services (Kirzner, 1999; Khin & Lim, 2018). Some authors Shane (2000), and Venkataraman

(1997) have explained opportunity in a lovely way that it is the heart of a business process, and an entrepreneur is a person who can recognize, identify, evaluate the opportunity and create a new venture.

H2: Entrepreneurial Alertness influence New Venture Creation Indirectly via Opportunity Creation (M1)

H3: Entrepreneurial Alertness impact New Venture Creation Indirectly through Opportunity Creation (M1), which in turn influences opportunity Discovery (M2)

Waterman (1984), S.A. Alvarez and Barney (2007), Chang Che Hang et al. (2013), and Félix González et al. (2017) have well established in literature the relationship between opportunity recognition and entrepreneurial Alertness, but this framework is still lacking. The ability of entrepreneurial Alertness enables one to become sensitive about the possible opportunities where the recognition enhances the cognitive behavior of entrepreneurs to fetch opportunities for new venture creation (Khin and Lim, 2018). Through this, one can scan the environment for opportunity recognition.

The entrepreneurs could have more connecting ideas and market knowledge to recognize opportunities and have high levels of entrepreneurial Alertness (Kuckertz et al., 2017). Siegel and Renko (2012) reported a significant link between entrepreneurial alertness and opportunity discovery and creation in a survey. So, later on Scheaf et al. (2020) reported a positive impact of entrepreneurial Alertness on entrepreneurial innovativeness and the new venture creation. Consequently, we explored the literary link between perineurial Alertness with an innovative idea then opportunity discovery creation on new venture creation.

H4: Entrepreneurial Alertness impact New Venture Creation Indirectly through Opportunity Creation (M1), which in turn influences Opportunity Recognition (M3)

H5: Entrepreneurial Alertness impact New Venture Creation Indirectly through Opportunity Discovery (M2), which in turn influences Opportunity Recognition (M3)

H6: Entrepreneurial Alertness impact New Venture Creation Indirectly through Opportunity Creation (M1), which in turn influences opportunity Discovery (M2), which in turn influences Opportunity Recognition (M3)

Figure 5. Theoretical model

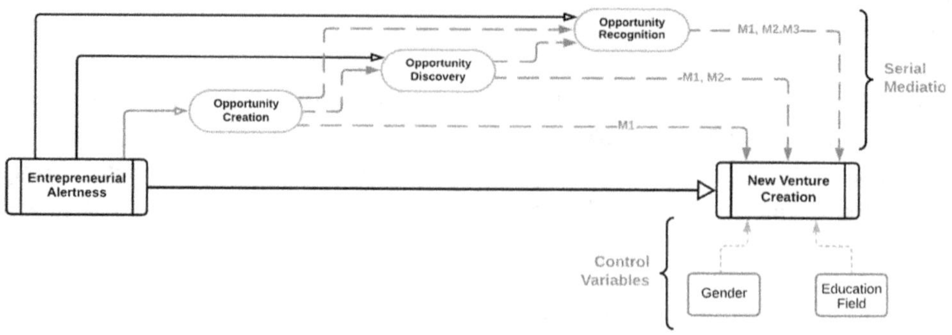

3. METHODS AND MATERIALS

3.1 Research Design

Sekaran (2000), Teece (2006), and Mackenzie and Knipe (2006) formation of new venture creation is an uncharted research area. The post-positivist school of thought influenced the study; the phenomenon is mind-dependent ontologically, positivist epistemology, and value-free axiology (Walter, 2006). The action research technique has been adopted to investigate to recognize the apparent causal relationship among variables (Ryan, 2006; Easterby-Smith et al., 2015). Ab Hamid et al. (2017) have utilized only primary data to answer the potential research questions. The data has been analyzed in IBM SPSS, AMOS v.26 (Al-Refaie, 2015; George & Mallery, 2016; IBM, 2019). The excel has also been used for relative data operations and techniques to evaluate the data. The techniques of data cleaning, screening, and missing values have been applied through a statistical tool pack taken from StatWiki developed by James Gaskin (Gaskin, 2012).

3.2 Population and Sampling

The respondents through which primary data has been collected via probability sampling (Kahle and Malhotra, 1994). The population definition comprises potential future entrepreneurs, most probably the master and doctorate scholars of business, entrepreneurship, management sciences, and other non-business degrees of different Universities from South-Asia and South-Europe through an e-survey form (Edwards and Lambert, 2007). Here, the stratified random sampling technique has been applied because authors need access to a highly qualified and expert population to get the actual data about existing gaps and developments (Cochran, 1948). Authors distributed the population into two strata, stratum-I (Pakistan, India & Bangladesh) for south Asian and stratum-II (Italy, Spain & Portugal) for south European universities (Morse, 1991; Etikan, 2016), respectively, to get the potential respondents with homogenous characteristics to achieve the desired numbers of respondents (Foreman, 1991). Because this population is infinite, researchers used the technique of sample size (Heinisch, 1965).

To enhance the generalizability of the results through multivariate regression analysis, one must maintain the ratio of 5 between the number of samples and independent variables. The one traditional threshold is to collect 10 observations per study variable. A rule of thumb shared by Stephen is to collect 15 observations per variable to achieve a higher level of satisfaction with the generalizability of the regression results. The following mathematical formula has been implemented in the current study to fetch the sample size:

$$5q \leq n \leq 15q$$

$$5*46 \leq n \leq 15*46$$

$$230 \leq n \leq 690$$

In the above formula, (q) represents the number of items which questionnaire has (i.e., 46) and (n) represents the appropriate sample size of the study. So, the calculation propelled to fix the sample size between the range of 230 to 690.

3.3 Data Collection

For data collection through online survey platforms like google forms used by the authors (Moradi et al., 2021). In addition, an electronic link of survey form was sent by e-mail to about 2160 master and doctorate scholars of business, entrepreneurship, management sciences, and other non-business degrees of 54 Universities, out of which 30 Universities belonged to south Asia, and the remaining 24 belonged to south Europe. We received 699 responses out of 2160 e-mails during four months with a response rate of 32.36% that was quite impressive; the details of responses have depicted in table no.1 below. After scrutinizing responses, 124 were eliminated because some were incomplete, and some were rejected due to unclear responses and missing values. Finally, we selected only 575 responses that fell within the calculated sample size range (i.e., 230 to 690) for further analysis to answer the study`s questions.

Table 1. Data collection process

Countries	#	Universities	E-surveys sent	E-surveys received	Response rate
Stratum-I					
Pakistan	1	Lahore University of Management Sciences	40	12	30.00%
	2	National University of Science and Technology	40	19	47.50%
	3	Iqra University	40	17	42.50%
	4	Sukkur, Institute of Business Administration	40	12	30.00%
	5	National College of Business Administration & Economics	40	14	35.00%
	6	GC University Faisalabad	40	18	45.00%
	7	Comsats	40	13	32.50%
	8	Quaid-e-Azam University Islamabad	40	6	15.00%
	9	Riphah International University Islamabad	40	16	40.00%
	10	Institute of Management Sciences Peshawar	40	12	30.00%
India	11	Indian Institute of Management	40	18	45.00%
	12	Indian School of Business (ISB)	40	14	35.00%
	13	Jamnalal Bajaj Institute of Management Studies	40	16	40.00%
	14	Department of Management Studies, IIT-Delhi	40	12	30.00%
	15	NMIMS School of Business Management	40	19	47.50%
	16	University Business School, Punjab University (UBS)	40	14	35.00%
	17	Taxila Business School	40	11	27.50%
	18	Loyola Institute of Business Administration	40	13	32.50%
	19	Jagan Institute of Management Studies	40	14	35.00%
	20	Jindal Global Business School	40	16	40.00%
Bangladesh	21	North-South University (NSU)	40	18	45.00%
	22	BRAC University	40	22	55.00%
	23	East-West University	40	18	45.00%
	24	Independent University	40	14	35.00%
	25	Daffodil International University (DIU)	40	16	40.00%
	26	United International University (UIU)	40	19	47.50%
	27	American International University Bangladesh (AIUB)	40	12	30.00%
	28	University of Asia Pacific	40	11	27.50%
	29	South East University	40	15	37.50%
	30	International Islamic University Chittagong	40	17	42.50%

continues on following page

Table 1. Continued

Countries	#	Universities	E-surveys sent	E-surveys received	Response rate
Stratum-II					
Italy	31	Università Carlo Cattaneo	40	8	20.00%
	32	Università degli Studi di Bari	40	7	17.50%
	33	Università degli Studi di Cagliari	40	9	22.50%
	34	Università degli Studi di Milano	40	5	12.50%
	35	Università degli Studi di Pavia	40	11	27.50%
	36	Università degli Studi di Perugia	40	4	10.00%
	37	Università degli Studi di Trieste	40	8	20.00%
	38	Università degli Studi di Verona	40	14	35.00%
	39	Università degli Studi Roma Tre	40	13	32.50%
	40	University of Milan (IULM)	40	14	35.00%
Spain	41	ESADE Business School (Barcelona)	40	9	22.50%
	42	ESERP Business School (Barcelona, Madrid, Palma de Mallorca)	40	17	42.50%
	43	Schellhammer Business School (Málaga)	40	12	30.00%
	44	IESE Business School (Barcelona, Madrid)	40	16	40.00%
	45	EADA Business School (Barcelona)	40	15	37.50%
	46	GBSB Global Business Schools in Spain (Barcelona, Madrid)	40	13	32.50%
	47	EU Business School (Barcelona)	40	18	45.00%
	48	United International Business Schools in Spain (Barcelona, Madrid)	40	12	30.00%
	49	Toulouse Business School (Barcelona)	40	9	22.50%
	50	Geneva Business Schools in Spain (Barcelona, Madrid)	40	15	37.50%
Portugal	51	University of Porto	40	4	10.00%
	52	University of Lisbon	40	8	20.00%
	53	University of Coimbra	40	7	17.50%
	54	Universidade NOVA de Lisboa	40	3	7.50%
Total			**2160**	**699**	**32.36%**

3.4 Measurement Instrument

The questionnaire has four sections; the first section is demographic characteristics based, the second is based on independent variables, the third is based on three mediators' items, and the last is based on dependent variable measurement items (Fornell and Larcker, 1981a). All our measurements were based on a 5-point Likert scale from "1= strongly disagree" to "5=strongly agree," except the dependent variable was based on a nominal scale. The control variables have also been measured as the respondents' demographic characteristics like age, gender, education field, and region (Norman, 2010).

Entrepreneurial Alertness - the researchers adapted 28 items from the study (Tang et al., 2012) to measure the only independent variable of entrepreneurial Alertness. Kaish and Gilad (1991) to measure the dimension of scanning and searching were based on these studies, so the second dimension of association and connection was based on the research work of (Gaglio & Katz, 2001; Kirzner, 1999). Lastly, the dimension of evaluation and judgment was based on published work (Crocker et al., 1984). Then, it was decided to adopt only thirteen items recently validated through scale validation (Tang et al., 2012).

Table 2. Descriptive analysis of social and demographic characteristics

Variables	Socio-Demographics	Percentage	Frequency	Mean	SD
Gender	Male	68.2%	392	0.32	0.467
	Female	31.8%	183		
Age	24-28	17.7%	102	2.30	0.855
	29-32	42.1%	242		
	33-36	31.8%	183		
	37-40	8.3%	48		
Edu_Field	Business	82.1%	472	0.18	0.385
	Nonbusiness	17.9%	103		
Region	South Asia	62.1%	375	0.38	.486
	South Europe	37.9%	218		

Note: SD = Standard Deviation.
Source: Self-generated

Opportunity recognition - (Shane et al., 2010) The first mediating variable is opportunity recognition; it has been measured through 8 adapted items from the mixture of three previous studies (McMullen & Shepherd, 2006). Opportunity discovery and creation - to measure two second and third mediating variables, the scholar has adapted five items for opportunity discovery and six items for opportunity creation from the study derived from the primary research (Craig and Johnson, 2006). New venture creation - the ability to turn the ideas into entrepreneurial action refers to entrepreneurial behavior and Alertness. The new venture creation process is understanding entrepreneurial opportunities and their implementation. The ten items have been selected based on previous studies and measured by nominal scale based on venture creation activities (Shirokova et al., 2016). First, each respondent attempted how many activities were divided by the total activities. Then, it was calculated through a summative approach for further analysis. The social and demographic characteristics of the study respondents have explained in Table 2.

3.5 Serial Mediation Model

The one thing that is very important to understand before pursuing a multiple mediation model is whether study variables have connections with each other or not. If they have connections, then it is a serial mediation and parallel mediation vice versa. In the current study, all the mediators have well-established connections theoretically. We developed a serial mediation model on that foundation, with three indirect and one direct relation. It is based on model-6 prescribed by (Hayes, 2015; Yang et al., 2021) in templates for SPSS and SAS. Furthermore, we have matured the mathematical expression for the said serial mediation model to enhance its generalizability and understanding widely.

This mathematical expression describes the direct relation from one to three mediators through X to Y:

$$X \to M_1 \to Y$$

$$X \to M_1 \to M_2 \to Y$$

$$X \to M_1 \to M_3 \to Y$$

$$X \to M_2 \to M_3 \to Y$$

$$X \to M_1 \to M_2 \to M_3 \to Y$$

Figure 6. Structural model

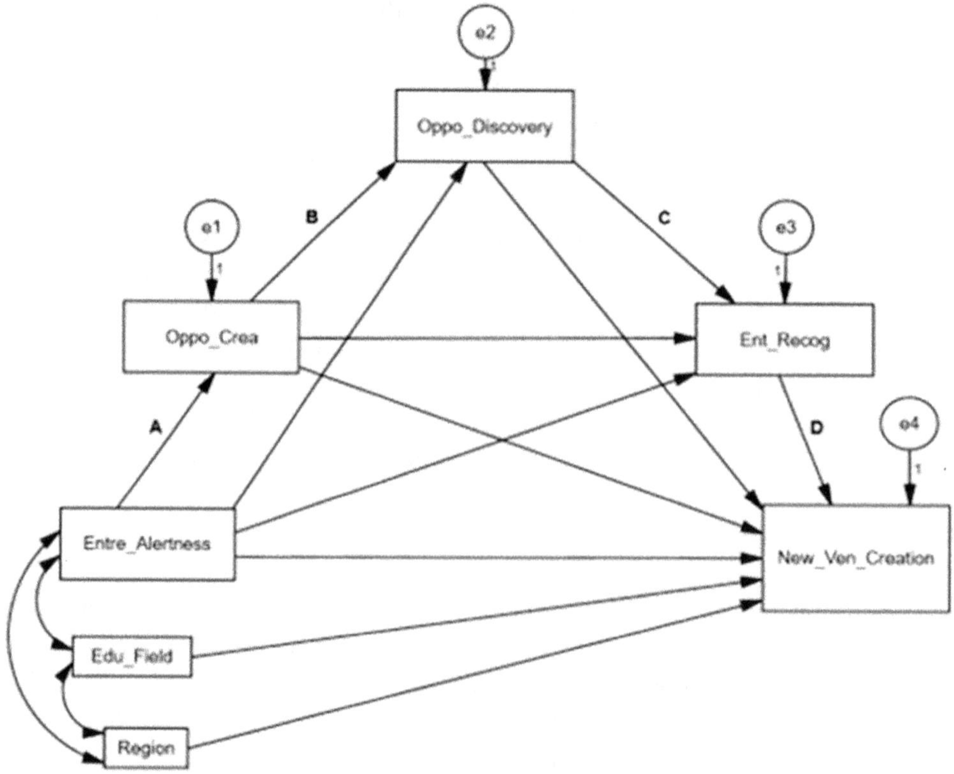

The serial mediation model for three mediators has been expressed into five equations. The first indirect effect of X (EA) on Y (NVC) through the first mediator (OC) is M1(a1 b1), the second indirect effect of X (EA) on Y (NVC) through first (OC) and second (OD) mediators is M1*M2 (a1 d21 b2). The third indirect effect of X (EA) on Y (NVC) through first (OC) and third (ER) mediators are M1*M2(a1 d31 b3), the fourth indirect effect of X (EA) on Y (NVC) through second (OD) and third (ER) mediators are M2*M3(a2 d32 b3). Finally, the serial mediation of X (EA) on Y (NVC) through first (OC), second (OD), and third (ER) mediators is M1*M2*M3(a1 d21 d32 b3). In this paper, we have used one of the best testing methods approved by antecedent studies (Hassan, Zhang, and Ahmad 2021), the bootstrapping method for serial mediation. In this study, we have used IBM SPSS AMOS v.26 to test this complex model for parametric analysis (IBM, 2019). Our mathematician author has developed a syntax to run AMOS in one shot through user-defined estimand (Gill et al., 2021). The estimand has developed through a syntax based on the labels provided in Figure 6.

4. RESULTS AND ANALYSIS

4.1 Measurement Model

Different approaches are used to analyze the structural relationships among latent and measured variables. This research paper is based on structural equation modeling (SEM) (Islam et al., 2018; Networks & Dhesi, 2020), which is the best approach to conduct multivariate statistical analysis (Kaish & Gilad, 1991; Ahmad et al., 2021). This approach tested the structural model through regression and factor analysis based on some pre-defined theoretical foundation. Furthermore, to develop a robust multivariate statistical model, SEM is advanced in estimating latent and observed variables, testing the imposed structural model for data fitness, and precisely assessing measurement error (Dedahanov et al., 2021).

To conduct SEM, we have applied the exploratory factor analysis (EFA) and confirmatory factor analysis (CFA) based on the results of EFA through principal component analysis (PCA) (Liu et al., 2003; Shirokova et al., 2016). The results of CFA demonstrated that the value of Kaiser-Meyer-Olkin (KMO) was (0.89>0.7) that was excellent to move for further statistical operations. In addition, Bartlett's test of Sphericity was significant; it established that our collected data had desired structural validity to perform factor analysis. The components above (eigenvalue> 1) explained 74.86% variation and were equal to study variables (Edelbroek et al., 2019).

Table 3. Measurement model fit during CFA

		First Model Fit		Revised Model Fit	
Measure	**Threshold**	**Estimate**	**Interpretation**	**Estimate**	**Interpretation**
CMIN/DF	Between 1 and 3	5.619	Terrible	2.470	Excellent
CFI	>0.95	0.850	Need More DF	0.954	Excellent
SRMR	<0.08	0.045	Excellent	0.037	Excellent
RMSEA	<0.06	0.108	Terrible	0.058	Excellent

Note: CMIN =chi square fit, DF = degree of freedom, CFI = Comparative Fit Index, RMSEA = Root Mean Square Error of Approximation, SRMR = Standardized Root Mean Square Residual

Source of Threshold: Hu, L., Bentler, P.M. (1999), "Cutoff Criteria for Fit Indexes in Covariance Structure Analysis: Conventional Criteria Versus New Alternatives" SEM vol. 6(1), pp. 1-55.

Source: Self-generated

During the first test of model fit, measures like CMIN/DF (5.619; Between 1 and 3) were terrible, CFI (0.85 >0.95) needed more DF, and RMSEA (0.108 <0.06) was terrible also. However, after the suggested revision, All the measures have improved in extraordinary was like CMIN/DF (2.47; Between 1 and 3) was excellent, CFI (0.954 >0.95) was excellent, SRMS (0.037 <0.08) was excellent, and RMSEA (0.058 <0.06) was also excellent (Fornell and Larcker, 1981b). So, our model has achieved the required level of data fitness exhibited in Table 3.

The integral part of the parametric analysis of the measurement model is the validity and reliability test (Rosenbach et al., 2009). It has been discussed in the following sequence: construct reliability, convergent validity, discriminant validity, and Nomological validity. Table 3 exhibits the measurement of master validity, including all the said parameters. Firstly, to measure the construct reliability that is more related to respondents has the approaches of Cronbach alpha (Cronbach, 1951) and composite reliability (CR) have been implemented (Raykov, 1997).

The computed values of Cronbach alpha ranged from 0.791 to 0.959 expressed the excellent degree of inter-item consistency ratio, and the values of CR ranged from 0.775 to 0.958 threshold (*ie., CR*>0.7), referred the excellent reliability foundation of the construct. Secondly, to assess the convergent validity the average variance extracted (AVE) has computed and found that all the values are above the threshold (*i.e., AVE*>0.5), and the attainment of this expression (*i.e., CR*>*AVE*), table no. 4 confirms the satisfactory level of convergent validity. Thirdly, this study computed the square roots of the AVEs values more excellent than the correlation between other factors to find out the discriminant validity. Based on their approach, it has been determined that the diagonal value of each factor is greater than the sum of square roots of its correlation (Fornell and Larcker, 1981b), and the result is satisfactorily exhibited in Table 4.

This study has applied the second and recently more common approach of heterotrait–monotrait (HTMT) ratio (Voorhees et al., 2016). This technique provides more significant results as compared to the first approach. To determine HTMT, we found that the average of the correlations between the study factors was below the threshold (*i.e., HTMT*<0.85), has achieved (Henseler et al., 2015). Related to construct reliability and validity, before moving to the next step of structural model evaluation, we tested nomological validity to develop a robust model (Watson, 2015). The convergent validity assured that the construct is correlated with other know constructs of the concept and literature. The discriminant validity confirmed the theoretical concepts and similar literature dichotomy. So, the nomological validity demonstrated that the scale successfully established the relationship between antecedent studies and theories. This nomological network confirmed the relationship between this research's theoretical framework and structural model (Spiro and Weitz, 1990).

Table 4. Master validity and reliability model

Variables	CR	AVE	MSV	Alpha	1	2	3	4	5	Collinearity Statistics	
										Tolera	VIF
Ent_Alert	0.958	0.639	0.040	0.959	**0.79**					.726	1.378
Ent_Rec	0.957	0.735	0.179	0.957	0.04	**0.86**				.920	1.087
Oppo_Cre	0.949	0.756	0.167	0.959	0.20***	0.24***	**0.87**			.808	1.237
Oppo_Dis	0.942	0.766	0.179	0.944	0.17***	0.43***	0.41***	**0.87**		.806	1.240
NVC	0.775	0.714	0.124	0.791	0.154	0.236	0.35	0.48	**0.71**	.718	1.457

Note: † $p < 0.100$, * $p < 0.050$, ** $p < 0.010$, *** $p < 0.001$, CR =composite reliability, AVE=average extracted value, MSV=maximum shared value, VIF=Variance Inflation Factor.

Values between the diagonal are the correlations between constructs.

Source of Threshold: Hu, L., Bentler, P.M. (1999), "Cutoff Criteria for Fit Indexes in Covariance Structure Analysis: Conventional Criteria Versus New Alternatives" SEM vol. 6(1), pp. 1-55.

Source: Self-generated.

Common Method Variance (CMV) Bias- this research collected data for exogenous and endogenous variables from the same source and within the same period. So, there could be the problem of common method variance (CMV) bias. Although, the questionnaire has been validated through different modern techniques, including content and constructs reliability. Even though we have utilized the two most commonly used statistical tools to identify the possibility of CMV, firstly, the data has processed through Harmon single-factor techniques by adding all the items and fixed number of factors as one and found that it explained only 31.53% variation that eliminates the existence of CMV (Podsakoff et al., 2003). Secondly, this study treated to implement the common latent factor (CLF) in AMOS; after comparing the standardized and unstandardized regression weights, we did not find any considerable difference among items more than 0.02%. This is how the latest technique also ruled out the possible existence of CMV (Williams & McGonagle, 2016; Gill et al., 2021).

4.2 Structural Model

In multiple regression analysis, the variance inflation factor (VIF) was tested to measure the possibility of multicollinearity (Neter et al., 1990). It would indicate the expected presence of multicollinearity if the variance increased for the regression coefficient. To verify this assumption, we have calculated the collinearity statistics and the values of VIF are between the threshold range ($1 > VIF < 10$), based on the results the data has ruled out the symptoms of multicollinearity (Kalnins, 2018). A robust regression model must not be the case with the symptoms of heteroskedasticity

(Breusch and Pagan, 1979). We tested this study model because it has five variables to deal with regression to verify the evidence of heteroskedasticity. After computing the square of residuals (sqres), we run the regression model by taking (sqres) as the outcome variable against the four predictors. The results of regression analysis supported the threshold (*Sig*>0.05), proved true against all the p-values of this study predictors (eg., X:0.134>0.05, M1:0.262>0.05, M2:0.475>0.05, M3:0.367>0.05) (Halunga et al., 2017).

Hayes (2015) based on his study, the results of serial mediation through user-defined estimands have been performed and exhibited in Tables 5 and 6. The entrepreneurial Alertness influenced positively to opportunity creation (A: β = 0.184, p-value .00 < 0.05), this phenomenon verified the H1. The entrepreneurial Alertness has positive and direct relationship with new venture creation (par_8: β = 0.106, p-value .02 < 0.05), opportunity creation has impacted positively on new venture creation (par_7: β = 0.028, p-value .04 < 0.05). The indirect impact has decreased on new venture creation compared to direct impact. So, H2 has verified partial mediation. The first mediator opportunity creation has positive and significant relationship with second mediator opportunity discovery (B: β = 0.381, p-value .000 < 0.05), opportunity discovery has positive and significant impact on new venture creation (par_5: β = 0.21, p-value .002 < 0.05). The indirect impacts of the first mediator and second mediator have increased compared to direct impact, so H3 verified a full serial mediation of opportunity creation and opportunity discovery between entrepreneurial Alertness and new venture creation.

Table 5. Analysis of structural model

			Label	β	SE-SE	Bootstrap	95%CI
Entre_Alertness	→	Oppo_Crea	A	.184	.001	.070	.290
Oppo_Crea	→	Oppo_Discovery	B	.381	.001	.278	.475
Entre_Alertness	→	Oppo_Discovery	par_12	.097	.000	.010	.183
Oppo_Crea	→	Ent_Recog	par_6	.118	.001	.008	.218
Oppo_Discovery	→	Ent_Recog	C	.377	.001	.259	.488
Entre_Alertness	→	Ent_Recog	par_13	.100	.000	.011	.185
Oppo_Discovery	→	New_Ven_Creation	par_5	.210	.001	.108	.226
Ent_Recog	→	New_Ven_Creation	D	.031	.001	.056	.112
Oppo_Crea	→	New_Ven_Creation	par_7	.028	.001	.075	.131
Entre_Alertness	→	New_Ven_Creation	par_8	.106	.000	.089	.235
Edu_Field	→	New_Ven_Creation	par_9	.023	.000	-.074	.120
Region	→	New_Ven_Creation	par_10	.034	.000	-.061	.133

Note: Label=The paths of the model, CI=Confidence Interval
Source: Self-generated

The path (A: $\beta = 0.184$, p-value $.00 < 0.05$) has already been proved positive, (par_6: $\beta = 0.118$, p-value $.03 < 0.05$) also emerged positively significant. The path (D: $\beta = 0.31$, p-value $.04 < 0.05$) proved a significantly positive indirect relation of mediator one opportunity creation and mediator third entrepreneurial recognition. Consequently (D: $\beta = 0.31$, p-value $.04 < 0.05$) showed an increased mediated impact than that of (par_8: $\beta = 0.106$, p-value $.02 < 0.05$) the direct relationship that observed partial mediation and hypothesis H4 has been accepted based on the discussion. The path (par_12: $\beta = 0.97$, p-value $.03 < 0.05$) evident significantly positive direct relation between entrepreneurial alertness and opportunity discovery.

Whereas path (C: $\beta = 0.377$, p-value $.00 < 0.05$) demonstrated a strong positively significant relation between opportunity discover and opportunity recognition. During the analysis of the H4, path D has been tested positively significantly. It has been concluded that opportunity discovery and opportunity recognition also mediated the direct relationship partially. However, all the direct and indirect relationships have been tested and proved positively significant. It also depicted the partial mediation relations between single and double mediation and accepted the hypothesis H5 of this study. Nevertheless, this study's most interesting and real contribution was the one-shot calculation of serial mediation through user-defined estimation (Serial mediation = 0.15, p-value $.04 < 0.05$). Indeed the direct relation was (par_8: $\beta = 0.106$, p-value $.04 < 0.05$), and serial mediation enhanced the serial impact in a positive direction that proved a partial serial mediation and results accepted hypothesis H6 categorically.

5. DISCUSSION

5.1 Theoretical Contributions

This study has accepted H1 that entrepreneurial Alertness positively impacted opportunity creation. That aligned with the study of (Tang and Tang, 2012), where he investigated that entrepreneurial Alertness has a positive relationship with innovative business ideas and ventures. Because new entrepreneurial opportunities could easily be dragged through entrepreneur alertness. Scheaf et al. (2020) witnessed that entrepreneurial Alertness developed the cognitive domain of individuals to muster up their knowledge, skill, and expertise to start a business venture. A recent study Sassetti et al. (2021) established a positive relationship of entrepreneurial Alertness including two dimensions only (e.g., searching and scanning) between the decision-making about business creation. So, the current study contributed a shred of solid literature evidence to the scholarly discussion about the role of entrepreneurial Alertness towards new venture creation .

Table 6. Hypothesis testing

Hypotheses			Label	Estimate	Lower	Upper	P-value
Entre_Alertness	→	Oppo_Crea	A	.184	.070	.290	.001
Oppo_Crea	→	Oppo_Discovery	B	.381	.278	.475	.000
Entre_Alertness	→	Oppo_Discovery	par_12	.097	.010	.183	.030
Oppo_Crea	→	Ent_Recog	par_6	.118	.008	.218	.037
Oppo_Discovery	→	Ent_Recog	C	.377	.259	.488	.000
Entre_Alertness	→	Ent_Recog	par_13	.100	.011	.185	.031
Oppo_Discovery	→	New_Ven_Creation	par_5	.210	.108	.226	.025
Ent_Recog	→	New_Ven_Creation	D	.031	.056	.112	.041
Oppo_Crea	→	New_Ven_Creation	par_7	.028	.075	.131	.042
Entre_Alertness	→	New_Ven_Creation	par_8	.106	.089	.235	.025
Edu_Field	→	New_Ven_Creation	par_9	.023	-.074	.120	.631
Region	→	New_Ven_Creation	par_10	.034	.061	.133	.492
User-defined estimands							
Serial Mediation				**.15**	**.068**	**.285**	**.004**

Note: Label=The paths of model, P=Significant level
Source: Self-generated

The H2 of this study proved a significantly positive relationship between opportunity creation and opportunity discovery. That unfolded the importance of studying the combination of these two variables. In contrast, a confused discussion was reported between the scholars of the theory of opportunity and discovery. There are two schools of thought on this phenomenon that were the reason to study these variables again. A recent study conducted in Pakistani perspective (Li et al., 2020) emphasized the strongly correlated association of opportunity discovery and creation on business creation behaviour. Simultaneously Jiatong et al. (2021) added in the literature that there is no need to study opportunity discovery and creation at the same time because opportunity creation has more strength than opportunity discovery. However, current research concluded the confusion of the literature through an endorsement to study both the variables simultaneously.

The H3 of this study has tested partial mediation of opportunity creation and discovery between entrepreneurial Alertness and new venture creation. Once again, enhance the need to study the opportunity creation and discovery juxtaposed as mediators. Lins et al. (2017), and Shane (2013) studied the mediation role of opportunity discovery and established a partial mediation so, the result of H3 has extended the finding of this cited study. In another study Puhakka (2011) the mediation role of opportunity creation has been studied. A weak scholarly discussion is available on the multiple mediations of opportunity creation and discovery that this study has filled.

In the same way Bhave (1994), and J. Tang et al. (2012) developed the positive relationship of opportunity recognition with entrepreneurial Alertness, but very few studies investigated its mediated role in the particular relationship between entrepreneurial Alertness and new venture creation. However, strong connections in literature have been developed about the positive role of entrepreneurial recognition on venture creation (Chang Chieh Hang & Garnsey, 2012; Félix Gonzâlez et al., 2017). So, the H4 and H5 have turned to be a unique relationship in this study settings.

The last but historical relationship of hypothesis H6 tested a partial serial mediation of opportunity creation, opportunity discovery, and entrepreneurial recognition between the relationship of entrepreneurial Alertness and new venture creation. The current study has categorically claimed that no literature has covered this gap addressed by H6. Indeed, all these variables have been studied in previously published work separately or with different settings (Kirzner, 1999; Lins et al., 2017). However, the current study served the entrepreneurship theory with a comprehensive model of new venture creation through the systematic coordination of entrepreneurial opportunities and Alertness (Boudreaux et al., 2019; Sassetti et al., 2021; Gill et al., 2021).

5.2 Practical Implications

The ultimate findings of this research have numerous practical implications that could impact multifaceted dimensions. This study has empirically developed a single robust model with solid theoretical roots. One looking to establish a business venture could promptly get guidance from this model. Individuals with entrepreneurial intentions tried to get an expert opinion from the field scholars to find the right path, so this model presented a squeezed solution. The entrepreneurs have to start from entrepreneurial Alertness, and they need to enhance their understanding about their sounding to collect the information. They must respond to the developments happing in the business market. To get the knowledge on industry or relevant sector entrepreneurs connected with the mainstream business activities to adopt more business sensitivity.

The investors used to attain more knowledge about the business rivulet they are interested in, and if the opportunities are not coming to them, they have to be equipped to create the opportunities. If they have less investment and a short time, they cannot wait for an opportunity to overtake. They can create an appropriate environment to start a business venture in this situation. Exclusively the results of this study connected individuals with the stages of new venture creation established in this robust model. Once the investors and individuals with entrepreneurial mindset have time and space, they would wait for an opportunity to discover. Nevertheless, it would happen if they continuously searched the economic activities in the economy. They should be well informed, educated, or knowledgeable about the market competition. The results revealed that entrepreneurial recognition played a pivotal role in aligning entrepreneurial Alertness and opportunities towards new venture creation.

It was purported that management is a GOD gifted skill and nobody can learn it in the far age. The modern World understands that management is a skill set that can be learned through a well-defined education process. An inevitable facet of this research also belonged to business or entrepreneurial education. Sassetti et al. (2021) based on their results, the entrepreneurial skill could be developed in more effectuated manners (Gaglio and Katz, 2001). The present study endorsed the strategy they suggested adopting for educational institutions or Universities. The targeted sector of the current study is specifically Universities of south Asia and Europe, so it suggested adding a practice-based curriculum for business and entrepreneurial programs learners. Universities need to get guidance from the model developed in this study to articulate their scheme of studies to increase the impact of the learners' entrepreneurial skills. It would enhance their capacity to drive their educational learning towards the creation of business venture that is the pivotal objective of business and entrepreneurial education. Whereas, it has resulted in the present study through control variables that there is no role of regional and education field factors on the overall study settings and model formation. However, both regions need to study the impact of this model based on its generalizability. Indeed, the entrepreneurial skill-based pedagogy has similar benefits for business and non-business education fields.

Developing countries are already facing the unemployment crisis that is increasing poverty. Woefully the pandemic of Covid-19 surges the ratio of unemployment through job reduction globally. However, the most pernicious consequences have been faced by the developing countries. Well, the present study presented a robust model to confront the challenge. The policymakers devoured to develop allure with entrepreneurial opportunities. They need to articulate social protection policies by considering the provision of entrepreneurial opportunities for the establishment to new venture creation. It would decrease the unemployment ratio and economic problems of the marginalized population sector. The assimilation of educationist and economist policymakers could develop a rivulet of opportunities for unemployed youth.

5.3 Implications for Future Research

The current research might have some limitations and constraints in its morphed. The outcome variable has been measured on the nominal scale because the literature on venture creation has not reported a Likert scale construct yet. In the future, scholars could adopt or develop a construct based on the Likert scale to eliminate the construct scale dichotomy. The present study respondents were University students of master's and doctorate. In future research, the under graduation students could be included or studied separately. That would enhance the scope of the study and sample size.

To deal with this research in the pandemic, the authors adopted the electronic survey technique to collect the data. The upcoming researcher could find international collaborations to collect data physically and from multiple regions of the World. The present study only emphasized and targeted the pedagogical articulation rather than incorporating the extra curriculum activities for entrepreneurial skill development. The model developed in this study did not provide fully comprehensive, and in the future, it could be tested with the inclusion of behavioral constructs like entrepreneurial self-efficacy and entrepreneurial intentions.

Finally concluded with the inclusion of some stereotype limitations the most studies (Zhao et al. 2021) have, in pursuit of enhancing the generalizability of this robust model, researchers from different regions of the World could replicate its testing in different study settings. The mixed-method approach of abductive research methodology could add value to these results. To analyze the propensity of this model the temporal investigation could define its effectiveness in a more sophisticated manner rather than cross-sectional.

5.4 Conclusion

This research submitted value in the body of knowledge that researchers have left in the literature unanswered about the simplified model for new venture creation. The conceptual framework identified and answered helps the authors and practitioners of entrepreneurship carry this research as the plinth of their future research and practice about the formation of new ventures. This paper also established a solid literary foundation to explore the relationship between entrepreneurial Alertness and new venture creation. Furthermore, it explored a simplified and overt role of entrepreneurial opportunities available to study and followed by the researchers and entrepreneurs. Finally, our research intensified the entrepreneurial activities even more by the researchers and scholars of the field that promoted the subject and practice of entrepreneurship theory.

REFERENCES

Ab Hamid, M. R., Sami, W., & Mohmad Sidek, M. H. (2017). Discriminant Validity Assessment: Use of Fornell & Larcker criterion versus HTMT Criterion. *Journal of Physics: Conference Series*, *890*, 012163. doi:10.1088/1742-6596/890/1/012163

Adomako, S., Danso, A., Boso, N., & Narteh, B. (2018). Entrepreneurial Alertness and new venture performance: Facilitating roles of networking capability. *Int. Small Bus. J. Res. Entrep.* doi:10.1177/0266242617747667

Ahmad, A. R., Hassan, A., Alhammadi, Y., & Jameel, A. S. (2021). National Culture. *Leadership Styles and Job Satisfaction : An Empirical Study in the United Arab Emirates*, *8*, 1111–1120. doi:10.13106/jafeb.2021.vol8.no6.1111

Al-Refaie, A. (2015). Effects of human resource management on hotel performance using structural equation modeling. *Computers in Human Behavior*, *43*, 293–303. doi:10.1016/j.chb.2014.11.016

Alvarez, S. A., & Barney, J. B. (2007). *Discovery and Creation: Alternative Theories of Entrepreneurial Action*. Rev. Organ. em Context., doi:10.15603/1982-8756/roc.v3n6p123-152

Alvarez, S. A., & Barney, J. B. (2010). *Entrepreneurship and epistemology: The philosophical underpinnings of the study of entrepreneurial opportunities*. Acad. Manag. Ann. doi:10.1080/19416520.2010.495521

Alvarez, S. A., Barney, J. B., & Newman, A. M. B. (2015). The poverty problem and the industrialization solution. *Asia Pacific Journal of Management*, *32*(1), 23–37. doi:10.100710490-014-9397-5

Barreto, H., & Kirzner, I. (1986). Discovery and the Capitalist Process. *Southern Economic Journal*, *53*(2), 529. doi:10.2307/1059434

Begley, T.M., & Boyd, D.P. (1987). Psychological characteristics associated with performence in entrepreneurial firms and smaller businesses. *J. Bus. Ventur.* doi:10.1016/0883-9026(87)90020-6

Bergner, S., Kanape, A., & Rybnicek, R. (2019). Taking an Interest in Taking the Lead: The Influence of Vocational Interests, Leadership Experience and Success on the Motivation to Lead. *Applied Psychology*, *68*(1), 202–219. doi:10.1111/apps.12150

Bhave, M. P. (1994). A process model of entrepreneurial venture creation. Journal of Business Venturing. doi:10.1016/0883-9026(94)90031-0

Boudreaux, C.J., Nikolaev, B.N., & Klein, P. (2019). Socio-cognitive traits and entrepreneurship: The moderating role of economic institutions. *J. Bus. Ventur.* doi:10.1016/j.jbusvent.2018.08.003

Breusch, T. S., & Pagan, A. R. (1979). A Simple Test for Heteroscedasticity and Random Coefficient Variation. *Econometrica, 47*(5), 1287. doi:10.2307/1911963

Burnham, J. F. (2006). Scopus database: A review. *Biomedical Digital Libraries, 3*(1), 1. doi:10.1186/1742-5581-3-1 PMID:16522216

Busenitz, L. W., & Lau, C.-M. (1996). A Cross-Cultural Cognitive Model of New Venture Creation. *Entrepreneurship Theory and Practice, 20*(4), 25–40. doi:10.1177/104225879602000403

Carland, J. & Carland, J. (2000). New Venture Creation Model. *J. Bus. Entrep.*

Cochran, W. G. (1948). *Sampling survey techniques. North Carolina State University.* Dept. of Statistics.

Cox, K. C., & Castrogiovanni, G. (2016). Entrepreneurial Alertness, Metacognition, and Opportunity Identification. *Proceedings - Academy of Management, 15008*(1), 15008. doi:10.5465/ambpp.2016.15008abstract

Craig, J. B. L., & Johnson, D. (2006). Establishing individual differences related to opportunity alertness and innovation dependent on academic-career training. *Journal of Management Development, 25*(1), 28–39. doi:10.1108/02621710610637945

Crocker, J., Fiske, S. T., & Taylor, S. E. (1984). Schematic Bases of Belief Change. Attitudinal Judgment. doi:10.1007/978-1-4613-8251-5_10

Cronbach, L. J. (1951). Coefficient alpha and the internal structure of tests. *Psychometrika, 16*(3), 297–334. doi:10.1007/BF02310555

Dedahanov, A. T., Miao, S., & Semyonov, A. A. (2021). When does abusive supervision mitigate work effort? Moderating roles of cognitive reappraisal and rumination. *Leadership and Organization Development Journal, 42*(3), 467–479. doi:10.1108/LODJ-07-2020-0312

Dimov, D. (2011). Grappling With the Unbearable Elusiveness of Entrepreneurial Opportunities. *Entrepreneurship Theory and Practice, 35*(1), 57–81. doi:10.1111/j.1540-6520.2010.00423.x

Easterby-Smith, M., Thorpe, R., & Jackson, P. R. (2015). *Designing Management and Business Research* (5th ed.). Designing Management and Business Research. Manag. Bus. Res.

Edelbroek, R., Peters, P., & Blomme, R. J. (2019). Engaging in open innovation: The mediating role of work engagement in the relationship between transformational and transactional leadership and the quality of the open innovation process as perceived by employees. *Journal of General Management, 45*(1), 5–17. doi:10.1177/0306307019844633

Edwards, J. R., & Lambert, L. S. (2007). Methods for integrating moderation and mediation: A general analytical framework using moderated path analysis. *Psychological Methods, 12*(1), 1–22. doi:10.1037/1082-989X.12.1.1 PMID:17402809

Ekelund, R. B., & Kirzner, I. M. (1974). Competition and Entrepreneurship. *Southern Economic Journal, 41*(1), 155. doi:10.2307/1056112

Etikan, I. (2016). *Comparision of Snowball Sampling and Sequential Sampling Technique*. Biometrics Biostat. Int. J., doi:10.15406/bbij.2016.03.00055

Félix González, M., Husted, B. W., & Aigner, D. J. (2017). Opportunity discovery and creation in social entrepreneurship: An exploratory study in Mexico. *Journal of Business Research, 81*, 212–220. doi:10.1016/j.jbusres.2016.10.032

Forbes, D. P. (1999). Cognitive approaches to new venture creation. *International Journal of Management Reviews, 1*(4), 415–439. doi:10.1111/1468-2370.00021

Foreman, E. K. (1991). *Survey sampling principles*. CRC Press.

Fornell, C., & Larcker, D. F. (1981a). Evaluating Structural Equation Models with Unobservable Variables and Measurement Error. *JMR, Journal of Marketing Research, 18*(1), 39–50. doi:10.1177/002224378101800104

Fornell, C., & Larcker, D.F. (1981b). *Structural equation models with unobservable variables and measurement error: Algebra and statistics.*

Gaglio, C. M., & Katz, J. A. (2001). The Psychological Basis of Opportunity Identification: Entrepreneurial Alertness. *Small Business Economics, 16*(2), 95–111. doi:10.1023/A:1011132102464

Gaskin, J. (2012). Common method bias using common latent factor. [Video]. Youtube, Gaskination's Stat. http//youtube. com/Gaskination,

George, D., & Mallery, P. (2016). *IBM SPSS statistics 23 step by step: A simple guide and reference*. Routledge. doi:10.4324/9781315545899

Gielnik, M.M., Barabas, S., Frese, M., Namatovu-Dawa, R., Scholz, F.A., Metzger, J.R., Walter, T. (2014). A temporal analysis of how entrepreneurial goal intentions, positive fantasies, and action planning affect starting a new venture and when the effects wear off. *J. Bus. Ventur.* doi:10.1016/j.jbusvent.2013.09.002

Gill, S. A., Bencheva, N., Karayel, S., & Usman, M. (2021). Does entrepreneurial self-efficacy moderate effects of cognitive flexibility and entrepreneurial Alertness on entrepreneurial intentions? *Entrepreneurial Business and Economics Review, 9*(3), 25–41. doi:10.15678/EBER.2021.090302

Gozukara, I., & Colakoglu, N. (2016). Enhancing Entrepreneurial Intention and Innovativeness of University Students: The Mediating Role of Entrepreneurial Alertness. *International Business Research, 9*(2), 34. doi:10.5539/ibr.v9n2p34

Halunga, A. G., Orme, C. D., & Yamagata, T. (2017). A heteroskedasticity robust Breusch–Pagan test for Contemporaneous correlation in dynamic panel data models. *Journal of Econometrics, 198*(2), 209–230. doi:10.1016/j.jeconom.2016.12.005

Hang, C. C., Garnsey, E., & Ruan, Y. (2013). Opportunity Discovery and Creation in Disruptive Innovation Centre for Technology. *Manag. Work. Pap. Ser.* 1–44.

Hang, C. C., & Garnsey, E. W. 2012. Opportunities and Resources for Disruptive Technological Innovation. SSRN *Electron. J.* doi:10.2139/ssrn.1923036

Hattwick, R. E. (1979). Perception, opportunity and profit. *The Journal of Behavioral Economics, 8*(2), 183–188. doi:10.1016/0090-5720(79)90012-3

Hayes, A. F. (2015). An Index and Test of Linear Moderated Mediation. *Multivariate Behavioral Research, 50*(1), 1–22. doi:10.1080/00273171.2014.962683 PMID:26609740

Hayton, J., Chandler, G. N., & DeTienne, D. R. (2011). Entrepreneurial opportunity identification and new firm development processes: A comparison of family and non-family new ventures. *International Journal of Entrepreneurship and Innovation Management, 13*(1), 12–31. doi:10.1504/IJEIM.2011.038445

Heinisch, O. & Cochran, W. G. (1965). Sampling Techniques, 2. John Wiley and Sons. doi:10.1002/bimj.19650070312

Helfat, C. E., & Peteraf, M. A. (2015). Managerial cognitive capabilities and the microfoundations of dynamic capabilities. *Strategic Management Journal, 36*(6), 831–850. doi:10.1002mj.2247

Henseler, J., Ringle, C. M., & Sarstedt, M. (2015). A new criterion for assessing discriminant validity in variance-based structural equation modeling. *Journal of the Academy of Marketing Science*, *43*(1), 115–135. doi:10.100711747-014-0403-8

IBM. (2019). *KMO and Bartlett's Test* [WWW Document]. IBM Knowl. Cent.

Islam, T., Ali, G., Aziz Khan Niazi, A., Ramzan, M., & Yousaf, U. (2018). Employees' Response to CSR: Role of Organizational Identification and Organizational Trust. *Pakistan J. Commer. Soc. Sci.*, *12*, 153–166. doi:10.1111/j.0001-6349.2005.00765.x

Jiao, H., Cui, Y., Zhu, Y., & Chen, J. (2014). Building entrepreneurs' innovativeness through knowledge management: The mediating effect of entrepreneurial Alertness. *Technology Analysis and Strategic Management*, *26*(5), 501–516. doi:10.1080/09537325.2013.872774

Jiatong, W., Murad, M., Li, C., Gill, S. A., & Ashraf, S. F. (2021). Linking cognitive flexibility to entrepreneurial Alertness and entrepreneurial intention among medical students with the moderating role of entrepreneurial self-efficacy: A second-order moderated mediation model. *PLoS One*, *16*(9), e0256420. doi:10.1371/journal.pone.0256420 PMID:34559823

Kahle, L. R., & Malhotra, N. K. (1994). Marketing Research: An Applied Orientation. *JMR, Journal of Marketing Research*, *31*(1), 137. doi:10.2307/3151953

Kaish, S., Gilad, B., 1991. Characteristics of opportunities search of entrepreneurs versus executives: Sources, interests, general Alertness. *J. Bus. Ventur.* doi:10.1016/0883-9026(91)90005-X

Kalnins, A. (2018). Multicollinearity: How common factors cause Type 1 errors in multivariate regression. *Strategic Management Journal*, *39*(8), 2362–2385. doi:10.1002mj.2783

Khin, S., & Lim, T. H. (2018). Entrepreneurial opportunity recognition, exploitation and new venture success: Moderating role of prior market and technology knowledge. *J. Leg. Ethical Regul*, (22), 1–6.

Kirzner, I. M. (1999). Creativity and/or Alertness: A reconsideration of the schumpeterian entrepreneur. *The Review of Austrian Economics*, *11*(1/2), 5–17. doi:10.1023/A:1007719905868

Kirzner, I. M. (2000). Entrepreneurial discovery and the competitive market process: an Austrian approach. In *The Driving Force of the Market* (pp. 15–52). Routledge. doi:10.4324/9780203465974-5

Kirzner, I. M., Hebert, R. F., & Link, A. N. (1983). The Entrepreneur, Mainstream Views and Radical Critiques. *Southern Economic Journal*, *50*(2), 611. doi:10.2307/1058249

Kuckertz, A., Kollmann, T., Krell, P., & Stöckmann, C. (2017). Understanding, differentiating, and measuring opportunity recognition and opportunity exploitation. *International Journal of Entrepreneurial Behaviour & Research*, *23*(1), 78–97. doi:10.1108/IJEBR-12-2015-0290

Li, C., Murad, M., Ashraf, S. F., Syed, N., & Riaz, M. (2020). Entrepreneurial nascent behaviour: The role of causation process in opportunity discovery and creation. *Entrepreneurial Business and Economics Review*, *8*(4), 183–200. doi:10.15678/EBER.2020.080410

Lins, F.A., Doktor, R.H., Park, J.Y., Sung, C.S., Im, I., Davidsson, P., & Alvarez, S., Barney, J.B., Waterman, A.S., Vodă, A.I., Florea, N., Hang, C.C., Garnsey, E., Ruan, Y., Félix González, M., Husted, B.W., Aigner, D.J., Kerr, S.P., Kerr, W.R., Xu, T., Mahmood, T.M.A.T., Al Mamun, A., Bin Ahmad, G., Ibrahim, M.D., Alvarez, S. a, Barney, J.B., Shane, S., Abbasianchavari, A., Moritz, A., Frese, M., & Gielnik, M.M. (. (2017). Personality traits of entrepreneurs: A review of recent literature. *Sustain.*, *11*, 123–152. doi:10.3390u11041192

Liu, R. X., Kuang, J., Gong, Q., & Hou, X. L. (2003). Principal component regression analysis with SPSS. *Computer Methods and Programs in Biomedicine*, *71*(2), 141–147. doi:10.1016/S0169-2607(02)00058-5 PMID:12758135

Lumpkin, G. T., & Dess, G. G. (1996). Clarifying the entrepreneurial orientation construct and linking it to performance. *Academy of Management Review*, *21*(1), 135. doi:10.2307/258632

Mackenzie, N., & Knipe, S. (2006). Research dilemmas: Paradigms, methods and methodology. *Issues in Educational Research*, *16*, 193–205.

McDonald, S., Gan, B. C., Fraser, S. S., Oke, A., & Anderson, A. R. (2015). A review of research methods in entrepreneurship 1985-2013. *International Journal of Entrepreneurial Behaviour & Research*, *21*(3), 291–315. doi:10.1108/IJEBR-02-2014-0021

Mehmood, T., Alzoubi, H. M., Alshurideh, M., Al-Gasaymeh, A., & Ahmed, G. (2019). Schumpeterian entrepreneurship theory: Evolution and relevance. *Academy of Entrepreneurship Journal*, *25*, 1–10.

Messersmith, J. G., & Wales, W. J. (2013). Entrepreneurial orientation and performance in young firms: The role of human resource management. *International Small Business Journal*, *31*(2), 115–136. doi:10.1177/0266242611416141

Moradi, E., Jafari, S. M., Doorbash, Z. M., & Mirzaei, A. (2021). *Impact of organizational inertia on business model innovation, open innovation and corporate performance*. Asia Pacific Manag. Rev., doi:10.1016/j.apmrv.2021.01.003

Morse, J.M. (1991). Strategies for sampling. *Qual. Nurs. Res. A Contemp. dialogue* 127–145.

Neter, J., Wasserman, W., & Kutner, M. H. (1990). Multicollinearity diagnostics—Variance inflation factor. Appl. linear. *Statistical Modelling*, 407–411.

Networks, R.A.S. & Dhesi, G. (2020). *Alertness Mixed Approach.*

Norman, G. (2010). Likert scales, levels of measurement and the "laws" of statistics. *Advances in Health Sciences Education : Theory and Practice, 15*(5), 625–632. doi:10.100710459-010-9222-y PMID:20146096

Ozgen, E. & Baron, R.A. (2007). Social sources of information in opportunity recognition: Effects of mentors, industry networks, and professional forums. *J. Bus. Ventur.* doi:10.1016/j.jbusvent.2005.12.001

Podsakoff, P. M., MacKenzie, S. B., Lee, J.-Y., & Podsakoff, N. P. (2003). Common method biases in behavioral research: A critical review of the literature and recommended remedies. *The Journal of Applied Psychology*, *88*(5), 879–903. doi:10.1037/0021-9010.88.5.879 PMID:14516251

Puhakka, V. (2011). Developing a Creative-Cognitive Model of Entrepreneurial Alertness to Business Opportunities. *J. Manag. Strateg.*, *2*(4). doi:10.5430/jms.v2n4p85

Raykov, T. (1997). Estimation of composite reliability for congeneric measures. *Applied Psychological Measurement*, *21*(2), 173–184. doi:10.1177/01466216970212006

Rosenbach, M., Murrell, D. F., Bystryn, J.-C., Dulay, S., Dick, S., Fakharzadeh, S., Hall, R., Korman, N. J., Lin, J., Okawa, J., Pandya, A. G., Payne, A. S., Rose, M., Rubenstein, D., Woodley, D., Vittorio, C., Werth, B. B., Williams, E. A., Taylor, L., & Werth, V. P. (2009). Reliability and Convergent Validity of Two Outcome Instruments for Pemphigus. *The Journal of Investigative Dermatology*, *129*(10), 2404–2410. doi:10.1038/jid.2009.72 PMID:19357707

Ryan, A. B. (2006). Post-Positivist Approaches to Research. In: *Researching and Writing your thesis: a guide for postgraduate students.*

Sassetti, S., Cavaliere, V., & Lombardi, S. (2021). The rhythm of effective entrepreneurs' decision-making process. The pathways of alertness scanning and search and cognitive style. A mediation model. *The International Entrepreneurship and Management Journal*. doi:10.100711365-021-00759-1

Scheaf, D. J., Loignon, A. C., Webb, J. W., Heggestad, E. D., & Wood, M. S. (2020). Measuring opportunity evaluation: Conceptual synthesis and scale development. *Journal of Business Venturing*, *35*(2), 1–26. doi:10.1016/j.jbusvent.2019.04.003

Seerat, S. (2016). Entrepreneurship and Economic Development. *IOSR Journal of Business and Management*, *2*(2), 98–105. doi:10.9790/487X-15010020298-105

Sekaran, U. (2000). *Research methods for business: A skill-building approach*. John Wiley & Sons.

Shambare, R., & Shambare, R. (2019). Presenting a PhD research proposal : A guide for commerce students. *African Journal of Science, Technology, Innovation and Development*, *0*, 1–15. doi:10.1080/20421338.2019.1638586

Shane, S. (2013). The Discovery of Entrepreneurial Opportunities. In *A General Theory of Entrepreneurship* (pp. 448–469). Edward Elgar Publishing. doi:10.4337/9781781007990.00010

Shane, S., Nicolaou, N., Cherkas, L., & Spector, T. D. (2010). Do openness to experience and recognizing opportunities have the same genetic source? *Human Resource Management*, *49*(2), 291–303. doi:10.1002/hrm.20343

Shane, S., & Venkataraman, S. (2000). The Promise of Enterpreneurship as a Field of Research. *Academy of Management Review*, *25*(1), 217. doi:10.2307/259271

Shirokova, G., Osiyevskyy, O., & Bogatyreva, K. (2016). Exploring the intention–behavior link in student entrepreneurship: Moderating effects of individual and environmental characteristics. *European Management Journal*, *34*(4), 386–399. doi:10.1016/j.emj.2015.12.007

Siegel, D. S., & Renko, M. (2012). The role of market and technological knowledge in recognizing entrepreneurial opportunities. *Management Decision*, *50*(5), 797–816. doi:10.1108/00251741211227500

Spiro, R. L., & Weitz, B. A. (1990). Adaptive Selling: Conceptualization, Measurement, and Nomological Validity. *JMR, Journal of Marketing Research*, *27*(1), 61–69. doi:10.1177/002224379002700106

Sternberg, R., & Wennekers, S. (2005). Determinants and effects of new business creation using global entrepreneurship monitor data. *Small Business Economics*, *24*(3), 193–203. doi:10.100711187-005-1974-z

Sweezy, P. (1943). Professpr Schumpter's theory of innovation. *The Review of Economics and Statistics*, *25*(1), 93. doi:10.2307/1924551

Tang, J., Kacmar, K.M.M., & Busenitz, L. (2012). Entrepreneurial Alertness in the pursuit of new opportunities. *J. Bus. Ventur.* doi:10.1016/j.jbusvent.2010.07.001

Tang, Z., & Tang, J. (2012). Entrepreneurial orientation and SME performance in China's changing environment: The moderating effects of strategies. *Asia Pacific Journal of Management*, *29*(2), 409–431. doi:10.100710490-010-9200-1

Teece, D. J. (2006). Reflections on "Profiting from Innovation. *Research Policy*, *35*(8), 1131–1146. doi:10.1016/j.respol.2006.09.009

Voorhees, C. M., Brady, M. K., Calantone, R., & Ramirez, E. (2016). Discriminant validity testing in marketing: An analysis, causes for concern, and proposed remedies. *Journal of the Academy of Marketing Science*, *44*(1), 119–134. doi:10.100711747-015-0455-4

Walter, M. (2006). The Nature of Social Science Research: Asking Social Questions, Seeking Social Answers. *Nat. Soc. Sci. Res.*

Waterman, A. S. (1984). Identity Formation: Discovery or Creation? *The Journal of Early Adolescence*, *4*(4), 329–341. doi:10.1177/0272431684044004

Watson, R. (2015). Quantitative research. *Nursing Standard*, *29*(31), 44–48. doi:10.7748/ns.29.31.44.e8681 PMID:25828021

Wiklund, J., & Shepherd, D. (2003). Knowledge-based resources, entrepreneurial orientation, and the performance of small and medium-sized businesses. *Strategic Management Journal*, *24*(13), 1307–1314. doi:10.1002mj.360

Williams, L. J., & McGonagle, A. K. (2016). Four Research Designs and a Comprehensive Analysis Strategy for Investigating Common Method Variance with Self-Report Measures Using Latent Variables. *Journal of Business and Psychology*, *31*(3), 339–359. doi:10.100710869-015-9422-9

Yang, J., Chang, M., Chen, Z., Zhou, L., & Zhang, J. (2021). The chain mediation effect of spiritual leadership on employees' innovative behavior. *Leadership and Organization Development Journal*, *42*(1), 114–129. doi:10.1108/LODJ-10-2019-0442

Chapter 8
Concept of Microenterprises' Supply Chain Management and Active Flexibility of Micro-Organizations in Bangladesh:
Impact on COVID-19 Aftermath and Russia-Ukraine War

José G. Vargas-Hernandez
Budapest Centre for Long-term Sustainability, Hungary

Muhammad Mahboob Ali
Dhaka School of Economics, University of Dhaka, Bangladesh

ABSTRACT

Microenterprises have a substantial impact on Bangladesh's economy. Supply chain management and dynamic flexibility of a micro-organization in Bangladesh are very important. As such the research question is whether supply chain management and dynamic flexibility for uplifting micro-entrepreneurial organizations are feasible in Bangladesh. The time of the study is 1st September 2022 to 5th January 2023. The study observed that microenterprises' supply chain management and dynamic flexibility of a micro-organization in Bangladesh are yet to be properly developed. Both the public and private sectors should work simultaneously to get rid of the problem. Local-level planning, the raising of the local economy, and projects/programs for the local sector in both urban and rural areas are being required to properly utilize mega projects as commented by the authors which in turn help to raise purchasing power, removing income inequality and help to develop the economy of the country.

DOI: 10.4018/978-1-6684-7140-1.ch008

INTRODUCTION

Micro Entrepreneurial Organizations have a considerable influence on Bangladesh's economy as they sustain job creation, and family income rise, reduce social and economic inequality, and economic development. These establishments assist in allowing communities to become fruitful entrepreneurs and finish the sequence of the deficiency by generous entree to financial facilities, training, consultancies, and assistance. According to World Bank (2022) in Bangladesh microenterprises create 56% of the country's entire job creation and 25% of the country's gross domestic product. For economic development in Bangladesh micro-entrepreneurship is playing a tremendous role including income-generating activities and trying to arrange gender equality. Yesminet al. described that (2021) in Bangladesh "micro-enterprises have no management strategies; nevertheless, their mitigation of a crisis appears more ad hoc.

Entrepreneurship seemed to be demonstrated in their company by implementing product delivery and marketing recovery strategies while managing to stay alive in the market. "Flexible and active conditions of microbusiness procedures may perform a multitasking character on the border sense of fundamental issues with synchronization of environmental scanning. Line management is the bottommost near of the management pyramid, a situation which is an extremely significant part that performs as the basis aimed at altogether fruitful micro businesses. These foremost leads help to create microentrepreneurial organizations in the financial market of the country either semi-formal or informal way with the help of microfinance organizations. Beznos (2023) urged that the microservice's architectural elegance is a method to emerging a sole tender by way of a set of minor facilities, apiece successively in its specific procedure and interactive by frivolous devices.

Bangladesh is now preparing to convert the country to SMART Bangladesh. Smart data is digital information that is configured as such it contains to perform upon the group opinion beforehand existence directed to a downside analysis stage aimed at additional data alliance and analytical ability. Microenterprises will be benefitted by using smart data for sustainable business processes. Dynamic flexibility can assist entrepreneurial growth for which an entrepreneurial mindset is very much required. The organizational dynamic flexibility perspective indicates the growing flexibility to maintain a positive position to develop systematic capital investment for the poor income stratum. This will help to remove poverty through financial inclusion, especially for unbanked people of the country. According to World Bank (2018), it will endure efforts in a dynamic and hardy country, to decrease poverty and carry wealth to all Bangladeshis, particularly the poor.

Micro-organizational flexibility is related to change phenomena such as ecological unexpected and disruptive events and to environmental characteristics such as complexity, uncertainty, turbulence, dynamics, etc. Flexibility is the organizational function of the overall awareness, management of vulnerabilities, and adaptive capacity in a complex, uncertain, dynamic, and interconnected environment. Micro-entrepreneurial organizational flexibility is a function of the situation awareness, management of vulnerabilities, adaptive capacity of an organization in a complex, uncertain, dynamic, and interdependent environment in a rural environment and urban areas for downtrodden people. Yousef et al. (2022) found that in Iran rural entrepreneurial business managers should have a long-term vision for the continuation of their business.

The economic, social, political, and cultural organizational environment are being considered as dynamic trait that may enhance organizational flexibility. The contribution of the flexibility conceptualization is critical to understand the dynamics or microentrepreneurial organizational flexibility capabilities related to the issues where there are gaps of information, such as in areas of the role of structural knowledge, culture, diversity, determinants of the flexibility process, preparation for unexpected events, abilities to deal with threatening events at different levels of analysis. The microentrepreneurial flexibility akin to self-restoring equilibrium dynamics in mainstream economics. The study intends to observe capability performance provides insights into the complex dynamics to rebuild opportunities and development of microentrepreneurs in a turbulent situation. World Bank (2020) described that Bangladesh's economy is dependent on its 7 million microenterprises, which provide 56 percent of all jobs.

The assumptions of flexibility can be accommodated in the dynamic capabilities framework as the platform to build the foundations for the conceptualization of organizational flexibility. Micro-Organizational flexibility is the ability to strengthen firms by harnessing experience to become adaptive, robust, agile, and competitive in an increasingly ever-changing, dynamic, and complex environment and embracing opportunities. Flexibility is conceptualized as a generic quality linked to dynamic capabilities. The impact of flexibility the on dynamic capabilities of the entrepreneurial organization is well known. Micro-Organizational flexibility encourages recovery and growth from the adversity that may involve adopting an entrepreneurial mindset and develops dynamic capabilities that turn adverse experiences into opportunities for strategic renewal. Micro-Organizations build dynamic capabilities in flexibility to design strategic opportunities out of adversity. Entrepreneurial organizational flexibility is the dynamic organizational capability to facilitate organizational change through the development of abilities to anticipate, cope and learn from potential threats, unexpected events, and trends. Flexibility is conceptualized as a normative construct of the system of capabilities for dynamic adaptive processes outcomes.

The sociological flexibility of the organization system is more dynamic and determined by the adaptation process undergone during the adaptive cycle. Dynamic and operating capabilities and division of routines in the context of entrepreneurial organizational flexibility contribute to building adaptations through segmented actions at several levels. The notion of micro-organizational flexibility is related to the concept of dynamic capabilities. Polasky et al. (2019) raised the question of what way to decrease poverty and discourse increasing inequality in the expression of environmental fluctuations increase significant social and economic features of sustainable development in adding to the environmental dimensions. Now in Figure1, the study has shown supply chain management processes:

Figure 1. Supply chain management processes

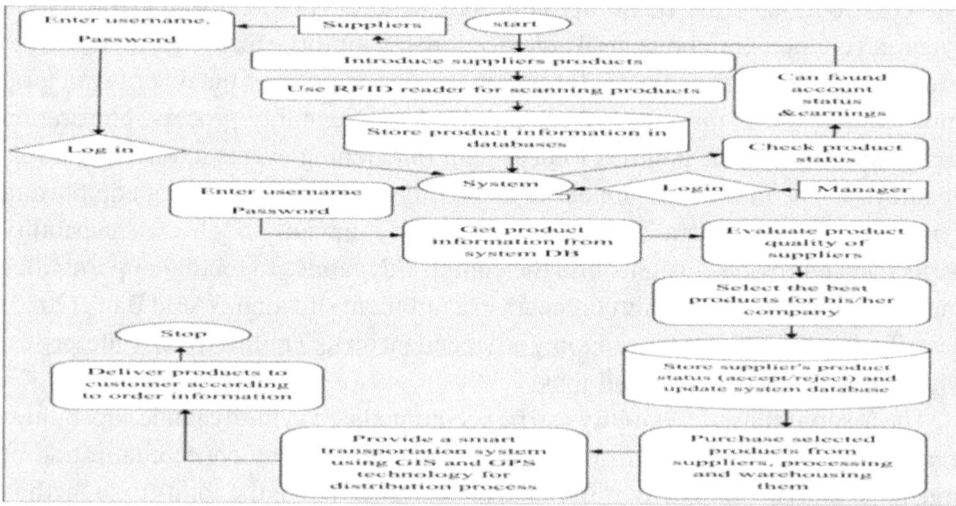

In the Figure 1, the part occupy by performs like order processing, production time, lead time, customer care service, prompt response, and product availability drive an extended method in ornamental an affable association amid group of actors including clients and entrepreneurs in the supply chain to distribute worth to the ultimate client. They generate can provide importance correspondingly on retrograde and onward connections in directive to form client satisfaction by the microentrepreneurs. In supposition, the client's desired fulfillment container be attained no solitary through a substantial position to the purchasers nonetheless also by generous equivalent reputation to all individuals tangled in the supply chain management method. The behavior pattern of the microentrepreneurs and the clients are very much significant.

Entrepreneurial micro-organizational flexibility is an intrinsic attribute to the ethos of the organization and provides a shared common platform adapted to the dynamic complexity of the organizational environment, providing confidence to take measured risks and respond appropriately. To ensure micro-organizational flexibility is important to develop dynamic leadership, understand the needs of all the stakeholders involved, and have well-trained staff. The different nature of organizational flexibility capabilities is based on the background either a heuristics-based dynamic capability or the adoption of routine actions in the absence of survival conditions.

When dynamism can be created it may be feasible for the organization to have better access to finance and get the benefits of financial inclusion. However, depending on the age, income, and provide areas situated offered micro-organizations depend on their resilient capabilities. Modern technological innovations may be feasible when benefits forms to financial institutions are feasible. The concept of micro-organizational flexibility informs organizational practices to bring more experiential learning and knowledge to prevent challenges of future scenarios, such as demographic, social, and economic changes (Bento, & Garotti, 2019) such as in the situation of post-covid-19 and current ongoing Russia -Ukraine war.

From March 2020 to February 2022, Bangladesh faced different times lockdowns, maintenance of social distances, and disruption of supply chain management with some gap time due to the COVID-19 pandemic. Now due to the war between Russia and Ukraine, the whole world is facing high inflation, negative externalities, a decline in purchasing power capabilities, especially poor income stratum, and the failure of the US Dollar as a vehicle currency due to shortage rather than the importance needed bilateral exchange rate as an adverse effect is also felt in Bangladesh. The situation has occurred due to global supply chain disruption and USA sanctions. The further ongoing war between Russia and Ukraine may play a negative impact on the local economy of the country. For the study purpose, the definition of microenterprises provided by the Bangladesh Bureau of Statistics stated that enterprises with fixed assets, excluding land and buildings, valued at Bangladesh Taka 0. 5 million to Bangladesh Taka 5 million, or with 10–24 or fewer workers can be used.

Objectives of the Study

1. To assess the supply chain management impact of microentrepreneurs in Bangladesh's economy.
2. To investigate microentrepreneurs based dynamic flexibility in Bangladesh.
3. To provide some Implications of the study.

As such the study intends to know whether micro-entrepreneurial organizations in Bangladesh have any need for supply chain management and dynamism of flexibility for competencies.

Research Question

Based on the aforesaid discussion, the study-built research question of the study is whether supply chain management and dynamic flexibility for uplifting micro-entrepreneurial organizations are feasible in Bangladesh.

The plan of the study includes an introduction followed by a literature review, Justification of the research work, methodology of the study, hypotheses, estimated results, case study, discussion followed by a conclusion, and implications.

LITERATURE REVIEW

In search of the answer to the research question, the study did literature reviews: A reliable action of flexibility beyond the evolution and revolution phases addresses sequences of crisis for the growth and maturity functioning of the organization (Greiner, 1972). Social sciences refer to flexibility as the anticipated effort to predict and prevent potential dangers and the capacity to cope after the dangers manifest, learning to bounce back (Wildavsky, 1988). The development of organizational flexibility enhances organizational learning enacted through routines oriented toward specific targets (Levitt, & March,1988). Organizational flexibility is a dynamic capacity that develops over time (Wildavsky, 1988). Adaptation is a key capability that includes reflection, learning, and organizational change aimed to avoid and reduce the negative effects of unexpected events (Carley, 1991; Carley, & Harrald, 1997). Liedholm, &Mead (1999) commented that Micro and small enterprises (MSEs) have been familiar as a main modern basis of employment and salary in a rising number of emerging nations.

The experience of mild and strong dysfunctional events and disruptions may be used for learning organizational flexibility reintegration with cognitive and behavioral solutions and predominant heuristic-based responses (March 1991). Organizational learning after these events can develop new flexibility and adaptation capacities (March et al., 2003). The socio-ecological systems have derived in flexibility (Folke, 2006) referring to a dynamic capacity of adaptation and to the system's capacity to absorb internal and external disruption and perturbations and return to a stable state. Organizational Flexibility is about learning to bounce back (Wildavsky,1988) and the ability to bounce forward (Manyena, O'Brien, O'Keefe, & Rose, 2011) to grow and prosper (Reich, 2006) through the mechanisms of performance optimization and adaptive innovation.

Organizational flexibility is the response to a crisis and learning over time how to face new challenges (Sutcliffe, & Vogus, 2003). Organizational flexibility is linked to overcoming the crisis and emerging strengthened successful growth (Freeman et al., 2004; Sutcliffe, & Vogus 2003; Teo et al., 2017) and learning to develop new capabilities and the ability to thrive despite diversity (Dalgaard-Nielsen, 2017; Stewart & O'Donnell, 2007; Teo et al., 2017; Wildavsky, 1988; Williams et al., 2017; Chan, 2011). Research on organizational flexibility has been undertaken in high-reliability organizations operating in uncertain, complex, and dynamic environments where errors may lead to catastrophic consequences (Bigley, & Roberts, 2001; Weick & Roberts, 1993; Weick & Sutcliffe, 2001; Weick et al., 2005).

Flexibility offers different thinking to contribute to the theoretical debates based on resource-based and dynamic capabilities. Theory building of organizational development is focusing on heuristic-based dynamic capabilities under strategic and resource collapse conditions (McGrath, 1999; Mellahi & Wilkinson, 2004; Probst & Raisch, 2005; Sheppard, & Chowdhury, 2005). Organizational flexibility is the intrinsic ability of a system to maintain a dynamic stable state and continue operations after a mishap in the presence of continuous stress (Woods & Hollnagel, 2006). Organizational flexibility is the ability to thrive in a dynamic environment (Cho et al., 2006). ADB (2007) described that microfinance projects need to be more focused and deliberate in targeting poor households. Organizational flexibility is essentially a dynamic capability used to manage unstable organizational systems to develop reliable functions (Weick & Sutcliffe, 2007).

Economic theories assert that organizations aim for an efficient economy balanced by turnarounds and dynamic capabilities (Barker, & Duhaime, 1997; Morrow, Sirmon, Hitt, & Holcomb, 2007; Shein, 2011) and dynamic capabilities (Helfat et al., 2007; Teece, 2007; Zahra, Sapienza, & Davidsson, 2006) and the ability of organizations to endure, recover and adapt from distress. Leadership enhances organizational flexibility in times of change as the capacity to respond adaptively to disruptive change implies the ability to withstand shocks and the capacity for adaptation and learning (Stewart, & O'Donnell, 2007).

The flexibility of an organization developing through lops the ability to be dynamic and stable to continue operations after any major mishap (Woods, & Hollnagel, 2006). Flexibility is an emergent property of complex systems related to the capacity of a system to reorganize after internal or external disturbances (Folke, 2006). Adapt to organizational settings through the emergence of new behavioral patterns, learning, and changes in the structure of social interactions. Flexibility is a mechanism of learning and change to foster practices for stability (Bingham, Eisenhard, & Davis 2007). The dynamic integration of logistics capabilities facilitates readiness, response, and recovery of the supply chain flexibility (Ponomarov & Holcomb, 2009).

Flexibility as stability and change (Farjoun, 2010) provides empirical evidence to facilitate learning and capability development for organizational change (Bingham, Eisenhard, & Davis, 2007).

Organizations are complex and dynamic systems continuously changing (Norris et al., 2008; Tyler, & Moench, 2012; Young, 2010). Fafchamps et al. (2011) described that the change in the belongings of cash and in-kind grants is related to additional through an absence of self-discipline than with outside compression funding is providing moves to microenterprise growth. Flexibility is shaped by an adaptive system based on multilevel dynamics interaction aiming to change (Masten, 2007, p. 926) which in turn resists increasing vulnerability and enhances flexibility (Walker, & Salt, 2012). Burger-Helmchen (2013) described that an entrepreneurial organization combines several aspects of entrepreneurship and firm flexibility. Specific attention processes make it possible for junior and senior managers to attract the attention of the decision-makers, Exact decision mechanisms that explain the acceptance of ideas, and a flexible, agile structure to allow the implementation.

"Organizational flexibility frameworks align to build a system adaptation based on dynamic capabilities constructs (Limnios et al., 2014). The concept of flexibility is complex and dynamic. Organizational flexibility includes several attributes and elements (Gibson & Tarrant, 2010). Flexibility is a dynamic concept and evolves over time from fragile to antifragile (Taleb, 2014). Organizational flexibility is dynamic and incremental (Alexiou, 2014; Kamalahmadi, & Parast, 2016; Ortiz-de-Mandojana, & Bansal, 2015). SMEs flexibility is tied to strategic planning and its aspirations in terms of development of dynamic capabilities in response to a crisis, such as innovativeness, responsiveness, competition, renewal, uncertainty, etc. (Macpherson, Herbane, & Jones, 2015).

Ecological flexibility requires the anticipation of risks, reduction of environmental degradation, and organizational preparedness of ecosystem dynamics dependent upon natural resources (Whiteman & Cooper 2011). The conceptual and empirical study of organizational flexibility provide evidence of the dual change mechanism of dynamic capabilities construct used as a framework to reconfigure existent routines and resources, creating opportunities through alliances and entrepreneurial actions (Peteraf et al., 2013, Zahra, Sapienza, & Davidsson, 2006, Alvarez, & Barney, 2007; Barreto, 2012). Organizational flexibility is a strategic ability to adapt, integrate and reconfigure internal and external organizational skills, resources, and functional competencies to match the requirements of a changing environment resulting from a set of dynamic capabilities (Limnios et al., 2014). Organizational flexibility is the dynamic capability of exploitative adaptations or engineering flexibility, explorative transformation, or ecological flexibility to maintain performance and longevity (Eltantawy, 2016). Organizational flexibility is the ability to anticipate, cope effectively, and learn from these events from trends and potential threats with unexpected events to produce a dynamic capability directed toward organizational change (Duchek, 2014).

Organizational flexibility is the ability to continually evolve and thrive over time in the face of adverse and hostile circumstances which naturally arise in dynamic environments (Demmer *et al.*,2011). Organizational flexibility is a trait to thrive in a dynamic and volatile business environment (Chan, 2011). Organizational flexibility is concerned with the adaptation process to challenge complex environmental conditions through the capability dynamic alignment aimed to avoid a path dependency approach and rebuild efficient performance (Lengnick-Hall, & Beck, 2009; Sydow, Schreyögg, & Koch, 2009; Eisenhardt et al., 2010). Organizational flexibility is the ability and the dynamic capability of an organization to resist, absorb, cope, recover, and adapt to the altered environment following a disaster (Kahan, Allen, George, & Thompson, 2009; McManus, Seville, Vargo, & Brunsdon, 2008).

Flexibility is conceptualized as a dynamic process of ongoing and reciprocal transactions between the organizations and the environment (Vanderbilt-Adriance, & Shaw, 2008). The flexibility capability perspective incorporates a hierarchy of activities that yield competitive advantages while reconfiguring responses as dynamic capabilities to environmental changes (Ambrosini et al., 2009; Danneels, 2012; Hine, Parker, Pregelj, & Verreynne, 2014). Luthar et al. (2000) define flexibility as the dynamic processes encompassing positive adaptation in the context of significant adversity (p. 543) and adapting to sudden changes. The flexibility process-oriented is a dynamic nature interaction between the organization and the environment (Williams et al. 2017, p. 20) responding before, during, and after adverse events (Linnenluecke et al. 2012; Alliger et al., 2015; Williams et al., 2017).

Organizational flexibility as an emergent system is a dynamic property that integrates the processes of adaptation and integration processes inter-systemic in nature (Clement, & Rivera, 2017, p. 30). The dynamic nature of organizational flexibility provides the inference of causality in a longitudinal evaluation that contributes to organizational renewal based on employee work-role performance (Gover & Duxbury, 2018). Organizational flexibility uses the interactions of assets, attributes and routines that recognize the effects of risk over time and their emergence in unexpected ways (Vanderbilt-Adriance, & Shaw, 2008, 30-31). As a dynamical property, organizational flexibility requires new core properties of the system's capacity to be ready to respond by anticipating and synchronizing events and proactively learning (Hollnagel & Woods, 2017). Flexibility can be desirable and non-desirable depending on the proactive development and adaptation of dynamic capabilities (Limnios et al., 2014).

Microentrepreneurial flexibility analysis as a dynamic property requires building inter and transdisciplinary bridges. It aimed at integrating processes of both organizational adaptation and transformation of the operative ecosystems and dependent networks to build and enhance flexibility aligned to more holistic sustainable development goals (Folke et al., 2010). Risk readiness is a concept developed in a dynamic model associated with flexibility (Cook & Rasmussen, 2005). The concept of flexibility links to the change from a static to a more dynamic paradigm of safety management. This must be accompanied by proper utilization of supply chain management.

Microentrepreneurs flexibility in the safety of complex systems copes with highly risky variability (Bergstr¨om et al., 2015). Although safety is a dynamic non-event and dealing with shocks and unexpected events (Weick and Sutcliffe 2001).It remains unclear how organizations may achieve flexibility (Boin, & van Eeten, 2013; Duit, 2016) and their antecedents, relationships, interactions and drivers between the different stages in an explicit conceptual framework for a comprehensive, conceptual and dynamics understanding (Lynham, 2002, p. 232; Meredith, 1993; Jabareen, 2009; Burnard and Bhamra, 2011). Some principles of organizational flexibility are the learning, flexibility, and adaptability. An organizational flexible capability loop can be based on heuristic dynamic capabilities. Heuristics in organizational flexibility are linked with the dynamic capabilities (Bingham, & Eisenhardt, 2011).

Dynamic organizational flexibility capabilities flexibility focuses on the shift from the capability hierarchy perspective to heuristics-based capabilities (Barreto, 2010; Hine et al., 2014). The heuristics insight provides a decision structure to assess the organizational flexibility preserving behavioral flexibility to deal with the collapse in any dynamic nature of a specific context. Organizational flexibility can be assessed based on the functions of monitoring, responding, anticipating, and learning (Apneseth et al., 2013). The flexibility orientations framework of Teece (2007) argued that the reintegration, homeostasis, and loss have different dynamic capabilities for sensing, seizing, and transforming. Organizational flexibility is the capacity and ability to respond positively, adaptively for adaptation, for learning and withstand in disruptive change and external shocks (Stewart, & O'Donnel, 2007).

Organizational culture, learning from past experiences and professional servant leadership are some of the factors that affect organizational flexibility (Erol et al., 2010; Boin & McConnell, 2007). Organizational learning from incidents experience at facing external environmental, socio ecosystems, spatial, societal, sectoral, etc., crises events, has an influence on the adoption of responses and other flexibility activities (Toft, & Reynolds, 1997) through isomorphic learning from events of other organizations with improvements and planning (Deverell, 2009; Weick & Sutcliffe, 2003). Cross-sectional learning is implicit in organizational flexibility to avoid failure and cope with crisis (Crichton et al., 2009).

Each type of disorganizations requires deployment of different heuristic flexibility dynamic capability at different times and across the processes of sensing, seizing, and transforming. The result of these processes differs in flexibility outcomes. The heuristics-based dynamic capabilities (Bingham et al., 2007) and the operating capabilities built on routines (Helfat et al., 2007) for organizational flexibility under conditions of sustainability and competitive advantage (Peteraf, di Stefano & Verona, 2013). The organizational flexibility process model is a framework to build and develop dynamic capabilities as high order process to respond to tensions created by adverse unknown events and disturbances. This requires reconfiguration of organizational resources and activities and changing environmental negative circumstances (Burnard & Bhamra, 2011).

Microenterprises flexibility building covers the management of human resources, cognitive adaptation to environmental situations, and supply chain management. It is reducing vulnerabilities and propensity to disruptive events and desirability of dynamic situations (Limnios et al., 2014; Lengnick-Hall, Beck, & Lengnick-Hall, 2011; Watts & Paciga, 2011; Sheffi, 2005). The concept of flexibility has gradually moved from an assumption of single equilibrium to multiple equilibrium in socio-ecological systems with the increasing recognition of complexity, uncertainty, variation and learning in living systems (Folke 2006).

Socio-ecology systems flexibility can be supported by heuristics to build anticipation, recovery, learning and adaptation (Walker et al., 2006; Madni, & Jackson, 2009). Organizational flexibility may result of learning from disasters (Roberts, Madsen, & Desai, 2005) and from unexpected events. Organizational flexibility includes adaptation capabilities to critical events and the ability to adjust using change for organizational long term learning and advancement and increasing the knowledge for anticipation (Limnios et al., 2014; Madni & Jackson, 2009).

An elaborate dynamic organizational flexibility capability supported by a portfolio of heuristics (Gigerenzer, & Brighton, 2009) the organization is challenged to deploy sensing, seizing and transformation. The heuristic-based dynamic organizational flexibility capability portfolio is more critical for an unstable organization more than resources and routines. Under stable conditions of resource management and strategy, the heuristic-based dynamic capabilities can configure and re-configure the operating routing-based and entrepreneurial capabilities (Hine, Parker, Pregelj, & Verreynne, 2014; Teece, 2012; Teece et al., 1997).

Global health actors can harness the opportunities offered by pathways of change, according to Held, Kickbusch, McNally, Piselli, &Told, (2019), degree of organizational learning and active feedback loops. This helps organizational epistemological and practice communities aimed to enhance a polycentric system of governance and the political leadership for governance innovation. An organizational dynamic flexibility perspective from the capability perspective considers that flexibility is a dynamic development and progressive process-based of organizations in improvisational response to crisis and involving identity management (Ishak, and Williams, 2018; McCarthy, Collard, & Johnson, 2017).

A theoretical organizational learning framework has been developed by Willems, Busscher, van den Brink, & Arts, (2018) to analyze the anticipation of change in agencies and the empirical research implications into the practice of waterway renewal in practice in which change is pragmatic. The dynamic capability perspective of organizational flexibility research is based on evolutionary economics, the resource base view, and capabilities (Davies, & Brady, 2016). Cycles of organizational learning and unlearning achieve strategic organizational flexibility (Morais-Storz, & Nguyen, 2017). Flexible and changing organizations only can thrive to keep aligned in a volatile environment enhancing the ability to be able to respond to crisis and supported by organizational learning, the organization can develop the dynamic resilient capacities to promote change (Duchek, 2014).

Organizational learning theory is incorporated into organizational flexibility by Umoh et al. (2014) and developed a measurement scale based on McManus *et al.*, (2008) to include planning capacity, organizational learning capacity, dynamic capacity, and adaptive capacity. Only flexible, changing, and agile organizations can thrive in dynamic and evolving environments (Lengnick-Hall et al., 2011). Organizational flexibility comprises adaptation implying long-term learning (Madni, & Jackson, 2009). Long-term adaptation of anticipatory adjustments and learning to respond to the impacts on ecological discontinuities from climate vulnerabilities and weather extremes should be considered in the design and implementation of flexibility strategies. Flexibility is a learning process of protective actions to build flexibility against perceived vulnerabilities over time that needs to be explicit for organizations (Hale, & Heijer, 2006; Masten, 2001).

Microenterprises flexibility can be increased to achieve robustness by learning from previous failures. Learning from failures facilitates organizational flexibility (Crichton et al., 2009). Personal networks and norms of generalized reciprocity for organizational development can be identified in the context of flexibility, social learning, community recovery of disasters (Chamlee-Wright, 2010). Group flexibility develops the capacity of learning through the imperfections and failures with the combination of accountability and psychological safety as critical ingredients (Edmonson, 2007). Organizational flexibility strategies aim to mitigate errors and error recovery (Weick & Sutcliffe, 2007), to overcome barriers and incentive adaptation and learning (Howard & Irving, 2013; Li et al., 2012).

One of the promised perspectives is the theory of organizational flexibility based on the dynamic capability theory considered as the ability of firms to perceive threats and opportunities, make decisions, solve problems, and change their resource bases

(Barreto, 2010). Internalized the dynamic capability as the organizational flexibility based on the safety audit of flexibility engineering by Huber *et al.* (2009), the results of their research show that the organizational dynamic capability determined the safety performance. Organizational flexibility is an iterative practice of learning the dynamic capabilities to reconfigure resources and activities for strategic opportunities by enhancing change and unintended consequences (Teece, 2007, 1343).

Wise & Ali (2009) said that CRM can be most effective with the use of the technologies. Behind the technologies human resources i.e., personnel works. They must be innovative and dedicated to their service structure. The flexibility learning capability enable organizational survival and growth to exploit advantages (McGrat, 2013). Unlearning facilitates organizational flexibility (Morais-Storz & Nguyen, 2017) causes problem. The transformational perspective of organizational flexibility capacity is tied to a dynamic process embedded in the individuals' knowledge, skills, and abilities (King et al., 2016; Kuntz et al., 2017). Organizational flexibility relates to the redundancy of humans and equipment (Azadeh et al., 2016). This promotes the robustness of the system and implies learning and adaptive changes.

Organizational flexibility can be trait-like stable of the individual, team, group, and organization (Luthans, 2002; Coutu, 2002). In a dialectic process, flexibility is influenced by different levels considered as the capability of individuals, groups, and organizations to cope in dynamic context (Cho et al., 2006). Flexibility stages depend on the prior organizational knowledge former crisis, the environment, actions, etc., and influence learning and knowledge base to be used in anticipation as learning for crisis, in coping by learning as crisis and adaptation as learning from crisis (Smith, &Elliott, 2007). Action learning facilitates organizational learning and change leading to organizational flexibility as the ability to recover unexpected exogenous environmental change (O'Hara et al., 2007).

Heuristics is an efficient mechanism embedding learning from adversity to become more resilient (Gigerenzer, 2008). The strategic flexibility enables the organizations to reinvent dynamic models and strategies as the circumstances and situations change (Hamel & Vaelikangas, 2003; Vaelikangas & Romme, 2013). This conceptualization is like the strategic offense (Limnios et al., 2014). The dynamics of organizational flexibility when facing challenges of unknow events, natural disasters, socio-economic trends, etc., requires organizations to respond, to adapt and protect continuing sustainable performance and growth (Stephenson, 2010). The dynamics of emerging organizational behaviors may arise from environmental changes such as disasters and unknown events (Burnard & Bhamra, 2011). Flexibility are optimization and renewal as lagged indicators, and protective factors as proactive indicators are equal partners leading to the ability to evolve and thrive in the face of adversity which arise in dynamic environments (Demmer et al. 2011).

Organizational flexibility is an approach to disaster management based on identification of resources and assets that can support adaptive response and dynamic recovery (O'Sullivan, Corneil, Kuziemsky, & Toal-Sullivan, 2015).The organizational knowledge base is enhanced by learning for and through rare unexpected events in close relationship between the anticipation and coping phases of organizational flexibility (Christianson et al., 2009) and also illustrated by the feedback loop between the anticipation and adaptation. The perspective of the systems, the organizational systems is a multifaceted concept used to develop capabilities to implement adaptive responses to disruptions and create organizational learning (Francis & Bekera, 2014; Lee et al., 2013; Maitlis, & Christianson, 2014; Thiel et al., 2012). Richardson (2016) applied the metatheory of flexibility postulating the qualities inquiring and learning to achieve mastery as the result of change.

Past experiences, learning and creativity are resources that influence facilitates flexibility in smaller businesses (Glover, 2012; Richtnér &Löfsten, 2014). The best organizational flexibility response occurs when strategies are designed to specific disturbances although may be cognitively demanding but still manageable (Masten, 2014).

Organizational suppleness is the function of the ability of adaptation to the dynamic environment of the organization (Wicker, Filo, &Cuskelly, 2013; Mcmanus, Seville, Vargo, & Brunsdon, 2008). Dynamic capabilities evolve with the changing environment where learning plays an important role (Zollo, & Winter, 2002). The organizational dynamic capability was proposed by Teece *et al.* (1997) as the ability of the firm to establish and reconfigure its internal and external resources to gain competitive advantage in the turbulent and changing environment. The improvement of organizational flexibility learning from multiple past failures in the network and disaster recovery, quickly identify, locate, and assess the grid flexibility elements of previous errors for critical missions aimed to correct and improve processes, optimize recovery efforts, and mitigate the impacts (Chen et al., 2014).

The elasticity is the combination of anticipating, learning, responding, and monitoring sociotechnical systems comply with the variability of activities, the nature of work and the nonlinear activities (Patriarca, Di Gravio, Constantino, Falegnami, & Bilotta, 2017). Ali (2017) described that micro savings should under the employing horizon of the micro investment for this social networking and community banking is desirable. Organizational flexibility is the ability to handle and respond threats and hazards to unexpected trouble, using pre-existing and pre-planned capabilities, by learning, changing, and developing new capabilities (Dalgaard-Nielson, 2017). Ali (2018) opined that job-related alteration was due to climate alteration and natural catastrophe that also be contingent on socio-economic condition of the public of the coastal part in Bangladesh.

Fatoki (2018) described that small business owners to develop strategies to improve flexibility by attending training and seminars on entrepreneurship especially in the areas of energy, pressure, change, failure management, and coping strategies (p.10). Bhuiyan, & Ivlevs (2019) opined that in Bangladesh micro-borrowers with advanced stages of properties involvement an upsurge in gratification by monetary safety. Organizations must manage their specific resources, structures, capabilities, etc. Some building blocks affect anticipating, coping with and adapting and learning from adversity, entailing leadership, environmental scanning, initiating change processes and flexibility planning in the complexity and uncertainty of the world (Vakilzadeh & Haase, 2020). Hamedi & Mehdiabadi (2020) described that flexibility construction is essential as appear to prime to entrepreneurial act which is the organization's dimensions to retort certainly or nominally to disturbances that demonstrations that there is not only confrontation to outside tremors nonetheless also the bulk for variation and knowledge.

The micro foundations of the dynamic capabilities are explored by Tabaklar, Sorkun, Yurt, & Yu (2021) and propose a social innovation framework in highly dynamic settings to build and reconfigure capabilities that may apply in organizational flexibility. Organizational flexibility is an effective means to achieve sustainable growth in crisis situations, Chen, Liu, & Zhou (2021), using the mapping and literature analysis methods, have developed an organizational flexibility framework for research. Hernåndez-Chea, Mahdad, Minh, & Hjorts (2021) observed that intermediate organizations, outside their main role of arranging space, grid, and guidance to entrepreneurs, in entrepreneurial ecosystems can perform an important character in scoring associations. Agile supply chain practices can be effective at improving the supply of products and the key to this process is incorporating an overall system into a supply chain that can provide real-time information, improve efficiency and continuity, and increase productivity(Knowledge Center,2023).This will help microentrepreneurs for their organizational capability and flexibility.

JUSTIFICATION OF THE RESEARCH WORK

From the aforesaid literature review though the study observed that lot of studies were done but non-profit organizations termed micro entrepreneurial institutions work in Bangladesh to encourage the poor people especially poverty prone people do have little study in Bangladesh. To discuss on micro entrepreneurial organizational flexibility, it is necessary to clarify and use some assumptions to underlie different orientations to enable the building and development of dynamic capabilities in the micro sector. Proper supply chain management is one of the prerequisites to develop organizations. These micro-organizations which aim at giving people who want to launch their own microbusinesses access to financial services, training, and assistance were properly evaluates were very scanty. These dynamic but flexible institutions seek to end the measurement and analysis of poverty in their communities and to grow Bangladesh. As such economic progress through production possibility frontier by providing individuals with the information, assets, and tools and macro perspectives they necessity to succeed need to be evaluated.

Micro financial institutions frequently deliver its customers through a diversity of facilities, such as mentorship programs, microbusiness training, and micro financial facilities but still in Bangladesh it was not unbiasedly done. These organizations provide microloans with relaxed payback periods and low interest rates to people who under poverty line to start or grow their microbusinesses to come out from the vicious circle of poverty. But most important thing to sustain in the business process is supply chain management which maximum authors did not develop or examine. In direction to contribution clients in acquiring the skills essential to become successful microentrepreneurs, they also offer microbusiness training and mentoring whether it is expressive method or not? As such it is necessary to address the research question for which following methodology of the study researchers have been undertaken.

METHODOLOGY OF THE STUDY

The study did extensive literature review in search of the research question mentioned above. Exact sources of secondary sources have been mentioned. Meanwhile, for primary sources a closed ended questionnaire was prepared and total 73 questionnaires were distributed to the owners of the microenterprises set up in the urban and the rural areas at Dhaka District, Cumilla District and Khulna District in Bangladesh among the male and female respondents through using random sampling technique which is a share of the sampling method in which respectively sample takes an equivalent probability of existence to be selected. However, for the respondent purposes, the research work was considered only owners of the micro enterprises. Out of them sixty-five (65) were responds the questionnaire.

Based on below noted hypotheses testing, the study did three chi-square test statistics. The study will also collect information from a rural area and prepare a case study at named "Dublar char". Time period of the study is 1st September, 2022 to 5th January, 2023. First hypothesis will be tested based on male and female categories. In case of second hypothesis, the study tested based on the category of income level below and above 20,000 Bangladesh Taka per month. Third test is done based on the on-age level of owners of the micro entrepreneurs considering the category below or above 30 years.

HYPOTHESES

Hypothesis One

Ho1: No supply chain management problem for dynamic flexibility upliftment between urban and rural micro entrepreneurs are prevailing.
Ha1: Supply chain management problem for dynamic flexibility upliftment between urban and rural micro entrepreneurs are prevailing.

Hypothesis Two

Ho2: Based on income level, micro entrepreneurs may not be capable to attain dynamic flexibility to do business.
Ha2: Based on income level, micro entrepreneurs may be capable to attain dynamic flexibility to do business.

Hypothesis Three

Ho3: There is no difference between dynamic flexibility based on age level of owners of the micro entrepreneurs.
Ha3: Difference between dynamic flexibility based on age level of owners of the micro entrepreneurs prevails.

ESTIMATED RESULTS

The following table 1 summarized the results of the Chi square test statistics:

Table 1. Summary of the empirical test

Sl. No.	Hypothesis no.	Chi-square test statistics	p-value	Significance	Decision
1.	One	5.1593	.0023123	Significant at p <.05	Rejected Null hypothesis
2.	Two	13.2708	.00027	Significant at p <.05	Rejected Null hypothesis
3.	Three	3.9196	.047727	Significant at p <.05	Rejected Null hypothesis

CASE STUDY

For the study purpose, to prepare a case study, one of the researchers went to Dublar char on 8 th May,2022, which place is isolated from the mainland in the Bangladesh and is an island. The char is very much interesting for microbusiness of dry fish. However, for collecting data one of the most inspiring success stories from active but flexible is that of named "Indrani Roy" a small business entrepreneur who produces spices. Indrani was around 24 years was aged and mother of three kids and her religion is Hindu. Indrani had been running her business for several years but was struggling to grow due to lack of access to capital. With the help of active but flexible micro business, she was able to secure a small loan from Mahajan (who is relatively Rich and give lending at a much higher interest rate than the market interest rate i.e at 67% compound interest rate per annum) in the year 2017 that allowed her to purchase additional raw of species and tried to increase production in the forthcoming years.

With the increase in production, Indrani was able to grow her micro business and increase her income by 85%within 5 years after getting that small loan, besides repayment of loan. She tried to take help of dry fishermen including her husband and brother. Indrani story is just one example of the impact that active but flexible has had on the economic well-being of micro-entrepreneurs in Bangladesh. While talking with the researcher, Indrani said in Bengali that though others are working directly dry fishing but she from her childhood wanted to do microbusiness on spices. She also argued that without the help of her husband and brother she cannot do this micro business. Now in her micro-organization eight female workers are working including packaging and her husband and brother not directly working but they help to sell the product in the mainland Khulna. She though a remote area lady but still she expressed her view that she wanted to maintain quality of spices.

OBSERVATIONS

By providing access to capital and support services, the micro-organization has helped to create job opportunities and increase income for many of its clients. Additionally, by supporting micro-entrepreneurs like: Indrani, women empowerment rises. Active but flexible micro-organizations had assisted to produce an additional dynamic and diverse economic countryside in Bangladesh like Indrani, with additional chances for communities to start and produce their own microbusinesses. Despite its achievement, dynamic but supple appearances some trials in its vision, mission, and super goal to empower micro-entrepreneurs in Bangladesh. The producer faces the problem of supply chain management.

One of the main trials is the nonexistence of financial literacy amid its customers, which can brand it problematic for them to comprehend the terms of them loans and achieve their moneys successfully. Additional trial is the trouble in accomplishment from remote rural communities to urban areas, which are often underserved by financial inclusions and lack of access to microbusiness advancement facilities. Financial institutions should come forward to give lower interest rate to new microentrepreneurs at the formal sector or semi formal sector. Supply chain management of the country is yet to develop,

DISCUSSION

From the aforesaid Table:1, the study observed that there may be relationship with supply chain management problem for dynamic resilient upliftment between urban and rural micro entrepreneurs. This is since COVID-19 created problem due to lockdown, maintenance of social distance in the economy despite govt. of Bangladesh was tried to help microentrepreneurs. But financial institutions of the country are not very much willing to help microentrepreneurs. Income level of micro entrepreneurs may be capable to attain dynamic flexibility to do business as per the empirical findings. Difference between dynamic flexibility based on age level of owners of the micro entrepreneurs have relationship as found from the empirical test. Value chain domination with the help of supply chain management in Bangladesh should properly developed. Otherwise, corner stone of value chain creation won't be feasible which is very much needed for the microentrepreneurs.

The micro-organization can evaluate its flexibility and learn after the event in terms of the resources employed and the capacity to absorb the impact of the climate change and extreme weather event and recover. Heuristic processes with recovery and growth from adversity can be invoked to build a dynamic flexibility building with the support or sensing, seizing, and transforming processes in response to specific threats. A comprehensive heuristic dynamic capability model characterizes threats for the types of strategic, operating and resource disorganization. Micro organizational flexibility is critical in a volatile environment and adversity where some organizations survive, others try to thrive, and others perishes. The social-ecological perspective of flexibility incorporates learning, adaptation and transformation beyond constancy and recovery. Flexible capabilities can be state-like open to development through training programs or on-the-job training in dynamic capability to cope and bounce back with significant change from risk and adversities.

A cultural learning process of micro-organizational flexibility enables the abilities and capabilities needed by the microfacial institutions to respond properly to deal with incidents, accumulations, allocations, and disturbances. Some cultural factors identified include the micro-organizational learning and learning from past experiences. Nevertheless, large organizations have organizational flexibility rooted in both locations and relationships, rather than flexibility formalization and isomorphous learning from other vicinities and neighborhoods characterized by their strategic flexibility planning formalization activities, resources, roles, and agreements to recover from disruptive events. Staying ahead in a competitive request requires applying creativity and invention to every area of micro entrepreneurship. Currently micro entrepreneurship is driven by creativity and invention to attain commercial objects. In technology, business, just in time services entrepreneurship, and ingesting in the new period is the result of ongoing invention. Further to entrepreneurship than simply developing new goods and services and to sale the products and services not only customer awareness but needed supply chain management.

Developed a business plan by the microenterprise that outlined vision, mission, super goal, and specific measures are being required. Microenterprises plan may be focused on achieving sustainable growth and profitability and to include a detail marketing strategy, financial projections, and risk management, distribution channel in the plan. He was aware of the importance of market coordination and therefore microenterprises should be worked closely with suppliers, manufacturers, and distributors to ensure that his /her products and services can be delivered on time and to the right customers. Microentrepreneurs also need to establish partnerships with key customers and worked with marketing and sales teams to increase visibility and fairness. Seizing from reintegration flexibility is learning from threats and become open to medium scale organizational change as part of the micro-organizational growth in response to uncertainty and adversity. The flexibility reintegration orientation engages in a deep learning process against threats. Communities approach towards flexibility with other associated concepts and terms seeking to recover it by learning from demonstration to achieve robust designs, high-reliability, and complex adaptive systems.

Microenterprises flexibility helps dynamic capabilities but do not have any boundaries, rather is dynamic consisting in a repertoire of knowledge, skills, processes, and heuristics learnt from experiences of adversity events. The dynamic capability of micro-organizational flexibility is based on learning integration skills to reduce vulnerability. Microenterprises' flexibility as a dynamic capability is a multidisciplinary concept is an acceptance the mechanisms of learning. Micro organizations may increase flexibility by learning from errors and dynamic plans. But they must prepare a strategic plan for proper supply chain management in Bangladesh. Micro organizations develop different flexibility capacities subject to their past experiences and leading to different threats, high risks, and disorganizations disturbances, which may require behavioral flexibility and heuristics in dynamic capabilities.

Micro organizations develop flexibility capability after coping with collapse aligned with the decision dynamic context, constraints in resources, opportunities and heuristics with a decision making. Micro organizational collapses are source of learning flexibility capabilities to build organizational flexibility an applied across the operating conditions. The application of Bayesian network models in organizational flexibility has implications with business models to open spaces for communication, learning and adaptation to prevent crisis. Unless product can be delivered from the producer/vendor to the client smoothly microenterprises vision, mission and super goal will drastically fail.

The adaptation processes in micro-organizational flexibility have implications in operational safety practices and others, becoming relevant for the emergence of learning and knowledge creation as a respond to crisis and unexpected events. Heuristics-based dynamic capabilities must be pertinent to some contextual circumstances while others may require routine-based capabilities to provide the micro- organizational flexibility. Micro- Organizations at microstructure need to use more heuristic-based flexibility dynamic capabilities in scenarios of major resource loss and uncertainty. As such regular repayment of loan from the microentrepreneurs are very important for micro financial institutions and capital accumulation and micro investment is very much needed.

Micro entrepreneurial organizational flexibility dynamic capability building proceeds across the decline, collapse, and re-building stages to withstand failure and manage collapse. Hamedi, & Mehdiabadi (2020) 's observation is applied for micro entrepreneurial organizations of the country. The flexibility dynamic capability development of the organization requires to learn heuristics and skills emerging from specific events and cases triggered by the different stakeholders in boundary and rebuilding transitions. An organization should learn to develop a dynamic organizational flexibility-based view of capability using heuristics instead of routines, enabling strategic change and reducing the threats of collapse. The organizational flexibility-based view may develop supported by dynamic capabilities and heuristics to regain stability after adversity. The process model of flexibility capability integrates the insights to provide flexibility dynamic capability by deploying a set of skills and heuristics to bounce back from collapse.

Microentrepreneurs need to get access to finance without any sort of hindrances. Entree of knowledge, innovation, and creativity for the microentrepreneurs are necessary for becoming sustainable. Technology transfer mechanism should properly work. Contact with market getting symmetric information and corruption free transportation mechanism is also needed for dynamic flexibility of the micro enterprises. Regular interval training and learning must be arranged by the govt. organizations and banks and NGOs for microentrepreneurs so that they can have the latest knowledge, and skills for doing business. Technical know-how should be transferred to them as per the microenterprises need-based, affordability can concern. For doing business, all sorts of support services including digitalization facilities must be ensured for the micro entrepreneurs for attaining competencies.

Micro organizational flexibility is a strategy aimed to face the challenges of a dynamic, complex, and uncertain and continually changing environment. Organizational flexibility is a strategy based on the adoption of best practices to survive, improve, and prosper in a context of dynamic global environment by building capabilities across all the organizational areas. Design and implementation of organizational flexibility strategies requires information availability and flexibility and adaptability processes through sharing of information flow and mission flexibility awareness and assurance of the dynamic environment.

Poor people in Bangladesh carry out variety of activities in their domestic lives and possess basic indigenous understanding, skill set, and resources which can be utilized to establish and manage microenterprises. All they require are awareness, motivation, sound business plans and an integrated external support. Insightful emphasis on developing microenterprises will eventually integrate them with export orientation through a sub-contracting linkage with larger export-oriented enterprises. With right amount of support coming from institutional as well as non-institutional factors micro-entrepreneurs can strengthen their own capacities to be able to contribute to the family and national earnings. Since micro-entrepreneurial contributions and capacity building are imperative for economic and social development in Bangladesh, scope of Flexible financing needs to be widened.

BRAC (Bangladesh Rural Advancement Committee) is in performance a self-same significant part in this respect. BRAC's active flexibility in loan processing is designed to empower its clients and help them build a better future for themselves and their families. By offering a range of financial products and services that are tailored to meet the unique needs of its clients, BRAC is helping to promote financial inclusion and reduce poverty in Bangladesh. An approach to micro-organizational supply chain management requires a balance of efficiency and reliability through suppleness and realizing measures of information availability to detect potential disruptions in the supply chain management process and overcome through using plan-do-check act. Measures for organizational flexibility in the context of specific goal may require moderate implementation of a feedback loop development for building dynamic emergency procedures to integrate the information required for the assessment of risks.

As stated by Chen, Liu, & Zhou 2021) in Bangladesh also during COVID-19 pandemic, the study observed that organizational flexibility is an effective means to achieve sustainable growth in crisis situations. The intra and inter-groups dynamics assess the organizational flexibility in which the different occupational groups distribute their activities. The notion of flexibility qualifies better based on informal arrangements affected by the inter-group dynamics with negotiated and articulated tasks. The flexibility of a team group increases in the face of unexpected events managed in a strong community practice. Assessing flexibility requires the costs of change representing the involved working groups in their intra- and inter-group dynamics confronted with the crisis.

An organizational flexibility approach of containing crises regards high reliable organizations as the essence of flexibility, the ability to maintain and regain a dynamic stable state in the presence of an uncertainty and vulnerability. The dynamic capability model development has implications for the organizational flexibility when resources dissipate the strategy fails to foster a long-term adversity period. The flexibility dynamic capability operates the ability to manage collapse and shift towards stability and re-building. Entrepreneurial organizational resiliency is a relevant attribute when dealing during crisis through preparation, dynamic and flexible planning and proactive behavior built with specific training on psychological capital of personnel. Yousef et al. (2022) suggestion is also applied for microentrepreneurs of the country for organizational flexibility.

Micro financial institutions energetic, elastic achievement and influence in Bangladesh validate the possible of microfinance and microbusiness nourishment amenities to generate economic prospects for marginalized peoples of the country. The micro-organization's emphasis on as long as microloans and support services to micro-entrepreneurs has acceptable it to take an important influence on the economic well-being of people of the country. Ali (2017)'s proposal to set up a societal banking for developing microentrepreneurs in the name of community banking or societal banking is urgently needed. Through as long as contact to capital and provision of support services, these micro-organizations can aid to generate job opportunities and upsurge salary for public who are marginalized and take restricted access to semi-formal and informal financial services.

Energetic stretchy achievement and influence on Bangladesh can prove the possible of microfinance and enterprises provision facilities to generate economic chances for disregarded inhabitants. The

association emphasis on if credits and provision facilities to microentrepreneurs has permissible it to take a noteworthy influence on the financial welfare of people of the country. If entree to money and provision, then institution container assistance to generate occupation openings and upsurge revenue for public who are marginalized, and pauper take very scanty entree to conventional financial facilities.

CONCLUSION AND IMPLICATION

In Bangladesh, there is a crucial necessity for different sectors starting from agriculture to industry and service sector, to accept an active method towards client pleasure by accepting supply chain management performs that deliver real-time and precise comebacks to client necessities by the entrepreneurs. Flexibility is addressed through turnaround and dynamic capabilities. Microentrepreneur works micro-organizational flexibility is a critical to possessing dynamic capabilities attracting new resources, design strategies and learn to overcome rigidity and regain stability.

Micro organizational flexibility of enterprises is the ability to manage workflow disturbances and regain a dynamic stable state. A dynamic capabilities perspective of micro-organizational flexibility provides more understanding of adaptive conditions of adversity with the purpose. If micro foundation is strong than macro foundation of the organizational ability will be more stable. However, to reduce poverty, proper analysis with right definition may be used by Bangladesh Bureau of statistics and reducing poverty must get higher priority by creating microentrepreneurs by formal, semi-formal and informal sector. Microenterprises must entangle with supply chain management with the purview of domestic, regional, and global perspective.

Youth employment opportunities through growth with equity is very much important in Bangladesh. Those who are working as a consultant in Bangladesh must be honest and give well-defined data and information so that policy makers can take right decisions in right time so that micro-organizations can get proper support of the government, public and private sectors so that institutionalist and welfarist activities can perform through microentrepreneurs. Micro Entrepreneurial organizations have a considerable influence on Bangladesh's economy meanwhile they care job creation, household income growth, and economic progress. These micro-organizations assist in allowing societies to develop fruitful microentrepreneurs and reducing poverty by the micro financial institutions through entree to financial facilities, training, consultancies, and assistances.

Digitalization process in the micro-organization will stipulate improvement of supply chain management and redistribution channel among producers, vendors, and customers. During COVID-19 online microbusiness raised in Bangladesh. But aftermath of COVID-19, it is observed that physically around 90 percent people want to purchase product and only 10 percent by online (Ali,2023). However, due to Russia-Ukraine war whole global economic order is now stuck up. But dynamic rationalization of a trade's supply-side doings to make the most of client worth and expansion a competitive advantage in the marketplace through better utilization process of supply chain management by the microentrepreneurs. As such, microentrepreneurs needs support services to provide better supply chain management and use active distribution channel. At the grass root level, active support should be arranged.

Micro-Organizational flexibility and adaptation of micro-enterprises focus on a dynamic interplay between organizational activities and diversified variabilities. Micro-Organizational flexibility involves more than a strategic imperative and the ability of the micro financial institutions to survive but enables to harness its experience and flourishes embracing the opportunities in a dynamic, complex, and interconnected environment. Saving, capital accumulation and investment for micro entrepreneurship development in Bangladesh is very much needed. Action priority can build micro enterprises organizational flexibility through the access to information and learning. Micro enterprise clusters may be developed without corruption free of the country by the govt. organizations.

Some of the ex-ante decisions are planning, learning and back-up systems and some of the ex-post adjustments are changing routines, minimizing strains on infrastructure and external support is necessary for micro enterprises. Micro enterprises must evolve and growth from a disturbance through the transformation processes by learning, flourish, and progress. Corruption free society and too ease doing business is necessary. New definition of micro, cottage, small and medium and large enterprises in Bangladesh is required as current definition is not pro cottage, micro and small industries to get access to the financial services from the formal sector. Still 50 per cent of the total population are only financially included in Bangladesh which needs to speed up economic development as the Bangladesh government has taken a special drive for creating competencies among the cottage, micro, small, and medium enterprises.

Implementation will help to get financial access of micro and cottage industries to remain included for doing business assistance from the formal sector. Micro saving is very important to channel micro investment for which saving, and capital accumulation must be done by the micro financial institution not only depending on donor agencies but through accumulating fund from the beneficiaries to reinvest. Elastic emphasizes knowledge from failures and success to become reliable for micro-organizations. Micro-organizational flexibility of micro-enterprises cannot be boosted on trial and error due to the high cost but by focusing on learning from failures. Moreover, microentrepreneurs' are relatively come from poor income stratum. Intermediary organization must help microentrepreneurs' for smooth networking to sell the products not only within the country but also outside the country. Supply chain management need to be promoted by the interactions between individuals developing micro-organizational learning and flexibility and an integrated manner so that distribution channel at domestic, regional, and global can work. Regional connectivity issue should get priority by the policy makers.

Flexibility can integrate findings from other areas and disciplines which can be related to other flexibility stages and levels such as the anticipation through high reliability organizations, coping using crisis management adaptation to unexpected events supported by organizational learning. During the COVID-19 pandemic, microentrepreneurs' in Bangladesh must find difficult situations but try to overcome the problem where role of Govt. organizations, commercial banks, non-scheduled banks, and non-bank financial institutions have been very slow despite the directives of the Honorable prime minister of Bangladesh's directives. Ongoing war between Russia and Ukraine will have also created difficulties for microenterprises global supply chain management's disruption. The micro-organizational flexibility needs to leverage through learning and experience, precautionary activities. This in turn will help to adjust and forge new micro-organizational growth with the support from public -private. Local level economy in Bangladesh should be strengthened.

The advancement of the flexible capability occurs when learning is embedded into the conscious mind of individuals in the organization. It becomes experiential knowledge to be used in future adversity events for which holistic basis microenterprises should act. The flexibility model becomes a litheness planning and implementing tool for micro enterprises which contributes to learn from mistakes and events so that the pro-people community to uplift socio-economic conditions and gradual participation through continuous development processes with adaption and mitigation in any changing environment if occur. Skill gap mismatching is prevailing in the country for which microenterprises cannot be properly developed.

The study is mainly done secondary literatures along with a primary survey-based questionnaire to test three hypotheses and one case study development. Flexibility of micro-organizations may be studied in future in broad spectrum considering not only micro-organizations but also cottage, small, medium, and large enterprises. To compare efficiency among these five types of organizations may be data envelopment analysis done for which input and output can be considered. A separate study may be undertaken to find out diversified characteristics at the border of fundamental influences foremost to entrepreneurship development. As such structural equation model may be considered to examine the internal and external influencing factors on smooth running of resilient of dynamism for upliftment of socio-economic condition of micro-organization with sustainability and competency. An independent study on "Smart data, Smart Bangladesh" may be done.

REFERENCES

Abdel-Basset, M, Manogaran, G. (2018). Internet of Things and its Impact on supply chain: A framework for building smart, secure, and efficient systems. *Future Generation Computer system, 86, 614-626*. doi:10.1016/j.future.2018.04.051

ADB. (2007). *Effect of Microfinance Operations on Poor Rural Households and the Status of Women.* ADB evaluation report. https://www.oecd.org/countries/bangladesh/39503711.pdf.

Alexiou, A. (2014). Taming the waves of adversity: Exploring the multidimensional construct of organizational flexibility. In D. G. Assimakopoulos, I. Oshri, & K. Pandza (Eds.), *Managing Emerging Technologies for Socio-Economic Impact.* Edward Elgar Publishing. doi:10.4337/9781782547884.00026

Ali, M. M. (2017). Testing Hypothesis on Theory of Social Networking, Community Banking and Empowerment of People: A Conceptual View. *Psychology and Behavioral Sciences (New York, N.Y.)*, *6*(5), 96–104. doi:10.11648/j.pbs.20170605.14

Ali, N. M. (2018). Impact of climate change and natural catastrophe on the occupational changes in the coastal areas of Bangladesh: An empirical study. *Environment and Ecology*, *9*(1), 22–37. doi:10.21511/ee.09(1).2018.02 PMID:30005645

Alliger, G. M., Cerasoli, C. P., Tannenbaum, S. I., & Vessey, W. B. (2015). Team flexibility: How teams flourish under pressure. *Organizational Dynamics*, *44*, 176–184. doi:10.1016/j.orgdyn.2015.05.003

Alvarez, S. A., & Barney, J. B. (2007). Discovery and Creation: Alternative Theories of Entrepreneurial Action. *Strategic Entrepreneurship Journal*, *1*(1), 11–26. doi:10.1002ej.4

Ambrosini, V., Bowman, C., & Collier, N. (2009). Dynamic Capabilities: An Exploration of How Firms Renew their Resource Base. *British Journal of Management*, *20*(S1), S9–S24. doi:10.1111/j.1467-8551.2008.00610.x

Apneseth, K., Wahl, A., & Hollnagel, E. (2013). Measuring flexibility in integrated planning. In E. Albrechtsen & D. Besnard (Eds.), *Oil and Gas, Technology and Humans: Assessing the Human Factors of Technological Change*. CRC press.

Azadeh, A., Hasannia Kolaee, M., & Salehi, V. (2016). The impact of redundancy on flexibility engineering in a petrochemical plant by data envelopment analysis. *Proceedings of the Institution of Mechanical Engineers. Part O, Journal of Risk and Reliability*, *230*(3), 285–296. doi:10.1177/1748006X16629866

Barker, V. L. III, & Duhaime, I. M. (1997). Strategic Change in the Turnaround Process: Theory and Empirical Evidence. *Strategic Management Journal*, *18*(1), 13–38. doi:10.1002/(SICI)1097-0266(199701)18:1<13::AID-SMJ843>3.0.CO;2-X

Barreto, I. (2010). Dynamic Capabilities: A Review of Past Research and an Agenda for the Future. *Journal of Management*, *36*(1), 256–280. doi:10.1177/0149206309350776

Barreto, I. (2012). Solving the Entrepreneurial Puzzle: The Role of Entrepreneurial Interpretation in Opportunity Formation and Related Processes. *Journal of Management Studies*, *49*(2), 356–380. doi:10.1111/j.1467-6486.2011.01023.x

Bento, F., & Garotti, L. (2019). Flexibility beyond Formal Structures: A Network Perspective towards the Challenges of an Aging Workforce in the Oil and Gas Industry. *Journal of Open Innovation*, *5*(1), 1–15. doi:10.3390/joitmc5010015

Bergstr̈om, J., van Winsen, R., & Henriqson, E. (2015). On the rationale of flexibility in the domain of safety: A literature review, *Reliab. Eng. Syst. Saf. 141,* 131–141. . doi:10.1016/j.ress.2015.03.008

Beznos, M. (2023). Microservices vs monolith: Which architecture is the best choice for your business? *N-iX*. https://www.n-ix.com/microservices-vs-monolith-which-architecture-best-choice-your-business/(Viewed on 31, Janaury,2023)

Bhuiyan, M. F., & Ivlevs, A. (2019). Micro-entrepreneurship and subjective well-being: Evidence from rural Bangladesh, *Journal of Business Venturing*, *34*(4), 625-645. https:// doi:10.1016/j.jbusvent.2018.09.005

Bigley, G. A., & Roberts, K. H. (2001). The incident command system: High reliability organizing for complex and volatile task environments. *Academy of Management Journal*, *44*(6), 1281–1299. doi:10.2307/3069401

Bingham, C. B., & Eisenhardt, K. M. (2011). Rational Heuristics: The 'Simple Rules' that Strategists Learn from Process Experience. *Strategic Management Journal*, *32*(13), 1437–1464. doi:10.1002mj.965

Bingham, C. B., Eisenhardt, K. M., & Davis, J. P. (2007). *Opening the black box of organizational expertise: understanding what firms learn from their process experience and how that learning unfolds over time*. University of Maryland working paper.

Bingham, C. B., Eisenhardt, K. M., & Furr, N. R. (2007). What Makes a Process a Capability? Heuristics, Strategy and Effective Capture of Opportunities. *Strategic Entrepreneurship Journal*, *1*(1), 27–47. doi:10.1002ej.1

Boin, A., & McConnell, A. (2007). Preparing for critical infrastructure breakdowns: The limits of crisis management and the need for flexibility. *Journal of Contingencies and Crisis Management*, *15*(1), 50–59. doi:10.1111/j.1468-5973.2007.00504.x

Boin, A., & van Eeten, M. J. B. (2013). The Resilient Organization—A critical appraisal. *Public Management Review*, *15*(3), 429–445. doi:10.1080/14719037.2013.769856

Burger-Helmchen, T. (2013). Entrepreneurial Organizations. In E. G. Carayannis (Ed.), *Encyclopedia of Creativity, Invention, Innovation and Entrepreneurship*. Springer., doi:10.1007/978-1-4614-3858-8_208

Burnard, K., & Bhamra, R. (2011). Organisational flexibility: Development of a conceptual framework for organisational responses. *International Journal of Production Research*, *49*(18), 5581–5599. doi:10.1080/00207543.2011.563827

Carley, K. M. (1991). Designing organizational structures to cope with communication breakdowns: A simulation model. *Industrial Crisis Quarterly*, *5*(1), 19–57. doi:10.1177/108602669100500102

Carley, K. M., & Harrald, J. R. (1997). Organizational learning under fire: Theory and practice. *The American Behavioral Scientist*, *40*(3), 310–332. doi:10.1177/0002764297040003007

Chamlee-Wright, E. (2010). *The Cultural and Political Economy of Recovery: Social Learning in a Post-Disaster Environment* (Vol. 12). Routledge. doi:10.4324/9780203855928

Chan, J. K. (2011). Enhancing Organisational Flexibility: Application of Viable System Model and MCDA in a Small Hong Kong Company. *International Journal of Production Research*, *49*(18), 5545–5563. doi:10.1080/00207543.2011.563829

Chen, J.-C., Li, W. T., Wen, C. K., Teng, J. H., & Ting, P. (2014, July). Efficient Identification Methods for Power Line Outages in the Smart Power Grid. *IEEE Transactions on Power Systems*, *29*(4), 1788–1800. doi:10.1109/TPWRS.2013.2296897

Chen, R., Liu, Y., & Zhou, F. (2021). Turning Danger into Safety: The Origin, Research Context and Theoretical Framework of Organizational Flexibility. IEEE Access, 9, 48899-48913. doi:10.1109/ACCESS.2021.3069301

Cho, S., Mathiassen, L., & Robey, D. (2006). *The Dialectics of Flexibility: A Multilevel Analysis of a Telehealth Innovation*. International Federation for Information Processing. 10.1007/0-387-34410-1_22

Christianson, M. K., Farkas, M. T., Sutcliffe, K. M., & Weick, K. E. (2009). Learning through rare events: Significant interruptions at the Baltimore and Ohio Railroad Museum. *Organization Science*, *20*(5), 846–860. doi:10.1287/orsc.1080.0389

Clement, V., & Rivera, J. (2017). From adaptation to transformation: An extended research agenda for organizational flexibility to adversity in the natural environment. *Organization & Environment*, *30*(4), 346–365. doi:10.1177/1086026616658333

Cook, R., & Rasmussen, J. (2005). Going Solid: A Model of System Dynamics and Consequences for Patient Safety. *Quality & Safety in Health Care, 14*(2), 130–134. doi:10.1136/qshc.2003.009530 PMID:15805459

Coutu, D. L. (2002). How flexibility works. *Harvard Business Review, 80*(5), 46–55. PMID:12024758

Crichton, M. T., Ramsay, C. G., & Kelly, T. (2009). Enhancing organizational flexibility through emergency planning: Learnings from cross-sectorial lessons. *Journal of Contingencies and Crisis Management, 17*(1), 24–37. doi:10.1111/j.1468-5973.2009.00556.x

Dalgaard-Nielsen, A. (2017). Organizational flexibility in national security bureaucracies: Realistic and practicable? *Journal of Contingencies and Crisis Management, 25*(4), 341–349. doi:10.1111/1468-5973.12164

Danneels, E. (2012). Second-order competences and Schumpeterian rents. *Strategic Entrepreneurship Journal, 6*(1), 42–58. doi:10.1002ej.1127

Davies, A., & Brady, T. (2016). Explicating the dynamics of project capabilities. *International Journal of Project Management, 34*(2), 314–327. doi:10.1016/j.ijproman.2015.04.006

Demmer, W. A., Vickery, S. K., & Calantone, R. (2011). Engendering flexibility in small-and medium-sized enterprises (SMEs): A case study of Demmer Corporation. *International Journal of Production Research, 49*(18), 5395–5413. doi:10.1080/00207543.2011.563903

Deverell, E. (2009). Crises as Learning Triggers: Exploring a Conceptual Framework of Crisis-Induced Learning. *Journal of Contingencies and Crisis Management, 17*(3), 179–188. doi:10.1111/j.1468-5973.2009.00578.x

Duchek, S. (2014). Growth in the face of crisis: The role of organizational flexibility capabilities. *Proceedings - Academy of Management, 2014*(1), 13487. doi:10.5465/ambpp.2014.225

Duit, A. (2016). Flexibility thinking: Lessons for Public Administration. *Public Administration, 94*(2), 364–380. doi:10.1111/padm.12182

Edmondson, A. C. (2007). The competitive imperative of learning. *Harvard Business Review, 86*(7-8), 60–67. PMID:18681298

Eisenhardt, K. M., Furr, N. R., & Bingham, C. B. (2010). Micro foundations of Performance: Balancing Efficiency and Flexibility in Dynamic Environments. *Organization Science, 21*(6), 1263–1273. doi:10.1287/orsc.1100.0564

Eltantawy, R. A. (2016). The role of supply management flexibility in attaining ambidexterity: A dynamic capabilities approach. *Journal of Business and Industrial Marketing*, *31*(1), 123–134. doi:10.1108/JBIM-05-2014-0091

Erol, O., Sauser, B., & Mansouri, M. (2010). A framework for investigation into extended enterprise flexibility. *Enterprise Information Systems*, *4*(2), 111–136. doi:10.1080/17517570903474304

Fafchamps, M. (2011). *When is capital enough to get female microenterprises growing? Evidence from a randomized experiment in Ghana.* National Bureau of Economic Research, Inc.

Farjoun, M. (2010). Beyond dualism: Stability and change as a duality. *Academy of Management Review*, *35*(2), 202–225.

Fatoki, O. (2018). The Impact of Entrepreneurial Flexibility on the Success of Small and Medium Enterprises in South Africa. *Sustainability (Basel)*, *10*(7), 2527. doi:10.3390u10072527

Folke, C. (2006). Flexibility: The emergence of a perspective for social–ecological systems analyses, *Global Environ. Change, 16*(3), 253–267. https://doi.org/. gloenvcha.2006.04.002. doi:10.1016/j

Folke, C., Carpenter, S. R., Walker, B., Scheffer, M., Chapin, T., & Rockström, J. (2010). Flexibility thinking: Integrating flexibility, adaptability, and transformability. *Ecology and Society*, *15*(4). doi:10.5751/ES-03610-150420

Francis, R., & Bekera, B. (2014). A metric and frameworks for flexibility analysis of engineered and infrastructure systems. *Reliability Engineering & System Safety*, *121*, 90–103. doi:10.1016/j.ress.2013.07.004

Freeman, S. F., Hirschhorn, L., & Maltz, M. (2004). *Organizational flexibility and moral purpose: Sandler O'Neill & Partners in the aftermath of 9/11/01*. Paper presented at the Annual Meeting of the Academy of Management, New Orleans.

Gibson, C., & Tarrant, M. (2010). A "Conceptual Models" approach to organisational flexibility. *Australian Journal of Emergency Management*, *25*(2), 8–14.

Gigerenzer, G. (2008). Why Heuristics Work. *Perspectives on Psychological Science*, *3*(1), 20–29. doi:10.1111/j.1745-6916.2008.00058.x PMID:26158666

Gigerenzer, G., & Brighton, H. (2009). Homo Heuristicus: Why Biased Minds Makes Better inferences. *Topics in Cognitive Science*, *1*(1), 107–143. doi:10.1111/j.1756-8765.2008.01006.x PMID:25164802

Glover, J. (2012). Rural flexibility through continued learning and innovation. *Local Economy, 27*(4), 355–372. doi:10.1177/0269094212437833

Gover, L., & Duxbury, L. (2018). Making sense of organizational change: Is hindsight really 20/20. *Journal of Organizational Behavior, 39*(1), 39–51. doi:10.1002/job.2208

Greiner, L. E. (1972). Evolution and Revolution as Organizations Grow. *Harvard Business Review, 50*(4), 37–46. PMID:10179654

Hale, A., & Heijer, T. (2006). Defining Flexibility. In E. Hollnagel, D. D. Woods, & N. Leveson (Eds.), *Flexibility Engineering: Concepts and Precepts* (pp. 35–40). Ashgate.

Hamedi, H., & Mehdiabadi, A. (2020). Entrepreneurship flexibility and Iranian organizations: Application of the fuzzy DANP technique. *Asia Pacific Journal of Innovation and Entrepreneurship, 14*(3), 231–247. doi:10.1108/APJIE-10-2019-0074

Hamel, G. and Välikangas, L. (2003). The quest for flexibility. *Harvard Business Review, 81*(9), 52–63. 5.

Held, D., Kickbusch, I., McNally, K., Piselli, D., & Told, M. (2019). Gridlock, Innovation and Flexibility in Global Health Governance. *Global Policy, 10*(2), 161–177. doi:10.1111/1758-5899.12654

Helfat, C. E., Finklestein, S., Mitchell, W., Peteraf, M. A., Singh, H., Teece, D. J., & Winter, S. G. (2007). *Dynamic Capabilities: understanding strategic change in organizations*. Blackwell Publishing.

Hernández-Chea, R., Mahdad, M., Minh, T. T., & Hjortsø, C. N. (2021). Moving beyond intermediation: How intermediary organizations shape collaboration dynamics in entrepreneurial ecosystems. *Technovation, 108*(102332), 102332. doi:10.1016/j.technovation.2021.102332

Hine, D., Parker, R., Pregelj, L., & Verreynne, M.-L. (2014). Deconstructing and Reconstructing the Capability Hierarchy. *Industrial and Corporate Change, 23*(5), 1299–1325. doi:10.1093/icc/dtt046

Hollnagel, E., & Woods, D. D. (2017). Epilogue: Flexibility engineering precepts. In E. Hollnagel, D. D. Woods, & N. Leveson (Eds.), *Flexibility engineering: Concepts and precepts* (pp. 347–358). CRC Press. doi:10.1201/9781315605685-30

Huber, S., van Wijgerden, I., de Witt, A., & Dekker, S. W. A. (2009). Learning from organizational incidents: Flexibility engineering for high-risk process environments. *Process Safety Progress, 28*(1), 90–95. doi:10.1002/prs.10286

Ishak, A. W., & Williams, E. A. (2018). A dynamic model of organizational flexibility: Adaptive and anchored approaches. *Editorial Advisory Board, 23*(2), 180–196.

Jabareen, Y. (2009). Building a conceptual framework: Philosophy, definitions, and procedure. *International Journal of Qualitative Methods, 8*(4), 49–62. doi:10.1177/160940690900800406

Kahan, J., Allen, A., George, J., & Thompson, W. (2009). *Concept development: An operational framework for flexibility.* VA: Homeland Security Studies and Analysis Institute. http://www.homelandsecurity.org/

Kamalahmadi, M., & Parast, M. M. (2016). A review of the literature on the principles of enterprise and supply chain flexibility: Major findings and directions for future research. *International Journal of Production Economics, 171*, 116–133. doi:10.1016/j.ijpe.2015.10.023

King, D. D., Newman, A., & Luthans, F. (2016). Not if, but when we need flexibility in the workplace. *Journal of Organizational Behavior, 37*(5), 782–786. doi:10.1002/job.2063

Knowledge Center. (2023). *Agile Supply Chain: What It Is, Benefits, and Applications.* Knowledge Center https://www.inboundlogistics.com/articles/agile-supply-chain/

Kuntz, J. R., Malinen, S., & Näswall, K. (2017). Employee flexibility: Directions for flexibility development. *Consulting Psychology Journal, 69*(3), 223–242. doi:10.1037/cpb0000097

Lee, A. V., Vargo, J., & Seville, E. (2013). Developing a tool to measure and compare organizations' flexibility. *Natural Hazards Review, 14*(1), 29–41. doi:10.1061/(ASCE)NH.1527-6996.0000075

Lengnick-Hall, C. A., & Beck, T. E. (2009). Flexibility capacity and strategic agility: Prerequisites for thriving in a dynamic environment. In Flexibility engineering perspectives, Volume 2. Preparation and restoration, ed. Christopher P. Nemeth, Erik Hollnagel, and Sidney Dekker, 39–70, Aldershot: Ashgate Publishing.

Lengnick-Hall, C. A., Beck, T. E., & Lengnick-Hall, M. L. (2011). Developing a Capacity for Organizational Flexibility through Strategic Human Resource Management. *Human Resource Management Review, 21*(3), 243–255. doi:10.1016/j.hrmr.2010.07.001

Levitt, B., & March, J. G. (1988). Organizational Learning. *Annual Review of Sociology, 14*(1), 319–340. doi:10.1146/annurev.so.14.080188.001535

Liedholm, C. E., & Mead, D. C. (1999). *Small Enterprises and Economic Development: The Dynamics of Micro and Small Enterprises* (1st ed.). Routledge. doi:10.4324/9780203354735

Limnios, E. A. M., Mazzarol, T., Ghadouani, A., & Schilizzi, S. G. M. (2014). The flexibility architecture framework: Four organizational archetypes. *European Management Journal, 32*(1), 104–116. doi:10.1016/j.emj.2012.11.007

Linnenluecke, M. K., & Griffiths, A. (2012). Assessing organizational flexibility to climate and weather extremes: Complexities and methodological pathways. *Climatic Change, 113*(3-4), 933–947. doi:10.100710584-011-0380-6

Luthans, F. (2002). Positive organizational behavior: Developing and managing psychological strengths. *The Academy of Management Perspectives, 16*(1), 57–72. doi:10.5465/ame.2002.6640181

Luthar, S. S., Cicchetti, D., & Becker, B. (2000). T*he construct of flexibility: A critical evaluation and guidelines for future work. Child Development, 71*(3), 543–562. doi:10.1111/1467-8624.00164 PMID:10953923

Lynham, S. A. (2002). The general method of theory-building research in applied disciplines. *Advances in Developing Human Resources, 4*(3), 221–241. doi:10.1177/1523422302043002

Macpherson, A., Herbane, B., & Jones, O. (2015). Developing Dynamic Capabilities through Resource Accretion: Expanding the Entrepreneurial Solution Space. *Entrepreneurship and Regional Development, 27*(5–6), 259–291. doi:10.1080/08985626.2015.1038598

Madni, A. M., & Jackson, S. (2009). Towards a conceptual framework for Flexibility Engineering. *IEEE Systems Journal, 3*(2), 181–191. doi:10.1109/JSYST.2009.2017397

Maitlis, S., & Christianson, M. (2014). Sense making in organizations: Taking stock and moving forward. *The Academy of Management Annals, 8*(1), 57–125. doi:10.5465/19416520.2014.873177

Manyena, S. B., O'Brien, G., O'Keefe, P., & Rose, J. (2011). Disaster flexibility: A bounce back or bounce forward ability? *Local Environment, 16*(5), 417–424. doi:10.1080/13549839.2011.583049

March, J. G. (1991). Exploration and Exploitation in Organizational Learning. *Organization Science, 2*(1), 71–87. doi:10.1287/orsc.2.1.71

March, J. G., Sproull, L. S., & Tamuz, M. (2003). Learning from samples of one or fewer. *Organization Science*, *2*(1), 1–13. doi:10.1287/orsc.2.1.1 PMID:14645764

Masten, A. S. (2001). Ordinary magic: Flexibility processes in development. *The American Psychologist*, *56*(3), 227–238. doi:10.1037/0003-066X.56.3.227 PMID:11315249

Masten, A. S. (2007). Flexibility in Developing Systems: Progress and Promise as the Fourth Wave Rises. *Development and Psychopathology*, *19*(3), 921–930. doi:10.1017/S0954579407000442 PMID:17705908

Masten, A. S. (2014). *Ordinary Magic: Flexibility in Development*. Guilford Press.

McCarthy, I. P., Collard, M., & Johnson, M. (2017). Adaptive organizational flexibility: An evolutionary perspective [Oct.]. *Current Opinion in Environmental Sustainability*, *28*, 33–40. doi:10.1016/j.cosust.2017.07.005

McGrath, R. G. (1999). Falling Forward: Real Options Reasoning and Entrepreneurial Failure. *Academy of Management Review*, *24*(1), 13–30. doi:10.2307/259034

McGrath, R. G. (2013). *The End of Competitive Advantage: How to Keep your Strategy Moving as Fast as your Business*. Harvard Business Review Press.

Mcmanus, S., Seville, E., Vargo, J., & Brunsdon, D. (2008). Facilitated process for improving organizational flexibility [May.]. *Natural Hazards Review*, *9*(2), 81–90. doi:10.1061/(ASCE)1527-6988(2008)9:2(81)

McManus, S., Seville, E., Vargo, J., & Brunsdon, D. (2008). Facilitated process for improving organizational flexibility. *Natural Hazards Review*, *9*(2), 81–90. doi:10.1061/(ASCE)1527-6988(2008)9:2(81)

Mellahi, K., & Wilkinson, A. (2004). Organizational Failure: A Critique of Recent Research and a Proposed Integrative Framework. *International Journal of Management Reviews*, *5/6*(1), 21–41. doi:10.1111/j.1460-8545.2004.00095.x

Meredith, J. (1993). Theory building through conceptual methods. *International Journal of Operations & Production Management*, *13*, 3–11.

Morais-Storz, M., & Nguyen, N. (2017). The role of unlearning in metamorphosis and strategic flexibility. *The Learning Organization*, *24*(2), 93–106. doi:10.1108/TLO-12-2016-0091

Morrow, J. L., Sirmon, D. G., Hitt, M. A., & Holcomb, T. R. (2007). Creating Value in the Face of Declining Performance: Firm Strategies and Organizational Recovery. *Strategic Management Journal*, *28*(3), 271–283. doi:10.1002mj.579

Norris, F. H., Stevens, S. P., Pfefferbaum, B., Wyche, K. F., & Pfeffer-baum, R. L. (2008). Community flexibility as a metaphor, theory, set of capacities, and strategy for disaster readiness. *American Journal of Community Psychology*, *41*(1–2), 127–150. doi:10.100710464-007-9156-6 PMID:18157631

O'Hara, S., Murphy, L., & Reeve, S. (2007). Action learning as leverage for strategic transformation: A case study reflection. *Strategic Change*, *16*(4), 177–190. doi:10.1002/jsc.792

O'Sullivan, T. L., Corneil, W., Kuziemsky, C. E., & Toal-Sullivan, D. (2015). Use of the structured interview matrix to enhance community flexibility through collaboration and inclusive engagement. *Systems Research and Behavioral Science*, *32*(6), 616–628. doi:10.1002res.2250

Ortiz-de-Mandojana, N., & Bansal, P. (2015). The long-term benefits of organizational flexibility through sustainable business practices. *Strategic Management Journal*. doi:10.1002mj.2410

Patriarca, R., Di Gravio, G., Constantino, F., Falegnami, A., & Bilotta, F. (2017). An Analytic Framework to Assess Organizational Flexibility. *Safety and Health at work, 9*. doi:10.1016/j.shaw.2017.10.005

Peteraf, M., Di Stefano, G., & Verona, G. (2013). The Elephant in the Room of Dynamic Capabilities: Bringing Two Diverging Conversations Together. *Strategic Management Journal*, *34*(12), 1389–1410. doi:10.1002mj.2078

Polask, S. (2019). Role of economics in analyzing the environment and sustainable development. *PNAS, 116* (12), 5233-5238. doi:10.1073/pnas.1901616116

Ponomarov, S. Y., & Holcolmb, M. C. (2009). Understanding the Concept of Supply Chain Flexibility. *International Journal of Logistics Management*, *20*(1), 124–143. doi:10.1108/09574090910954873

Probst, G., & Raisch, S. (2005). Organizational Crisis: The Logic of Failure. *The Academy of Management Perspectives*, *19*(1), 90–105. doi:10.5465/ame.2005.15841958

Reich, J. W. (2006). Three psychological principles of flexibility in natural disasters. *Disaster Prevention and Management*, *15*(5), 793–798. doi:10.1108/09653560610712739

Richardson, G. E. (2016). The applied metatheory of flexibility and resiliency. In U. Kumar (Ed.), *The Routledge International Handbook of Psychological Flexibility* (pp. 124–135). Routledge.

Richtnér, A., & Löfsten, H. (2014). Managing in turbulence: How the capacity for flexibility influences creativity. *R & D Management*, *44*(2), 137–151. doi:10.1111/radm.12050

Roberts, K. H., Madsen, P. M., & Desait, V. M. (2005). The space between in space transportation: A relational analysis of the failure of STS-107. In W. H. Starbuck & M. Farjoun (Eds.), *Organization at the limit—NASA and the Columbia Disaster* (pp. 81–98). Blackwell.

Sheffi, Y. (2005). Building a Resilient Supply Chain. *Harvard Business Review Supply Chain Strategy*. https://sheffi.mit.edu/sites/default/files/genmedia.buildingresilientsupplychain.pdf

Sheppard, J. P., & Chowdhury, S. D. (2005). Riding the Wrong Wave: Organizational Failure as a Failed Turnaround. *Long Range Planning*, *38*(3), 239–260. doi:10.1016/j.lrp.2005.03.009

Smith, D., & Elliott, D. (2007). Exploring the barriers to learning from crisis -Organizational learning and crisis. *Management Learning*, *38*(5), 519–538. doi:10.1177/1350507607083205

Stephenson, A. (2010). *Benchmarking the Flexibility of Organizations*. [Unpublished PhD Thesis, Civil and Natural Resources Engineering Department, University of Canterbury].

Stewart, J., & O'Donnell, M. (2007). Implementing change in a public agency. *International Journal of Public Sector Management*, *20*(3), 239–251. doi:10.1108/09513550710740634

Sutcliffe, K. M., & Vogus, T. J. (2003). Organizing for flexibility. *Positive organizational scholarship*, 94-110.

Sydow, J., Schreyögg, G., & Koch, J. (2009). Organizational Path Dependence: Opening the Black Box. *Academy of Management Review*, *34*(4), 689–709.

Tabaklar, T., Sorkun, M. F., Yurt, O., & Yu, W. (2021). Exploring the microfoundations of dynamic capabilities for social innovation in a humanitarian aid supply network setting. *Industrial Marketing Management*, *96*, 147–162. https://www.sciencedirect.com/science/article/pii/S0019850121000845. doi:10.1016/j.indmarman.2021.04.012

Taleb, N. N. N. (2014). *Antifragile: Things that Gain from Disorder* (3rd ed.). Random House.

Teece, D. J. (2007). Explicating Dynamic Capabilities: The Nature and Micro foundations of (Sustainable) Enterprise Performance. *Strategic Management Journal*, *28*(13), 1319–1350. doi:10.1002mj.640

Teece, D. J. (2012). Dynamic Capabilities: Routines versus Entrepreneurial Action. *Journal of Management Studies*, *49*(8), 1395–1401. doi:10.1111/j.1467-6486.2012.01080.x

Teece, D. J., Pisano, G., & Shuen, A. (1997). Dynamic capabilities and strategic management. *Strategic Management Journal*, *18*(7), 509–533. doi:10.1002/(SICI)1097-0266(199708)18:7<509::AID-SMJ882>3.0.CO;2-Z

Teo, W. L., Lee, M., & Lim, W.-S. (2017). The relational activation of flexibility model: How leadership activates flexibility in an organizational crisis. *Journal of Contingencies and Crisis Management*, *25*, 136–147. doi:10.1111/1468-5973.12179

Thiel, C. E., Bagdasarov, Z., Harkrider, L., Johnson, J. F., & Mumford, M. D. (2012). Leader ethical decision-making in organizations: Strategies for sense making. *Journal of Business Ethics*, *107*(1), 49–64. doi:10.100710551-012-1299-1

Toft, B., & Reynolds, S. (1997). *Learning from Disasters* (2nd ed.). Perpetuity Press.

Tyler, S., & Moench, M. (2012). A framework for urban climate flexibility. *Climate and Development*, *4*(4), 311–326. doi:10.1080/17565529.2012.745389

Umoh, G. I., Amah, E., & Wokocha, H. I. (2014). Management development and organizational flexibility: A case study of some selected manufacturing firms in Rivers State, Nigeria,'. *IOSR Journal of Business and Management*, *16*(2), 7–16. doi:10.9790/487X-16230716

Vaelikangas, L., & Romme, A. G. L. (2013). How to design for strategic flexibility: A case study in retailing. *Journal of Organization Design*, *2*(2), 44–53. doi:10.7146/jod.7360

Vakilzadeh, K., & Haase, A. (2020). *The building blocks of organizational flexibility: a review of the empirical literature*. Continuity & Flexibility Review., doi:10.1108/CRR-04-2020-0002

Vanderbilt-Adriance, E., & Shaw, D. S. (2008). Conceptualizing and re-evaluating flexibility across levels of risk, time, and domains of competence. *Clinical Child and Family Psychology Review*, *11*(1-2), 30–58. doi:10.100710567-008-0031-2 PMID:18379875

Walker, B. H., & Salt, D. A. (2006). *Flexibility Thinking: Sustaining Ecosystems and People in a Changing World*. Island Press.

Watts, G., & Paciga, J. J. (2011). Conscious Adaptation: Building Resilient Organizations. In T. Carmichael (Ed.), *Complex Adaptive Systems: Energy, Information, and Intelligence*, (pp. 158-167). Arlington VA: AAAI Fall Symposium Series.

Weick, K. E., & Roberts, K. H. (1993). Collective mind in organizations: Heedful interrelating on flight decks. *Administrative Science Quarterly, 38*(3), 357–381. doi:10.2307/2393372

Weick, K. E., & Sutcliffe, K. M. (2001). *Managing the Unexpected: Assuring High Performance in an Age of Complexity*. Jossey-Bass.

Weick, K. E., & Sutcliffe, K. M. (2003). Hospitals as Cultures of Entrapment: A Re-Analysis of the Bristol Royal Infirmary. *California Management Review, 45*(2), 73–84. doi:10.2307/41166166

Weick, K. E., & Sutcliffe, K. M. (2007). Managing the unexpected: Resilient performance in an age of uncertainty (2. ed.). San Francisco, CA: Jossey-Bass.

Weick, K. E., Sutcliffe, K. M., & Obstfeld, D. (2005). Organizing and the process of sensemaking. *Organization Science, 16*(4), 409–421. doi:10.1287/orsc.1050.0133

Whiteman, G., & Cooper, W. H. (2011). Ecological sensemaking. *Academy of Management Journal, 43*(6), 1265–1282. doi:10.2307/1556349

Wicker, P., Filo, K., & Cuskelly, G. (2013). Organizational flexibility of community sport clubs impacted by natural disasters [Nov.]. *Journal of Sport Management, 27*(6), 510–525. doi:10.1123/jsm.27.6.510

Wildavsky, A. (1988). *Searching for Safety*. Transaction Press.

Willems, J. J., Busscher, T., van den Brink, M., & Arts, J. (2018). Anticipating water infrastructure renewal: A framing perspective on organizational learning in public agencies Environment and Planning C. *Politics and Space, 36*(6), 1088–1108.

Williams, T. A., Gruber, D. A., Sutcliffe, K. M., Shepherd, D. A., & Zhao, E. Y. (2017). Organizational response to adversity: Fusing crisis management and flexibility research streams. *The Academy of Management Annals, 11*(2), 733–769. doi:10.5465/annals.2015.0134

Wise, V., & Ali, M. M. (2009). *Customer Relationship Management of Commercial Banks in Bangladesh with special reference to automation process: an empirical study*. Research Gate. https://www.researchgate.net/publication/318725722_Customer_Relationship_Management_of_Commercial_Banks_in_Bangladesh_with_special_reference_to_automation_process_an_empirical_study

Woods, D. D., & Hollnagel, E. (2006). *Joint Cognitive Systems: Patterns in Cognitive Systems Engineering*. Taylor, and Francis. doi:10.1201/9781420005684

World Bank. (2018). *Bangladesh: Reducing Poverty and Sharing Prosperity*. World Bank. https://www.worldbank.org/en/results/2018/11/15/bangladesh-reducing-poverty-and-sharing-prosperity

World Bank. (2020). *Bangladesh's microenterprises embraced green growth and thrived–then COVID-19 hit.* World Bank. https://blogs.worldbank.org/endpovertyinsouthasia/bangladeshs-microenterprises-embraced-green-growth-and-thrived-then-covid-19(Viewed on 3rd June,2022)

World Bank. (2022). Micro Enterprise Owners in Bangladesh Go Green. World Bank. https://www.worldbank.org/en/results/2022/09/06/micro-enterprise-owners-in-bangladesh-go-green

Yesmin, A. (2021). Microbusiness Continuity and Resilience Strategies for COVID-19 Crisis: Entrepreneurs' Insight from Bangladesh. *International Journal of Academic Research in Accounting Finance and Management Sciences*, *10*(2), 33–48.

Young, O. (2010). *Institutional dynamics: Emergent patters in international environmental governance*. MIT Press. doi:10.7551/mitpress/8457.001.0001

Yousef, M. (2022). Developing a Paradigm Model for Flexibility of Rural Entrepreneurial Businesses in Dealing With the COVID-19 Crisis; Application of Grounded Theory in Western of Iran. *Frontiers in Public Health*, *10*, 833909. Advance online publication. doi:10.3389/fpubh.2022.833909

Zahra, S. A., Sapienza, H. J., & Davidsson, P. (2006). Entrepreneurship and Dynamic Capabilities: A review, model, and research agenda. *Journal of Management Studies*, *43*(4), 917–955. doi:10.1111/j.1467-6486.2006.00616.x

Zollo, M., & Winter, S. G. (2002). Deliberate learning and the evolution of dynamic capabilities [June.]. *Organization Science*, *13*(3), 339–351. doi:10.1287/orsc.13.3.339.2780

Chapter 9
How Policies Foster Regional Development:
An Italian Entrepreneurial Ecosystem Analysis

Nicoletta Cangiano
https://orcid.org/0000-0002-4394-0188
Parthenope University of Naples, Italy

ABSTRACT

The entrepreneurial ecosystem literature paid little attention to policies' effects on the evolution of the regional ecosystem. Scholars underlined the development of the entrepreneurial ecosystem and how different actors affect its dynamics. However, no study focused on the dynamic role and different types of policies in an entrepreneurial ecosystem that evolves or changes. This chapter aims to fill this gap by highlighting the policy directions in addressing regional entrepreneurial ecosystem development. The author presents the results of the thematic content analysis exploring the regional operational programme of three Italian regions - Lombardy, Campania, and Calabria - representative of different development levels. Taking evidence from the analysis, implementing a specific policy direction indicates the entrepreneurial ecosystem stage covered by each region. Results highlight measures employed at different stages of the entrepreneurial ecosystem - nascent, strengthening, and resilient - and identify three policy directions: recovery, reinforcing, and shooting.

DOI: 10.4018/978-1-6684-7140-1.ch009

INTRODUCTION

Given the great importance of entrepreneurship and innovation topics in explaining the development of a territory, in the last decade, some questions emerged in scientific circles regarding the relationship between entrepreneurship and its local context. Indeed, the specific territory's community and culture could have a meaningful impact on entrepreneurship (Autio et al., 2014). Furthermore, the interaction between the agents leads to a regional environment that fosters the firms' and territory's competitiveness. In accordance with these arguments, literature has presented contributions to the entrepreneurial ecosystem (hereafter EE) phenomenon. It is strictly related to the territory it is established, affecting its development and creating networks and relationships between all the actors within the same territory and with other territories. An EE enables entrepreneurship and value creation and fosters and stimulates economic growth by promoting entrepreneurship, social change, and innovation.

Literature on EE is still developing. Although different definitions exist, they share some essential attributes and identify specific components. In this vein, Stam (2015) framed core elements that compose an EE, defining the ecosystem as a set of interdependent actors and factors coordinated to enable productive entrepreneurship. In this definition, three components are shared. The first two are actors - i.e., firms, government institutions, capital providers, academia sector, and the market - and factors, i.e., information, human capital, knowledge, support services, entrepreneurship capability and opportunity, and social culture. Finally, the third component is productive entrepreneurship, i.e., a system that produces "any entrepreneurial activity that contributes directly or indirectly to the net or additional output of the economy" (Baumol, 1993, p. 30).

The literature underlined three critical features of EE, namely dynamism, evolution, and context. Indeed, an EE works through cooperation and synergies among its elements. This means that EE is a highly dynamic phenomenon that changes over time according to the interaction between the different actors and attributes that develop in tandem, influencing and reproducing each other (Spigel, 2017). These interactions also explain the evolutionary aspect. When all the elements within the EE are developed and strictly connected, the ecosystem evolves, leading to the development of the territory in which it is established. Finally, each EE has a different configuration related to the spatial component that can explain the different outcomes. Indeed, an EE reflects the characteristics of the context in which it arises and develops, which explains why every EE is "unique and impossible to replicate" (Fernandes & Ferreira, 2022, p. 190). The context characteristics shape the configurations, the networks, and the actors giving rise to EE with different elements and profiles.

Scholars investigating the influence of single actors in explaining the development of EE have focused mainly on firms, universities, capital providers, and financial intermediaries. At the same time, few studies pointed out the contribution and effects of policies. Regarding the evolutionary aspect over time, some studies have explored the dynamic view of EE development to find evolutive patterns. In this vein, scholars defined different stages of development and different characteristics (Mack & Mayer, 2016). They also studied the different policies adopted by regions with diverse ecosystems (Brown & Mason, 2017). However, no studies focused on the policy types in the different stages of EE, grouping them according to the goals towards which they are directed.

To the best author's knowledge, no studies investigate the regional policy directions according to the development level in the management domain. To fill this research gap, this study classifies the policies and measures typology and characteristics from the regions studied.

Therefore, this study aims to achieve the following research objectives:

RO1: To identify the main measures related to entrepreneurship and innovation topics, studying the policy documents of three selected regional EEs;

RO2: To categorize and analyse these measures based on the EE's different development levels to gain more insights into the EE phenomenon.

For the research objectives, the author conducts a Thematic Content Analysis to derive the policy objectives and synthesize the literature for a future-focused research agenda. To achieve this goal, this chapter analysed policy documents, investigating measures to distinguish three policy directions, i.e., recovery, reinforcing, and shooting. These perspectives represent the regions' policies and measures objects.

This chapter aims to fill this gap deepening how EE develops and changes over time. It focuses on the policy types within a regional EE to investigate their influence through the implementation of specific measures, adopted taking into account the peculiarities of the context. Furthermore, it investigates policy directions, i.e., policy measures types adopted, exploring how EEs address the issue of entrepreneurship and innovation at a regional policy level.

The chapter is organized as follows. Section 1 presents the main topics of the investigation and the literature review. Section 2 introduces the methodology adopted. The main findings are presented in Section 3 and discussed in Section 4. Section 5 indicates the study's perspective for the future before concluding in section 6.

BACKGROUND AND LITERATURE REVIEW

This section shares definitions and existing literature for a better understanding of the EE related to the evolutionary process, governance, policy directions, and regional policy topics.

The Entrepreneurial Ecosystem Evolutionary Process

Studies on EE evolution explored the dynamic perspective of ecosystem development. Indeed, several efforts have been made to find patterns to inform policymaking on how best to lead the EE toward more advanced stages of maturity. In this vein, scholars identified different stages as birth, growth, sustainment, and decline or re-emerge (Mack & Mayer, 2016; Cantner et al., 2021). A different configuration describes each stage concerning the number of firms, financial capital, support infrastructure, and regional policies. These critical components and mutual interaction drive the EE evolution from stage to stage. Indeed, institutions, culture, politics, support structures, and entrepreneurship evolve together and influence each other (Spigel, 2017). According to the different levels of development, the focus shifts from the new firm creation - to reinforce the regional entrepreneurial climate - to creating partnerships, strong networks, and sharing knowledge, skills, and expertise. This evolution involves transitioning from an embryonic EE to a scale-up EE (Brown & Mason, 2017) or an emerging EE to a developed EE (Roundy et al., 2017). These differences imply that specific policy approaches should reflect the EE size and variation (Pita, Costa, & Carrizo Moreira, 2021). Finally, Spigel and Harrison (2018) presented an EE's evolutionary model based on two elements, i.e., their network strengths and available resources. They identified three stages of EE development as nascent, strengthening, and resilient. A nascent ecosystem is characterized by few links between entrepreneurs because of the lack of resources and the culture that fosters these interactions. A strengthening ecosystem is defined by entrepreneurial success, which leads to new resource creation and sharing. More investments are addressed towards labor up-skilling and the new firm's creation. Finally, a resilient ecosystem presents a strong entrepreneurial culture that sustains the ecosystem and attracts more resources, entrepreneurs, and workers to it. The connections and interactions between these actors become more solid and allow the ecosystem to resist an external shock.

This study aims to highlight the dynamic characteristic of EE and employs the classification developed by Spigel and Harrison (2018) to describe the development stages, defining the regional EE as nascent, strengthening, and resilient.

The Entrepreneurial Ecosystem Governance

Focusing on the EE evolution, the author considers the role of an actor as the regional policymaker that changes over time to address better the policies and measures to implement in the EE. The government institution is one of the actors within the EE that could foster and help its development. Despite its relevance, regional policy's contribution to including missing elements and enabling interaction between components is rarely discussed. The EE literature describes governance as the actor that sets rules and norms to coordinate and drive entrepreneurial activity and entrepreneurial networks (Colombo, 2019). Indeed, the institutional context influences the entrepreneurial attitude, characteristics, and performance of startups and small and medium-sized enterprises (hereafter SMEs). It fosters long-term economic development by creating a favorable climate for entrepreneurship to flourish through innovation promotion.

Governance may take different forms depending on the primary economic conditions, relational links among the agents, and the historical and cultural factors related to the EE territory. Every configuration - i.e., a specific setting given by the different mix of these elements - coordinates the interaction between actors and individuals in a certain way (Colombo, 2019). In decision-making contexts, different EE exhibits diverse institutional configurations and interactions among the actors based on political, economic, social, and historical differences. The government institutions act within the EE through policies defined as programs and regulations that support entrepreneurship with direct funding or foster the launching of new firms (Spiegel, 2017). In recent decades, governments have increasingly adopted a policy direction to innovation and entrepreneurship policies aimed at developing EE. Indeed, entrepreneurship and innovation are two critical topics for competitiveness, social development, regional development, and EE development. Therefore, the policies and measures, adopted in a territory, influence EE development in terms of output, relationships, networking, innovation, and entrepreneurship levels.

Policy Directions and European Union Regional Policy

This chapter investigates the policy directions adopted by regions, defined as a "collection of strategies, policy statements, committed reports, and scientific studies that express the will of the government" (Stahl et al., 2002, p. 236). However, the role of public policy in supporting and creating EE is unclear. There is often a search for best practices, which are adopted from other successful places, without sufficient consideration of the characteristics and peculiarities of the local context. Therefore, creating and implementing entrepreneurship and innovation policies is insufficient to ensure EE development. Policies need to be calibrated to the specific territory to be successful and effective. For the region is crucial to decide what types of policies and measures to apply to achieve the objectives. Entrepreneurship policies take into account entrepreneurial actions. These actions, however, depend on individual considerations and the territory in which they are established. Without evidence on the EE framework and what factors encourage entrepreneurship in a certain context, policies could be ineffective and fail to achieve the aim (Pita, Costa, & Carrizo Moreira, 2021). These policy tools should be chosen to respond precisely to the goals. Whether these tools are not carefully selected, there is a risk of not reaching the goals and producing the expected result. The objectives could change from region to region because they depend on the development level.

Among the different types of policies, this chapter focuses more on entrepreneurial policies, i.e., measures aiming to increase the quantity and quality of businesses within a specific territory (Ortega-Agiles, 2022). Indeed, entrepreneurial action depends on individual motivations and the context in which they are inserted. Entrepreneurial policies are classified as hard policies or soft policies (Storey, 2005; Banerjee, Savani, and Shreedhar, 2021). The former refers to measures that aim to support financially businesses (Ortega-Argiles, 2022; Storey 2005). The latter includes counseling activities to entrepreneurs, fostering technology adoption; creating mechanisms for facilitating interactions among the regional actors; SME support; educational measures; and incentives in green energy adoption.

Besides, the author investigates the direction referred to the policy measures adopted in the EE. The policy direction is a dynamic concept, and often, according to the implementation results of policies, regions have to change their strategies to achieve the main objectives. Indeed, whether policies or measures fail to reach the objective, they need to be reformulated and adjusted to new goals that respond to the needs of the EE.

In this vein, the European Union (hereafter EU) Cohesion Policy, known as regional policy, intends to help the regions create the proper measures that better fit their characteristics. It aims to prevent regional disparities and enhance the economic prosperity of EU regions. It attempts to eliminate economic, social, and territorial inequities, restructure failing industrial districts, and diversify rural regions with failing agriculture. By doing this, the regional policy aims to increase regional competitiveness, promote economic growth, and generate employment. This regional policy covers all European regions belonging to member states, but different objectives are assigned to regions, primarily based on their economic and development levels. In this vein, the EU in 2000 classified regions into two categories, i.e., less developed and more developed regions. A third category has been foreseen since 2007, i.e., transition regions.

The EU's poorest regions, with a Gross Domestic Product (hereafter GDP) per capita less than 75% of the EU average, are grouped under the heading of "less developed regions." Almost all of the territories of the new Member States are included in this group, along with the majority of Southern Italy, Greece, Portugal, some areas of the United Kingdom, and parts of Spain. Most regional policy funding is earmarked for these regions to encourage development. In these regions, financial constraints are frequent, particularly for SMEs, which share a higher percentage of financial issues.

In the more developed regions category, the EU regions with a GDP per capita higher than 90% of the EU average are included. The funding's main objective regards these areas is to increase competitiveness and make the regions more attractive to firms and investors to generate employment. Investing in sustainability, assisting research facilities, universities, start-ups, and SMEs, as well as offering training and generating employment, are all potential projects typical in these regions.

Alongside these two classifications, the EU has also provided for transition regions group, i.e., regions with a GDP per capita between 75 and 90% of the EU average. Regions classified as transitions obtain less funding than less developed regions but more financing than the more developed ones.

SOLUTIONS AND RACCOMANDATIONS

Methodological Approach

This chapter investigates policies, measures, and different stages of EE maturity. To address this issue, the author studies the regional policies of three EEs and defines the policy directions and their characteristics during each EE stage. Therefore, the objective of the analysis is twofold: i) understanding how the policy direction changes when EE evolves; and ii) regional policy characteristics during the EE's stages.

To this purpose, the author takes empirical evidence from the case of three Italian regions.

Italy presents a particular regional development framework. Indeed, regions display different socioeconomic development levels and entrepreneurial climates due to the country's demographic dynamics, history, and economy. All these reasons make the Italian social and economic structure particularly heterogeneous between the regions.

To achieve the objectives, the author has conducted a qualitative analysis of policy in the Italian context. Policy programs and measures of three Italian regions (Lombardy, Campania, and Calabria) are analysed. These regions represent three different EE scenarios and facing evolutionary challenges. Each region has a different entrepreneurial climate and regional development level.

To compare programs and measures, the author has carried out a Thematic Content Analysis (TCA) inspecting "Regional Operational Programs" (ROPs) in twenty years from 2000 to 2020. The TCA organizes and describes data sets in detail, identifying, analysing, and extracting themes within data (Braun & Clarke, 2006). In other words, TCA supported the analysis by organising and describing regional programs and measures and tracing regional policy direction. The dataset comprises ROP documents containing measures and policies applied by regions to increase regional development. Nevertheless, coherently with the study's purpose, only policies and measures related to EE are selected. The analysis results identify three policy directions that the region covers in different EE stages.

The Italian Context and Selection Criteria

Italy presents a particular regional development framework, highly fragmented and historically divided into three macro-areas: the Northern, Central, and Southern regions. The first two areas are characterized by a good level of development, which is higher in the North compared to the central regions, while the South is generally less developed. The differences in the levels of development refer: to the levels of per capita GDP, the levels of employment rates and job opportunities, the number of services offered to the citizen, the urban infrastructural assets, and the quality of life. From this perspective, the Italian regions represent the optimal sample to analyse as they fit the purpose of the analysis, presenting different development levels and entrepreneurial climates. Indeed, this analysis aims to study the different policy types, i.e., policy direction, to capture the elements and characteristics that describe the EE stage.

The path of each region over time was studied, starting from different development and entrepreneurial levels.

As mentioned above, the EU classified regions into three groups: more developed, transitions, and less developed. In addition, the sample selection is confirmed by the Regional Innovation Scoreboard (hereafter RIS), a composite index that describes the innovation performance of all the regions belonging to the EU. It identifies three main groups of innovators: strong, moderate, and modest.

This analysis addresses a twenty-year time study from 2000 to 2020. The indicators chosen to select the sample were evaluated during the initial year of the analysis. In 2000 the EU classification considered only more developed and less developed regions. The transition regions group was established in 2007. Molise was the only Italian region in 2007 to fall into this group. In this vein, the author analysed the situation of this region in 2000. The Molise was a modest innovator and classified as a less developed region. Consistent with the purpose of the analysis, the author decided to discard this region from the potential sample as its development level for the indicators used was higher than the Calabria region. Therefore, the author included Calabria as a representative region of a low stage of development and then analyse its path up to 2020. Equally, in 2000, in Italy, no region was labeled as a strong innovator, according to the RIS. However, Lombardy had the highest level in the country for this indicator. Therefore, the author selected Lombardy as the representative region of an already-formed ecosystem.

Regarding Campania, the region was classified as less developed like Calabria and a moderate innovator like Lombardy, but different in levels. Therefore, the author selected it as the region representative of the medium-level development in the sample.

The analysis of the other indexes allowed it to gather important information about the three regions, highlighting the distance in development level between Campania and Calabria, which were less developed regions but with different RIS labels. The same evidence occurred for Campania compared to Lombardy, classified as moderate innovators but with different development classifications according to the EU. Indeed, the analysis considered other equally relevant indexes for the EEs study, which confirmed the different levels of development.

The additional information taken from the indexes are the number of startups in 2014 and the number of graduates employed 1-3 years after graduation in 2006 (before data are unavailable). These indicators photograph the level of regional development and the entrepreneurial climate.

Regarding the number of startups (available from 2014), Lombardy covered the first position with 341 companies; Campania is the first region of the South with 83 startups; and finally, Calabria is the region with lower numbers, with 20 startups launched. Likewise, the number of graduates employed from 1 to 3 years after graduation represents the ability of the region to employ more qualified people. *Table 1* presents the values that support the clustering.

Table 1. Indexes of regions. Source: authors' adaption

Index Region	RIS value	Startups' number	Graduates employed numbers from 1-3 years	EU classification
Lombardy	Moderate	341	80,1	More developed
Campania	Moderate	83	57,8	Less developed
Calabria	Modest	10	43.5	Less developed

Therefore, according to the EU, Lombardy is the most developed region, meanwhile, among less developed regions, this study individuated a region presenting a value near the average value and a region that negatively diverged from the medium value, considering the RIS index, number of startups, and graduates employed. The second region selected is Campania, and the last one is Calabria. Therefore, the sample of regions was not randomly selected. The author has individuated the regions searching for the optimal sample for the analysis, i.e., focusing on the differences between the regions. According to the arguments abovementioned, the heterogeneity between the regions in the sample is demonstrated. The analysis looked at the regional design of the ROP documents from 2000 to 2020.

The Regional Operational Programme

The ROP is a regional operational programme that describes how regions use the European Regional Development Fund (ERDF) to implement economic growth. It covers seven years and represents the most important and descriptive program of the regional strategic plan that a region develops and applies. The first ROP was launched in 2000, followed by the second in 2007, and the third in 2014. The last one has been in force since 2021. Therefore, in this analysis, the author discards the 2021-2027 ROP as it is still ongoing and focuses on 2000-2006 ROPs, 2007-2013 ROPs, and 2014-2020 ROPs, as their outcomes have already been realised.

The regions are responsible for their policymaking decisions, and ROP documents contain measures they intend to adopt employing European funds. However, in 2000 the EU fixed some macro objectives based on the region's development level, creating different programs for higher and lower-developed regions. In the first programming period, from 2000 to 2006, EU regional policy consisted of three objectives known as Objectives 1, 2, and 3. The EU created Single Programming Documents (DoCup) to guide Central and Northern European Regions (including Lombardy) in promoting economic reconversion and the revitalization of the territory, which represented Objective 1 regions; Regional Operational Programs (ROPs), otherwise, guiding Southern European (such as Campania, and Calabria) in creating a homogeneous and solid basis of development, which represented Objective 2 regions. Finally, for the most developed regions, the EU foresaw Objective 3, which focuses on the adaptation and modernisation of EU and national policies on employment, education, and training. Despite three different ROP documents existing in the EU, for the Italian regions, only two types have been developed: the Objective 1 ROP and the Objective 2 ROP, defined as a "Single Programming Document." These two documents represent the dataset for the period 2000-2006.

Regarding the second programming period, from 2007 to 2013, the EU proposed different macro objectives again among developed and less developed regions asking for the redaction of ROPs for Convergence (hereafter ROP CONV) to Southern Regions; and ROPs for Competitiveness and Employment (hereafter ROP RCE) to Central and Northern Regions; and European Territorial Cooperation, by strengthening regional cooperation to reduce the boundaries within and between territories, foreseeing three cooperation types, i.e., cross-border, transnational, and interregional cooperation. For the second programming period, Italian regions developed only two ROP types: the ROP CONV (Campania and Calabria) and ROP RCE (Lombardy).

Finally, for the 2014-2020 ROP, no different programs have been foreseen. The EU fixed common objectives among all the regions concerning research and innovation (hereafter R&I), information and communication technologies (hereafter ITC), and the competitiveness of SMEs.

More precisely, the analysis TCA concerns the following nine documents presented in Table 2:

Table 2. Regions' Operational Programmes analysed from 2000 to 2020. Source Authors' adaption

Period Region	2000-2006	2007-2013	2014-2020
Lombardy	Single Programming Document 2000-2006	ROP RCE 2007-2013	ROP 2014-2020
Campania	ROP 2000-2006	ROP CONV 2007-2013	ROP 2014-2020
Calabria	ROP 2000-2006	ROP CONV 2007-2013	ROP 2014-2020

The ROP has a specific structure composed of a)the thematic objectives; b) the priority axes; c) the specific objectives; d) the expected results; and finally, e) the actions. The "priority axis" includes the thematic objectives and represents regional investment priorities based on the analysis of the socio-economic context. Each investment priority is related to a specific objective. Then, the ROP reports the expected results, actions, and allocated resources linked to each specific objective. Table 3 shows the documents' characteristics for each region of the sample.

Table 3. ROP documents details of the analysis from 2000 to 2020. Source: Author adaption

Region	Pages	Priority axes	Specific objectives	Priority axes entrepreneurship-related	Specific objectives entrepreneurship-related
2000-2006					
Lombardy	295	3	13	3	11
Campania	755	7	77	5	44
Calabria	513	7	44	7	34
2007-2013					
Lombardy	136	5	6	3	4
Campania	294	7	17	6	13
Calabria	396	9	20	7	15
2014-2020					
Lombardy	291	7	18	6	13
Campania	585	10	25	6	13
Calabria	550	14	46	8	19

The Codification Process

The analysis focused on the specific objectives related to regional entrepreneurial development. Specifically, the author focused on measures that stimulate EE assets, i.e., firm creation, network development, startups, university partnerships, technology adoption, innovation, and job qualification. The objectives and measures that respond to these characteristics were selected and codified through Atlas.ti.7, a Computer-Assisted qualitative data analysis software (CAQDAS). According to the TCA process, the author marked data segments in ROP paragraphs describing the specific objectives and actions in detail. In the following step, the author associated codes at the level of sentences and categories at the level of codes. Codes and categories represent the units of analysis of this study. Codes allowed for the organization, structure, and retrieval of data, supporting the identification of decisive themes for document interpretation. Although many codes already exist in the literature on policy design (Acs & Szerb, 2007), the author proceeded to create new codes inductively, as the existing codes did not cover all the aspects of the topic wanted to study.

At the end of the codification process, sixty codes are produced, focusing on specific objectives and actions included in ROP documents. Codes are grouped by the themes they represent, forming the category. Therefore, the TCA process presented fourteen categories: Competencies building; Qualification; Credit; Entrepreneurship; Innovative Industry; Structure framework; Know-how; Innovation sharing;

Employment; Traditional Industry; Strategic partnership; Equality; technology; and Support activities. *Table 4* illustrates codes and categories.

The code's frequency and the weight of codes to value categories are used as a metric to analyse codes and categories defined. The former refers to the total number where a code has been used in the document. The category's weight is a measure given by the sum of the code frequencies that make up the category.

Regarding the interpretation of codes, the analysis does not set a fixed cut-off value. The ROP documents examined presented many differences in terms of the number of pages and the structure. For this reason, the author has defined values with higher frequency as descriptive of the strategy of the regional policy according to the number of codes and categories for regions and in the same programming periods.

Table 4. Description of codes and categories. Source: Author Adaption

Category	Codes
Competencies building	Attractiveness, Competitiveness, Internationalization, Promotion, Investment attractiveness.
Qualification	Education, Graduation, Specialisation.
Credit	Access to credit, Credit expansion, Financial innovation, Micro-credit, Secured credit, Risk capital, Private Equity.
Entrepreneurship	Enterprise, Micro-enterprise, Social business, Spinoff, Startup.
Innovative Industry	Knowledge-Intensive, Strategic Sector.
Structure framework	Physical assets, Logistics, Research facility, Urban development.
Know-how	Emerging Technology, Technology development, Manufacturing Research, Innovation, Research and Development, Research and Innovation, Sustainable Innovation.
Innovation sharing	Innovation sharing, Technology sharing, Digitalization, Know-how transfer, Open Innovation.
Employment	Employment, Skilled employees.
Traditional Industry	Primary sector, Secondary sector, Public Interest issue, Natural environment, Tertiary sector, Traditional Industry.
Strategic Partnership	Micro-supplying, Closeness, Public-private agreement, Private-Private agreement.
Equality	Gender Equality, Legality, Social Equality, Sustainability.
Technology	Tech-innovation, Technology, Technological & Industrial development, Advanced technology.
Support activities	Firm services, Support for innovation & technology.

EMERGING FINDINGS OF THE THEMATIC CONTENT ANALYSIS

This section presents the major insights the author has gathered from the analysis.

Calabria

In the 2000-2006 ROP, Calabria region worked on macro-areas such as qualification, competencies building, traditional industry, and structural framework. As an Objective 1 region, Calabria shared issues such as unemployment, GDP degrowth, insufficient infrastructure endowments, weak productive structure, inequalities, industrial structure with the predominance of SMEs in traditional sectors, and weak investment in technologies and innovation. To face these issues, ROP implemented measures and actions addressed to existing firms and to support infrastructure and equipment. In this vein, the document showed a high frequency for the "Physical assets" code and incentives for technology adoption. Measures for education and training programs are included through the codes "Employment" and "Education." These codes co-occurred, often with "Enterprise" and "Firm services." These measures highlighted two policy purposes, i.e., to create educational and training programs - reinforcing the capabilities and knowledge of unemployed people, women, and students – and to help firms in activities as incentives for business development. Another predominant category is the "Traditional Industry," and "Primary sector" and "Tertiary sector" codes are the most frequent. Calabria's territorial extension and characteristics could explain this value, in which the importance of the primary sector in the economy was much more marked in Calabria compared to the Italian average. The weight of agriculture - in terms of employment and income produced - is approximately double the national average.

For 2007-2013 Calabria implemented the ROP CONV and still focused on measures relating to the "Qualification" category. Regarding "Entrepreneurship," this region insisted more on measures relating to enterprises and micro-enterprises. Furthermore, it tries to implement measures aimed at encouraging innovation in firms ("Know-how" category) and also on technology transfer and the diffusion of innovation within firms ("Know-how transfer" category). Calabria again presented measures for the "Employment" to tackle unemployment which still represents an important issue in the region; and insisted on the "Traditional Industry" sector, implementing measures and actions for the tourism (tertiary sector) and public interest issue. Finally, there are also measures related to the "Technology" category.

For the period 2014-2020, there is only one type of ROP which is developed by all regions. However, Calabria was still considered a less developed region. In this vein, ROP presented measures and actions still addressed to the "Employment" code. In 2013 the region had an unemployment rate higher than 15%, with a predominance of unemployed women. This code often co-occurs with the "Education" and "Enterprise" codes and, to a lesser extent, with the "Gender Equality" code. The explanation for this co-occurrence is that the region tried to increase the employment rate through the launch of new businesses and the qualification of human resources and also to grant more gender equality for women in firms. Calabria developed some measures referred to as the "Enterprise" code, which co-occurs with "Education."

Table 5 shows the results of the ROPs analysis for the Calabria region.

Table 5. Metrics of Calabria Regional Operational Programs 2000-2020. Source: Author adaption

Code	Frequency			Category	Weight of category		
	2000-2006	2007-2013	2014-2020		2000-2006	2007-2013	2014-2020
Competitiveness	6	8	6	Competences building	19	23	16
Promotion	8	8	4				
Internationalization	2	1	2				
Attractiveness	2	4	2				
Investment attractiveness	1	2	2				
Education	9	7	5	Qualification	11	7	7
Graduation	1	0	2				
Specialisation	1	0	0				
Access to credit	1	0	0	Credit	5	5	6
Credit expansion	0	0	1				
Financial innovation	1	1	1				
Micro-credit	0	0	1				
Secured credit	2	1	1				
Risk capital	1	2	1				
Private Equity	0	1	1				
Enterprise	12	3	8	Entrepreneurship	17	10	17
Micro-enterprise	1	3	2				
Social business	0	0	2				
Spinoff	4	3	2				
Startup	0	1	3				
Knowledge-intensive	0	0	1	Innovative Industry	0	0	2
Strategic sector	0	0	1				

continues on following page

Table 5. Continued

Code	Frequency			Category	Weight of category		
	2000-2006	2007-2013	2014-2020		2000-2006	2007-2013	2014-2020
Research facility	1	4	2	Structural framework	18	19	14
Physical assets	15	13	12				
Logistics	0	0	0				
Urban development	2	2	0				
Manufacturing research	0	3	2	Know-how	10	15	20
Research and Development	1	0	4				
Innovation	6	7	6				
Technology Development	2	3	1				
Emerging technology	0	1	0				
Sustainable Innovation	0	0	4				
Research and Innovation	1	1	3				
Know-how transfer	2	4	3	Innovation sharing	5	8	11
Innovation sharing	2	1	2				
Technology sharing	0	1	1				
Digitalisation	1	2	4				
Open innovation	0	0	1				
Employment	12	3	7	Employment	12	3	8
Skilled employees	0	0	1				
Primary sector	13	1	1	Traditional Industry	39	25	12
Secondary sector	3	1	0				
Public Interest issue	8	9	4				
Natural environment	7	3	3				
Tertiary sector	7	10	4				
Traditional Industry	1	1	0				
Micro-supplying	1	2	1	Strategic Partnership	8	10	13
Closeness	3	0	3				
Private-Private Agreement	2	3	4				
Public-private Agreement	2	5	5				

continues on following page

Table 5. Continued

<table>
<tr><th rowspan="2">Code</th><th colspan="3">Frequency</th><th rowspan="2">Category</th><th colspan="3">Weight of category</th></tr>
<tr><th>2000-2006</th><th>2007-2013</th><th>2014-2020</th><th>2000-2006</th><th>2007-2013</th><th>2014-2020</th></tr>
<tr><td>Legality</td><td>2</td><td>1</td><td>0</td><td rowspan="4">Equality</td><td rowspan="4">9</td><td rowspan="4">10</td><td rowspan="4">5</td></tr>
<tr><td>Social Equality</td><td>0</td><td>1</td><td>0</td></tr>
<tr><td>Gender equality</td><td>2</td><td>1</td><td>3</td></tr>
<tr><td>Sustainability</td><td>5</td><td>7</td><td>2</td></tr>
<tr><td>Technology</td><td>4</td><td>7</td><td>6</td><td rowspan="4">Technology</td><td rowspan="4">13</td><td rowspan="4">12</td><td rowspan="4">13</td></tr>
<tr><td>Technology Innovation</td><td>5</td><td>4</td><td>4</td></tr>
<tr><td>Technological & Industrial development</td><td>4</td><td>1</td><td>2</td></tr>
<tr><td>Advanced technology</td><td>0</td><td>0</td><td>1</td></tr>
<tr><td>Firm services</td><td>13</td><td>5</td><td>6</td><td rowspan="2">Support activities</td><td rowspan="2">14</td><td rowspan="2">5</td><td rowspan="2">9</td></tr>
<tr><td>Support for innovation & technology</td><td>1</td><td>0</td><td>3</td></tr>
</table>

Campania

Campania aimed to achieve Objective 1 in the 2000-2006 ROP. As for Calabria, also Campania shared the Objective 1 regions issues abovementioned. For these reasons, ROP measures were addressed to existing firms, infrastructure, and equipment support - in fact, the document shows a high frequency for the "Physical assets" code - and incentives for technology adoption. There are also measures for education and training programs, individuating with the code "Employment" and "Education," to reduce unemployment and increase the employees' and unemployed skills and knowledge to be more qualified. These two codes co-occurred, often also with "Enterprise" and "Firm services" codes. About the code "Firm services," the ROP showed the willingness of the region to help firms in several activities.

For 2007-2013 Campania presented the ROP CONV. The region had no "Qualification" or "Employment" measures. It stressed the "Structural framework" category by focusing more on measures relating to "Logistics" and "Physical assets" and also on the finance sector with measures relating to attracting investment and the use of "Financial innovation." Furthermore, Campania focused on the "Innovative Industry" with measures relating above all to the "Strategic Sector." The number of measures relating to the "Structural framework" category is significantly high, demonstrating Campania's effort to make the region more attractive and more efficiently connected. For the "Strategic Partnership" category, Campania presents measures aimed at agreements between the public and private sectors. The region presented higher values in categories: Competencies building, Innovative Industry, Structural framework, and Strategic Partnership. These levels showed that Campania had mainly pushed certain sectors to increase the level of innovation and development of the region. Specifically, concerning the "Competences building" category, many policies concerned the increase in competitiveness and attractiveness; while for what concerns the "Innovative Industry" category, it has begun to develop policies aimed at encouraging the creation of spinoffs and strategic industries. Finally, for the "Structural framework" category, the region has invested in the logistics and physical assets with the ultimate aim of making the connections on the territory more effective and efficient, increasing the region's attractiveness. Furthermore, as regards the "Strategic Partnership" category, the Campania region has invested more in establishing agreements between the public and private sectors and encouraging partnerships between private companies to help companies develop.

Table 6. Metrics of Campania Regional Operational Programs 2000-2020. Source: Author adaption

Code	Frequency			Category	Weight of category		
	2000-2006	2007-2013	2014-2020		2000-2006	2007-2013	2014-2020
Competitiveness	6	10	9	Competences building	12	27	28
Promotion	4	1	3				
Internationalization	2	4	4				
attractiveness	0	12	11				
Investment attractiveness	0	0	1				
Education	15	0	1	Qualification	17	1	4
Graduation	2	1	1				
Specialisation	0	0	2				
Access to credit	0	0	2	Credit	0	6	10
Credit expansion	0	2	3				
Financial innovation	0	2	0				
micro-credit	0	0	1				
Secured credit	0	0	2				
Risk capital	0	2	1				
Private Equity	0	0	1				

continues on following page

Table 6. Continued

Code	Frequency			Category	Weight of category		
	2000-2006	2007-2013	2014-2020		2000-2006	2007-2013	2014-2020
Enterprise	12	4	6				
Micro-enterprise	2	1	6				
Social business	1	0	3	Entrepreneurship	15	7	29
Spinoff	0	2	4				
Startup	0	0	10				
Knowledge-intensive	0	1	1	Innovative Industry	0	6	13
Strategic sectors	0	5	12				
Research facility	1	2	4				
Physical assets	17	16	11				
Logistics	1	13	6	Structural framework	20	36	23
Urban development	1	5	2				
Manufacturing research	2	2	4				
Research and Development	2	1	6				
Innovation	3	4	5				
Technology development	0	1	0	Know-how	7	8	27
Emerging technology	0	0	3				
Sustainable Innovation	0	0	5				
Research and Innovation	0	0	4				
Know-how Transfer	4	1	7				
Innovation sharing	0	0	5				
Technology sharing	0	1	9	Innovation sharing	4	4	31
Digitalisation	0	2	5				
Open innovation	0	0	5				
Employment	15	0	0	Employment	15	0	0
Skilled employees	0	0	0				
Primary sector	9	0	2				
Secondary sector	5	1	2				
Public Interest issue	4	4	8				
Natural environment	5	2	5	Traditional Industry	32	13	29
Tertiary sector	9	5	7				
Traditional Industry	0	1	5				

continues on following page

Table 6. Continued

Code	Frequency			Category	Weight of category		
	2000-2006	2007-2013	2014-2020		2000-2006	2007-2013	2014-2020
Micro-supplying	1	1	0	Strategic Partnership	8	13	23
Closeness	2	4	3				
Private-Private Agreement	2	3	9				
Public-private Agreement	3	5	11				
Legality	1	0	0	Equality	5	8	11
Social Equality	1	3	3				
Gender equality	0	0	0				
Sustainability	3	5	8				
Technology	6	3	8	Technology	12	9	25
Tech-Innovation	2	4	9				
Thecnological & industrial development	4	0	8				
Advanced technology	0	2	0				
Firm services	11	1	7	Support activities	11	3	13
Support for innovation & technology	0	2	6				

The 2007-2013 ROP document, which launched an improvement of the ecosystem structure, was strengthened and fortified by the 2014–2020 ROP for all the regions analysed but at a different level. Campania focused on startups; in fact, the "startup" code has a high frequency and is related to knowledge-intensive, private-private agreements and the strategic sectors. The ROP documents aim to increase and enhance partnerships among different actors, such as universities and research structures with firms, but also large companies with SMEs and startups. In fact, "Public-private Agreement" and "Private-private Agreement" indicated measures that stimulate cooperation and innovation. The code "Strategic Sector" co-occurs with "Research and Development," "startup," and "spinoff." Campania has made an important effort in many sectors for the number of measures to encourage the region's development above all. The higher differences are found in the categories: "Competencies building," "Entrepreneurship," "Innovative industry," "Structural framework," "Know-how," "Innovation sharing," "Traditional Industry," and "Strategic Partnership." *Table 6* presents the results of the TCA on Campania ROPs.

Lombardy

Regarding Lombardy, which is the Objective 2 ROP region, it mainly, developed measures focused on increasing the level of innovation and also technology in firms. This is the most important difference between the other two regions; in fact, the category "Technology" and "Know-how" are higher in this region than the others. Besides, the category "Traditional Industry" still has importance, but with the difference that there is no measure for the sector as agriculture but instead for craftsmanship (secondary sector), tourism (tertiary sector), and traditional firms. There is no measure for the "Qualification" category and a weak intervention for the "Employment" code. This could be explained by the development level of this region, which had already achieved Objective 1 for the EU, and the regional policy had to reach different goals relative to innovation and technology measures, support the existing firms, and create new ones. In 2000 only Lombardy presented a real EE. In the other two regions, however, there were some important elements determinant for the development of an ecosystem. Finally, the 2000-2006 Single Programming Document focused on measures for "Competences building," "Traditional Industry," "Know-how," and "Technology."

For 2007-2013 Lombardy presented the ROP RCE. The ROP RCE aimed to achieve the common objectives of increasing regional competitiveness and employment. The Lombardy "Structure framework" category and the "Strategic partnership" category presented more measures. In the second programming period, Lombardy still presented a higher level of development compared to the other two regions analysed.

For the period 2014-2020, there is only one type of ROP which is developed by all regions. This document reinforced and fortified the 2007-2013 ROP, which launched an improvement of the ecosystem structure in all the regions analysed but at a different level. Lombardy is the most developed Italian region, whose per capita GDP is over 90% of the EU average. The region aimed to enhance the attractiveness and competitiveness level of the regional EE and foster the development of innovation level. *Table 7* presents the results.

Table 7. Metrics of Lombardy regional operational programs 2000-2020. Source: Author adaptation

Code	Frequency			Category	Weight of category		
	2000-2006	2007-2013	2014-2020		2000-2006	2007-2013	2014-2020
Competitiveness	4	2	4				
Promotion	3	2	5				
Internationalization	1	0	2	Competences building	11	5	18
Attractiveness	2	1	5				
Investment attractiveness	1	0	2				
Education	0	0	2				
Graduation	0	0	0	Qualification	0	0	2
Specialisation	0	0	0				
Access to credit	1	1	1				
Credit expansion	0	0	0				
Financial innovation	0	1	2				
Micro-credit	0	0	0	Credit	2	2	6
Secured credit	1	0	1				
Risk capital	0	0	1				
Private Equity	0	0	1				
Enterprise	5	2	4				
Micro-enterprise	0	0	1				
Social business	0	0	1	Entrepreneurship	6	4	9
Spinoff	1	1	1				
Startup	0	1	2				
Knowledge-intensive	0	0	0	Innovative Industry	0	0	0
Strategic sector	0	0	0				
Research facility	0	1	1				
Physical asset	6	1	4				
Logistics	0	0	0	Structural framework	7	2	6
Urban development	1	0	1				

continues on following page

Table 7. Continued

Code	Frequency			Category	Weight of category		
	2000-2006	2007-2013	2014-2020		2000-2006	2007-2013	2014-2020
Manufacturing research	0	1	1	Know-how	9	8	16
Research and development	1	1	3				
Innovation	8	3	8				
Technology development	0	1	1				
Emerging technology	0	0	2				
Sustainable Innovation	0	0	0				
Research and Innovation	0	2	1				
Know-how Transfer	0	0	0	Innovation sharing	2	0	6
Innovation sharing	0	0	2				
Technology sharing	2	0	2				
Digitalisation	0	0	1				
Open innovation	0	0	1				
Employment	2	0	2	Employment	2	0	2
Skilled employees	0	0	0				
Primary sector	0	0	1	Traditional Industry	13	3	9
Secondary sector	4	0	0				
Public Interest issue	3	1	3				
Natural Environment	2	1	2				
Tertiary sector	4	1	3				
Traditional Industry	0	0	0				
Micro-supplying	0	0	0	Strategic Partnership	3	2	6
Closeness	2	1	0				
Private-Private Agreement	0	0	4				
Public-private Agreement	1	1	2				
Legality	0	0	0	Equality	7	3	7
Social Equality	0	1	2				
Gender equality	1	0	0				
Sustainability	6	2	5				

continues on following page

Table 7. Continued

Code	Frequency			Category	Weight of category		
	2000-2006	2007-2013	2014-2020		2000-2006	2007-2013	2014-2020
Technology	6	2	7	Technology	12	3	11
Tech-Innovation	3	0	1				
Technological & Industrial development	3	1	1				
Advanced technology	0	0	2				
Firm services	5	2	5	Support activities	5	2	6
Support for innovation & technology	0	0	1				

DISCUSSION

This paragraph discusses the results of the TCA derived from the nine ROP documents. The 2000-2006 ROPs developed by Campania and Calabria contained some measures and actions but were not much articulated. These documents promote the development and structural adjustment of regions experiencing developmental delays. The measures are addressed to the infrastructure creation and equipment for private and public firms, educational and training programs for unemployed people, incentives to entrepreneurship, firm services to facilitate recruiting and technology adoption, competencies building, and know-how production. On the contrary, the Lombardy ROP focused on encouraging the economic and social transformation of regions with structural issues. This document was more oriented toward technology and entrepreneurship and less toward qualification and measures to reduce unemployment.

The second programming period faced an international financial crisis that negatively affected regions' economies and development levels. Despite the crisis, some changes in the regional EEs have been verified. Campania ROP was more articulated and covered new themes such as credit issues and the innovative industry. At the same time, the attention to firms' creation is reduced, and no measures are presented for employment and qualification. Furthermore, more attention was devoted to the attractiveness and competitiveness of firms, structural framework, and strategic partnerships. This document still supported economic development and employment through programs aimed at the modernization and diversification of economic structures and creating and maintaining stable jobs. Concerning the ROP of Lombardy, it focused on strengthening Research and Development (hereafter R&D) and innovation through its promotion in industry, SMEs, and technology transfer; and fostering innovation and entrepreneurship in all sectors of the regional economy. The ROP also fixed objectives for supporting and granting better access to finance by SMEs. It aimed to promote cooperation networks between firms and research institutions and the launching of new businesses. In this document, Lombardy presented important measures to increase the competencies building, the firms' access to credit, and actions for stimulating the adoption of technology for all regional businesses. Calabria's document focused on the attractiveness and competitiveness of firms, structural framework, and strategic partnerships, and less attention was given to entrepreneurship, employment, and qualification.

Finally, regarding the 2014-2020 ROPs documents, they are diversified. They focus on measures to enhance know-how, innovation sharing, and technology. Besides, the documents encouraged agreements among actors such as universities and research structures with private firms and big companies with SMEs and startups.

The Evolutionary Stages

The measures highlighted in the analysis respond to the diverse EE stages.

In 2000 only Lombardy presented a developing EE. This condition is confirmed by the type of policies and measures applied, focused more on investment in R&D, enhancing their regional network, on technology adoption. These measures are addressed to all SMEs and large companies in the regional territory. Regarding the other two regions, some important elements were determinants for an ecosystem but were still in development. In these cases, our analysis defined an embryonic EE. The ROPs focus on reinforcing and expanding the current entrepreneurial climate in the traditional industry; and on investing in qualification and employment policies to increase these regional indexes.

In the second programming period, generally, there has been an evolution for all the regions. Campania became a developing EE, but Calabria, albeit knowing a development, was still an embryonic EE because its ROP insisted on measures typical of this type of ecosystem. Lombardy evolved in the EE maturity phase as its policies and measures focused more on achieving a nodal position relative to managing relational and financial resources by inserting them in firms, industries, and innovative projects, using technology and innovation.

Finally, about the 2014-2020 ROP, all the regions have shown a higher but different level of development. Lombardy remained mature, but it knew some improvement compared to previous programming periods. The Campania EE evolved into a maturity phase. Finally, Calabria remained anchored to the developing phase.

The Policy Directions

In analysing the ROPs for the period 2000-2020, the author highlights policy direction and governance approaches, as the policy types implemented in the EE could be explained through the measures and actions applied in the region (Colombelli, Paolucci, and Ughetto, 2019). The policy direction of the 2000-2006 ROPs for Campania and Calabria focused on three main goals: to increase the regional employment rates, generating new jobs; to enhance the skills of human resources through training programs; to strengthen and support traditional sectors of specialization and production, creating new firms.

The policies and measures aimed to restore and create a new regional economy are characterised by launching new firms in traditional sectors and creating new jobs to reduce unemployment. Taking these elements into account, the policy direction is defined as recovery, as it implemented a long-term regional strategy aimed at restoring territorial weaknesses, investing resources and policies to reinforce traditional sectors, and helping existing firms to grow and develop. In this phase, there were the first steps that led to the creation of an EE with measures on qualification and employment; and also on ecosystem infrastructure and traditional industry. It was a still nascent ecosystem that was forming, first strengthening its basic structure. The regions that fell into this category were both Campania and Calabria. However, Campania presented a more significant number of measures in the qualification category, physical assets, employment policies, and the traditional sector of the low-tech industry. Alongside these, it also showed few measures in R&D, manufacturing research, and know-how transfer.

For this reason, even if the framework that delineates the regional development of this group fell - for the elements that most characterised the territories - in a recovery policy direction, the presence of measures covering different sectors configured this direction as more advanced than Calabria. Regarding Lombardy, the region presented the signs of an already existing EE. In this phase, the policy assumed a reinforcing direction, where the measures supported and helped create a network of actors to promote regional innovation and strengthen the overall attractiveness and competitiveness of the region. The policies and measures were driven by a strategy aimed at investing in regional specializations representing each region's peculiarity and economic value to exploit the local competitive advantage. The reinforcing policy direction aimed to create an extended regional network of entrepreneurs that initiated many collaborations. The ecosystem began to have a stronger and more cohesive structure allowing the region to grow and develop even more.

Moving on to the analysis of the 2007-2013 ROPs documents, Campania showed signs of effective development by creating and expanding its regional network. In this phase, the policy assumed a reinforcing direction and was committed to supporting and helping create a network and enhancing the innovation and competitiveness of the region. The measures aimed to invest in regional specializations, conquering a competitive advantage. Regarding Lombardy, the region focused on increasing competitiveness and attractiveness, as well as the creation of firms, in particular, startups and spinoffs. Measures aiming to encourage innovation and technology in the firms were also highlighted. This type of approach is defined as shooting and entailed that the region could attract investments from outside and - through policies to enhance competitiveness - made the EE prepared to compete with actors outside the region.

The policy direction in Calabria was not yet reinforcing because the region still presented some policies that focused on the sector as education and employment. However, some elements also brought it closer to the reinforcing approach, but it was still in a recovery direction. In the 2014-2020 ROP, Calabria applied measures typical of a reinforcing approach. Concerning the Campania policy direction, it adopted an approach defined as shooting, as the region covered a nodal position relative to managing the relational and financial resources by inserting them in firms, industries, and innovative and technological projects.

Finally, Lombardy's ROP showed elements still classified as a shooting approach but also different measures. Indeed, the policy direction focused on measures typical of that group, but there were different policies to increase technology, innovation, and technology sharing. This means that the region continued to develop during the 2014-2020 ROP. *Table 8* shows the policy directions compared to the regions analysed.

Table 8. Regional policy direction evolution. Source: Author adaption

Policy direction	2000-2006 ROP	2007-2013 ROP	2014-2020 ROP
RECOVERY	Calabria		
	Campania	Calabria	
REINFORCING	Lombardy	Campania	Calabria
SHOOTING		Lombardy	Campania
			Lombardy

Table 9. The policy directions during the evolution of the regional entrepreneurial ecosystem. Source: Author adaption

<table>
<tr><th></th><th colspan="2">Stage 1: Nascent Entrepreneurial Ecosystem</th><th colspan="2">Stage 2: Strengthening Entrepreneurial Ecosystem</th><th colspan="2">Stage 3: Resilient entrepreneurial ecosystem</th></tr>
<tr><td rowspan="5">MEASURES</td><td>· Support to manufacturing firms' infrastructure and equipment</td><td rowspan="2">Financing and investment in R&D</td><td>Investments in regional transport and logistics infrastructure</td><td rowspan="2">Funding in startups' creation</td><td>Funding in startups' creation</td><td rowspan="2">Investment in the diffusion of technology and technology projects</td></tr>
<tr><td>Incentives for new technologies' adoption</td><td>Investments in regional cultural amenities</td><td>Investment in startup support programs managed by accelerators and incubators</td></tr>
<tr><td>Financial incentives for new business generation</td><td rowspan="3">investments in regional transport and logistics infrastructures</td><td>Financing the acquisition of new plants, machinery, and equipment</td><td rowspan="3">Funding opportunities for innovation projects</td><td>Funding opportunities for innovation projects</td><td rowspan="3">Investment in innovation</td></tr>
<tr><td>Provision of business consultancy services.</td><td>Financing R&D projects and new technology adoption</td><td>· Financial acquisition of digital assets and new technologies</td></tr>
<tr><td>Training programs for enhancing individuals' capabilities and skills</td><td>Financing the establishment of networks for the R&D cooperation</td><td>Financial support for investments in emerging technologies</td></tr>
<tr><td rowspan="3">OBJECTIVES</td><td colspan="2">Reduction of regional unemployment rates</td><td colspan="2">Improvement of the region's overall attractiveness</td><td colspan="2">Fostering the development of cutting-edge innovation throughout the whole community of the ecosystem</td></tr>
<tr><td colspan="2">Empowering human resources</td><td colspan="2">Development of innovation-driven networks</td><td colspan="2">Increasing the level of attractiveness and competitiveness of the ecosystems' actors at the international</td></tr>
<tr><td colspan="2">Strengthening the traditional regional areas of specialization</td><td colspan="2">Improvement of existing firms' competitiveness</td><td colspan="2"></td></tr>
<tr><td></td><td colspan="2">RECOVERY</td><td colspan="2">REINFORCING</td><td colspan="2">SHOOTING</td></tr>
</table>

Finally, in *Table 9* the author presents the evolution of the policy directions during the development of the regional EE referred to measures, objectives, and EE stages. The parts highlighted in grey represent the adding measures that regions adopted during different programming periods, i.e., Campania during the 2000-2006 ROP, Calabria in the 2007-2013 ROP, and finally, Lombardy in the 2014-2020 ROP. These additional measures have shown that, although there are patterns, similar objectives, and measures shared by regions in the same EE development stages, depending on the peculiarities and specific characteristics of each context, some differences are found.

FUTURE RESEARCH DIRECTIONS

Introducing the limits weighting this study, which are addressing the sample's size and the qualitative methodology used, this research highlights the contribution to the EE development given by the adoption of specific groups of policies aimed at the real needs of EE and based on the context characteristics in which they are implemented. Future research should continue in this direction, examining more measures and actions aiming to individuate other policy groups.

The contributions of this study are threefold: i) it provides a dynamic view of policy types from an EE perspective; ii) it delineates a categorization of policy and measures typical in each different EE's phases; iii) it identifies three policy directions adopted by the regions.

Therefore, future research may involve adopting a quantitative approach to analyze documents. In addition, the tiny sample may neglect other policy direction peculiarities; thus, we may extend the analysis to the entire Italian sample of regions to gain more insights into the direction adopted in other EU regions.

CONCLUSION

To underline the topic of policy direction within the EE, this chapter presents the analysis of the ROP, the most important and descriptive program of the regional strategic plan that a region develops and applies. It includes all the main objectives, measures, and policies the region aims to achieve in seven years. This document represents an attempt to achieve a balanced result considering all the actors within a specific context, the regional EE. Each region has to present this document, filling up all the objectives and measures they want to implement, taking into account all the entrepreneurial climate's characteristics and peculiarities within the EE.

The sample is composed of three Italian regions - Lombardy, Campania, and Calabria - and covers a period of twenty years, studying 2000-2006 ROP, 2007-2014 ROP, and 2014-2020 ROP.

The analysis of the documents is focused on answering a series of key questions about policy directions adopted by the regions and their contribution to EE development.

In the first place, this chapter, shedding light on the government institution's actor, focuses on the EE policies. It underlines its influence and dynamics over time, defining three policy directions adopted: recovery, reinforcing, and shooting. These approaches are defined on the EE development stages, entrepreneurial measures, and entrepreneurial objectives. In addition, this analysis presents insights related to the EE stages. Indeed, the recovery direction is typical of a nascent EE, still immature and forming. The entrepreneurial climate has to reshape and recover, and many investments are required in human capital development, new firm creation, and educational sectors. The reinforcing direction belongs to a strengthening EE, and the objectives address investing in innovation and start-ups and creating networks and links among the actors. Finally, the shooting direction regards a resilient EE with network relationships, a high innovation level, and investment in advanced technology. It focuses more on specialisations, a high level of qualified employees, and the creation of external networks.

Secondly, this chapter is interested in presenting a TCA analysis and mapping the dynamic and evolution of the policy types in the regions analysed, i.e., Lombardy, Campania, and Calabria. It shows an evolution path for each region lasting twenty years, highlighting the changes in directions adopted and, consequently, the dynamic characteristics of policy groups within the EE. These changes respond to a different configuration of the EE and the entrepreneurial and innovation climate.

Third, based on the evolution of paths and trends, this chapter considers which future is drawn for the policies tool within the EE and how to address the positive contributions highlighted in the results.

REFERENCES

Acs, Z.J., Autio, E., & Szerb, L. (2014). National systems of entrepreneurship: Measurement issues and policy implications. *Research Policy*, *43*(3), 476-494. Doi:. 2013.08.016 doi:10.1016/j.respol

Autio, E., Kenney, M., Mustar, P., Siegel, D., & Wright, M. (2014). Entrepreneurial innovation: The importance of context. *Research Policy*, *43*(7), 1097–1108. doi:10.1016/j.respol.2014.01.015

Banerjee, S., Savani, M., & Shreedhar, G. (2021). Public support for 'soft' versus 'hard' public policies: Review of the evidence. *Journal of Behavioral Public Administration*, *4*(2), 1–24. doi:10.30636/jbpa.42.220

Baumol, W. J. (1993). Formal entrepreneurship theory in economics: Existence and bounds. *Journal of Business Venturing*, *8*(3), 197–210. doi:10.1016/0883-9026(93)90027-3

Braun, V., & Clarke, V. (2006). Using thematic analysis in psychology. *Qualitative Research in Psychology*, *3*(2), 77–101. doi:10.1191/1478088706qp063oa

Brown, R., & Mason, C. (2017). Looking inside the spiky bits: A critical review and conceptualisation of entrepreneurial ecosystems. *Small Business Economics*, *49*(1), 11–30. doi:10.100711187-017-9865-7

Cantner, U., Cunningham, J. A., Lehmann, E. E., & Menter, M. (2021). Entrepreneurial ecosystems: A dynamic lifecycle model. *Small Business Economics*, *57*(1), 407–423. doi:10.100711187-020-00316-0

Colombelli, A., Paolucci, E., & Ughetto, E. (2019). Hierarchical and relational governance and the life cycle of entrepreneurial ecosystems. *Small Business Economics*, *52*(2), 505–521. doi:10.100711187-017-9957-4

Colombo, M. G., Dagnino, G. B., Lehmann, E. E., & Salmador, M. (2019). The governance of entrepreneurial ecosystems. *Small Business Economics*, *52*(2), 419–428. doi:10.100711187-017-9952-9

Fernandes, A. J., & Ferreira, J. J. (2022). Entrepreneurial ecosystems and networks: A literature review and research agenda. *Review of Managerial Science*, *16*(1), 189–247. doi:10.100711846-020-00437-6

Mack, E., & Mayer, H. (2016). The evolutionary dynamics of entrepreneurial ecosystems. *Urban Studies (Edinburgh, Scotland)*, *53*(10), 2118–2133. doi:10.1177/0042098015586547

Malecki, E. J. (2018). Entrepreneurship and entrepreneurial ecosystems. *Geography Compass*, *12*(3), 12359. doi:10.1111/gec3.12359

Ortega-Argilés, R. (2022). The evolution of regional entrepreneurship policies: "No one size fits all". *The Annals of Regional Science*, *69*(3), 585–610. doi:10.100700168-022-01128-8

Pita, M., Costa, J., & Carrizo Moreira, A. (2021). Entrepreneurial Ecosystems and Entrepreneurial Initiative: Building a Multi-Country Taxonomy. *Sustainability (Basel)*, *13*(7), 4065. doi:10.3390u13074065

Roundy, P. T., Brockman, B. K., & Bradshaw, M. (2017). The resilience of entrepreneurial ecosystems. *Journal of Business Venturing Insights*, *8*, 99–104. doi:10.1016/j.jbvi.2017.08.002

Spigel, B. (2017). The relational organization of entrepreneurial ecosystems. *Entrepreneurship Theory and Practice*, *41*(1), 49–72. doi:10.1111/etap.12167

Stam, E. (2015). Entrepreneurial ecosystems and regional policy: A sympathetic critique. *European Planning Studies*, *23*(9), 1759–1769. doi:10.1080/09654313.2015.1061484

Storey, J. (2005). What Next for Strategic-level Leadership Research? *Leadership*, *1*(1), 89–104. doi:10.1177/1742715005049353

KEY TERMS AND DEFINITIONS

EE: This stands for entrepreneurial ecosystem.

Policy Direction: All the measures, actions, and specific policy types implemented by the region and adopted in the EE, exploring how EEs address the issue of entrepreneurship and innovation at a regional policy level.

RIS: This stands for Regional Innovation Scoreboard.

ROP: This stands for Regional Operational Programme.

TCA: This stands for Thematic Content Analysis.

Compilation of References

Ab Hamid, M. R., Sami, W., & Mohmad Sidek, M. H. (2017). Discriminant Validity Assessment: Use of Fornell & Larcker criterion versus HTMT Criterion. *Journal of Physics: Conference Series*, *890*, 012163. doi:10.1088/1742-6596/890/1/012163

Abdel-Basset, M, Manogaran, G. (2018). Internet of Things and its Impact on supply chain: A framework for building smart, secure, and efficient systems. *Future Generation Computer system, 86, 614-626*. doi:10.1016/j.future.2018.04.051

Abdul-Halim, H., Ahmad, N. H., Geare, A., & Thurasamy, R. (2019). Innovation culture in SMEs: The importance of organizational culture, organizational learning and market orientation. *Entrepreneurship Research Journal*, *9*(3), 20170014. doi:10.1515/erj-2017-0014

Abualoush, S., Bataineh, K., & Alrowwad, A. A. (2018). The role of knowledge management process and intellectual capital as intermediary variables between knowledge management infrastructure and organization performance. *Interdisciplinary Journal of Information, Knowledge, and Management*, *13*, 279–309. doi:10.28945/4088

Acs, Z.J., Autio, E., & Szerb, L. (2014). National systems of entrepreneurship: Measurement issues and policy implications. *Research Policy*, *43*(3), 476-494. Doi:. 2013.08.016 doi:10.1016/j.respol

Acs, Z., Desaid, S., & Hessels, J. (2008). Entrepreneurship, economic development, and institutions. *Small Business Economics*, *31*(1), 219–234. doi:10.100711187-008-9135-9

ADB. (2007). *Effect of Microfinance Operations on Poor Rural Households and the Status of Women*. ADB evaluation report. https://www.oecd.org/countries/bangladesh/39503711.pdf.

Adler, P. S. (2012). Perspective – the sociological ambivalence of bureaucracy: From Weber via Gouldner to Marx. *Organization Science*, *23*(1), 244–266. doi:10.1287/orsc.1100.0615

Adomako, S., Danso, A., Boso, N., & Narteh, B. (2018). Entrepreneurial Alertness and new venture performance: Facilitating roles of networking capability. *Int. Small Bus. J. Res. Entrep.* doi:10.1177/0266242617747667

Adusei, M. (2016). Does entrepreneurship promote economic growth in Africa? *African Development Review*, *28*(2), 201–214. doi:10.1111/1467-8268.12190

Ahmad, A. R., Hassan, A., Alhammadi, Y., & Jameel, A. S. (2021). National Culture. *Leadership Styles and Job Satisfaction : An Empirical Study in the United Arab Emirates*, *8*, 1111–1120. doi:10.13106/jafeb.2021.vol8.no6.1111

Ahmad, N. H., Halim, H. A., Ramayah, T., & Rahman, S. A. (2015). Green entrepreneurship inclination among generation Y: The road towards a green economy. *Problems and Perspectives in Management*, *13*(2), 211–218. https://www.businessperspectives.org/images/pdf/applications/publishing/templates/article/assets/6626/PPM_2015_02cont_Ahmad.pdf

Ahmed, J. U., Talukdar, A., & Ahmed, A. (2023). *Dignity Kitchen: Social Enterprise for Differently Abled People in the Labor Market*. SAGE Publications: SAGE Business Cases Originals.

Ahmed, R. R., and Streimikiene, D. (2021). Environmental issues and strategic corporate social responsibility for organizational competitiveness. *Journal of Competitiveness*, (2).

Ajagbe, M. A., Peter, O. F., Ekanem, E. U. U., Uduimoh, A. A., & Akpan, E. S. (2016). Business strategy as a contributor to organizational performance. *International Journal of Advanced Academic Research*, *2*(3), 1–19.

Ajzen, I. (1987). Attitudes, traits, and actions—Dispositional prediction of behavior in personality and social-psychology. *Advances in Experimental Social Psychology*, *20*, 1–63. doi:10.1016/S0065-2601(08)60411-6

Ajzen, I. (1991). The theory of planned behavior. *Organizational Behavior and Human Decision Processes*, *50*(2), 179–211. doi:10.1016/0749-5978(91)90020-T

Akingbola, K., & Phaetthayanan, S. (2021). The paradox of employee–volunteer interchangeability in a supported social enterprise. *Journal of Public and Nonprofit Affairs*, *7*(1), 89–107. doi:10.20899/jpna.7.1.89-107

Akpa, V. O., Asikhia, O. U., & Nneji, N. E. (2021). Organizational culture and organizational performance: A review of literature. *International Journal of Advances in Engineering and Management*, *3*(1), 361–372.

Alarifi, G., & Alrubaishi, D. (2018). The Social Entrepreneurship Landscape in Saudi Arabia. *Academy of Entrepreneurship Journal*, *24*(4), 1–8.

Alexiou, A. (2014). Taming the waves of adversity: Exploring the multidimensional construct of organizational flexibility. In D. G. Assimakopoulos, I. Oshri, & K. Pandza (Eds.), *Managing Emerging Technologies for Socio-Economic Impact*. Edward Elgar Publishing. doi:10.4337/9781782547884.00026

Ali, M. M. (2017). Testing Hypothesis on Theory of Social Networking, Community Banking and Empowerment of People: A Conceptual View. *Psychology and Behavioral Sciences (New York, N.Y.)*, *6*(5), 96–104. doi:10.11648/j.pbs.20170605.14

Ali, N. M. (2018). Impact of climate change and natural catastrophe on the occupational changes in the coastal areas of Bangladesh: An empirical study. *Environment and Ecology*, *9*(1), 22–37. doi:10.21511/ee.09(1).2018.02 PMID:30005645

Allaire, Y., & Firsirotu, M. E. (1984). Theories of organizational culture. *Organization Studies*, *5*(3), 193–226. doi:10.1177/017084068400500301

Alliger, G. M., Cerasoli, C. P., Tannenbaum, S. I., & Vessey, W. B. (2015). Team flexibility: How teams flourish under pressure. *Organizational Dynamics*, *44*, 176–184. doi:10.1016/j.orgdyn.2015.05.003

Al-Refaie, A. (2015). Effects of human resource management on hotel performance using structural equation modeling. *Computers in Human Behavior*, *43*, 293–303. doi:10.1016/j.chb.2014.11.016

Alter, S. K. (2008). Social enterprise models and their mission and money relationship. In A. Nicholls (Ed.), *Social entrepreneurship: New models of sustainable social change* (pp. 205–232). Oxford University Press.

Alvarez, S. A., & Barney, J. B. (2007). *Discovery and Creation: Alternative Theories of Entrepreneurial Action*. Rev. Organ. em Context., doi:10.15603/1982-8756/roc.v3n6p123-152

Alvarez, S. A., & Barney, J. B. (2007). Discovery and Creation: Alternative Theories of Entrepreneurial Action. *Strategic Entrepreneurship Journal*, *1*(1), 11–26. doi:10.1002ej.4

Alvarez, S. A., & Barney, J. B. (2010). *Entrepreneurship and epistemology: The philosophical underpinnings of the study of entrepreneurial opportunities*. Acad. Manag. Ann. doi:10.1080/19416520.2010.495521

Alvarez, S. A., Barney, J. B., & Newman, A. M. B. (2015). The poverty problem and the industrialization solution. *Asia Pacific Journal of Management*, *32*(1), 23–37. doi:10.100710490-014-9397-5

Alwakid, W., Aparicio, S., & Urbano, D. (2021). The influence of green entrepreneurship on sustainable development in Saudi Arabia: The role of formal institutions. *International Journal of Environmental Research and Public Health*, *18*(10), 1–23. doi:10.3390/ijerph18105433 PMID:34069588

Alwakid, W., Sebastian, A., & David, U. (2020). Cultural antecedents of green entrepreneurship in Saudi Arabia: An institutional approach. *Sustainability (Basel)*, *12*(9), 36–73. doi:10.3390u12093673

Ambrosini, V., Bowman, C., & Collier, N. (2009). Dynamic Capabilities: An Exploration of How Firms Renew their Resource Base. *British Journal of Management*, *20*(S1), S9–S24. doi:10.1111/j.1467-8551.2008.00610.x

Amburgey, T. L., & Dacin, T. M. (1994). As the left foot follows the right? The dynamics of strategic and structural change. *Academy of Management Journal*, *37*(6), 1427–1452. doi:10.2307/256794

Andresen, M., & Bergdolt, F. (2017). A systematic literature review on the definitions of global mindset and cultural intelligence merging two different research streams. *International Journal of Human Resource Management*, *28*(1), 170–195. doi:10.1080/09585192.2016.1243568

Andrews, K. (1971). *The concept of corporate strategy*. Dow Jones-Irwin.

Anh, D. B. H., Duc, L. D. M., Yen, N. T. H., Hung, N. T., & Tien, N. H. (2022). Sustainable development of social entrepreneurship: Evidence from Vietnam. *International Journal of Entrepreneurship and Small Business*, *45*(1), 62–76. doi:10.1504/IJESB.2022.120553

Anheier, H. K. (2000). *Managing nonprofit organizations: Towards a new approach*. Civil Society.

Anning-Dorson, T. (2021). Organizational culture and leadership as antecedents to organizational flexibility: Implications for SME competitiveness. *Journal of Entrepreneurship in Emerging Economies*, *13*(5), 1309–1325. doi:10.1108/JEEE-08-2020-0288

Ansari, Z. N., and Qureshi, M. N. (). Sustainability in supply chain management: An overview. *IUP Journal of Supply Chain Management, 12*(2)," 2015.

Ansoff, H. I. (1965). *Corporate strategy: An analytic approach to business policy for growth and expansion*. McGraw-Hill.

Apneseth, K., Wahl, A., & Hollnagel, E. (2013). Measuring flexibility in integrated planning. In E. Albrechtsen & D. Besnard (Eds.), *Oil and Gas, Technology and Humans: Assessing the Human Factors of Technological Change*. CRC press.

Ardichvili, A., Cardozo, R., & Ray, S. (2003). A theory of entrepreneurial opportunity identification and development. *Journal of Business Venturing*, *18*(1), 105–123. doi:10.1016/S0883-9026(01)00068-4

Armanious, M., & Padgett, J. D. (2021). Agile learning strategies to compete in an uncertain business environment. *Journal of Workplace Learning*, *33*(8), 635–647. doi:10.1108/JWL-11-2020-0181

Armitage, C. J., & Conner, M. (2001). Efficacy of the theory of planned behaviour: A meta-analytic review. *British Journal of Social Psychology*, *40*(4), 471–499. doi:10.1348/014466601164939 PMID:11795063

Arregle, J. L., Batjargal, B., Hitt, M. A., Webb, J. W., Miller, T., & Tsui, A. S. (2015). Family ties in entrepreneurs' social networks and new venture growth. *Entrepreneurship Theory and Practice*, *39*(2), 313–344. doi:10.1111/etap.12044

Ashforth, B. E., Rogers, K. M., Pratt, M. G., & Pradies, C. (2014). Ambivalence in organizations: A multilevel approach. *Organization Science*, *25*(5), 1453–1478. doi:10.1287/orsc.2014.0909

Ashraf, S. N., & Singh, A. K. (2019). Does entrepreneurship ecosystem have a long-term relationship with economic Growth in selected economies? A statistical investigation. In Misra S., Shukla S. and Batthini G. (Eds.), *Proceedings of the 13th Biennial Conference on Entrepreneurship, EDII Ahmedabad,* (pp. 176-187). Bookwell Publishing House, New Delhi.

Ashraf, S. N., & Singh, A. K. (2022). Implications of appropriate technology and farm inputs in the agricultural sector of Gujarat: Empirical analysis based on primary data. *Agricultural Economics Research Review*, *35*(2), 59–77. doi:10.5958/0974-0279.2022.00031.3

Astrachan, C. B., Patel, V. K., & Wanzenried, G. (2014). A comparative study of CB-SEM and PLS-SEM for theory development in family firm research. *Journal of Family Business Strategy*, *5*(1), 116–128. doi:10.1016/j.jfbs.2013.12.002

Audretsch, D. B., Belitski, M., & Desai, S. (2015). Entrepreneurship and economic development in cities. *The Annals of Regional Science*, *55*(1), 33–60. doi:10.100700168-015-0685-x

Austin, J., Stevenson, H., & Wei-Skillern, J. (2006). Social and commercial entrepreneurship: Same, different, or both? *Entrepreneurship Theory and Practice*, *30*(1), 1–22. doi:10.1111/j.1540-6520.2006.00107.x

Autio, E., Keeley, R. H., Klofsten, M., Parker, G. G. C., & Hay, M. (2001). Entrepreneurial Intent Among Students in Scandinavia and in the USA. *Enterprise and Innovation Management Studies*, *2*(2), 145–160. doi:10.1080/14632440110094632

Autio, E., Kenney, M., Mustar, P., Siegel, D., & Wright, M. (2014). Entrepreneurial innovation: The importance of context. *Research Policy*, *43*(7), 1097–1108. doi:10.1016/j.respol.2014.01.015

Azadeh, A., Hasannia Kolaee, M., & Salehi, V. (2016). The impact of redundancy on flexibility engineering in a petrochemical plant by data envelopment analysis. *Proceedings of the Institution of Mechanical Engineers. Part O, Journal of Risk and Reliability*, *230*(3), 285–296. doi:10.1177/1748006X16629866

Babajide, A., Lawal, A., Asaleye, A., Okafor, T., & Osuma, G. (2020). Financial stability and entrepreneurship development in sub-Sahara Africa: Implications for sustainable development goals. *Cogent Social Sciences*, *6*(1), 1798330. doi:10.1080/23311886.2020.1798330

Bacq, S., & Eddleston, K. A. (2018). A resource-based view of social entrepreneurship: How stewardship culture benefits scale of social impact. *Journal of Business Ethics*, *152*(3), 589–611. doi:10.100710551-016-3317-1

Bageac, D., Furrer, O., & Reynaud, E. (2011). Management students' attitudes toward business ethics: A comparison between France and Romania. *Journal of Business Ethics*, *98*(3), 391–406. doi:10.100710551-010-0555-5

Bagozzi, R. P., & Yi, Y. (1988). On the evaluation of structural equation models. *Journal of the Academy of Marketing Science*, *16*(1), 74–94. doi:10.1007/BF02723327

Bakotic, D., & Kruzic, D. (2010). Students' perceptions and intentions towards entrepreneurship: The empirical findings from Croatia. *The Business Review, Cambridge*, *14*(2), 209.

Balabanis, G., & Katsikea, E. (2004). Being an entrepreneurial exporter: Does it pay? *International Business Review*, *12*(2), 233–252. doi:10.1016/S0969-5931(02)00098-7

Bandura, A. (1977). Self-efficacy: Toward a unifying theory of behavioral change. *Psychological Review*, *84*(2), 191–215. doi:10.1037/0033-295X.84.2.191 PMID:847061

Bandura, A. (1986). *The Social Foundations of Thought and Action*. Prentice-Hall.

Banerjee, S., Savani, M., & Shreedhar, G. (2021). Public support for 'soft' versus 'hard' public policies: Review of the evidence. *Journal of Behavioral Public Administration*, *4*(2), 1–24. doi:10.30636/jbpa.42.220

Barbieri, J. (2003). *Organizações inovadoras: estudos e casos brasileiros*. FGV Editora.

Barker, V. L. III, & Duhaime, I. M. (1997). Strategic Change in the Turnaround Process: Theory and Empirical Evidence. *Strategic Management Journal*, *18*(1), 13–38. doi:10.1002/(SICI)1097-0266(199701)18:1<13::AID-SMJ843>3.0.CO;2-X

Barney, J. B., & Hoskisson, R. E. (1990). Strategic groups: Untested assertions and research proposals. *MDE. Managerial and Decision Economics*, *11*(3), 187–198. doi:10.1002/mde.4090110306

Baron, R. M., & Kenny, D. A. (1986). The moderator–mediator variable distinction in social psychological research: Conceptual, strategic, and statistical considerations. *Journal of Personality and Social Psychology*, *51*(6), 1173–1182. doi:10.1037/0022-3514.51.6.1173 PMID:3806354

Barratt, M., & Choi, T. (2007). Mandated RFID and institutional responses: Cases of decentralised business units. *Production and Operations Management*, *16*(5), 569–585. doi:10.1111/j.1937-5956.2007.tb00281.x

Barreto, H., & Kirzner, I. (1986). Discovery and the Capitalist Process. *Southern Economic Journal*, *53*(2), 529. doi:10.2307/1059434

Barreto, I. (2010). Dynamic Capabilities: A Review of Past Research and an Agenda for the Future. *Journal of Management*, *36*(1), 256–280. doi:10.1177/0149206309350776

Barreto, I. (2012). Solving the Entrepreneurial Puzzle: The Role of Entrepreneurial Interpretation in Opportunity Formation and Related Processes. *Journal of Management Studies*, *49*(2), 356–380. doi:10.1111/j.1467-6486.2011.01023.x

Barringer, R. B., & Bluedon, A. C. (1990). The relationship between corporate entrepreneurship and strategic management. *Strategic Management Journal*, *20*(5), 421–444. doi:10.1002/(SICI)1097-0266(199905)20:5<421::AID-SMJ30>3.0.CO;2-O

Bastian, B. L., Sidani, Y. M., & El Amine, Y. (2018). Women entrepreneurship in the Middle East and North Africa: A review of knowledge areas and research gaps. *Gender in Management*, *33*(1), 14–29. doi:10.1108/GM-07-2016-0141

Batjargal, B. (2010). Network dynamics and new ventures in China: A longitudinal study. *Entrepreneurship and Regional Development*, *22*(2), 139–153. doi:10.1080/08985620802628864

Battilana, J., & Dorado, S. (2010). Building sustainable hybrid organizations: The case of commercial microfinance organizations. *Academy of Management Journal*, *53*(6), 1419–1440. doi:10.5465/amj.2010.57318391

Battilana, J., & Lee, M. (2014). Advancing research on hybrid organizing – Insights from the study of social enterprises. *The Academy of Management Annals*, *8*(1), 397–441. doi:10.5465/19416520.2014.893615

Battilana, J., Sengul, M., Pache, A. C., & Model, J. (2014). Harnessing productive tensions in hybrid organizations: The case of work integration social enterprises. *Academy of Management Journal*.

Baumol, W. J. (1990). Entrepreneurship: Productive, unproductive and destructive. *Journal of Political Economy*, *80*(5), 893–921. doi:10.1086/261712

Baumol, W. J. (1993). Formal entrepreneurship theory in economics: Existence and bounds. *Journal of Business Venturing*, *8*(3), 197–210. doi:10.1016/0883-9026(93)90027-3

Bauwens, T., Huybrechts, B., & Dufays, F. (2020). Understanding the diverse scaling strategies of social enterprises as hybrid organizations: The case of renewable energy cooperatives. *Organization & Environment*, *33*(2), 195–219. doi:10.1177/1086026619837126

Beer, M. (2021). Reflections: Towards a normative and actionable theory of planned organizational change and development. *Journal of Change Management*, *21*(1), 14–29. doi:10.1080/14697017.2021.1861699

Beer, M., & Eisenstat, R. A. (2000). The silent killers of strategy implementation and learning. *Sloan Management Review*, *41*, 29–40.

Begley, T.M., & Boyd, D.P. (1987). Psychological characteristics associated with performence in entrepreneurial firms and smaller businesses. *J. Bus. Ventur.* doi:10.1016/0883-9026(87)90020-6

Belitski, M., Guenther, C., Kritikos, A. S., & Thurik, R. (2021). *Economic effects of the COVID-19 pandemic on entrepreneurship and small businesses* (Issue 14630).

Benner, M. J., & Tushman, M. L. (2003). Exploitation, exploration, and process management: The productivity dilemma revisited. *Academy of Management Review*, *28*(2), 238–256. doi:10.2307/30040711

Bensaou, M., & Venkatraman, N. (1995). Configurations of inter-organizational relationships: A comparison between the US and Japanese automakers. *Management Science*, *41*(9), 1471–1492. doi:10.1287/mnsc.41.9.1471

Bento, F., & Garotti, L. (2019). Flexibility beyond Formal Structures: A Network Perspective towards the Challenges of an Aging Workforce in the Oil and Gas Industry. *Journal of Open Innovation*, *5*(1), 1–15. doi:10.3390/joitmc5010015

Bergman, E. M. (2009). Embedding network analysis in spatial studies of innovation. *The Annals of Regional Science*, *43*(3), 559–565. doi:10.100700168-008-0250-y

Bergner, S., Kanape, A., & Rybnicek, R. (2019). Taking an Interest in Taking the Lead: The Influence of Vocational Interests, Leadership Experience and Success on the Motivation to Lead. *Applied Psychology*, *68*(1), 202–219. doi:10.1111/apps.12150

Bergstr¨om, J., van Winsen, R., & Henriqson, E. (2015). On the rationale of flexibility in the domain of safety: A literature review, *Reliab. Eng. Syst. Saf. 141,* 131–141. . doi:10.1016/j.ress.2015.03.008

Bertrand, J. L., & Parnaudeau, M. (2019). Understanding the economic effects of abnormal weather to mitigate the risk of business failures. *Journal of Business Research, 98*, 391–402. doi:10.1016/j.jbusres.2017.09.016

Besharov, M. L., & Smith, W. K. (2013). *Multiple logics within organizations: An integrative framework and model of organizational hybridity*. Cornell University.

Beznos, M. (2023). Microservices vs monolith: Which architecture is the best choice for your business? *N-iX*. https://www.n-ix.com/microservices-vs-monolith-which-architecture-best-choice-your-business/(Viewed on 31, Janaury,2023)

Bezzina, F. (2010). Characteristics of the Maltese entrepreneur. *The International Journal of the Arts in Society, 3*(7), 292–312.

Bhagchandani, R. (2017). How India can up its startup game by bolstering student entrepreneurship. *Your Story*. https://yourstory.com/2017/01/india-startup-game-bolstering-student-entrepreneurship

Bhave, M. P. (1994). A process model of entrepreneurial venture creation. *Journal of Business Venturing, 9*(3), 233–242. doi:10.1016/0883-9026(94)90031-0

Bhuiyan, M. F., & Ivlevs, A. (2019). Micro-entrepreneurship and subjective well-being: Evidence from rural Bangladesh, *Journal of Business Venturing, 34*(4), 625-645. https:// doi:10.1016/j.jbusvent.2018.09.005

Bigley, G. A., & Roberts, K. H. (2001). The incident command system: High reliability organizing for complex and volatile task environments. *Academy of Management Journal, 44*(6), 1281–1299. doi:10.2307/3069401

Bingham, C. B., Eisenhardt, K. M., & Davis, J. P. (2007). *Opening the black box of organizational expertise: understanding what firms learn from their process experience and how that learning unfolds over time*. University of Maryland working paper.

Bingham, C. B., & Eisenhardt, K. M. (2011). Rational Heuristics: The 'Simple Rules' that Strategists Learn from Process Experience. *Strategic Management Journal, 32*(13), 1437–1464. doi:10.1002mj.965

Bingham, C. B., Eisenhardt, K. M., & Furr, N. R. (2007). What Makes a Process a Capability? Heuristics, Strategy and Effective Capture of Opportunities. *Strategic Entrepreneurship Journal, 1*(1), 27–47. doi:10.1002ej.1

Bird, B. (1988). Implementing entrepreneurial ideas—The case for intention. *Academy of Management Review, 13*(3), 442–453. doi:10.2307/258091

Bird, B. J., & West, G. P. III. (1998). *Time and Entrepreneurship*. Entrepreneurship. doi:10.1177/104225879802200201

Bissola, R., & Imperatori, B. (2012). Sustaining the stakeholder engagement in the social enterprise: the human resource architecture. *Patterns in Social Entrepreneurship Research*, 137-160.

Bloom, P. N., & Chatterji, A. K. (2009). Scaling social entrepreneurial impact. *California Management Review*, *51*(3), 114–133. doi:10.2307/41166496

Boin, A., & McConnell, A. (2007). Preparing for critical infrastructure breakdowns: The limits of crisis management and the need for flexibility. *Journal of Contingencies and Crisis Management*, *15*(1), 50–59. doi:10.1111/j.1468-5973.2007.00504.x

Boin, A., & van Eeten, M. J. B. (2013). The Resilient Organization—A critical appraisal. *Public Management Review*, *15*(3), 429–445. doi:10.1080/14719037.2013.769856

Boudreaux, C.J., Nikolaev, B.N., & Klein, P. (2019). Socio-cognitive traits and entrepreneurship: The moderating role of economic institutions. *J. Bus. Ventur.* doi:10.1016/j.jbusvent.2018.08.003

Boyd, N. G., & Vozikis, G. S. (1994). The influence of self-efficacy on the development of entrepreneurial intentions and actions. *Entrepreneurship Theory and Practice*, *18*(4), 63–77. doi:10.1177/104225879401800404

Bradač Hojnik, B., & Crnogaj, K. (2020). Social impact, innovations, and market activity of social enterprises: Comparison of European countries. *Sustainability (Basel)*, *12*(5), 1915. doi:10.3390u12051915

Brandsen, T., & Karré, P. M. (2011). Hybrid organizations: No cause for concern. *International Journal of Public Administration*, *34*(13), 827–836. doi:10.1080/01900692.2011.605090

Braun, V., & Clarke, V. (2006). Using thematic analysis in psychology. *Qualitative Research in Psychology*, *3*(2), 77–101. doi:10.1191/1478088706qp063oa

Breusch, T. S., & Pagan, A. R. (1979). A Simple Test for Heteroscedasticity and Random Coefficient Variation. *Econometrica*, *47*(5), 1287. doi:10.2307/1911963

Brickley, J., Smith, C., Zimmerman, J. L., & Willett, J. (2002). *Designing organizations to create value: From strategy to structure*. McGraw-Hill.

Brockhaus, R. H. Sr. (1980). Risk taking propensity of entrepreneurs. *Academy of Management Journal*, *23*(3), 509–520. doi:10.2307/255515

Brown, R., & Mason, C. (2017). Looking inside the spiky bits: A critical review and conceptualisation of entrepreneurial ecosystems. *Small Business Economics*, *49*(1), 11–30. doi:10.100711187-017-9865-7

Bruhn, N. C. P., Alcântara, J. N. & Calegário, C. L. L. (2016). Multinational enterprises and spillover effects: A study on the factors associated with the innovation capacity of SMEs in Brazil. *Espacios*, *37*(10).

Bubicz, M. E., Barbosa-Póvoa, A. P. F. D., & Carvalho, A. (2019). Incorporating social aspects in sustainable supply chains: Trends and future directions. *Journal of Cleaner Production*, *237*, 117500. doi:10.1016/j.jclepro.2019.06.331

Bull, M., & Crompton, H. (2006). () "Business practices in social enterprises. *Social Enterprise Journal*, *2*(1), 42–60. doi:10.1108/17508610680000712

Bunduchi, R., Smart, A. U., Crisan-Mitra, C., & Cooper, S. (2023). Legitimacy and innovation in social enterprises. *International Small Business Journal*, *41*(4), 371–400. doi:10.1177/02662426221102860

Burger-Helmchen, T. (2013). Entrepreneurial Organizations. In E. G. Carayannis (Ed.), *Encyclopedia of Creativity, Invention, Innovation and Entrepreneurship*. Springer., doi:10.1007/978-1-4614-3858-8_208

Burnard, K., & Bhamra, R. (2011). Organisational flexibility: Development of a conceptual framework for organisational responses. *International Journal of Production Research*, *49*(18), 5581–5599. doi:10.1080/00207543.2011.563827

Burnham, J. F. (2006). Scopus database: A review. *Biomedical Digital Libraries*, *3*(1), 1. doi:10.1186/1742-5581-3-1 PMID:16522216

Busenitz, L. W., & Lau, C.-M. (1996). A Cross-Cultural Cognitive Model of New Venture Creation. *Entrepreneurship Theory and Practice*, *20*(4), 25–40. doi:10.1177/104225879602000403

Calik, E., Calisir, F., & Centigue, B. (2017). A scale development for innovation capability measurement. *Journal of Advanced Management Science*, *5*(2), 69–76. doi:10.18178/joams.5.2.69-76

Cameron, K. S., & Quinn, R. E. (2005). Diagnosing and changing organizational culture: Based on the competing values framework. Jossey-Bass.

Campos-Blázquez, J. R., Rubio-Andrada, L., & Celemín-Pedroche, M. S. (2023). Voices from within. To what extent can internal crowdsourcing drive a change in organizational culture? *Journal of Business Research*, *157*, 113618. doi:10.1016/j.jbusres.2022.113618

Cantner, U., Cunningham, J. A., Lehmann, E. E., & Menter, M. (2021). Entrepreneurial ecosystems: A dynamic lifecycle model. *Small Business Economics*, *57*(1), 407–423. doi:10.100711187-020-00316-0

Cardoza, G., & Fornes, G. (2011). The internationalisation of SMEs from China: The case of Ningxia Hui autonomous region. *Asia Pacific Journal of Management*, *28*(4), 737–759. doi:10.100710490-009-9174-z

Carland, J. & Carland, J. (2000). New Venture Creation Model. *J. Bus. Entrep.*

Carley, K. M. (1991). Designing organizational structures to cope with communication breakdowns: A simulation model. *Industrial Crisis Quarterly*, *5*(1), 19–57. doi:10.1177/108602669100500102

Carley, K. M., & Harrald, J. R. (1997). Organizational learning under fire: Theory and practice. *The American Behavioral Scientist*, *40*(3), 310–332. doi:10.1177/0002764297040003007

Carneiro, J., & Brenes, E. R. (2014). Latin American firms competing in the global economy. *Journal of Business Research*, *67*(5), 831–836. doi:10.1016/j.jbusres.2013.07.001

Carr, J. C., & Sequeira, J. M. (2007). Prior family business exposure as intergenerational influence and entrepreneurial intent: A theory of planned behavior approach. *Journal of Business Research*, *60*(10), 1090–1098. doi:10.1016/j.jbusres.2006.12.016

Carter, C., & Easton, P. L. (2011). Sustainable supply chain management: Evolution and future directions. *International Journal of Physical Distribution & Logistics Management*, *41*(1), 46–62. doi:10.1108/09600031111101420

Cartwright, S., & Cooper, C. L. (1993). The role of culture compatibility in successful organizational marriage. *The Academy of Management Perspectives*, *7*(2), 57–70. doi:10.5465/ame.1993.9411302324

Cepeda, G., Henseler, J., Ringle, C., & Roldán, J. L. (2016). Prediction-oriented modeling in business research by means of partial least squares path modeling. *Journal of Business Research*, *69*, 4545–4551. doi:10.1016/j.jbusres.2016.03.048

Chamlee-Wright, E. (2010). *The Cultural and Political Economy of Recovery: Social Learning in a Post-Disaster Environment* (Vol. 12). Routledge. doi:10.4324/9780203855928

Chandel, T. A. (2022). Green entrepreneurship and sustainable development. In M. Magd, D. Singh, D. Spicer, & R. T. Syed (Eds.), *International Perspectives on Value Creation and Sustainability Through Social Entrepreneurship*. IGI Global. doi:10.4018/978-1-6684-4666-9.ch009

Chandler, A. D. (2003) Strategy and structure: Chapters in the history of the American industrial enterprise. Beard Books.

Chandra, Y., & Shang, L. (2017). Unpacking the biographical antecedents of the emergence of social enterprises: A narrative perspective. *Voluntas*, *28*(6), 2498–2529. doi:10.100711266-017-9860-2

Chan, J. K. (2011). Enhancing Organisational Flexibility: Application of Viable System Model and MCDA in a Small Hong Kong Company. *International Journal of Production Research*, *49*(18), 5545–5563. doi:10.1080/00207543.2011.563829

Chatterjee, S., Lubatkin, M. H., Schweiger, D. M., & Weber, Y. (1992). Cultural differences and shareholder value in related mergers: Linking equity and human capital. *Strategic Management Journal*, *13*(5), 319–334. doi:10.1002mj.4250130502

Cheah, J., Amran, A., & Yahya, S. (2019). Internal oriented resources and social enterprises' performance: How can social enterprises help themselves before helping others? *Journal of Cleaner Production*, *211*, 607–619. doi:10.1016/j.jclepro.2018.11.203

Chell, E. (2008). *The Entrepreneurial Personality: A Social Construction* (2nd ed.). Routledge. doi:10.4324/9780203938638

Chen, R., Liu, Y., & Zhou, F. (2021). Turning Danger into Safety: The Origin, Research Context and Theoretical Framework of Organizational Flexibility. IEEE Access, 9, 48899-48913. doi:10.1109/ACCESS.2021.3069301

Chen, C. C., Greene, P. G., & Crick, A. (1998). Does entrepreneurial self-efficacy distinguish entrepreneurs from managers? *Journal of Business Venturing*, *13*(4), 295–316. doi:10.1016/S0883-9026(97)00029-3

Chen, J.-C., Li, W. T., Wen, C. K., Teng, J. H., & Ting, P. (2014, July). Efficient Identification Methods for Power Line Outages in the Smart Power Grid. *IEEE Transactions on Power Systems*, *29*(4), 1788–1800. doi:10.1109/TPWRS.2013.2296897

Chen, S., Shen, W., Qiu, Z., Liu, R., & Mardani, A. (2023). Who are the green entrepreneurs in China? The relationship between entrepreneurs' characteristics, green entrepreneurship orientation, and corporate financial performance. *Journal of Business Research*, *165*, 113960. doi:10.1016/j.jbusres.2023.113960

Chetty, S., Karami, M., & Martín, O. M. (2018). Opportunity discovery and creation as duality: Evidence from small firms' foreign market entries. *Journal of International Marketing*, *26*(3), 70–93. doi:10.1509/jim.17.0005

Chien, S. Y. (2014). Franchisor resources, spousal resources, entrepreneurial orientation, and performance in a couple-owned franchise outlet. *Management Decision*, *52*(5), 916–933. doi:10.1108/MD-07-2013-0368

Child, J. (1984). *Organization: A Guide to Problems and Practice*. SAGE. doi:10.4135/9781446280348

Chirico, F., Sirmon, D. G., Sciascia, S., & Mazzola, P. (2011). Resource orchestration in family firms: Investigating how entrepreneurial orientation, generational involvement, and participative strategy affect performance. *Strategic Entrepreneurship Journal*, *5*(4), 307–326. doi:10.1002ej.121

Cho, S., Mathiassen, L., & Robey, D. (2006). *The Dialectics of Flexibility: A Multilevel Analysis of a Telehealth Innovation*. International Federation for Information Processing. 10.1007/0-387-34410-1_22

Choi, D., Lee, K. H., & Hur, H. (2020). Social enterprises' social orientation: The impact on the organizational commitment of employees. *Journal of Public and Nonprofit Affairs*, *6*(1), 44–62. doi:10.20899/jpna.6.1.44-62

Christianson, M. K., Farkas, M. T., Sutcliffe, K. M., & Weick, K. E. (2009). Learning through rare events: Significant interruptions at the Baltimore and Ohio Railroad Museum. *Organization Science*, *20*(5), 846–860. doi:10.1287/orsc.1080.0389

Clement, V., & Rivera, J. (2017). From adaptation to transformation: An extended research agenda for organizational flexibility to adversity in the natural environment. *Organization & Environment*, *30*(4), 346–365. doi:10.1177/1086026616658333

Cochran, W. G. (1948). *Sampling survey techniques. North Carolina State University*. Dept. of Statistics.

Cohen, J. (1992). A power primer. *Psychological Bulletin, 112*(1), 155–159. doi:10.1037/0033-2909.112.1.155 PMID:19565683

Colombelli, A., Paolucci, E., & Ughetto, E. (2019). Hierarchical and relational governance and the life cycle of entrepreneurial ecosystems. *Small Business Economics, 52*(2), 505–521. doi:10.100711187-017-9957-4

Colombo, M. G., Dagnino, G. B., Lehmann, E. E., & Salmador, M. (2019). The governance of entrepreneurial ecosystems. *Small Business Economics, 52*(2), 419–428. doi:10.100711187-017-9952-9

Congressional Research Service. (2021). *Global economic effects of COVID-19*. CRS.

Conti, T. (2002). Human and Social Implications of Excellence Models: Are They Really Accepted by the Business Community. *Managing Service Quality, 12*(3), 151–158. doi:10.1108/09604520210429213

Cook, R., & Rasmussen, J. (2005). Going Solid: A Model of System Dynamics and Consequences for Patient Safety. *Quality & Safety in Health Care, 14*(2), 130–134. doi:10.1136/qshc.2003.009530 PMID:15805459

Cooper, A. C., Dunkelberg, W. C. & Woo, C. Y. (1988). Survival and failure: A longitudinal study. *Frontiers of entrepreneurship research, 1*, 225-237.

Cooper, A. C. (1985). The role of incubator organizations in the founding of growth-oriented firms. *Journal of Business Venturing, 1*(1), 75–86. doi:10.1016/0883-9026(85)90008-4

Cooper, A. C. (1993). Challenges in predicting new firm performance. *Journal of Business Venturing, 8*(3), 241–253. doi:10.1016/0883-9026(93)90030-9

Cooper, S. Y., & Park, J. S. (2008). The impact of incubator' organizations on opportunity recognition and technology innovation in new, entrepreneurial high-technology ventures. *International Small Business Journal, 26*(1), 27–56. doi:10.1177/0266242607084658

Corkindale, G. (2011). *The Importance of Organizational Design and Structure*. HBR. https://hbr.org/2011/02/the-importance-of-organization

Costa, E., & Andreaus, M. (2020). Social impact and performance measurement systems in an Italian social enterprise: A participatory action research project. *Journal of Public Budgeting, Accounting & Financial Management*.

Coutu, D. L. (2002). How flexibility works. *Harvard Business Review, 80*(5), 46–55. PMID:12024758

Coviello, N. E., McDougall, P. P., & Oviatt, B. M. (2011). The emergence, advance and future of international entrepreneurship research: An introduction to the special forum. *Journal of Business Venturing, 26*(6), 625–631. doi:10.1016/j.jbusvent.2011.07.002

Covin, J. G., & Miller, D. (2014). International entrepreneurial orientation: Conceptual considerations, research themes, measurement issues, and future research directions. *Entrepreneurship Theory and Practice*, *38*(1), 11–44. doi:10.1111/etap.12027

Covin, J. G., & Slevin, D. P. (1989). Strategic management of small firms in hostile and benign environments. *Strategic Management Journal*, *10*(1), 75–87. doi:10.1002mj.4250100107

Cox, K. C., & Castrogiovanni, G. (2016). Entrepreneurial Alertness, Metacognition, and Opportunity Identification. *Proceedings - Academy of Management*, *15008*(1), 15008. doi:10.5465/ambpp.2016.15008abstract

Craig, J. B. L., & Johnson, D. (2006). Establishing individual differences related to opportunity alertness and innovation dependent on academic-career training. *Journal of Management Development*, *25*(1), 28–39. doi:10.1108/02621710610637945

Crichton, M. T., Ramsay, C. G., & Kelly, T. (2009). Enhancing organizational flexibility through emergency planning: Learnings from cross-sectorial lessons. *Journal of Contingencies and Crisis Management*, *17*(1), 24–37. doi:10.1111/j.1468-5973.2009.00556.x

Crick, D. (2009). The internationalisation of born global and international new venture SMEs. *International Marketing Review*, *26*(4), 453–476. doi:10.1108/02651330910971986

Crocker, J., Fiske, S. T., & Taylor, S. E. (1984). Schematic Bases of Belief Change. Attitudinal Judgment. doi:10.1007/978-1-4613-8251-5_10

Cronbach, L. J. (1951). Coefficient alpha and the internal structure of tests. *Psychometrika*, *16*(3), 297–334. doi:10.1007/BF02310555

Cunha, N., & Santos, A. (2005). As práticas gerenciais e a inovação empresarial: Estudo de empresas líderes em inovação. *Revista Alcance*, *12*(3), 353–372.

Dacin, P. A., Dacin, M. T., & Matear, M. (2010). Social entrepreneurship: Why we don't need a new theory and how we move forward from here. *The Academy of Management Perspectives*, *24*(3), 37–57.

Dada, O., & Watson, A. (2013). Entrepreneurial orientation and the franchise system: Organizational antecedents and performance outcomes. *European Journal of Marketing*, *47*(6), 790–812. doi:10.1108/03090561311306877

Daft, R.L. (2009). Organization theory and design. *South-Western Publication*, *17*.

Dalgaard-Nielsen, A. (2017). Organizational flexibility in national security bureaucracies: Realistic and practicable? *Journal of Contingencies and Crisis Management*, *25*(4), 341–349. doi:10.1111/1468-5973.12164

Danneels, E. (2012). Second-order competences and Schumpeterian rents. *Strategic Entrepreneurship Journal*, *6*(1), 42–58. doi:10.1002ej.1127

Dauber, D., Fink, G., & Yolles, M. (2012). A configuration model of organizational culture. *SAGE Open*, *2*(1). doi:10.1177/2158244012441482

Davidsson, P., & Honig, B. L. (2003). The role of social and human capital among nascent entrepreneurs. *Journal of Business Venturing*, *18*(3), 301–331. doi:10.1016/S0883-9026(02)00097-6

Davidsson, P., Steffens, P., & Fitzsimmons, J. (2009). Growing profitable or growing from profits: Putting the horse in front of the cart? *Journal of Business Venturing*, *24*(4), 388–406. doi:10.1016/j.jbusvent.2008.04.003

Davies, A., & Brady, T. (2016). Explicating the dynamics of project capabilities. *International Journal of Project Management*, *34*(2), 314–327. doi:10.1016/j.ijproman.2015.04.006

Davis, P. E., Bendickson, J. S., Muldoon, J., & McDowell, W. C. (2021). Agency theory utility and social entrepreneurship: Issues of identity and role conflict. *Review of Managerial Science*, *15*(8), 2299–2318. doi:10.100711846-020-00423-y

De Mon, I. A., Gabaldón, P., & Nuñez, M. (2022). Social entrepreneurs: Making sense of tensions through the application of alternative strategies of hybrid organizations. *The International Entrepreneurship and Management Journal*, *18*(2), 975–997. doi:10.100711365-020-00731-5

Dedahanov, A. T., Miao, S., & Semyonov, A. A. (2021). When does abusive supervision mitigate work effort? Moderating roles of cognitive reappraisal and rumination. *Leadership and Organization Development Journal*, *42*(3), 467–479. doi:10.1108/LODJ-07-2020-0312

Dees, J. G. (2012). A tale of two cultures: Charity, problem-solving, and the future of Social Entrepreneurship. *Journal of Business Ethics*, *111*(3), 321–334. doi:10.100710551-012-1412-5

Dees, J. G., Battle Anderson, B., & Wei-Skillem, J. (2004). Scaling social entrepreneurship: Strategies for spreading social innovations. *Stanford Social Innovation Review*, *1*(4), 24–32.

Delery, J. E., & Doty, D. H. (1996). Modes of theorising in strategic human resource management: Tests of universalistic, contingency, and configurational performance predictions. *Academy of Management Journal*, *39*(4), 802–835. doi:10.2307/256713

Delmas, M. A., & Pekovic, S. (2018). Organizational configurations for sustainability and employee productivity: A qualitative comparative analysis approach. *Business & Society*, *57*(1), 216–251. doi:10.1177/0007650317703648

Demirel, P., Li, Q. C., Rentocchini, F., & Tamvada, J. P. (2017). Born to be green: New insights into the economics and management of green entrepreneurship. *Small Business Economics*, *52*(1), 759–771. doi:10.100711187-017-9933-z

Demmer, W. A., Vickery, S. K., & Calantone, R. (2011). Engendering flexibility in small-and medium-sized enterprises (SMEs): A case study of Demmer Corporation. *International Journal of Production Research*, *49*(18), 5395–5413. doi:10.1080/00207543.2011.563903

Desmarchelier, B., Djellal, F., & Gallouj, F. (2019). *Towards a servitization of innovation networks: a mapping. Public Management Review, Taylor and Francis*. Routledge.

Deverell, E. (2009). Crises as Learning Triggers: Exploring a Conceptual Framework of Crisis-Induced Learning. *Journal of Contingencies and Crisis Management, 17*(3), 179–188. doi:10.1111/j.1468-5973.2009.00578.x

Dhahri, S., & Omri, A. (2018). Entrepreneurship contribution to the three pillars of sustainable development: What does the evidence really say? *World Development, 106*(1), 64–77. doi:10.1016/j.worlddev.2018.01.008

Dhillon, M. K., Rafi-Ul-Shan, P. M., Amar, H., Sher, F., & Ahmed, S. (2023). Flexible Green Supply Chain Management in Emerging Economies: A Systematic Literature Review. *Global Journal of Flexible Systems Managment, 24*(1), 1–28. doi:10.100740171-022-00321-0 PMID:37519431

Di Domenico, M., Haugh, H., & Tracey, P. (2010). Social bricolage: Theorising social value creation in social enterprises. *Entrepreneurship Theory and Practice, 34*(4), 681–703. doi:10.1111/j.1540-6520.2010.00370.x

Diamantopoulos, A., & Winklhofer, H. M. (2001). Index construction with formative indicators: An alternative to scale development. *JMR, Journal of Marketing Research, 38*(2), 269–277. doi:10.1509/jmkr.38.2.269.18845

Dimov, D. (2011). Grappling With the Unbearable Elusiveness of Entrepreneurial Opportunities. *Entrepreneurship Theory and Practice, 35*(1), 57–81. doi:10.1111/j.1540-6520.2010.00423.x

Dionisio, M. (2019). The evolution of social entrepreneurship research: A bibliometric analysis. *Social Enterprise Journal, 15*(1), 22–45. doi:10.1108/SEJ-05-2018-0042

Distanont, A., & Khongmalai, O. (2020). The role of innovation in creating a competitive advantage. *Kasetsart Journal of Social Sciences, 41*(1), 15–21.

Djellal, F., & Gallouj, F. (2015). *The handbook of service business: management, marketing, innovation and internationalization*. Edward Elgar Publishers.

Dodgson, M. (1993). () “Organizational learning: A review of some literature. *Organization Studies, 14*(3), 375–394. doi:10.1177/017084069301400303

Doherty, B., Haugh, H., & Lyon, F. (2014). Social enterprises as hybrid organizations: A review and research agenda. *International Journal of Management Reviews, 16*(4), 417–436. doi:10.1111/ijmr.12028

Doll, J., & Ajzen, I. (1992). Accessibility and stability of predictors in the theory of planned behavior. *Journal of Personality and Social Psychology, 63*(5), 754–765. doi:10.1037/0022-3514.63.5.754

Domańska, A., Żukowska, B., & Zajkowski, R. (2018). Green entrepreneurship as a connector among social, environmental and economic pillars of sustainable development. Why some countries are more agile? *Problemy Ekorozwoju, 13*(2), 67-76. https://ekorozwoj.pollub.pl/no26/i.pdf

Donaldson, L. (1996). *For positive organization theory: Proving the hardcore. London*. SAGE. doi:10.4135/9781446280331

Donnelly-Cox, G., & O' Regan, A. (1999). *Resourcing organizational growth and development: A typology of third sector service delivery organizations*. IRSPMIII: Aston.

Doran, J., McCarthy, N., & O'Connor, M. (2018). The role of entrepreneurship in stimulating economic growth in developed and developing countries. *Cogent Economics & Finance*, *6*(1), 1442093. doi:10.1080/23322039.2018.1442093

Doty, D. H., & Glick, W. H. (1994). Typologies as a unique form of theory building: Toward improved understanding and modelling. *Academy of Management Review*, *19*(2), 230–251. doi:10.2307/258704

Douglas, E. J., & Shepherd, D. A. (2000). Entrepreneurship as a utility maximizing response. *Journal of Business Venturing*, *15*(3), 231–251. doi:10.1016/S0883-9026(98)00008-1

Drennan, J., Kennedy, J., & Renfrow, P. (2005). Impact of childhood experiences on the development of entrepreneurial intentions. *International Journal of Entrepreneurship and Innovation*, *6*(4), 231–238. doi:10.5367/000000005775179801

Drucker, P. (2004). *As fronteiras da administração: onde as decisões do amanhã estão sendo determinadas hoje*. Pioneira.

Drucker, P. F. (1985). Principles of successful innovation. *Research Management*, *28*(5), 10–12. doi:10.1080/00345334.1985.11756915

Duchek, S. (2014). Growth in the face of crisis: The role of organizational flexibility capabilities. *Proceedings - Academy of Management*, *2014*(1), 13487. doi:10.5465/ambpp.2014.225

Duit, A. (2016). Flexibility thinking: Lessons for Public Administration. *Public Administration*, *94*(2), 364–380. doi:10.1111/padm.12182

Easterby-Smith, M., Thorpe, R., & Jackson, P. R. (2015). *Designing Management and Business Research* (5th ed.). Designing Management and Business Research. Manag. Bus. Res.

Ebrahimi, P., & Mirbargkar, S. M. (2017). Green entrepreneurship and green innovation for SME development in market turbulence. *Eurasian Business Review*, *7*(2), 203–228. doi:10.100740821-017-0073-9

Edelbroek, R., Peters, P., & Blomme, R. J. (2019). Engaging in open innovation: The mediating role of work engagement in the relationship between transformational and transactional leadership and the quality of the open innovation process as perceived by employees. *Journal of General Management*, *45*(1), 5–17. doi:10.1177/0306307019844633

Edmondson, A. C. (2007). The competitive imperative of learning. *Harvard Business Review*, *86*(7-8), 60–67. PMID:18681298

Edwards, J. R., & Lambert, L. S. (2007). Methods for integrating moderation and mediation: A general analytical framework using moderated path analysis. *Psychological Methods, 12*(1), 1–22. doi:10.1037/1082-989X.12.1.1 PMID:17402809

Eisenhardt, K. M., Furr, N. R., & Bingham, C. B. (2010). Micro foundations of Performance: Balancing Efficiency and Flexibility in Dynamic Environments. *Organization Science, 21*(6), 1263–1273. doi:10.1287/orsc.1100.0564

Ekelund, R. B., & Kirzner, I. M. (1974). Competition and Entrepreneurship. *Southern Economic Journal, 41*(1), 155. doi:10.2307/1056112

Eltantawy, R. A. (2016). The role of supply management flexibility in attaining ambidexterity: A dynamic capabilities approach. *Journal of Business and Industrial Marketing, 31*(1), 123–134. doi:10.1108/JBIM-05-2014-0091

Erol, O., Sauser, B., & Mansouri, M. (2010). A framework for investigation into extended enterprise flexibility. *Enterprise Information Systems, 4*(2), 111–136. doi:10.1080/17517570903474304

Etikan, I. (2016). *Comparision of Snowball Sampling and Sequential Sampling Technique.* Biometrics Biostat. Int. J., doi:10.15406/bbij.2016.03.00055

Eze, S. C., Bello, A. O., & Adekola, T. A. (2017). The effects of organizational structure on the performance of organizations. *European Journal of Business and Innovation Research, 5*(6), 46–62. doi:10.37745/ejbir.vol5.no6.p46-62.2017

Fafchamps, M. (2011). *When is capital enough to get female microenterprises growing? Evidence from a randomized experiment in Ghana.* National Bureau of Economic Research, Inc.

Farid, M. (2007). Entrepreneurship in Egypt and the US compared: Directions for further research suggested. *Journal of Management Development, 26*(5), 428–440. doi:10.1108/02621710710748266

Farinelli, F., Bottini, M., Akkoyunlu, S., & Aerni, P. (2011). Green entrepreneurship: The mission link towards a greener economy. *ATDF Journal, 8*(3/4), 42–48.

Farjoun, M. (2010). Beyond dualism: Stability and change as a duality. *Academy of Management Review, 35*(2), 202–225.

Fatoki, O. (2018). The Impact of Entrepreneurial Flexibility on the Success of Small and Medium Enterprises in South Africa. *Sustainability (Basel), 10*(7), 2527. doi:10.3390u10072527

Fayol, H. (1937). The administrative theory in the state. *Papers on the Science of Administration.* 99-114.

Felício, J. A., Caldeirinha, V. R., and Ribeiro-Navarrete, B. (2015). Corporate and individual global mindset and internationalization of European SMEs. *Journal of Business Research, 68*(4), 797–802. doi:10.1016/j.jbusres.2014.11.031

Felício, J., Meidutė, I., & Kyvik, Ø. (2016). Global mindset, cultural context, and the internationalization of SMEs. *Journal of Business Research*, *69*(11), 4924–4932. doi:10.1016/j.jbusres.2016.04.054

Félix González, M., Husted, B. W., & Aigner, D. J. (2017). Opportunity discovery and creation in social entrepreneurship: An exploratory study in Mexico. *Journal of Business Research*, *81*, 212–220. doi:10.1016/j.jbusres.2016.10.032

Feranita, N. V., Nugraha, A., & Sukoco, S. A. (2019). The Role of Government Support for Innovation and Performance of SMEs. *Politico (Pavia, Italy)*, *19*(2), 5–10.

Ferguson, T. D., & Ketchen, D. J. Jr. (1999). Organizational configurations and performance: The role of statistical power in extant research. *Strategic Management Journal*, *20*(4), 385–395. doi:10.1002/(SICI)1097-0266(199904)20:4<385::AID-SMJ24>3.0.CO;2-X

Fernandes, A. J., & Ferreira, J. J. (2022). Entrepreneurial ecosystems and networks: A literature review and research agenda. *Review of Managerial Science*, *16*(1), 189–247. doi:10.100711846-020-00437-6

Ferreira, F. A. F., Marques, C. S. E., Bento, P., Ferreira, J. J. M., & Jalali, M. S. (2015). Operationalizing and measuring individual entrepreneurial orientation using cognitive mapping and MCDA techniques. *Journal of Business Research*, *68*(12), 2691–2702. doi:10.1016/j.jbusres.2015.04.002

Ferrell, O. C., Fraedrich, J., & Ferrell, L. (2013). *Business Ethics: Ethical Decision Making and Cases* (10th ed.). Cengage Learning.

Fink, G., & Mayrhofer, W. (2009). Cross-cultural competence and management–setting the stage. *European Journal of Cross-Cultural Competence and Management*, *1*(1), 42–65. doi:10.1504/EJCCM.2009.026733

Fiss, P. C. (2007). A Set-Theoretic Approach to Organizational Configurations. *Academy of Management Review*, *32*(4), 1180–1198. doi:10.5465/amr.2007.26586092

Fitriasari, F. (2020). How do Small and Medium Enterprise (SME) survive the COVID-19 outbreak? *Journal Inovasi Ekonomi*, *5*(02). doi:10.22219/jiko.v5i3.11838

Folke, C. (2006). Flexibility: The emergence of a perspective for social–ecological systems analyses, *Global Environ. Change, 16*(3), 253–267. https://doi.org/. gloenvcha.2006.04.002. doi:10.1016/j

Folke, C., Carpenter, S. R., Walker, B., Scheffer, M., Chapin, T., & Rockström, J. (2010). Flexibility thinking: Integrating flexibility, adaptability, and transformability. *Ecology and Society*, *15*(4). doi:10.5751/ES-03610-150420

Forbes, D. P. (1999). Cognitive approaches to new venture creation. *International Journal of Management Reviews*, *1*(4), 415–439. doi:10.1111/1468-2370.00021

Foreman, E. K. (1991). *Survey sampling principles*. CRC Press.

Fornell, C., & Larcker, D.F. (1981b). *Structural equation models with unobservable variables and measurement error: Algebra and statistics.*

Fornell, C., & Larcker, D. F. (1981). Evaluating Structural Equation Models with Unobservable Variables and Measurement Error. *JMR, Journal of Marketing Research, 18*(1), 39–50. doi:10.1177/002224378101800104

Francis, R., & Bekera, B. (2014). A metric and frameworks for flexibility analysis of engineered and infrastructure systems. *Reliability Engineering & System Safety, 121*, 90–103. doi:10.1016/j.ress.2013.07.004

Franks, J., & Mayer, C. (1995). Ownership and control. In H. Siebert (Ed.), *Trends in business organization: Do participation and cooperation increase cometitiveness?* Mohr.

Freeman, S. F., Hirschhorn, L., & Maltz, M. (2004). *Organizational flexibility and moral purpose: Sandler O'Neill & Partners in the aftermath of 9/11/01.* Paper presented at the Annual Meeting of the Academy of Management, New Orleans.

Freeman, R. E. (1994). The politics of stakeholder theory: Some future directions. *Business Ethics Quarterly, 4*(4), 409–421. doi:10.2307/3857340

Freeman, R. E., Harrison, J. S., & Wicks, A. C. (2007). *Managing for Stakeholders: Survival, Reputation, and Success.* Yale University Press.

Freeman, S., & Cavusgil, S. T. (2007). Toward a typology of commitment states among managers of born-global firms: A study of accelerated internationalization. *Journal of International Marketing, 15*(4), 1–40. doi:10.1509/jimk.15.4.1

Freixanet, J., Renart, G., & Rialp-Criado, A. (2018). The Impact of Managers' Global Orientation on SME Export and Economic Performance. *MIR. Management International Review, 58*(4), 571–604. doi:10.100711575-018-0358-y

FSB. (2020). *COVID-19 Pandemic: Financial stability implications and policy measures taken.* Issue July.

Gadanecz, B., & Jayaram, K. (2009). Measures of financial stability – a review. Irving Fisher Committee (IFC) - Bank for International Settlements.

Gaglio, C. M., & Katz, J. A. (2001). The Psychological Basis of Opportunity Identification: Entrepreneurial Alertness. *Small Business Economics, 16*(2), 95–111. doi:10.1023/A:1011132102464

Galindo, M. Á., & Méndez, M. T. (2013). Entrepreneurship, economic growth, and innovation: Are feedback effects at work? *Journal of Business Research, 67*(5), 825–829. Advance online publication. doi:10.1016/j.jbusres.2013.11.052

Galindo-Martín, M. A., Castaño-Martínez, M. S., & Méndez-Picazo, M. T. (2020). The relationship between green innovation, social entrepreneurship, and sustainable development. *Sustainability (Basel), 12*(11), 1–19. doi:10.3390u12114467

Gallego-Álvarez, I., & Ortas, E. (2017). Corporate environmental sustainability reporting in the context of national cultures: A quantile regression approach. *International Business Review*, *26*(2), 337–353. doi:10.1016/j.ibusrev.2016.09.003

Gallouj, F., Rubalcaba, L. & Windrum, P. (2013). Public–Private innovation networks in services. *Economics*.

Gamble, E. N., Parker, S. C., & Moroz, P. W. (2020). Measuring the integration of social and environmental missions in hybrid organizations. *Journal of Business Ethics*, *167*(2), 271–284. doi:10.100710551-019-04146-3

Gandhi, T., & Raina, R. (2018). Social entrepreneurship: The need, relevance, facets and constraints. *Journal of Global Entrepreneurship Research*, *8*(1), 1–13. doi:10.118640497-018-0094-6

Gao, Y., & Qin, X. (2022). Entrepreneurship education and entrepreneurial intention of Chinese college students: Evidence from a moderated multi-mediation model. *Frontiers in Psychology*, *13*(1), 1–12. doi:10.3389/fpsyg.2022.1049232 PMID:36524159

Gartner, W. B. (1985). A conceptual framework for describing the phenomenon of new venture Creation. *Academy of Management Review*, *10*(4), 696–706. doi:10.2307/258039

Gartner, W. B., Shaver, K. G., Gatewood, E. J., & Katz, J. (1994). Finding the entrepreneur in entrepreneurship. *Entrepreneurship Theory and Practice*, *18*(3), 5–10. doi:10.1177/104225879401800301

Gaskin, J. (2012). Common method bias using common latent factor. [Video]. Youtube, Gaskination's Stat. http//youtube. com/Gaskination,

Gentile-Lüdecke, S., R.T. de Oliveira, & Paul, J. (2020). Does organizational structure facilitate inbound and outbound open innovation in SMEs? *Small Business Economics*, *55*(4), 091-1112.

George, D., & Mallery, P. (2016). *IBM SPSS statistics 23 step by step: A simple guide and reference*. Routledge. doi:10.4324/9781315545899

George, G., & Zahra, S. (2002). Culture and its consequences for entrepreneurship. *Entrepreneurship Theory and Practice*, *26*(4), 5–8. doi:10.1177/104225870202600401

Ghafar, A., Nair, M., Elalfy, S., & Fenech, R. (2023). The Pursuit of Gaining Legitimacy through Marketing Strategy: A Case of Social Enterprises in UAE. *Journal of Social Entrepreneurship*, 1–23. doi:10.1080/19420676.2023.2205865

Ghalwash, S., Tolba, A., & Ismail, A. (2017). What motivates social entrepreneurs to start social ventures? An exploratory study in the context of a developing economy. *Social Enterprise Journal*, *13*(3), 268–298. doi:10.1108/SEJ-05-2016-0014

Gibson, C., & Tarrant, M. (2010). A "Conceptual Models" approach to organisational flexibility. *Australian Journal of Emergency Management*, *25*(2), 8–14.

Gielnik, M.M., Barabas, S., Frese, M., Namatovu-Dawa, R., Scholz, F.A., Metzger, J.R., Walter, T. (2014). A temporal analysis of how entrepreneurial goal intentions, positive fantasies, and action planning affect starting a new venture and when the effects wear off. *J. Bus. Ventur.* doi:10.1016/j.jbusvent.2013.09.002

Gigerenzer, G. (2008). Why Heuristics Work. *Perspectives on Psychological Science*, *3*(1), 20–29. doi:10.1111/j.1745-6916.2008.00058.x PMID:26158666

Gigerenzer, G., & Brighton, H. (2009). Homo Heuristicus: Why Biased Minds Makes Better inferences. *Topics in Cognitive Science*, *1*(1), 107–143. doi:10.1111/j.1756-8765.2008.01006.x PMID:25164802

Gill, S. A., Bencheva, N., Karayel, S., & Usman, M. (2021). Does entrepreneurial self-efficacy moderate effects of cognitive flexibility and entrepreneurial Alertness on entrepreneurial intentions? *Entrepreneurial Business and Economics Review*, *9*(3), 25–41. doi:10.15678/EBER.2021.090302

Gimenez, C., & Tachizawa, E. (2012). Extending sustainability to suppliers: A systematic literature review. *Supply Chain Management*, *17*(5), 531–543. doi:10.1108/13598541211258591

Glancey, K. (1998). Determinants of growth and profitability in small entrepreneurial firms. *International Journal of Entrepreneurial Behaviour & Research*, *4*(1), 18–27. doi:10.1108/13552559810203948

Glover, J. (2012). Rural flexibility through continued learning and innovation. *Local Economy*, *27*(4), 355–372. doi:10.1177/0269094212437833

Gomez-Mejia, L. R., Cruz, C., Berrone, P., & De Castro, J. (2011). The bind that ties: Socioemotional wealth preservation in family firms. *The Academy of Management Annals*, *5*(1), 653–707. doi:10.5465/19416520.2011.593320

Gover, L., & Duxbury, L. (2018). Making sense of organizational change: Is hindsight really 20/20. *Journal of Organizational Behavior*, *39*(1), 39–51. doi:10.1002/job.2208

Gozukara, I., & Colakoglu, N. (2016). Enhancing Entrepreneurial Intention and Innovativeness of University Students: The Mediating Role of Entrepreneurial Alertness. *International Business Research*, *9*(2), 34. doi:10.5539/ibr.v9n2p34

Greenberg, J. (2011). *Behaviour in organizations* (10th ed.). Prentice-Hall.

Greenwood, R., Magán Díaz, A., Li, S. X., & Céspedes Lorente, J. (2010). The multiplicity of institutional logics and the heterogeneity of organizational responses. *Organization Science*, *21*(2), 521–539. doi:10.1287/orsc.1090.0453

Greiner, L. E. (1972). Evolution and Revolution as Organizations Grow. *Harvard Business Review*, *50*(4), 37–46. PMID:10179654

Gresov, C., & Drazin, R. (1997). Equifinality: Functional equivalence in organization design. *Academy of Management Review*, *22*(2), 403–428. doi:10.2307/259328

Grosskopf, S., & Barmeyer, C. (2021). Learning from multi-paradigmatic sensitivity in cross-cultural management? Empirical and theoretical considerations. *International Journal of Cross Cultural Management*, *21*(2), 181–202. doi:10.1177/14705958211019437

Guo, Y., Wang, L., & Chen, Y. (2020). Green entrepreneurial orientation and green innovation: The mediating effect of supply chain learning. *SAGE Open*, *10*(1), 1–24. doi:10.1177/2158244019898798

Gupta, A. K., Smith, K. G., & Shalley, C. E. (2006). The interplay between exploration and exploitation. *Academy of Management Journal*, *49*(4), 693–706. doi:10.5465/amj.2006.22083026

Gupta, M., & Dharwal, M. (2022). Green entrepreneurship and sustainable development: A conceptual framework. *Materials Today: Proceedings*, *49*(8), 3603–3606. doi:10.1016/j.matpr.2021.08.148

Gupta, V. K., & Batra, S. (2015). Entrepreneurial orientation and firm performance in Indian SMEs: Universal and contingency perspectives. *International Small Business Journal*, 1–23. doi:10.1177/0266242615577708

Hage, J. (1965). An axiomatic theory of organizations. *Administrative Science Quarterly*, *10*(3), 289–320. doi:10.2307/2391470

Haigh, N., & Hoffman, A. J. (2012). Hybrid organizations: The next chapter of sustainable business. *Organizational Dynamics*, *41*(2), 126–134. doi:10.1016/j.orgdyn.2012.01.006

Haigh, N., Kennedy, E. D., & Walker, J. (2015). E.D., Kennedy, and J. Walker, "Hybrid Organizations as Shape-Shifters: Altering Legal Structure for Strategic Gain.". *California Management Review*, *57*(3), 59–82. doi:10.1525/cmr.2015.57.3.59

Haigh, N., Walker, J., Bacq, S., & Kickul, J. (2015). Hybrid Organizations: Origins, Strategies, Impacts, and Implications. *California Management Review*, *57*(3), 5–12. doi:10.1525/cmr.2015.57.3.5

Haile, E. A., & Tüzüner, V. L. (2022). Organizational learning capability and its impact on organizational innovation. *Asia Pacific Journal of Innovation and Entrepreneurship*, *16*(1), 69–85. doi:10.1108/APJIE-03-2022-0015

Hair, J. F., Black, W. C., Babin, B. J., & Anderson, R. E. (2010). *Multivariate Data Analysis*. Pearson.

Hair, J. F., Black, W. C., Babin, B. J., & Anderson, R. E. (2010). *Multivariate data analysis: International version*. Pearson.

Haldar, S. (2019). Green entrepreneurship in the renewable energy sector – a case study of Gujarat. *Journal of Science and Technology Policy Management*, *10*(1), 234–250. doi:10.1108/JSTPM-12-2017-0070

Hale, A., & Heijer, T. (2006). Defining Flexibility. In E. Hollnagel, D. D. Woods, & N. Leveson (Eds.), *Flexibility Engineering: Concepts and Precepts* (pp. 35–40). Ashgate.

Hall, E. T. (1976). *Beyond culture*. Anchor Books.

Hall, J., Daneke, G. A., & Lenox, M. (2010). Sustainable development and entrepreneurship: Past contributions and future directions. *Journal of Business Venturing*, *25*(1), 439–448. doi:10.1016/j.jbusvent.2010.01.002

Hall, R. H., & Tolbert, P. S. (2009). *Organizations: structures, processes, and outcome* (9th ed.). Prentice-Hall.

Halunga, A. G., Orme, C. D., & Yamagata, T. (2017). A heteroskedasticity robust Breusch–Pagan test for Contemporaneous correlation in dynamic panel data models. *Journal of Econometrics*, *198*(2), 209–230. doi:10.1016/j.jeconom.2016.12.005

Hamedi, H., & Mehdiabadi, A. (2020). Entrepreneurship flexibility and Iranian organizations: Application of the fuzzy DANP technique. *Asia Pacific Journal of Innovation and Entrepreneurship*, *14*(3), 231–247. doi:10.1108/APJIE-10-2019-0074

Hamel, G. and Välikangas, L. (2003). The quest for flexibility. *Harvard Business Review, 81*(9), 52–63. 5.

Hamelin, A. (2013). Influence of family ownership on small business growth. Evidence from French SMEs. *Small Business Economics*, *41*(3), 563–579. doi:10.100711187-012-9452-x

Hamilton, R. T., & Shergill, G. S. (1993). *The logic of New Zealand business: Strategy, structure, and performance*. Oxford University Press.

Handrito, R. P., Slabbinck, H., & Vanderstraeten, J. (2020). Enjoying or Refraining from Risk? The Impact of Implicit Need for Achievement and Risk Perception on SME Internationalization. *Cross Cultural & Strategic Management*, *27*(3), 317–342. doi:10.1108/CCSM-03-2019-0068

Handy, C. B. (1993). *Understanding organizations*. Oxford University Press.

Hanelt, A., Bohnsack, R., Marz, D., & Antunes Marante, C. (2000). A systematic review of the literature on digital transformation: Insights and implications for strategy and organizational change. *Journal of Management Studies, 58*(5), 1159-1197

Hang, C. C., & Garnsey, E. W. 2012. Opportunities and Resources for Disruptive Technological Innovation. SSRN *Electron. J.* doi:10.2139/ssrn.1923036

Hang, C. C., Garnsey, E., & Ruan, Y. (2013). Opportunity Discovery and Creation in Disruptive Innovation Centre for Technology. *Manag. Work. Pap. Ser.* 1–44.

Hatch, M. J. (1993). The dynamics of organizational culture. *Academy of Management Review*, *18*(4), 657–693. doi:10.2307/258594

Hattab, H. (2011). *Towards understanding women entrepreneurship in MENA countries. 56th ICSB World Conference*, Stockholm, Sweden.

Hatten, T. S., & Ruhland, S. K. (1995). Student attitude toward entrepreneurship as affected by participation in an SBI program. *Journal of Education for Business*, *70*(4), 224–227. doi:10.1080/08832323.1995.10117754

Hattwick, R. E. (1979). Perception, opportunity and profit. *The Journal of Behavioral Economics*, *8*(2), 183–188. doi:10.1016/0090-5720(79)90012-3

Hayes, A. F. (2015). An Index and Test of Linear Moderated Mediation. *Multivariate Behavioral Research*, *50*(1), 1–22. doi:10.1080/00273171.2014.962683 PMID:26609740

Hayton, J. C., George, G., & Zahra, S. A. (2002). National culture and entrepreneurship: A review of behavioral research. *Entrepreneurship Theory and Practice*, *26*(4), 33–52. doi:10.1177/104225870202600403

Hayton, J., Chandler, G. N., & DeTienne, D. R. (2011). Entrepreneurial opportunity identification and new firm development processes: A comparison of family and non-family new ventures. *International Journal of Entrepreneurship and Innovation Management*, *13*(1), 12–31. doi:10.1504/IJEIM.2011.038445

Hazenberg, R., Bajwa-Patel, M., Mazzei, M., Roy, M. J., & Baglioni, S. (2016). The role of institutional and stakeholder networks in shaping social enterprise ecosystems in Europe. *Social Enterprise Journal*, *12*(3), 302–321. doi:10.1108/SEJ-10-2016-0044

Heinisch, O. & Cochran, W. G. (1965). Sampling Techniques, 2. John Wiley and Sons. doi:10.1002/bimj.19650070312

Held, D., Kickbusch, I., McNally, K., Piselli, D., & Told, M. (2019). Gridlock, Innovation and Flexibility in Global Health Governance. *Global Policy*, *10*(2), 161–177. doi:10.1111/1758-5899.12654

Helfat, C. E., Finklestein, S., Mitchell, W., Peteraf, M. A., Singh, H., Teece, D. J., & Winter, S. G. (2007). *Dynamic Capabilities: understanding strategic change in organizations*. Blackwell Publishing.

Helfat, C. E., & Peteraf, M. A. (2015). Managerial cognitive capabilities and the microfoundations of dynamic capabilities. *Strategic Management Journal*, *36*(6), 831–850. doi:10.1002mj.2247

Henseler, J., Ringle, C. M., & Sarstedt, M. (2015). A new criterion for assessing discriminant validity in variance-based structural equation modeling. *Journal of the Academy of Marketing Science*, *43*(1), 115–135. doi:10.100711747-014-0403-8

Hernández-Chea, R., Mahdad, M., Minh, T. T., & Hjortsø, C. N. (2021). Moving beyond intermediation: How intermediary organizations shape collaboration dynamics in entrepreneurial ecosystems. *Technovation*, *108*(102332), 102332. doi:10.1016/j.technovation.2021.102332

Hernández-Perlines, F., Moreno-García, J., & Yañez-Araque, B. (2016a). The mediating role of competitive strategy in international entrepreneurial orientation. *Journal of Business Research*, *69*(11), 5383–5389. doi:10.1016/j.jbusres.2016.04.142

Hine, D., Parker, R., Pregelj, L., & Verreynne, M.-L. (2014). Deconstructing and Reconstructing the Capability Hierarchy. *Industrial and Corporate Change*, *23*(5), 1299–1325. doi:10.1093/icc/dtt046

Hmieleski, K. M., & Corbett, A. C. (2006). Proclivity for improvisation as a predictor of entrepreneurial intentions. *Journal of Small Business Management*, *44*(1), 45–63. doi:10.1111/j.1540-627X.2006.00153.x

Ho, T. S. and Koh, H. C. (1992). Differences in psychological characteristics between entrepreneurially inclined and non-entrepreneurially inclined accounting graduates in Singapore. *Entrepreneurship, Innovation and Change: an international journal*, *1*(2), 243-254.

Hoang, H., & Antoncic, B. (2003). Network-based research in entrepreneurship: A critical review. *Journal of Business Venturing*, *18*(2), 165–187. doi:10.1016/S0883-9026(02)00081-2

Hoffman, A. J., Badiane, K. K., & Haigh, N. (2010). Hybrid organizations as agents of positive social change: Bridging the for-profit and nonprofit divide. Ross School of Business.

Hofstede, G. (2001). *Culture's consequences: Comparing values, behaviours, institutions and organizations across nations*. SAGE.

Hofstede, G., Neuijen, B., Ohayv, D. D., & Sanders, G. (1990). Measuring organizational cultures: A qualitative and quantitative study across twenty cases. *Administrative Science Quarterly*, *35*(2), 286–316. doi:10.2307/2393392

Ho, H., & Lu, R. (2015). Performance implications of marketing exploitation and exploration: Moderating role of supplier collaboration. *Journal of Business Research*, *68*(5), 1026–1034. doi:10.1016/j.jbusres.2014.10.004

Hollnagel, E., & Woods, D. D. (2017). Epilogue: Flexibility engineering precepts. In E. Hollnagel, D. D. Woods, & N. Leveson (Eds.), *Flexibility engineering: Concepts and precepts* (pp. 347–358). CRC Press. doi:10.1201/9781315605685-30

Homburg, C., & Pflesser, C. (2000). A multiple-layer model of market-oriented organizational culture: Measurement issues and performance outcomes. *JMR, Journal of Marketing Research*, *37*(4), 449–462. doi:10.1509/jmkr.37.4.449.18786

Honeyman, R., & Jana, T. (2019). *The B Corp handbook: How you can use business as a force for good*. Berrett-Koehler Publishers.

Hsieh, C.-M. (2003). Counting importance: The case of life satisfaction and relative domain importance. *Social Indicators Research*, *61*(2), 227–240. doi:10.1023/A:1021354132664

Hsu, W. T., Chen, H. L., & Cheng, C. Y. (2013). Internationalization and firm performance of SMEs: The moderating effects of CEO attributes. *Journal of World Business*, *48*(1), 1–1. doi:10.1016/j.jwb.2012.06.001

Huber, S., van Wijgerden, I., de Witt, A., & Dekker, S. W. A. (2009). Learning from organizational incidents: Flexibility engineering for high-risk process environments. *Process Safety Progress, 28*(1), 90–95. doi:10.1002/prs.10286

IBM. (2019). *KMO and Bartlett's Test* [WWW Document]. IBM Knowl. Cent.

Imperatori, B., & Ruta, D. D. (2015). Designing a social enterprise: Organization configuration and social stakeholders' work involvement. *Social Enterprise Journal, 11*(3), 321–346. doi:10.1108/SEJ-08-2014-0034

Inkpen, A., & Choudhury, N. (1995). The seeking of strategy is not: Towards a theory of strategy absence. *Strategic Management Journal, 16*(4), 313–323. doi:10.1002mj.4250160405

International Monetary Fund. (2006). *Financial soundness indicators: Compilation guide.* International Monetary Fund.

Isabelle, D. A., Han, Y., & Westerlund, M. (2022). A machine-learning analysis on the impacts of the COVID-19 pandemic on small business owners and implications from Canadian government policy response. *Canadian Public Policy, 48*(2), 1–50. doi:10.3138/cpp.2021-018 PMID:36039356

Ishak, A. W., & Williams, E. A. (2018). A dynamic model of organizational flexibility: Adaptive and anchored approaches. *Editorial Advisory Board, 23*(2), 180–196.

Iskandar, Y., & Kaltum, U. (2021). The Relationship Between Intellectual Capital and Performance of Social Enterprises: A Literature Review. *Academic Journal of Interdisciplinary Studies, 10*(5), 309–330. doi:10.36941/ajis-2021-0141

Islami, X., Mustafa, N., & Topuzovska Latkovikj, M. (2020). Linking Porter's generic strategies to firm performance. *Future Business Journal, 6*(1), 1–15. doi:10.118643093-020-0009-1

Islam, T., Ali, G., Aziz Khan Niazi, A., Ramzan, M., & Yousaf, U. (2018). Employees' Response to CSR: Role of Organizational Identification and Organizational Trust. *Pakistan J. Commer. Soc. Sci., 12*, 153–166. doi:10.1111/j.0001-6349.2005.00765.x

Ismail, N., Jaffar, N., & Hooi, T. S. (2013). Using EAO model to predict the self-employment intentions among the Universities' Undergraduates in Malaysia. *International Journal of Trade, Economics and Finance, 4*(5), 282–287. doi:10.7763/IJTEF.2013.V4.302

Iversen, J., Jørgensen, R., $ Malchow-Møller, N. (2008). Defining and measuring entrepreneurship. *Foundations and Trends R in Entrepreneurship, 4*(1), 1 – 63.

Jabareen, Y. (2009). Building a conceptual framework: Philosophy, definitions, and procedure. *International Journal of Qualitative Methods, 8*(4), 49–62. doi:10.1177/160940690900800406

Jafari Sadeghi, V., Kimiagari, S., & Biancone, P. (2019). Level of Education and Knowledge, Foresight Competency, and International Entrepreneurship: A Study of Human Capital Determinants in the European Countries. *European Business Review, 32*(2), 46–68. doi:10.1108/EBR-05-2018-0098

Jafari Sadeghi, V., Nkongolo-Bakenda, J.-M., Anderson, B., & Dana, L.-P. (2019). An institution-based view of international entrepreneurship: A comparison of context-based and universal determinants in developing and economically advanced countries. *International Business Review, 28*(6), 1–1. doi:10.1016/j.ibusrev.2019.101588

Jafari-Sadeghi, V. (2020). The motivational factors of business venturing: Opportunity versus necessity? A gendered perspective on European countries. *Journal of Business Research, 113*, 279–289. doi:10.1016/j.jbusres.2019.09.058

Jansen, J. J. P., Van Den Bosch, F. A. J., & Volberda, H. W. (2006). Exploratory innovation, exploitative innovation, and performance: Effects of organizational antecedents and environmental moderators. *Management Science, 52*(11), 1661–1674. doi:10.1287/mnsc.1060.0576

Javidan, M., Bullough, A., & Dibble, R. (2016). Mind the gap: Gender differences in global leadership self-efficacies. *The Academy of Management Perspectives, 30*(1), 59–73. doi:10.5465/amp.2015.0035

Jay, J. (2013). Navigating Paradox as a Mechanism of Change and Innovation in Hybrid Organizations. *Academy of Management Journal, 56*(1), 137–159. doi:10.5465/amj.2010.0772

Jiao, H., Cui, Y., Zhu, Y., & Chen, J. (2014). Building entrepreneurs' innovativeness through knowledge management: The mediating effect of entrepreneurial Alertness. *Technology Analysis and Strategic Management, 26*(5), 501–516. doi:10.1080/09537325.2013.872774

Jiatong, W., Murad, M., Li, C., Gill, S. A., & Ashraf, S. F. (2021). Linking cognitive flexibility to entrepreneurial Alertness and entrepreneurial intention among medical students with the moderating role of entrepreneurial self-efficacy: A second-order moderated mediation model. *PLoS One, 16*(9), e0256420. doi:10.1371/journal.pone.0256420 PMID:34559823

Jin, Z., Shang, Y., & Xu, J. (2018). he Impact of Government Subsidies on Private R&D and Firm Performance: Does Ownership Matter in China's Manufacturing Industry? *Sustainability (Basel), 10*(7), 2205. doi:10.3390u10072205

Joardar, A., & Wu, S. (2011). Examining the dual forces of individual entrepreneurial orientation and liability of foreignness on international entrepreneurs. *Canadian Journal of Administrative Sciences, 28*(3), 328–340. doi:10.1002/cjas.203

Johnson, J., Lenartowicz, T., & Apud, S. (2006). Cross-cultural competence in international business: Toward a definition and a model. *Journal of International Business Studies, 37*(4), 525–543. doi:10.1057/palgrave.jibs.8400205

Jones, M. V., & Coviello, N. E. (2005). Internationalisation: Conceptualising an entrepreneurial process of behaviour in time. *Journal of International Business Studies, 36*(3), 284–303. doi:10.1057/palgrave.jibs.8400138

Jones, M. V., Coviello, N., & Tang, Y. K. (2011). International Entrepreneurship research (1989-2009): A domain ontology and thematic analysis. *Journal of Business Venturing, 26*(6), 632–659. doi:10.1016/j.jbusvent.2011.04.001

Jyoti, B., & Singh, A. K. (2023). Does digitalization have a causal relationship with economic development? an experience from a country-wise panel data statistical analysis. In R. Sine Nazlı & G. Sari (Eds.), Handbook of Research on Perspectives on Society and Technology Addiction (pp. 34-61). IGI Global. doi:10.4018/978-1-6684-8397-8.ch003

Jyoti, B., & Singh, A. K. (2020). Characteristics and determinants of new start-ups in Gujarat, India. *Entrepreneurship Review, 1*(2), 1–25. doi:10.38157/entrepreneurship-review.v1i2.154

Jyoti, B., Singh, A. K., & Ashraf, S. N. (2023). Appropriate technologies and their implications in the agricultural sector. In P. H. Alex Khang (Ed.), *Advanced Technologies and AI-Equipped IoT Applications in High-Tech Agriculture* (pp. 65–87). IGI Global. doi:10.4018/978-1-6684-9231-4.ch004

Kahan, J., Allen, A., George, J., & Thompson, W. (2009). *Concept development: An operational framework for flexibility.* VA: Homeland Security Studies and Analysis Institute. http://www.homelandsecurity.org/

Kahle, L. R., & Malhotra, N. K. (1994). Marketing Research: An Applied Orientation. *JMR, Journal of Marketing Research, 31*(1), 137. doi:10.2307/3151953

Kaish, S., Gilad, B., 1991. Characteristics of opportunities search of entrepreneurs versus executives: Sources, interests, general Alertness. *J. Bus. Ventur.* doi:10.1016/0883-9026(91)90005-X

Kalnins, A. (2018). Multicollinearity: How common factors cause Type 1 errors in multivariate regression. *Strategic Management Journal, 39*(8), 2362–2385. doi:10.1002mj.2783

Kamalahmadi, M., & Parast, M. M. (2016). A review of the literature on the principles of enterprise and supply chain flexibility: Major findings and directions for future research. *International Journal of Production Economics, 171*, 116–133. doi:10.1016/j.ijpe.2015.10.023

Karimi, R. F., & Chashmi, S. A. N. (2019). Designing green entrepreneurship model in sustainable development consistent with the performance of Tehran industrial towns. *Journal of Business-To-Business Marketing, 26*(1), 95–102. doi:10.1080/1051712X.2019.1565143

Karré, P. M. (2023). The Thumbprint of a Hybrid Organization—A Multidimensional Model for Analysing Public/Private Hybrid Organizations. *Public Organization Review, 23*(2), 777–791. doi:10.100711115-021-00598-2

Katz, D. and Stotland, E. (1959). A preliminary statement to a theory of attitude structure and change. *Psychology: A study of a science, 3*, 423-475.

Katz, D., & Kahn, R. L. (1978). *The social psychology of organizations* (2nd ed.). Wiley.

Kaufman, Z. (2012). Social Entrepreneurship in the Age of Atrocities: Changing Our World. Cheltenham: Edward Elgar, 01-19.

Kautonen, T., Tornikoski, E. T., & Kibler, E. (2011). Entrepreneurial intentions in the third age: The impact of perceived age norms. *Small Business Economics, 37*(2), 219–234. doi:10.100711187-009-9238-y

Kautonen, T., van Gelderen, M., & Fink, M. (2015). Robustness of the Theory of Planned Behavior in Predicting Entrepreneurial Intentions and Actions. *Entrepreneurship Theory and Practice*, *39*(3), 655–674. doi:10.1111/etap.12056

Kedia, B., & Mukherji, A. (1999). Global managers: Developing a mindset for global competitiveness. *Journal of World Business*, *34*(3), 230–251. doi:10.1016/S1090-9516(99)00017-6

Ketchen, D. J. Jr, Combs, J. G., Russell, C. J., Shook, C., Dean, M. A., Runge, J., Lohrke, F. T., Naumann, S. E., Haptonstahl, D. E., Baker, R., Beckstein, B. A., Handler, C., Honig, H., & Lamoureux, S. (1997). Organizational configurations and performance: A meta-analysis. *Academy of Management Journal*, *40*(1), 223–240. doi:10.2307/257028

Ketchen, D. J. Jr, & Hult, G. T. (2007). Bridging organizational theory and supply chain management: The case of best value supply chains. *Journal of Operations Management*, *25*(2), 573–580. doi:10.1016/j.jom.2006.05.010

Ketprapakorn, N., & Kantabutra, S. (2019). Sustainable social enterprise model: Relationships and consequences. *Sustainability (Basel)*, *11*(14), 3772. doi:10.3390u11143772

Khan, H. U. R., Ali, M., Olya, H. G., Zulqarnain, M., & Khan, Z. R. (2018). Transformational leadership, corporate social responsibility, organizational innovation, and organizational performance: Symmetrical and asymmetrical analytical approaches. *Corporate Social Responsibility and Environmental Management*, *25*(6), 1270–1283. doi:10.1002/csr.1637

Khedhaouria, A., Gurău, C., & Torrès, O. (2014). Creativity, self-efficacy, and small-firm performance: The mediating role of entrepreneurial orientation. *Small Business Economics*, *44*(3), 485–504. doi:10.100711187-014-9608-y

Khin, S., & Lim, T. H. (2018). Entrepreneurial opportunity recognition, exploitation and new venture success: Moderating role of prior market and technology knowledge. *J. Leg. Ethical Regul*, (22), 1–6.

Kickert, W. J. M. (2001). Public Management of Hybrid Organizations: Governance of Quasi-Autonomous Executive Agencies. *International Public Management Journal*, *4*(2), 35–150. doi:10.1016/S1096-7494(01)00049-6

Kickul, J., Gundry, L. K., Barbosa, S. D., & Whitcanack, L. (2009). Intuition versus analysis? Testing differential models of cognitive style on entrepreneurial self-efficacy and the new venture creation process. *Entrepreneurship Theory and Practice*, *33*(2), 439–453. doi:10.1111/j.1540-6520.2009.00298.x

King, D. D., Newman, A., & Luthans, F. (2016). Not if, but when we need flexibility in the workplace. *Journal of Organizational Behavior*, *37*(5), 782–786. doi:10.1002/job.2063

Kirton, M. (1978). Field dependence and adaption-innovation theories. *Perceptual and Motor Skills*, *47*(3), 1239–1245. doi:10.2466/pms.1978.47.3f.1239 PMID:745906

Kirzner, I. M. (1999). Creativity and/or Alertness: A reconsideration of the schumpeterian entrepreneur. *The Review of Austrian Economics*, *11*(1/2), 5–17. doi:10.1023/A:1007719905868

Kirzner, I. M. (2000). Entrepreneurial discovery and the competitive market process: an Austrian approach. In *The Driving Force of the Market* (pp. 15–52). Routledge. doi:10.4324/9780203465974-5

Kirzner, I. M., Hebert, R. F., & Link, A. N. (1983). The Entrepreneur, Mainstream Views and Radical Critiques. *Southern Economic Journal, 50*(2), 611. doi:10.2307/1058249

Kiss, A., Williams, D., & Houghton, S. (2013). Risk bias and the link between motivation and new venture post-entry international growth. *International Business Review, 22*(6), 1068–1078. doi:10.1016/j.ibusrev.2013.02.007

Kleinbaum, D. G., Kupper, L. L., Muller, K. E., & Nizam, A. (1988). *One-Way Analysis of Variance. Applied Regression Analysis and Other Multivariable Methods*. PWS-Kent Publishing.

Knight, G. (2001). Entrepreneurship and strategy in the international SME. *Journal of International Management, 7*(3), 155–171. doi:10.1016/S1075-4253(01)00042-4

Knockaert, M., Ucbasaran, D., Wright, M., & Clarysse, B. (2011). The relationship between knowledge transfer, top management team composition, and performance: The case of science-based entrepreneurial firms. *Entrepreneurship Theory and Practice, 35*(4), 777–803. doi:10.1111/j.1540-6520.2010.00405.x

Knowledge Center. (2023). *Agile Supply Chain: What It Is, Benefits, and Applications*. Knowledge Center https://www.inboundlogistics.com/articles/agile-supply-chain/

Koh, H. C. (1996). Testing hypotheses of entrepreneurial characteristics. a study of Hong Kong MBA students. *Journal of Managerial Psychology, 11*(3), 12–25. doi:10.1108/02683949610113566

Kolvereid, L. (1996b). Prediction of employment status choice intentions. *Entrepreneurship Theory and Practice, 21*(1), 47–57. doi:10.1177/104225879602100104

Kolvereid, L., & Isaksen, E. (2006). New business start-up and subsequent entry into self-employment. *Journal of Business Venturing, 21*(6), 866–885. doi:10.1016/j.jbusvent.2005.06.008

Koppell, J. G. S. (2003). *The Politics of Quasi-Government: Hybrid Organizations and the Dynamics of Bureaucratic Control*. University Press.

Korepanov, G., Yatskevych, I., Popova, O., Shevtsiv, L., Marych, M., & Purtskhvanidze, O. (2020). Managing the financial stability potential of crisis enterprises. *International Journal of Advanced Research in Engineering and Technology, 11*(4), 359–371.

Korsakienė, R., & Tvaronavičienė, M. (2012). The internationalization of SMEs: An integrative approach. *Journal of Business Economics and Management, 13*(2), 294–307. doi:10.3846/16111699.2011.620138

Ko, W. W., & Liu, G. (2020). The transformation from traditional nonprofit organizations to social enterprises: An institutional entrepreneurship perspective. *Journal of Business Ethics*, 1–18.

Kropp, F., Lindsay, N. J., & Shoham, A. (2006). Entrepreneurial, market, and learning orientations and international entrepreneurial business venture performance in South African firms. *International Marketing Review*, *23*(5), 504–523. doi:10.1108/02651330610703427

Krueger, N. F. (1993). The impact of prior entrepreneurial exposure on perceptions of new venture feasibility and desirability. *Entrepreneurship Theory and Practice*, *18*(1), 5–21. doi:10.1177/104225879301800101

Krueger, N. F., & Carsrud, A. L. (1993). Entrepreneurial intentions: Applying the theory of planned behavior. *Entrepreneurship and Regional Development*, *5*(4), 315–330. doi:10.1080/08985629300000020

Krueger, N. F. Jr. (2000). The cognitive infrastructure of opportunity emergence. *Entrepreneurship Theory and Practice*, *24*(3), 5–22. doi:10.1177/104225870002400301

Krueger, N. F. Jr, & Brazeal, D. V. (1994). Entrepreneurial potential and potential entrepreneurs. *Entrepreneurship Theory and Practice*, *18*(3), 91–104. doi:10.1177/104225879401800307

Krueger, N. F. Jr, Reilly, M. D., & Carsrud, A. L. (2000). Competing models of entrepreneurial intentions. *Journal of Business Venturing*, *15*(5-6), 411–432. doi:10.1016/S0883-9026(98)00033-0

Krug, K., & Weinberg, C. B. (2004). Mission, Money and Merit: Strategic Decision Making by Nonprofit Managers. *Nonprofit Management & Leadership*, *14*(3), 325–342. doi:10.1002/nml.37

Kuckertz, A., Kollmann, T., Krell, P., & Stöckmann, C. (2017). Understanding, differentiating, and measuring opportunity recognition and opportunity exploitation. *International Journal of Entrepreneurial Behaviour & Research*, *23*(1), 78–97. doi:10.1108/IJEBR-12-2015-0290

Kuehn, K. W. (2008). Entrepreneurial intentions research: Implications for entrepreneurship education. *Journal of Entrepreneurship Education*, *11*, 87.

Kumar, A., Ahmad, M. M., & Sharma, P. (2015). Carbon emission and global food security: A cross country analysis. *PENCIL Publication of Agricultural Sciences*, *2*(1), 7–24.

Kumar, A., Ahmad, M. M., & Sharma, P. (2017). Influence of climatic and non-climatic factors on sustainable food security in India: A statistical investigation. *International Journal of Sustainable Agricultural Management and Informatics*, *3*(1), 1–30. doi:10.1504/IJSAMI.2017.082917

Kumar, A., Sharma, P., & Joshi, S. (2016). Assessing the impacts of climate change on land productivity in Indian crop agriculture: An evidence from panel data analysis. *Journal of Agricultural Science and Technology*, *18*(1), 1–13. https://jast.modares.ac.ir/article-23-4491-en.pdf

Kumar, P. (2015). An analytical study on mintzberg's framework: Managerial roles. *International Journal of Research in Management and Business Studies*, *2*(3), 12–19.

Kumar, S., & Singh, A. K. (2023). Modeling the effects of climate change on agricultural productivity: Evidence from Himachal Pradesh, India. *Asia-Pacific Journal of Regional Science*, *7*(2), 1–28. doi:10.100741685-023-00291-w

Küng, L. (2016). Strategic management in the media: Theory to practice. *Strategic Management in the Media*, 1-256.

Kuntz, J. R., Malinen, S., & Näswall, K. (2017). Employee flexibility: Directions for flexibility development. *Consulting Psychology Journal*, *69*(3), 223–242. doi:10.1037/cpb0000097

Lambert, D., Mccann, F., Mcquinn, J., Myers, S., Yao, F., Lambert, D., Mccann, F., Mcquinn, J., Myers, S., & Yao, F. (2020). *SME finances, the pandemic, and the design of enterprise support policies enterprise support policies.*

Lambooy, T., Anthoni, P., & Argyrou, A. (2020). Aren't we all pursuing societal goals in our businesses? Defining "societal purpose" as pursued by social enterprises. *Sustainable Development (Bradford)*, *28*(3), 485–494. doi:10.1002d.2039

Lamotte, O., & Colovic, A. (2013). Innovation and Internationalization of Young Entrepreneurial Firms. *Management International Review*, *18*(1), 87–103.

Lampel, J., & Mintzberg, H. (1996). Customising customisation. *Sloan Management Review*, *38*(1), 21.

Lee, A. V., Vargo, J., & Seville, E. (2013). Developing a tool to measure and compare organizations' flexibility. *Natural Hazards Review*, *14*(1), 29–41. doi:10.1061/(ASCE)NH.1527-6996.0000075

Lee, S. H., & Wong, P. K. (2004). An exploratory study of technopreneurial intentions: A career anchor Perspective. *Journal of Business Venturing*, *19*(1), 7–28. doi:10.1016/S0883-9026(02)00112-X

Lee, S., & Peterson, S. (2000). Culture, entrepreneurial orientation, and global competitiveness. *Journal of World Business*, *35*(4), 401–416. doi:10.1016/S1090-9516(00)00045-6

Lengnick-Hall, C. A., & Beck, T. E. (2009). Flexibility capacity and strategic agility: Prerequisites for thriving in a dynamic environment. In Flexibility engineering perspectives, Volume 2. Preparation and restoration, ed. Christopher P. Nemeth, Erik Hollnagel, and Sidney Dekker, 39–70, Aldershot: Ashgate Publishing.

Lengnick-Hall, C. A., Beck, T. E., & Lengnick-Hall, M. L. (2011). Developing a Capacity for Organizational Flexibility through Strategic Human Resource Management. *Human Resource Management Review*, *21*(3), 243–255. doi:10.1016/j.hrmr.2010.07.001

Lerner, M., & Sharir, M. (2006). Gauging the success of social ventures initiated by individual social entrepreneurs. *Journal of World Business*, *41*(1), 6–20. doi:10.1016/j.jwb.2005.09.004

Levesque, Moren and Minniti, M. (2006). The Effect of Aging on Entrepreneurial Behavior. *Journal of Business Venturing, 21* (2), 177-194.

Levitt, B., & March, J. G. (1988). Organizational Learning. *Annual Review of Sociology*, *14*(1), 319–340. doi:10.1146/annurev.so.14.080188.001535

Levy, O., Beechler, S., Taylor, S., & Boyacigiller, N. A. (2007). What we talk about when we talk about 'global mindset': Managerial cognition in multinational corporations. *Journal of International Business Studies*, *38*(2), 231–258. doi:10.1057/palgrave.jibs.8400265

Lewis, M. W., & Smith, W. K. (2011). Toward a theory of paradox: A dynamic equilibrium model of organising. *Academy of Management Review*, *36*(2), 381–403.

Li, C., Murad, M., & Ashraf, S. F. (2023). The influence of women's green entrepreneurial intention on green entrepreneurial behaviour through university and social support. *Sustainability (Basel)*, *15*(3), 1–17. doi:10.3390u151310123

Li, C., Murad, M., Ashraf, S. F., Syed, N., & Riaz, M. (2020). Entrepreneurial nascent behaviour: The role of causation process in opportunity discovery and creation. *Entrepreneurial Business and Economics Review*, *8*(4), 183–200. doi:10.15678/EBER.2020.080410

Li, D., Huang, M., Ren, S., Chen, X., & Ning, L. (2018). Environmental legitimacy, green innovation, and corporate carbon disclosure: Evidence from CDP China 100. *Journal of Business Ethics*, *150*(4), 1089–1104. doi:10.100710551-016-3187-6

Liedholm, C. E., & Mead, D. C. (1999). *Small Enterprises and Economic Development: The Dynamics of Micro and Small Enterprises* (1st ed.). Routledge. doi:10.4324/9780203354735

Limnios, E. A. M., Mazzarol, T., Ghadouani, A., & Schilizzi, S. G. M. (2014). The flexibility architecture framework: Four organizational archetypes. *European Management Journal*, *32*(1), 104–116. doi:10.1016/j.emj.2012.11.007

Lin˜an, F., Paul, J., & Fayolle, A. (2019). SMES and entrepreneurship in the era of globalization. *Small Business Economics*, *55*(3), 695–703. doi:10.100711187-019-00180-7

Liñán, F., & Chen, Y. W. (2009). Development and cross-cultural application of a specific instrument to measure entrepreneurial intentions. *Entrepreneurship Theory and Practice*, *33*(3), 593–617. doi:10.1111/j.1540-6520.2009.00318.x

Linnenluecke, M. K., & Griffiths, A. (2012). Assessing organizational flexibility to climate and weather extremes: Complexities and methodological pathways. *Climatic Change*, *113*(3-4), 933–947. doi:10.100710584-011-0380-6

Lins, F.A., Doktor, R.H., Park, J.Y., Sung, C.S., Im, I., Davidsson, P., & Alvarez, S., Barney, J.B., Waterman, A.S., Vodă, A.I., Florea, N., Hang, C.C., Garnsey, E., Ruan, Y., Félix González, M., Husted, B.W., Aigner, D.J., Kerr, S.P., Kerr, W.R., Xu, T., Mahmood, T.M.A.T., Al Mamun, A., Bin Ahmad, G., Ibrahim, M.D., Alvarez, S. a, Barney, J.B., Shane, S., Abbasianchavari, A., Moritz, A., Frese, M., & Gielnik, M.M. (. (2017). Personality traits of entrepreneurs: A review of recent literature. *Sustain.*, *11*, 123–152. doi:10.3390u11041192

Littlewood, D., & Holt, D. (2018). Social entrepreneurship in South Africa: Exploring the influence of environment. *Business & Society*, *57*(3), 525–561. doi:10.1177/0007650315613293

Liu, H., Ke, W., Wei, K. K., Gu, J., & Chen, H. (2009). The role of institutional pressures and organizational culture in the firm's intention to adopt Internet-enabled supply chain management systems. *Journal of Operations Management, 28*(5), 372–384. doi:10.1016/j.jom.2009.11.010

Liu, R. X., Kuang, J., Gong, Q., & Hou, X. L. (2003). Principal component regression analysis with SPSS. *Computer Methods and Programs in Biomedicine, 71*(2), 141–147. doi:10.1016/S0169-2607(02)00058-5 PMID:12758135

Low, W., & Davenport, E. (2006). Mainstreaming fair trade: Adoption, assimilation, appropriation. *Journal of Strategic Marketing, 14*(4), 315–327. doi:10.1080/09652540600947912

Lumpkin, G. T., & Dess, G. G. (1996). The entrepreneurial clarifying it construct and linking orientation. *Academy of Management Review, 21*(1), 135–172. doi:10.2307/258632

Lumpkin, G. T., & Dess, G. G. (2001). Linking two dimensions of entrepreneurial orientation to firm performance: The moderating role of environment and industry life cycle. *Journal of Business Venturing, 16*(5), 429–451. doi:10.1016/S0883-9026(00)00048-3

Lumpkin, G. T., Moss, T. W., Gras, D. M., Kato, S., & Amezcua, A. S. (2013). Entrepreneurial processes in social contexts: How are they different, if at all? *Small Business Economics, 40*(3), 61–783. doi:10.100711187-011-9399-3

Lunenberg, F.C. (2012). Organizational Structure: Mintzberg's Framework. *International Journal of Scholarly, Academic, Intellectual Diversity 14*, 01-08.

Luthans, F. (2002). Positive organizational behavior: Developing and managing psychological strengths. *The Academy of Management Perspectives, 16*(1), 57–72. doi:10.5465/ame.2002.6640181

Luthar, S. S., Cicchetti, D., & Becker, B. (2000). T*he construct of flexibility: A critical evaluation and guidelines for future work. Child Development, 71*(3), 543–562. doi:10.1111/1467-8624.00164 PMID:10953923

Lüthje, C., & Franke, N. (2003). The 'making' of an entrepreneur: Testing a model of entrepreneurial intent among engineering students at MIT. *R & D Management, 33*(2), 135–147. doi:10.1111/1467-9310.00288

Luthje, C., & Franke, N. (2003). The 'making' of an entrepreneur: Testing a model of entrepreneurial intent among engineering students at MIT. *Research Management, 33*(2), 135–147.

Lynham, S. A. (2002). The general method of theory-building research in applied disciplines. *Advances in Developing Human Resources, 4*(3), 221–241. doi:10.1177/1523422302043002

Lysaght, R., Krupa, T., & Bouchard, M. (2018). The Role of Social Enterprise in Creating Work Options for People With Intellectual and Developmental Disabilities. *Journal on Developmental Disabilities, 23*(3).

Mack, E., & Mayer, H. (2016). The evolutionary dynamics of entrepreneurial ecosystems. *Urban Studies (Edinburgh, Scotland), 53*(10), 2118–2133. doi:10.1177/0042098015586547

Mackenzie, N., & Knipe, S. (2006). Research dilemmas: Paradigms, methods and methodology. *Issues in Educational Research, 16*, 193–205.

Macpherson, A., Herbane, B., & Jones, O. (2015). Developing Dynamic Capabilities through Resource Accretion: Expanding the Entrepreneurial Solution Space. *Entrepreneurship and Regional Development, 27*(5–6), 259–291. doi:10.1080/08985626.2015.1038598

Madajova, M., Pallabi, P., & Mpumwire, S. (2017). *Social entrepreneurship: The dual role of Bricolage on Innovation.* Semantic Scholar.

Madni, A. M., & Jackson, S. (2009). Towards a conceptual framework for Flexibility Engineering. *IEEE Systems Journal, 3*(2), 181–191. doi:10.1109/JSYST.2009.2017397

Maitland, E., & Sammartino, A. (2015). Managerial cognition and internationalization. *Journal of International Business Studies, 46*(7), 733–760. doi:10.1057/jibs.2015.9

Maitlis, S., & Christianson, M. (2014). Sense making in organizations: Taking stock and moving forward. *The Academy of Management Annals, 8*(1), 57–125. doi:10.5465/19416520.2014.873177

Malecki, E. J. (2018). Entrepreneurship and entrepreneurial ecosystems. *Geography Compass, 12*(3), 12359. doi:10.1111/gec3.12359

Mamabolo, A., & Myres, K. (2020). Performance measurement in emerging market social enterprises using a balanced scorecard. *Journal of Social Entrepreneurship, 11*(1), 65–87. doi:10.1080/19420676.2018.1561499

Mani, V., Jabbour, C. J. C., & Mani, K. T. (2020). Supply chain social sustainability in small and medium manufacturing enterprises and firms' performance: Empirical evidence from an emerging Asian economy. *International Journal of Production Economics, 227*, 227. doi:10.1016/j.ijpe.2020.107656

Manyena, S. B., O'Brien, G., O'Keefe, P., & Rose, J. (2011). Disaster flexibility: A bounce back or bounce forward ability? *Local Environment, 16*(5), 417–424. doi:10.1080/13549839.2011.583049

March, J. G. (1991). Exploration and Exploitation in Organizational Learning. *Organization Science, 2*(1), 71–87. doi:10.1287/orsc.2.1.71

March, J. G., Sproull, L. S., & Tamuz, M. (2003). Learning from samples of one or fewer. *Organization Science, 2*(1), 1–13. doi:10.1287/orsc.2.1.1 PMID:14645764

Marcoulides, G. A., & Heck, R. H. (1993). Organizational culture and performance: Proposing and testing a model. *Organization Science, 4*(2), 209–225. doi:10.1287/orsc.4.2.209

Masten, A. S. (2001). Ordinary magic: Flexibility processes in development. *The American Psychologist, 56*(3), 227–238. doi:10.1037/0003-066X.56.3.227 PMID:11315249

Masten, A. S. (2007). Flexibility in Developing Systems: Progress and Promise as the Fourth Wave Rises. *Development and Psychopathology, 19*(3), 921–930. doi:10.1017/S0954579407000442 PMID:17705908

Masten, A. S. (2014). *Ordinary Magic: Flexibility in Development*. Guilford Press.

Mati, A., Machuki, V., Ogutu, M., & Njihia, J. M. (2020). The Joint Effect Of Organizational Strategy, Organizational Culture And External Environment On Organizational Performance Of Large Private Health Facilities In Kenya. *Dba Africa Management Review*, *10*(1), 11–27.

McCarthy, I. P., Collard, M., & Johnson, M. (2017). Adaptive organizational flexibility: An evolutionary perspective [Oct.]. *Current Opinion in Environmental Sustainability*, *28*, 33–40. doi:10.1016/j.cosust.2017.07.005

McCartney, S. (2020). Unlocking investment to scale innovation in fashion. *PR Newswire Association, LLC*, 1–4.

McClelland, D. C. (1961). *The Achieving Society*. D. Van Norstrand Co Inc. doi:10.1037/14359-000

McDonald, S., Gan, B. C., Fraser, S. S., Oke, A., & Anderson, A. R. (2015). A review of research methods in entrepreneurship 1985-2013. *International Journal of Entrepreneurial Behaviour & Research*, *21*(3), 291–315. doi:10.1108/IJEBR-02-2014-0021

McGrath, R. G. (1999). Falling Forward: Real Options Reasoning and Entrepreneurial Failure. *Academy of Management Review*, *24*(1), 13–30. doi:10.2307/259034

McGrath, R. G. (2013). *The End of Competitive Advantage: How to Keep your Strategy Moving as Fast as your Business*. Harvard Business Review Press.

McGregor, A., Glass, A., & Clark, S. (2003). *Revaluing the Social Economy, Training and Employment Research Unit*. The University of Glasgow.

Mcmanus, S., Seville, E., Vargo, J., & Brunsdon, D. (2008). Facilitated process for improving organizational flexibility [May.]. *Natural Hazards Review*, *9*(2), 81–90. doi:10.1061/(ASCE)1527-6988(2008)9:2(81)

Mehmood, T., Alzoubi, H. M., Alshurideh, M., Al-Gasaymeh, A., & Ahmed, G. (2019). Schumpeterian entrepreneurship theory: Evolution and relevance. *Academy of Entrepreneurship Journal*, *25*, 1–10.

Mellahi, K., & Wilkinson, A. (2004). Organizational Failure: A Critique of Recent Research and a Proposed Integrative Framework. *International Journal of Management Reviews*, *5/6*(1), 21–41. doi:10.1111/j.1460-8545.2004.00095.x

Meredith, J. (1993). Theory building through conceptual methods. *International Journal of Operations & Production Management*, *13*, 3–11.

Messersmith, J. G., & Wales, W. J. (2013). Entrepreneurial orientation and performance in young firms: The role of human resource management. *International Small Business Journal*, *31*(2), 115–136. doi:10.1177/0266242611416141

Meyer, A.D., Tsui, A.S., and Hinings, C.R. (1993) Configurational approaches to organizational analysis. *Academy of Management Journal, 36*, 1175-1195.

Mia, M. M., Rizwan, S., Zayed, N. M., Nitesenko, V., Miroshnyk, O., Kryshtal, H., & Ostapenko, R. (2022). The impact of green entrepreneurship on social change and factors influencing AMO theory. *System, 10*(5), 1–19. doi:10.3390ystems10050132

Miles, R. E., Snow, C. C., Meyer, A. D., & Coleman, H. J. (2011). *Organizational strategy, structure, and process*. Stanford University Press.

Miller, D. (1983). The correlates of entrepreneurship in three types of firms. *Management Science, 29*(7), 770–791. doi:10.1287/mnsc.29.7.770

Miller, D. (1996). Configurations revisited. *Strategic Management Journal, 17*(7), 505–512. doi:10.1002/(SICI)1097-0266(199607)17:7<505::AID-SMJ852>3.0.CO;2-I

Mimouni, F. (2010). *Implications of Islam on management theory and practice: A case study of two organizations in the Middle East*. Lambert Academic Publishing.

Minniti, M., & Nardone, C. (2007). Being in Someone Else's Shoes: The Role of Gender in Nascent Entrepreneurship. *Small Business Economics, 28*(3), 223–238. doi:10.100711187-006-9017-y

Mintzberg, H., Ahlstrand, B. W., & Lampel, J. (2009). *Strategy safari: The complete guide through the wilds of strategic management*. Financial Times Prentice Hall.

Mintzberg, H. (2009). *Tracking strategies: Toward a general theory of strategy formation*. Oxford University Press.

Mitchell, R. K., Smith, B., Seawright, K. W., & Morse, E. A. (2000). Cross cultural cognition and venture creation decision. *Academy of Management Review, 43*(5), 974–993.

Mitchell, R., Agle, B., & Wood, D. (1997). Toward a theory of stakeholder identification and salience: Defining the principle of who and what really counts. *Academy of Management Review, 22*(4), 853–886. doi:10.2307/259247

Mitton, D. G. (1989). The compleat entrepreneur. *Entrepreneurship Theory and Practice, 13*(3), 9–20. doi:10.1177/104225878901300303

Mocsary, G. A. (2016). Freedom of corporate purpose. *BYU L. Rev.*, 1319.

Molecke, G., & Pinkse, J. (2017). Accountability for social impact: A bricolage perspective on impact measurement in social enterprises. *Journal of Business Venturing, 32*(5), 550–568. doi:10.1016/j.jbusvent.2017.05.003

Mondal, S. (2023). The nexus between green entrepreneurship and sustainable development: An econometric study. *Global Business Review*, 09721509231157009. doi:10.1177/09721509231157009

Monteduro, F., Cecchetti, I., Lai, Y., & Allegrini, V. (2021). Does stakeholder engagement affect corruption risk management? *The Journal of Management and Governance, 25*(3), 759–785. doi:10.100710997-020-09527-9

Moradi, E., Jafari, S. M., Doorbash, Z. M., & Mirzaei, A. (2021). *Impact of organizational inertia on business model innovation, open innovation and corporate performance*. Asia Pacific Manag. Rev., doi:10.1016/j.apmrv.2021.01.003

Moraes, G. H. S. M. D., Iizuka, E. S., & Pedro, M. (2018). Effects of entrepreneurial characteristics and university environment on entrepreneurial intention. *RAC. Revista de Administração Contemporânea*, *22*(2), 226–248. doi:10.1590/1982-7849rac2018170133

Morais-Storz, M., & Nguyen, N. (2017). The role of unlearning in metamorphosis and strategic flexibility. *The Learning Organization*, *24*(2), 93–106. doi:10.1108/TLO-12-2016-0091

Morrison, A. (2000). Entrepreneurship: What triggers it? *International Journal of Entrepreneurial Behaviour & Research*, *6*(2), 59–71. doi:10.1108/13552550010335976

Morrow, J. L., Sirmon, D. G., Hitt, M. A., & Holcomb, T. R. (2007). Creating Value in the Face of Declining Performance: Firm Strategies and Organizational Recovery. *Strategic Management Journal*, *28*(3), 271–283. doi:10.1002mj.579

Morse, J.M. (1991). Strategies for sampling. *Qual. Nurs. Res. A Contemp. dialogue* 127–145.

Moya-Clemente, I., Ribes-Giner, G., & Pantoja-Dıaz, O. (2020). Identifying environmental and economic development factors in sustainable entrepreneurship over time by partial least squares (PLS). *PLoS One*, *15*(9), 1–17. doi:10.1371/journal.pone.0238462 PMID:32886680

Mrkajic, B., Murtinu, S., & Scalera, V. G. (2017). Is green the new gold? Venture capital and green entrepreneurship. *Small Business Economics*, *52*(4), 929–950. doi:10.100711187-017-9943-x

Mueller, S. L., & Thomas, A. S. (2001). Culture and entrepreneurial potential: A nine country study of locus of control and innovativeness. *Journal of Business Venturing*, *16*(1), 51–75. doi:10.1016/S0883-9026(99)00039-7

Muñoz, P., & Kimmitt, J. (2019). Social mission as competitive advantage: A configurational analysis of the strategic conditions of social entrepreneurship. *Journal of Business Research*, *101*, 854–861. doi:10.1016/j.jbusres.2018.11.044

Murphy, P. J., & Coombes, S. M. (2009). A model of social entrepreneurial discovery. *Journal of Business Ethics*, *87*(3), 325–336. doi:10.100710551-008-9921-y

Nabi, G., Liñán, F., Ertuna, Z. İ., & Gurel, E. (2011). The moderating role of higher education on entrepreneurship. *Education + Training*, *53*(5), 387–402. doi:10.1108/00400911111147703

Nagy, G., Bilgin-Wührer, Z., Akrout, H., Lioliou, E., Hofer, K. M., & Beracs, J. (2022). Achieving high international market performance via simple vs complex configuration of international managerial network ties: A set theoretic approach across two countries. *Journal of Small Business Management*, 1–48. doi:10.1080/00472778.2022.2046014

Navarathinam, K., & Amutha, V. (2022). Green entrepreneurship: A sustainable development initiative with special reference to selected districts. *Journal of Positive School Psychology*, *6*(3), 7517–7526.

Nayak, R., Akbari, M., & Far, S. M. (2019). Recent sustainable trends in Vietnam's fashion supply chain. *Journal of Cleaner Production, 225*, 291–303. doi:10.1016/j.jclepro.2019.03.239

Nelson, D. B., & Quick, J. C. (2011). *Understanding organizational behaviour.* South-Western Cengage Learning.

Neter, J., Wasserman, W., & Kutner, M. H. (1990). Multicollinearity diagnostics—Variance inflation factor. Appl. linear. *Statistical Modelling*, 407–411.

Networks, R.A.S. & Dhesi, G. (2020). *Alertness Mixed Approach.*

Neumann, T. (2022). Impact of green entrepreneurship on sustainable development: An ex-post empirical analysis. *Journal of Cleaner Production, 377*, 134317. doi:10.1016/j.jclepro.2022.134317

Nguyen, V. B. (2021). The digitalization – economic growth relationship in developing countries and the role of governance. *Scientific Annals of Economics and Business, 68*(4), 481–493. doi:10.47743aeb-2021-0028

Nicholls, Alex., and C. Opal, Fairtrade: Market-driven ethical consumption. (2004). Sage Publications.

Nicholls, A. (2010). The legitimacy of social entrepreneurship: Reflexive isomorphism in a pre-paradigmatic field. *Entrepreneurship Theory and Practice, 34*(4), 611–633. doi:10.1111/j.1540-6520.2010.00397.x

Norman, G. (2010). Likert scales, levels of measurement and the "laws" of statistics. *Advances in Health Sciences Education : Theory and Practice, 15*(5), 625–632. doi:10.100710459-010-9222-y PMID:20146096

Norris, F. H., Stevens, S. P., Pfefferbaum, B., Wyche, K. F., & Pfeffer-baum, R. L. (2008). Community flexibility as a metaphor, theory, set of capacities, and strategy for disaster readiness. *American Journal of Community Psychology, 41*(1–2), 127–150. doi:10.100710464-007-9156-6 PMID:18157631

North, D., Smallbone, D., & Vickers, I. (2001). Public Sector Support for Innovating SMEs. *Small Business Economics, 16*(4), 303–317. doi:10.1023/A:1011164801073

Nummela, N., Saarenketo, S., and Puumalainen, K. (2004). A global mindset – a prerequisite for successful internationalization? *Canadian Journal of Administrative Sciences/Revue Canadienne des Sciences de l'Administration, 21*(1), 51–64. https://doi.org/ doi:10.1111/j.1936-4490.2004.tb00322.x

Nunnally, J. C. (1978). An overview of psychological measurement, Clinical diagnosis of mental disorders, pp. 97-146. Springer. doi:10.1007/978-1-4684-2490-4_4

Nuringsih, K., & Nuryasman, M. N. (2020). Role of green entrepreneurship in raising the effect of green toward sustainable development. *International Journal of Economics, Business, and Entrepreneurship, 3*(2), 29–46. doi:10.23960/ijebe.v3i2.69

Nyarko, I. K., Dorkenoo, C. B., Semordey, E. Y., & Agbanu, P. (2016). Organizational Structure as a Logical Tool for Determining the Flow of Responsibility and Authority. *International Journal of Management and Administrative Sciences*, *3*(3), 1–19.

O' Toole, J., & Vogel, D. (2011). Two and a Half Cheers for Conscious Capitalism. *California Management Review*, *53*(3), 60–76. doi:10.1525/cmr.2011.53.3.60

O'Hara, S., Murphy, L., & Reeve, S. (2007). Action learning as leverage for strategic transformation: A case study reflection. *Strategic Change*, *16*(4), 177–190. doi:10.1002/jsc.792

O'Sullivan, T. L., Corneil, W., Kuziemsky, C. E., & Toal-Sullivan, D. (2015). Use of the structured interview matrix to enhance community flexibility through collaboration and inclusive engagement. *Systems Research and Behavioral Science*, *32*(6), 616–628. doi:10.1002res.2250

Oberoi, R., Halsall, J. P., & Snowden, M. (2021). Reinventing social entrepreneurship leadership in the COVID-19 era: Engaging with the new normal. *Entrepreneurship Education*, *4*(2), 117–136. doi:10.100741959-021-00051-x

OECD. (2012). *Recomendação do conselho sobre política regulatória e governança.* OECD. / doi:10.1787/9789264209084-pt

OECD. (2020). *The impact of the coronavirus (COVID-19) crisis on development finance*. Issue June.

Olejnik, E., & Swoboda, B. (2012). SMEs' internationalisation patterns: Descriptives, dynamics and Determinants. *International Marketing Review*, *29*(5), 466–495. doi:10.1108/02651331211260340

Oliveira, N., & Takahashi, N. (2012). *Automated organizations: Development and structure of the modern business firm.* Springer. doi:10.1007/978-3-7908-2759-0

Olson, P. D., & Bosserman, D. A. (1984). Attributes of the entrepreneurial type. *Business Horizons*, *27*(3), 53–56. doi:10.1016/0007-6813(84)90027-2

Omoruyi, E. M. M., Olamide, K. S., Gomolemo, G., & Donath, O. A. (2017). Entrepreneurship and economic growth: Does entrepreneurship bolster economic expansion in Africa? *Journal of Socialomics*, *6*(4), 1–11.

Onsay, E. A. (2021). The analysis of green growth indicators in predicting the economic development of southeast Asian countries. *Review of Socio -. Economic Perspectives*, *6*(3), 1–15. https://reviewsep.com/wp-content/uploads/2021/09/1_ONSAY-1.pdf

Ormiston, J., & Seymour, R. (2011). Understanding Value Creation in Social Entrepreneurship: The Importance of Aligning Mission, Strategy and Impact Measurement. *Journal of Social Entrepreneurship*, *2*(2), 125–150. doi:10.1080/19420676.2011.606331

Ortega-Argilés, R. (2022). The evolution of regional entrepreneurship policies: "No one size fits all". *The Annals of Regional Science*, *69*(3), 585–610. doi:10.100700168-022-01128-8

Ortiz-de-Mandojana, N., & Bansal, P. (2015). The long-term benefits of organizational flexibility through sustainable business practices. *Strategic Management Journal*. doi:10.1002mj.2410

Ouchi, W. G. (1980). Markets, bureaucracies, and clans. *Administrative Science Quarterly, 25*(1), 129–141. doi:10.2307/2392231

Oviatt, B., & McDougall, P. (1994). Toward a Theory of International New ventures. *Journal of International Business Studies, 25*(1), 45–64. doi:10.1057/palgrave.jibs.8490193

Oviatt, B., & McDougall, P. (2005). Defining international entrepreneurship and modeling the speed of internationalization. *Entrepreneurship Theory and Practice, 29*(5), 537–553. doi:10.1111/j.1540-6520.2005.00097.x

Ozgen, E. & Baron, R.A. (2007). Social sources of information in opportunity recognition: Effects of mentors, industry networks, and professional forums. *J. Bus. Ventur.* doi:10.1016/j.jbusvent.2005.12.001

Ozili, P. K. (2019). *Financial stability: Does social activism matter? 92192.*

Pache, A. C., & Santos, F. (2013). Embedded in hybrid contexts: How individuals in organizations respond to competing institutional logics. *Research in the Sociology of Organizations, 39*, 3–35. doi:10.1108/S0733-558X(2013)0039b014

Palma, M. A. M. (2004). *A capacidade de inovação como formadora de valor: análise dos vetores de valor em empresas brasileiras de biotecnologia* [Doctoral Thesis, São Paulo University].

Pandey, K. (2019). India's Unemployment Rate Doubled in Two Years: SoE in Figures. https://www.downtoearth.org.in/news/economy/india-s-unemployment-ratedoubled-in -two-years-soe-in-figures-64953

Pareja-Cano, B., Valor, C., & Benito, A. (2020). How Social Enterprises Nurture Empowerment: A Grounded Theoretical Model of Social Change. *Journal of Social Entrepreneurship*, 1–21.

Parida, V., Pesämaa, O., Wincent, J., & Westerberg, M. (2017). Network capability, innovativeness, and performance: A multidimensional extension for entrepreneurship. *Entrepreneurship and Regional Development, 29*(2), 94–115. doi:10.1080/08985626.2016.1255434

Parmar, B. L., Freeman, R. E., Harrison, J. S., Wicks, A. C., Purnell, L., & De Colle, S. (2010). Stakeholder theory: The state of the art. *The Academy of Management Annals, 4*(1), 403–445. doi:10.5465/19416520.2010.495581

Parrish, B. D. (2010). Sustainability-driven entrepreneurship: Principles of organization design. *Journal of Business Venturing, 25*(5), 510–523. doi:10.1016/j.jbusvent.2009.05.005

Parthasarthy, R., & Sethi, S. P. (2018). The impact of flexible automation on business strategy and organizational structure. In *Organizational Innovation* (pp. 319–344). Routledge.

Patriarca, R., Di Gravio, G., Constantino, F., Falegnami, A., & Bilotta, F. (2017). An Analytic Framework to Assess Organizational Flexibility. *Safety and Health at work, 9.* doi:10.1016/j.shaw.2017.10.005

Paul, H. (2000). Creating a global mindset. *Thunderbird International Business Review, 42*(2), 187–200. doi:10.1002/1520-6874(200003/04)42:2<187::AID-TIE4>3.0.CO;2-7

Paul, J., Parthasarathy, S., & Gupta, P. (2017). Exporting challenges of SMEs: A review and future research agenda. *Journal of World Business, 52*(3), 327–342. doi:10.1016/j.jwb.2017.01.003

Peattie, K., & Morley, A. (2008). Eight paradoxes of the social enterprise research agenda. *Social Enterprise Journal, 4*(2), 91–107. doi:10.1108/17508610810901995

Pelizza Vier Machado, H., Gaiotto, S. A. V., & Rovaris Machado, M. C. (2021). *Growth and social entrepreneurs: the challenge of conciliating economic and social values.* Revista de Gestão.

Pereira, A. C., & Romero, F. (2013). A review of the meanings and the implications of the Industry 4.0 concept. *Procedia Manufacturing, 13*, 1206–1214. doi:10.1016/j.promfg.2017.09.032

Peteraf, M., Di Stefano, G., & Verona, G. (2013). The Elephant in the Room of Dynamic Capabilities: Bringing Two Diverging Conversations Together. *Strategic Management Journal, 34*(12), 1389–1410. doi:10.1002mj.2078

Pfeilstetter, R., & Gómez Carrasco, I. (2020). Local meanings of social enterprise. A historical-particularist view on hybridity of organizations. *Revista de Estudios Cooperativos 134.*

Phan, P. H., Wong, P. K., & Wang, C. K. (2002). Antecedents to entrepreneurship among university students in Singapore: Beliefs, attitudes and background. *Journal of Enterprising Culture, 10*(2), 151–174. doi:10.1142/S0218495802000189

Pinho, J., & Prange, C. (2016). The effect of social networks and dynamic internationalization capabilities on international performance. *Journal of World Business, 51*(3), 391–403. doi:10.1016/j.jwb.2015.08.001

Pita, M., Costa, J., & Carrizo Moreira, A. (2021). Entrepreneurial Ecosystems and Entrepreneurial Initiative: Building a Multi-Country Taxonomy. *Sustainability (Basel), 13*(7), 4065. doi:10.3390u13074065

Podsakoff, P. M., MacKenzie, S. B., Lee, J.-Y., & Podsakoff, N. P. (2003). Common method biases in behavioral research: A critical review of the literature and recommended remedies. *The Journal of Applied Psychology, 88*(5), 879–903. doi:10.1037/0021-9010.88.5.879 PMID:14516251

Polask, S. (2019). Role of economics in analyzing the environment and sustainable development. *PNAS, 116* (12), 5233-5238. doi:10.1073/pnas.1901616116

Polonsky, M. J. (1995). A stakeholder theory approach to designing an environmental marketing strategy. *Journal of Business and Industrial Marketing, 10*(3), 29–46. doi:10.1108/08858629510096201

Ponomarov, S. Y., & Holcolmb, M. C. (2009). Understanding the Concept of Supply Chain Flexibility. *International Journal of Logistics Management*, *20*(1), 124–143. doi:10.1108/09574090910954873

Poon, J. M. L., Ainuddin, R. H., & Junit, S. A. (2006). Effects of self-concept traits and entrepreneurial orientation on firm performance. *International Small Business Journal*, *24*(1), 61–82. doi:10.1177/0266242606059779

Popadiuk, S., Vidal, P., & Franklin, M. (2010). Measuring knowledge exploitation and exploration: An empirical application in a technological development center in Brazil. *Revista Espacios*, *31*(3), 36.

Porter, M. E. (1986). *Estratégia competitiva: técnicas para análise de indústrias e da concorrência*. Editora Campus.

Post, J. E., & Waddock, S. (1991). Social entrepreneurs and catalytic change. *Public Administration Review*, *51*(5), 393–401. doi:10.2307/976408

Powell, M., Gillett, A., & Doherty, B. (2019). Sustainability in social enterprise: Hybrid organizing in public services. *Public Management Review*, *21*(2), 159–186. doi:10.1080/14719037.2018.1438504

Prahalad, C. K. (2006). *The fortune at the bottom of the pyramid*. Pearson Education, India.

Probst, G., & Raisch, S. (2005). Organizational Crisis: The Logic of Failure. *The Academy of Management Perspectives*, *19*(1), 90–105. doi:10.5465/ame.2005.15841958

Puhakka, V. (2011). Developing a Creative-Cognitive Model of Entrepreneurial Alertness to Business Opportunities. *J. Manag. Strateg.*, *2*(4). doi:10.5430/jms.v2n4p85

Ragin, C. C. (1987). *The comparative method: Moving beyond qualitative and quantitative strategies*. University of California Press.

Ramos, A. & Zilber, S. N. (2015). O Impacto do investimento na capacidade inovadora da empresa. *Review of Administration and Innovation - RAI*, *12*(1), 303. doi:10.11606/rai.v12i1.100326

Ramus, T., La Cara, B., Vaccaro, A., & Brusoni, S. (2018). Social or commercial? Innovation strategies in social enterprises at times of turbulence. *Business Ethics Quarterly*, *28*(4), 463–492. doi:10.1017/beq.2017.55

Ramus, T., & Vaccaro, A. (2017). Stakeholders matter: How social enterprises address mission drift. *Journal of Business Ethics*, *143*(2), 307–322. doi:10.100710551-014-2353-y

Rasheed, H. S., & Rasheed, B. Y. (2003). Developing entrepreneurial characteristics in minority youth: The effects of education and enterprise experience. In *Ethnic entrepreneurship: Structure and process*. Emerald Group Publishing Limited. doi:10.1016/S1074-7877(03)04012-1

Rauch, A., Wiklund, J., Lumpkin, G. T., & Frese, M. (2009). Entrepreneurial orientation and business performance: an assessment of past research and suggestions for the future. *Entrepreneurship Theory and Practice, 33,* 761–787. doi:. 00308.x doi:10.1111/j.1540-6520.2009

Raykov, T. (1997). Estimation of composite reliability for congeneric measures. *Applied Psychological Measurement, 21*(2), 173–184. doi:10.1177/01466216970212006

Reich, J. W. (2006). Three psychological principles of flexibility in natural disasters. *Disaster Prevention and Management, 15*(5), 793–798. doi:10.1108/09653560610712739

Reijonen, H., Hirvonen, S., Nagy, G., Laukkanen, T., & Gabrielsson, M. (2015). The impact of entrepreneurial orientation on B2B branding and business growth in emerging markets. *Industrial Marketing Management, 51*, 35–46. doi:10.1016/j.indmarman.2015.04.016

Richardson, G. E. (2016). The applied metatheory of flexibility and resiliency. In U. Kumar (Ed.), *The Routledge International Handbook of Psychological Flexibility* (pp. 124–135). Routledge.

Richtnér, A., & Löfsten, H. (2014). Managing in turbulence: How the capacity for flexibility influences creativity. *R & D Management, 44*(2), 137–151. doi:10.1111/radm.12050

Roberts, K. H., Madsen, P. M., & Desait, V. M. (2005). The space between in space transportation: A relational analysis of the failure of STS-107. In W. H. Starbuck & M. Farjoun (Eds.), *Organization at the limit—NASA and the Columbia Disaster* (pp. 81–98). Blackwell.

Robinson, P. B., Stimpson, D. V., Huefner, J. C., & Hunt, H. K. (1991). An attitude approach to the prediction of entrepreneurship. *Entrepreneurship Theory and Practice, 15*(4), 13–32. doi:10.1177/104225879101500405

Rocha, E. L. C., & Freitas, A. A. F. (2014). Evaluation of entrepreneurship teaching among university students through the entrepreneurial profile. *Contemporary Administration Magazine, 18*(4), 465–486.

Rodrigues, M., Silva, R., & Franco, M. (2021). Entrepreneurial Attitude and Intention in Higher Education Students: What Factors Matter? *Entrepreneurship Research Journal*. doi:10.1515/erj-2020-0107

Rong, B., & Wilkinson, I. F. (2011). What do managers' survey responses mean and what affects them? The case of market orientation and firm performance. *Australasian Marketing Journal, 19*(3), 137–147. doi:10.1016/j.ausmj.2011.04.001

Rosenbach, M., Murrell, D. F., Bystryn, J.-C., Dulay, S., Dick, S., Fakharzadeh, S., Hall, R., Korman, N. J., Lin, J., Okawa, J., Pandya, A. G., Payne, A. S., Rose, M., Rubenstein, D., Woodley, D., Vittorio, C., Werth, B. B., Williams, E. A., Taylor, L., & Werth, V. P. (2009). Reliability and Convergent Validity of Two Outcome Instruments for Pemphigus. *The Journal of Investigative Dermatology, 129*(10), 2404–2410. doi:10.1038/jid.2009.72 PMID:19357707

Rosenbusch, N., Rauch, A., & Bausch, A. (2013). The mediating role of entrepreneurial orientation in the task environment—Performance relationship: A meta-analysis. *Journal of Management, 39*(3), 633–659. doi:10.1177/0149206311425612

Roumpi, D., Magrizos, S., & Nicolopoulou, K. (2020). Virtuous circle: Human capital and human resource management in social enterprises. *Human Resource Management, 59*(5), 401–421. doi:10.1002/hrm.22002

Roundy, P. T., Brockman, B. K., & Bradshaw, M. (2017). The resilience of entrepreneurial ecosystems. *Journal of Business Venturing Insights*, *8*, 99–104. doi:10.1016/j.jbvi.2017.08.002

Ryan, A. B. (2006). Post-Positivist Approaches to Research. In: *Researching and Writing your thesis: a guide for postgraduate students.*

Saari, U. A., & Joensuu-Salo, S. (2019). Green entrepreneurship. In W. Leal Filho, A. Azul, L. Brandli, P. Özuyar, & T. Wall (Eds.), *Responsible Consumption and Production. Encyclopedia of the UN Sustainable Development Goals*. Springer. doi:10.1007/978-3-319-71062-4_6-1

Sagiv, L., & Schwartz, S. H. (2007). Cultural values in organizations: Insights for Europe. *European Journal of International Management*, *1*(3), 176–190. doi:10.1504/EJIM.2007.014692

Santika, I. W., Wardana, I. M., Setiawan, P. Y., & Widagda, I. G. N. J. A. (2022). Entrepreneurship education and green entrepreneurial intention: A conceptual framework. *Linguistics and Culture Review*, *6*(S1), 797–810. doi:10.21744/lingcure.v6nS1.2159

Santos, F., Pache, A. C., & Birkholz, C. (2015). Making hybrids work: Aligning business models and organizational design for social enterprises. *California Management Review*, *57*(3), 36–58. doi:10.1525/cmr.2015.57.3.36

Sapienza, H. J., Autio, E., George, G., & Zahra, S. A. (2006). A capabilities perspective on the effects of early internationalization on firm survival and growth. *Academy of Management Review*, *31*(4), 914–933. doi:10.5465/amr.2006.22527465

Sargiacomo, M., & Walker, S. P. (2022). Disaster governance and hybrid organizations: Accounting, performance challenges and evacuee housing. *Accounting. Accounting, Auditing & Accountability Journal*, *35*(3), 887–916. doi:10.1108/AAAJ-12-2019-4323

Sarkis, J., Zhu, Q., & Lai, K. H. (2011). An organizational theoretic review of green supply chain management literature. *International Journal of Production Economics*, *130*(1), 1–15. doi:10.1016/j.ijpe.2010.11.010

Sarstedt, M., Ringle, C. M., Smith, D., Reams, R., & Hair, J. F. Jr. (2014). Partial least squares structural equation modeling (PLS-SEM): A useful tool for family business researchers. *Journal of Family Business Strategy*, *5*(1), 105–115. doi:10.1016/j.jfbs.2014.01.002

Sassetti, S., Cavaliere, V., & Lombardi, S. (2021). The rhythm of effective entrepreneurs' decision-making process. The pathways of alertness scanning and search and cognitive style. A mediation model. *The International Entrepreneurship and Management Journal*. doi:10.100711365-021-00759-1

Saunila, M. (2020). Innovation capability in SMEs: A systematic review of the literature. *Journal of Innovation and Knowledge*, *5*(4), 260–265. doi:10.1016/j.jik.2019.11.002

Savchina, O., Bratanov, A., Savchina, O., & Shcherbachenko, P. (2019). Assessment of financial stability and business expansion of JSC Statoil in the context of economic instability. *Journal of Advanced Research in Law and Economics*, *10*(6), 1929–1938. doi:10.14505/jarle.v10.6(44).35

Savitz, A. (2013). *The triple bottom line: how today's best-run companies are achieving economic, social and environmental success and how you can too*. John Wiley and Sons.

Scandelari, V. R. N., & Cunha, J. C. (2013). Ambidestralidade e desempenho socioambiental de empresas do setor eletroeletrônico. *RAE, 53*(2), 183–198. doi:10.1590/S0034-75902013000200006

Scheaf, D. J., Loignon, A. C., Webb, J. W., Heggestad, E. D., & Wood, M. S. (2020). Measuring opportunity evaluation: Conceptual synthesis and scale development. *Journal of Business Venturing, 35*(2), 1–26. doi:10.1016/j.jbusvent.2019.04.003

Schein, E. H. (1985). *Organizational culture and leadership*. Jossey-Bass.

Schinasi, G. J. (2004). Defining Financial Stability. *IMF Working Paper, 04*(187), 1. doi:10.5089/9781451859546.001

Schmidt, T. (2006). *A review of Structure in Fives; Designing Effective Organizations* [Thesis, MSC]. http://www.thesis.msc-cse.com/pdf/article_mintzberg.pdf

Schmidt, S., & Bohnenberger, M. C. (2009). Entrepreneurial profile and organizational performance. *Contemporary Administration Magazine, 13*(3), 450–467.

Schreiber, D. (2012). *Inovação e desenvolvimento organizacional*. Editora Feevale.

Schumpeter, J. (2012). *Teoria do desenvolvimento económico*. Fundação Calouste Gulbenkian.

Scott, J. (1991). *Social Network Analysis*. Sage Publications.

Scott, W. R. (2008). *Institutions and organizations: Ideas and interests*. SAGE.

Seerat, S. (2016). Entrepreneurship and Economic Development. *IOSR Journal of Business and Management, 2*(2), 98–105. doi:10.9790/487X-15010020298-105

Segal, G., Borgia, D., & Schoenfeld, J. (2005). The motivation to become an entrepreneur. *International Journal of Entrepreneurial Behaviour & Research, 11*(1), 42–57. doi:10.1108/13552550510580834

Sekaran, U. (2000). *Research methods for business: A skill-building approach*. John Wiley & Sons.

Shafritz, J. M., Ott, J. S., & Jang, Y. S. (2015). *Classics of organization theory*. Cengage Learning.

Shambare, R., & Shambare, R. (2019). Presenting a PhD research proposal : A guide for commerce students. *African Journal of Science, Technology, Innovation and Development, 0*, 1–15. doi:10.1080/20421338.2019.1638586

Shamsudin, S., & Velmurugan, V. P. (2023). A study on the drivers of corporate culture impacting employee performance in IT industry. *International Journal of Professional Business Review: Int. J. Prof. Bus. Rev., 8*(2), 13. doi:10.26668/businessreview/2023.v8i2.1023

Shane, S. (2013). The Discovery of Entrepreneurial Opportunities. In *A General Theory of Entrepreneurship* (pp. 448–469). Edward Elgar Publishing. doi:10.4337/9781781007990.00010

Shane, S., & Nicolaou, N. (2015). Creative personality, opportunity recognition and the tendency to start businesses: A study of their genetic predispositions. *Journal of Business Venturing*, *30*(3), 407–419. doi:10.1016/j.jbusvent.2014.04.001

Shane, S., Nicolaou, N., Cherkas, L., & Spector, T. D. (2010). Do openness to experience and recognizing opportunities have the same genetic source? *Human Resource Management*, *49*(2), 291–303. doi:10.1002/hrm.20343

Shane, S., & Venkataraman, S. (2000). The Promise of Enterpreneurship as a Field of Research. *Academy of Management Review*, *25*(1), 217. doi:10.2307/259271

Sharaf, A., El-Gharbawy, A., & Ragheb, M. A. (2018). Factors That Influence Entrepreneurial Intention within University Students in Egypt. *OAlib*, *5*(10), 1–14. doi:10.4236/oalib.1104881

Sharma, A., Das, N., & Singh, S. P. (2023). Causal association of entrepreneurship ecosystem and financial inclusion. *Heliyon*, *9*(3), 1–13. doi:10.1016/j.heliyon.2023.e14596 PMID:36950562

Sharma, P., & Singh, A. K. (2017). Association of state-wise food security index with climatic factors in India: Evidence from state-wise panel data. *Journal of Global Agriculture and Ecology*, *6*(3), 196–205.

Sheffi, Y. (2005). Building a Resilient Supply Chain. *Harvard Business Review Supply Chain Strategy*. https://sheffi.mit.edu/sites/default/files/genmedia.buildingresilientsupplychain.pdf

Sheppard, J. P., & Chowdhury, S. D. (2005). Riding the Wrong Wave: Organizational Failure as a Failed Turnaround. *Long Range Planning*, *38*(3), 239–260. doi:10.1016/j.lrp.2005.03.009

Shi, H. X., Graves, C., & Barbera, F. (2019). Intergenerational succession and internationalization strategy of family SMEs: Evidence from China. *Long Range Planning*, *52*(4), 101838. doi:10.1016/j.lrp.2018.05.004

Shirokova, G., Osiyevskyy, O., & Bogatyreva, K. (2016). Exploring the intention–behavior link in student entrepreneurship: Moderating effects of individual and environmental characteristics. *European Management Journal*, *34*(4), 386–399. doi:10.1016/j.emj.2015.12.007

Short, J. C., Tyge Payne, G., & Jr Ketchen, D. J. (2008). Research on organizational configurations: Past accomplishment and future challenges. *Journal of Management*, *34*(6), 1053–1079. doi:10.1177/0149206308324324

Siegel, D. S., & Renko, M. (2012). The role of market and technological knowledge in recognizing entrepreneurial opportunities. *Management Decision*, *50*(5), 797–816. doi:10.1108/00251741211227500

Siegner, M., Pinkse, J., & Panwar, R. (2018). Managing tensions in a social enterprise: The complex balancing act to deliver a multi-faceted but coherent social mission. *Journal of Cleaner Production*, *174*, 1314–1324. doi:10.1016/j.jclepro.2017.11.076

Siemiński, M., Andruszkiewicz, K., & Pinho, T. (2022). Application of the 6D Hofstede Model in an Analysis of the Polish and Portuguese Business Culture. *Olsztyn Economic Journal, 17*(1), 59–69. doi:10.31648/oej.8651

Siepel, J., Camerani, R., & Masucci, M. (2019). Skills combinations and firm performance. *Small Business Economics, 5*, 1–23.

Singh, A. K., & Jyoti, B. (2021). Further research direction for indicators of technology entrepreneurship ecosystem, technology start-ups ecosystem and technology-business incubators: A conceptual review. *Dimensions International Journal of Management ICFAI Business School (IBS) Mumbai, 7*(1), 14-33.

Singh, A. K., & Jyoti, B. (2023c). Empirical evidence from a different income group countries on the interdependency between digitalization and economic development. In Patricia Ordóñez de Pablos and Xi Zhang (Eds.), 5G, Artificial Intelligence, and Next Generation Internet of Things: Digital Innovation for Green and Sustainable Economies, (pp. 44-85). IGI Global. doi:10.4018/978-1-6684-8634-4.ch003

Singh, A. K. (2020). Technology transfer and commercialization models and policies in India, USA, China and Malaysia: A conceptual review. *Asian Journal of Sociological Research, 3*(1), 19–45. https://globalpresshub.com/index.php/AJSR/article/view/916

Singh, A. K., Arya, A., & Jyoti, B. (2019b). A conceptual review on economic, business, intellectual property rights and science & technology related activities in Asian economies. *JNNCE Journal of Engineering & Management, 3*(2), 1–22.

Singh, A. K., & Ashraf, S. N. (2020). Association of entrepreneurship ecosystem with economic growth in selected countries: An empirical exploration. *Journal of Entrepreneurship. Business Economics (Cleveland, Ohio), 8*(2), 36–92.

Singh, A. K., Ashraf, S. N., & Arya, A. (2019c). Estimating factors affecting technical efficiency in Indian manufacturing sector. *Eurasian Journal of Business and Economics, 12*(24), 65–86. doi:10.17015/ejbe.2019.024.04

Singh, A. K., Ashraf, S. N., & Sharma, S. K. (2023f). Farmer's perception on climatic factors and social-economic characteristics in the agricultural sector of Gujarat. *Research on World Agricultural Economy, 4*(1), 36–53. doi:10.36956/rwae.v4i1.788

Singh, A. K., Ashraf, S. N., Sharma, S. K., & Kumar, S. (2023b). Factors affecting farm income and climate adaptation strategies in the farming sector of Gujarat state of India. In B. J. Sadhik, J. Adewole, A. Yeneneh, & L. Abidoye (Eds.), *Opportunities and Challenges in Climate-Friendly Clean Water and Energy Technologies* (pp. 122–147). IGI Global. doi:10.4018/978-1-6684-7303-0.ch006

Singh, A. K., Issac, J., & Narayanan, K. G. S. (2019a). Measurement of environmental sustainability index and its association with socio-economic indicators in selected Asian economies: An empirical investigation. *International Journal of Environment and Sustainable Development, 18*(1), 57–100. doi:10.1504/IJESD.2019.098641

Singh, A. K., & Jyoti, B. (2020). Factors affecting firm's annual turnover in selected manufacturing industries of India: An empirical study. *Business Perspectives and Research*, *2*(3), 33–59. doi:10.38157/business-perspective-review.v2i3.206

Singh, A. K., & Jyoti, B. (2023a). Does digitalization have a bi-directional causal relationship with the entrepreneurship ecosystem? evidence from a country-wise panel data analysis. In *Ramakrishna Yanamandra and Logaiswari Indiran (Edt.), Handbook of Research on Designing Sustainable Strategies to Develop Entrepreneurial Intention*. IGI Global. doi:10.4018/978-1-6684-8781-5.ch007

Singh, A. K., & Jyoti, B. (2023b). Appropriate technology and adaptation strategies mitigate the adverse impact of climate change on the agricultural sector: A case study in Gujarat, India. In P. H. Alex Khang (Ed.), *Advanced Technologies and AI-Equipped IoT Applications in High-Tech Agriculture* (pp. 389–416). IGI Global. doi:10.4018/978-1-6684-9231-4.ch023

Singh, A. K., Jyoti, B., Kumar, S., & Lenka, S. K. (2021). Assessment of global sustainable development, environmental sustainability, economic development and social development index in selected economies. *International Journal of Sustainable Development and Planning*, *16*(1), 123–138. doi:10.18280/ijsdp.160113

Singh, A. K., & Kumar, S. (2021). Assessing the performance and factors affecting industrial development in Indian states: An empirical analysis. *Journal of Social Economics Research*, *8*(2), 135–154. doi:10.18488/journal.35.2021.82.135.154

Singh, A. K., & Kumar, S. (2022a). Expert's perception on technology transfer and commercialization, and intellectual property rights in India: Evidence from selected research organizations. *Journal of Management, Economics, and Industrial Organization*, *6*(1), 1–33. doi:10.31039/jomeino.2022.6.1.1

Singh, A. K., & Kumar, S. (2022b). Factors influencing entrepreneurship ecosystem and economic development: Evidence from cross-sectional country-wise imbalanced panel data analysis. *The IUP Journal of Entrepreneurship Development*, *19*(3), 24–47.

Singh, A. K., & Kumar, S. (2022c). Exploring the impact of sustainable development on social-economic, and science and technological development in selected countries: A panel data analysis. *Society & Sustainability*, *4*(1), 55–83. doi:10.38157s.v4i1.405

Singh, A. K., Kumar, S., Ashraf, S. N., & Jyoti, B. (2022b). Implications of farmer's adaptation strategies to climate change in agricultural sector of Gujarat: Evidence from farm level data. *Research on World Agricultural Economy*, *3*(1), 42–57. doi:10.36956/rwae.v3i1.498

Singh, A. K., Kumar, S., & Jyoti, B. (2023c). Does entrepreneurship ecosystem have a causal relationship with economic development? A country-wise imbalanced panel data investigation. In H. Magd, S. A. Khan, N. D. Nte, & M. Sarim (Eds.), *Entrepreneurship and Economic Sustainability* (pp. 1–15). Prestige Publishers.

Singh, A. K., Kumar, S., & Sharma, A. K. (2023e). Does green entrepreneurship ecosystem have causal association with economic development? Evidence from country-wise panel data investigation. *Journal of International Business Research*, *22*(2), 1–18. https://www.abacademies.org/articles/Does-Green-Entrepreneurship-Ecosystem-have-1544-0230-22-2-191.pdf

Singh, A. K., Kumar, S., Sharma, A. K., & Sinha, S. (2022a). Does green entrepreneurship have an association with sustainable development and its components? Evidence from a country-wise panel data investigation. In M. Magd, D. Singh, D. Spicer, & R. T. Syed (Eds.), *International Perspectives on Value Creation and Sustainability Through Social Entrepreneurship* (pp. 132–172). IGI Global. doi:10.4018/978-1-6684-4666-9.ch008

Singh, A. K., Sharma, A. K., & Jyoti, B. (2023a). Does economic development have a causal relationship with environmental degradation? Experience from different income group countries. In G. Sart (Ed.), *Considerations on Education for Economic, Social, and Environmental Sustainability* (pp. 300–333). IGI Global. doi:10.4018/978-1-6684-8356-5.ch015

Singh, A. K., & Sharma, P. (2018). Implications of climatic and non-climatic variables on food security in developing economies: A conceptual review. *MOJ Food Processing & Technology*, *6*(1), 1–12. doi:10.15406/mojfpt.2018.06.00138

Singh, A. K., Sharma, S. K., & Lenka, S. K. (2023d). Causality between green entrepreneurship and sustainable development: A cross-country analysis using ARDL model. *The IUP Journal of Applied Economics*, *22*(1), 5–38.

Singh, A. K., Singh, B. J., & Negi, V. (2020b). Does sustainable development have a causal relationship with environmental development? Evidence from a country-wise panel data analysis. *International Journal of Technology Management & Sustainable Development*, *19*(2), 147–171. doi:10.1386/tmsd_00020_1

Singh, A. K., Singh, B., & Ashraf, S. N. (2020a). Implications of intellectual property protection, and science and technological development in the manufacturing sector in selected economies. *Journal of Advocacy. Research in Education*, *7*(1), 16–35.

Skordoulis, M., Kyriakopoulos, G., Ntanos, S., Galatsidas, S., Arabatzis, G., Chalikias, M., & Kalantonis, P. (2022). The mediating role of firm strategy in the relationship between green entrepreneurship, green innovation, and competitive advantage: The case of medium and large-sized firms in Greece. *Sustainability (Basel)*, *14*(6), 1–18. doi:10.3390u14063286

Slater, A. (2020). Coronavirus fallout threatens financial stability. *Economic Outlook*, *44*(2), 26–28. doi:10.1111/1468-0319.12481

Small Enterprise Development Agency (SEDA). (2016). *The small, medium and micro-enterprise sector of South Africa*. SEDA.

Smallbone, D., Evans, M., Ekanem, I., & Butters, S. (2001). *Researching Social Enterprise*. Small Business Service.

Smith, W.K., Leonard, H. & Epstein, M. (2007). Digital divide data: A social enterprise in action. *Harvard Business School Case Study*.

Smith, D., & Elliott, D. (2007). Exploring the barriers to learning from crisis -Organizational learning and crisis. *Management Learning*, *38*(5), 519–538. doi:10.1177/1350507607083205

Smith, P., McVilly, K. R., McGillivray, J., & Chan, J. (2018). Developing open employment outcomes for people with an intellectual disability utilising a Social Enterprise Framework. *Journal of Vocational Rehabilitation*, *48*(1), 59–77. doi:10.3233/JVR-170916

Smith, S. (2010). For love or money? Fairtrade business models in the UK supermarket sector. *Journal of Business Ethics*, *92*(S2, no. S2), 257–266. doi:10.100710551-010-0582-2

Söderholm, P. (2020). The green economy transition: The challenges of technology change for sustainability. *Sustainable Earth*, *3*(6), 1–11. doi:10.118642055-020-00029-y

Souitaris, V., Zerbinati, S., & Al-Laham, A. (2007). Do entrepreneurship programmes raise entrepreneurial intention of science and engineering students? The effect of learning, inspiration and resources. *Journal of Business Venturing*, *22*(4), 566–591. doi:10.1016/j.jbusvent.2006.05.002

Sparviero, S. (2019). The case for a socially oriented business model canvas: The social enterprise model canvas. *Journal of Social Entrepreneurship*, *10*(2), 232–251. doi:10.1080/19420676.2018.1541011

Spigel, B. (2017). The relational organization of entrepreneurial ecosystems. *Entrepreneurship Theory and Practice*, *41*(1), 49–72. doi:10.1111/etap.12167

Spiro, R. L., & Weitz, B. A. (1990). Adaptive Selling: Conceptualization, Measurement, and Nomological Validity. *JMR, Journal of Marketing Research*, *27*(1), 61–69. doi:10.1177/002224379002700106

Stam, E. (2015). Entrepreneurial ecosystems and regional policy: A sympathetic critique. *European Planning Studies*, *23*(9), 1759–1769. doi:10.1080/09654313.2015.1061484

Stam, W., & Elfring, T. (2008). Entrepreneurial orientation and new venture performance: The moderating role of intra-and extraindustry social capital. *Academy of Management Journal*, *51*(1), 97–111. doi:10.5465/amj.2008.30744031

Standish-Kuon, T., & Rice, M. P. (2002). Introducing engineering and science students to entrepreneurship: Models and influential factors at six American universities. *Journal of Engineering Education*, *91*(1), 33–39. doi:10.1002/j.2168-9830.2002.tb00670.x

Steel, P., & Koenig, C. J. (2006). Integrating theories of motivation. *Academy of Management Review*, *31*(4), 889–913. doi:10.5465/amr.2006.22527462

Stephan, U., & Folmer, E. (2017). Context and social enterprises: which environments enable social entrepreneurship? *European Policy Brief*, 1-5.

Stephenson, A. (2010). *Benchmarking the Flexibility of Organizations*. [Unpublished PhD Thesis, Civil and Natural Resources Engineering Department, University of Canterbury].

Sternberg, R., & Wennekers, S. (2005). Determinants and effects of new business creation using global entrepreneurship monitor data. *Small Business Economics*, *24*(3), 193–203. doi:10.100711187-005-1974-z

Stewart, J., & O'Donnell, M. (2007). Implementing change in a public agency. *International Journal of Public Sector Management*, *20*(3), 239–251. doi:10.1108/09513550710740634

Storey, J. (2005). What Next for Strategic-level Leadership Research? *Leadership*, *1*(1), 89–104. doi:10.1177/1742715005049353

Strielkowski, W. (2012). Factors that determine success of small and medium enterprises: The role of internal and external factors. *Journal of Applied Economic Sciences*, *7*(21), 326–333.

Suchman, M. C. (1995). Managing legitimacy: Strategic and institutional approaches. *Academy of Management Review*, *20*(3), 571–610. doi:10.2307/258788

Sullivan Mort, G., & Weerawardena, J. (2006). Investing social entrepreneurship: A multidimensional model. *Journal of World Business*, *41*(1), 21–35. doi:10.1016/j.jwb.2005.09.001

Sundqvist, S., Kyläheiko, K., Kuivalainen, O., & Cadogan, J. W. (2012). Kirznerian and Schumpeterian entrepreneurial– oriented behavior in turbulent export markets. *International Marketing Review*, *29*(2), 203–219. doi:10.1108/02651331211216989

Sutcliffe, K. M., & Vogus, T. J. (2003). Organizing for flexibility. *Positive organizational scholarship*, 94-110.

Sweezy, P. (1943). Professpr Schumpter's theory of innovation. *The Review of Economics and Statistics*, *25*(1), 93. doi:10.2307/1924551

Sydow, J., Schreyögg, G., & Koch, J. (2009). Organizational Path Dependence: Opening the Black Box. *Academy of Management Review*, *34*(4), 689–709.

Tabaklar, T., Sorkun, M. F., Yurt, O., & Yu, W. (2021). Exploring the microfoundations of dynamic capabilities for social innovation in a humanitarian aid supply network setting. *Industrial Marketing Management*, *96*, 147–162. https://www.sciencedirect.com/science/article/pii/S0019850121000845. doi:10.1016/j.indmarman.2021.04.012

Taghizadeh-hesary, F., Phoumin, H., & Rasoulinezhad, E. (2021). *COVID-19 and regional solutions for mitigating the risk of small and medium-sized enterprise finance in ASEAN member states* (Issue 399).

Taleb, N. N. N. (2014). *Antifragile: Things that Gain from Disorder* (3rd ed.). Random House.

Tang, J., Kacmar, K.M.M., & Busenitz, L. (2012). Entrepreneurial Alertness in the pursuit of new opportunities. *J. Bus. Ventur.* doi:10.1016/j.jbusvent.2010.07.001

Tang, Z., & Tang, J. (2012). Entrepreneurial orientation and SME performance in China's changing environment: The moderating effects of strategies. *Asia Pacific Journal of Management*, *29*(2), 409–431. doi:10.100710490-010-9200-1

Tawiah, V., Zakari, A., & Adedoyin, F. F. (2021). Determinants of green growth in developed and developing countries. *Environmental Science and Pollution Research International*, *28*(1), 39227–39242. doi:10.100711356-021-13429-0 PMID:33751350

Taylor, F. W. (1914). *The Principles of Scientific Management*. Harper.

Teece, D. J. (2006). Reflections on "Profiting from Innovation. *Research Policy*, *35*(8), 1131–1146. doi:10.1016/j.respol.2006.09.009

Teece, D. J. (2007). Explicating Dynamic Capabilities: The Nature and Micro foundations of (Sustainable) Enterprise Performance. *Strategic Management Journal*, *28*(13), 1319–1350. doi:10.1002mj.640

Teece, D. J. (2012). Dynamic Capabilities: Routines versus Entrepreneurial Action. *Journal of Management Studies*, *49*(8), 1395–1401. doi:10.1111/j.1467-6486.2012.01080.x

Teece, D. J., Pisano, G., & Shuen, A. (1997). Dynamic capabilities and strategic management. *Strategic Management Journal*, *18*(7), 509–533. doi:10.1002/(SICI)1097-0266(199708)18:7<509::AID-SMJ882>3.0.CO;2-Z

Tegtmeier. (2012). Empirical implications for promoting students' entrepreneurial intentions. *Journal of Enterprising Culture, 20*(2), 151–169.

Tencati, A., & Zsolnai, L. (2009). The collaborative enterprise.. *Journal of Business Ethics*, *85*(43), 367–376. doi:10.100710551-008-9775-3

Teo, W. L., Lee, M., & Lim, W.-S. (2017). The relational activation of flexibility model: How leadership activates flexibility in an organizational crisis. *Journal of Contingencies and Crisis Management*, *25*, 136–147. doi:10.1111/1468-5973.12179

Thiel, C. E., Bagdasarov, Z., Harkrider, L., Johnson, J. F., & Mumford, M. D. (2012). Leader ethical decision-making in organizations: Strategies for sense making. *Journal of Business Ethics*, *107*(1), 49–64. doi:10.100710551-012-1299-1

Thompson, J. D. (2003). *Organizations in action: Social science bases of administrative theory*. Transaction Publishers.

Thompson, J. L. (2002). The world of the social entrepreneur. *International Journal of Public Sector Management, 15*(5), 412–431. doi:10.1108/09513550210435746

Tian, Y., & Smith, W. K. (2014). Entrepreneurial Leadership of Social Enterprises: Challenges and Skills for Embracing Paradoxes. *Journal of Leadership Studies*, *8*(3), 42–45. doi:10.1002/jls.21339

Tidd, J., Bessant, J., & Pavitt, K. (1997). *Managing Innovation: integrating Technological, market and organizational change*. John Wiley and Sons Ltd.

Tlaiss, H. A. (2015). How Islamic business ethics impact women entrepreneurs: Insights from four Arab Middle Eastern countries. *Journal of Business Ethics, 129*(4), 859–877. doi:10.100710551-014-2138-3

Tlaiss, H. A., & McAdam, M. (2021). Unexpected lives: The intersection of Islam and Arab women's entrepreneurship. *Journal of Business Ethics, 171*(2), 253–272. doi:10.100710551-020-04437-0

Toft, B., & Reynolds, S. (1997). *Learning from Disasters* (2nd ed.). Perpetuity Press.

Tracey, P., & Phillips, N. (2007). The distinctive challenge of educating social entrepreneurs: A postscript and rejoinder to the special issue on entrepreneurship education. *Academy of Management Learning & Education, 6*(2), 264–271. doi:10.5465/amle.2007.25223465

Tracey, P., Phillips, N., & Jarvis, O. (2011). Bridging institutional entrepreneurship and the creation of new organizational forms: A multilevel model. *Organization Science, 22*(1), 60–80. doi:10.1287/orsc.1090.0522

Tsui, A. S., Nifadkar, S. S., & Ou, A. Y. (2007). Cross-national, cross-cultural organizational behaviour research: Advances, gaps, and recommendations. *Journal of Management, 33*(3), 26–478. doi:10.1177/0149206307300818

Tubbs, M. E., & Ekeberg, S. E. (1991). The role of intentions in work motivation: Implications for goal-setting theory and research. *Academy of Management Review, 16*(1), 180–199. doi:10.2307/258611

Twum, K. K., Kosiba, J. P. B., Hinson, R. E., Gabrah, A. Y. B., & Assabil, E. N. (2022). Determining mobile money service customer satisfaction and continuance usage through service quality. *Journal of Financial Services Marketing, 945*(2021), 1–13. doi:10.1057/s41264-021-00138-5

Tyler, S., & Moench, M. (2012). A framework for urban climate flexibility. *Climate and Development, 4*(4), 311–326. doi:10.1080/17565529.2012.745389

Umoh, G. I., Amah, E., & Wokocha, H. I. (2014). Management development and organizational flexibility: A case study of some selected manufacturing firms in Rivers State, Nigeria,'. *IOSR Journal of Business and Management, 16*(2), 7–16. doi:10.9790/487X-16230716

UNDP, & NBS. (2021). *The Impact of COVID-19 on Business Enterprises in Nigeria*. UNDP & NBS.

Vaelikangas, L., & Romme, A. G. L. (2013). How to design for strategic flexibility: A case study in retailing. *Journal of Organization Design, 2*(2), 44–53. doi:10.7146/jod.7360

Vakilzadeh, K., & Haase, A. (2020). *The building blocks of organizational flexibility: a review of the empirical literature*. Continuity & Flexibility Review., doi:10.1108/CRR-04-2020-0002

Vakkuri, J., Johanson, J. E., Feng, N. C., & Giordano, F. (2021). Governance and accountability in hybrid organizations–past, present and future. *Journal of Public Budgeting, Accounting & Financial Management, 33*(3), 245–260. doi:10.1108/JPBAFM-02-2021-0033

Van Gelderen, M., Brand, M., Van Praag, M., Bodewes, W., Poutsma, E., & Van Gils, A. (2008). Explaining entrepreneurial intentions by means of the theory of planned behaviour. *Career Development International, 13*(6), 538–559. doi:10.1108/13620430810901688

Vanderbilt-Adriance, E., & Shaw, D. S. (2008). Conceptualizing and re-evaluating flexibility across levels of risk, time, and domains of competence. *Clinical Child and Family Psychology Review, 11*(1-2), 30–58. doi:10.100710567-008-0031-2 PMID:18379875

Vasilescu, M. D., Dimian, G. C., & Gradinaru, G. I. (2023). Green entrepreneurship in challenging times: A quantitative approach for European countries. *Ekonomska Istrazivanja, 36*(1), 1828–1947. doi:10.1080/1331677X.2022.2093767

Verhoef, P. C., Broekhuizen, T., Bart, Y., Bhattacharya, A., Dong, J. Q., Fabian, N., & Haenlein, M. (2021). Digital transformation: A multidisciplinary reflection and research agenda. *Journal of Business Research, 122*, 889–901. doi:10.1016/j.jbusres.2019.09.022

Voorhees, C. M., Brady, M. K., Calantone, R., & Ramirez, E. (2016). Discriminant validity testing in marketing: An analysis, causes for concern, and proposed remedies. *Journal of the Academy of Marketing Science, 44*(1), 119–134. doi:10.100711747-015-0455-4

Wales, W., Monsen, E., & McKelvie, A. (2011). The organizational pervasiveness of entrepreneurial orientation. *Entrepreneurship Theory and Practice, 5,* 895–923. doi:. 00451.x doi:10.1111/j.1540-6520.2011

Walker, B. H., & Salt, D. A. (2006). *Flexibility Thinking: Sustaining Ecosystems and People in a Changing World.* Island Press.

Walter, M. (2006). The Nature of Social Science Research: Asking Social Questions, Seeking Social Answers. *Nat. Soc. Sci. Res.*

Wang, C. K., & Wong, P. K. (2004). Entrepreneurial interest of university students in Singapore. *Technovation, 24*(2), 163–172. doi:10.1016/S0166-4972(02)00016-0

Waterman, A. S. (1984). Identity Formation: Discovery or Creation? *The Journal of Early Adolescence, 4*(4), 329–341. doi:10.1177/0272431684044004

Watson, R. (2015). Quantitative research. *Nursing Standard, 29*(31), 44–48. doi:10.7748/ns.29.31.44.e8681 PMID:25828021

Watts, G., & Paciga, J. J. (2011). Conscious Adaptation: Building Resilient Organizations. In T. Carmichael (Ed.), *Complex Adaptive Systems: Energy, Information, and Intelligence*, (pp. 158-167). Arlington VA: AAAI Fall Symposium Series.

Weber, M. (1947). *The theory of social and economic organization.* Oxford University Press.

Webster, F. A. (1977). Entrepreneurs and ventures: An attempt at classification and clarification. *Academy of Management Review*, *2*(1), 54–61. doi:10.2307/257605

Weerawardena, J., Mort, G. S., Liesch, P. W., & Knight, G. (2007). Conceptualizing accelerated internationalization in the born global firm: A dynamic capabilities perspective. *Journal of World Business*, *42*(3), 294–306. doi:10.1016/j.jwb.2007.04.004

Weick, K. E., & Sutcliffe, K. M. (2007). Managing the unexpected: Resilient performance in an age of uncertainty (2. ed.). San Francisco, CA: Jossey-Bass.

Weick, K. E., & Roberts, K. H. (1993). Collective mind in organizations: Heedful interrelating on flight decks. *Administrative Science Quarterly*, *38*(3), 357–381. doi:10.2307/2393372

Weick, K. E., & Sutcliffe, K. M. (2001). *Managing the Unexpected: Assuring High Performance in an Age of Complexity*. Jossey-Bass.

Weick, K. E., & Sutcliffe, K. M. (2003). Hospitals as Cultures of Entrapment: A Re-Analysis of the Bristol Royal Infirmary. *California Management Review*, *45*(2), 73–84. doi:10.2307/41166166

Weick, K. E., Sutcliffe, K. M., & Obstfeld, D. (2005). Organizing and the process of sensemaking. *Organization Science*, *16*(4), 409–421. doi:10.1287/orsc.1050.0133

Wennekers, S., & Thurik, R. (1999). Linking Entrepreneurship and Economic Growth. *Small Business Economics*, *13*(1), 27–56. doi:10.1023/A:1008063200484

Whiteman, G., & Cooper, W. H. (2011). Ecological sensemaking. *Academy of Management Journal*, *43*(6), 1265–1282. doi:10.2307/1556349

Whittington, R. (2001). *What is a strategy—And does it matter?* Routledge.

Whittington, R., Pettigrew, A., Peck, S., Fenton, E., & Conyon, M. (1999). M. "Change and complementarities in the new competitive landscape: A European panel study, 1992–1996.". *Organization Science*, *10*(5), 583–600. doi:10.1287/orsc.10.5.583

Wicker, P., Filo, K., & Cuskelly, G. (2013). Organizational flexibility of community sport clubs impacted by natural disasters [Nov.]. *Journal of Sport Management*, *27*(6), 510–525. doi:10.1123/jsm.27.6.510

Wiklund, J., Patzelt, H., & Shepherd, D. A. (2009). Building an integrative model of small business growth. *Small Business Economics*, *32*(4), 351–374. doi:10.100711187-007-9084-8

Wiklund, J., & Shepherd, D. (2003). Knowledge-based resources, entrepreneurial orientation, and the performance of small and medium-sized businesses. *Strategic Management Journal*, *24*(13), 1307–1314. doi:10.1002mj.360

Wiklund, J., & Shepherd, D. (2005). Entrepreneurial orientation and small business performance: A configurational approach. *Journal of Business Venturing*, *20*(1), 71–91. doi:10.1016/j.jbusvent.2004.01.001

Wildavsky, A. (1988). *Searching for Safety*. Transaction Press.

Willems, J. J., Busscher, T., van den Brink, M., & Arts, J. (2018). Anticipating water infrastructure renewal: A framing perspective on organizational learning in public agencies Environment and Planning C. *Politics and Space*, *36*(6), 1088–1108.

Williams, L. J., & McGonagle, A. K. (2016). Four Research Designs and a Comprehensive Analysis Strategy for Investigating Common Method Variance with Self-Report Measures Using Latent Variables. *Journal of Business and Psychology*, *31*(3), 339–359. doi:10.100710869-015-9422-9

Williams, T. A., Gruber, D. A., Sutcliffe, K. M., Shepherd, D. A., & Zhao, E. Y. (2017). Organizational response to adversity: Fusing crisis management and flexibility research streams. *The Academy of Management Annals*, *11*(2), 733–769. doi:10.5465/annals.2015.0134

Wilson, F., Kickul, J., & Marlino, D. (2007). Gender, entrepreneurial self-efficacy, and entrepreneurial career intentions: Implications for entrepreneurship education. *Entrepreneurship Theory and Practice*, *31*(3), 387–406. doi:10.1111/j.1540-6520.2007.00179.x

Wise, V., & Ali, M. M. (2009). *Customer Relationship Management of Commercial Banks in Bangladesh with special reference to automation process: an empirical study*. Research Gate. https://www.researchgate.net/publication/318725722_Customer_Relationship_Management_of_Commercial_Banks_in_Bangladesh_with_special_reference_to_automation_process_an_empirical_study

Wolf, J., & Egelhoff, W. G. (2002). A reexamination and extension of the international strategy-structure theory. *Strategic Management Journal*, *23*(2), 181–189. doi:10.1002mj.210

Wolf, M., & Mair, J. (2019). Purpose, commitment and coordination around small wins: A proactive approach to governance in integrated hybrid organizations. *Voluntas*, *30*(3), 535–548. doi:10.100711266-019-00116-5

Woods, D. D., & Hollnagel, E. (2006). *Joint Cognitive Systems: Patterns in Cognitive Systems Engineering*. Taylor, and Francis. doi:10.1201/9781420005684

Woodside, A. G. (2013). Moving beyond multiple regression analysis to algorithms: Calling for adoption of a paradigm shift from symmetric to asymmetric thinking in data analysis and crafting theory. *Journal of Business Research*, *66*(4), 463–472. doi:10.1016/j.jbusres.2012.12.021

Woodside, A. G., Prentice, C., & Larsen, A. (2015). Revisiting problem gamblers' harsh gaze on casino services: Applying complexity theory to identify exceptional customers. *Psychology and Marketing*, *32*(1), 65–77. doi:10.1002/mar.20763

World Bank. (2018). *Bangladesh: Reducing Poverty and Sharing Prosperity*. World Bank. https://www.worldbank.org/en/results/2018/11/15/bangladesh-reducing-poverty-and-sharing-prosperity

World Bank. (2020). *Bangladesh's microenterprises embraced green growth and thrived–then COVID-19 hit.* World Bank. https://blogs.worldbank.org/endpovertyinsouthasia/bangladeshs-microenterprises-embraced-green-growth-and-thrived-then-covid-19(Viewed on 3rd June,2022)

World Bank. (2020). *COVID-19 to Plunge Global Economy into Worst Recession since World War II.* The World Bank. https://www.worldbank.org/en/news/press-release/2020/06/08/covid-19-to-plunge-global-economy-into-worst-recession-since-world-war-ii

World Bank. (2022). Micro Enterprise Owners in Bangladesh Go Green. World Bank. https://www.worldbank.org/en/results/2022/09/06/micro-enterprise-owners-in-bangladesh-go-green

Wright, M., Westhead, P., & Ucbasaran, D. (2007). Internationalization of small and medium-sized enterprises (SMEs) and international entrepreneurship: A critique and policy implications. *Regional Studies, 41*(7), 1013–1030. doi:10.1080/00343400601120288

Wright, R. T., Campbell, D. E., Thatcher, J. B., & Roberts, N. (2012). Operationalizing multidimensional constructs in structural equation modeling: Recommendations for IS research. *Communications of the Association for Information Systems, 30*, 367–412. doi:10.17705/1CAIS.03023

Yağcı, M. (2017). Institutional entrepreneurship and organisational learning: Financial stability policy design in Turkey. *Policy and Society, 36*(4), 539–555. doi:10.1080/14494035.2017.1369616

Yang. (2013). The theory of planned behavior and prediction of entrepreneurial intention among Chinese undergraduates. *Social Behavior and Personality,* 41(3), 367–376.

Yang, J., Chang, M., Chen, Z., Zhou, L., & Zhang, J. (2021). The chain mediation effect of spiritual leadership on employees' innovative behavior. *Leadership and Organization Development Journal, 42*(1), 114–129. doi:10.1108/LODJ-10-2019-0442

Yesmin, A. (2021). Microbusiness Continuity and Resilience Strategies for COVID-19 Crisis: Entrepreneurs' Insight from Bangladesh. *International Journal of Academic Research in Accounting Finance and Management Sciences, 10*(2), 33–48.

Yin, C., Salmador, M. P., Li, D., & Lloria, M. B. (2022). Green entrepreneurship and SME performance: The moderating effect of firm age. *The International Entrepreneurship and Management Journal, 18*(1), 255–275. doi:10.100711365-021-00757-3

Young, O. (2010). *Institutional dynamics: Emergent patters in international environmental governance.* MIT Press. doi:10.7551/mitpress/8457.001.0001

Yousef, M. (2022). Developing a Paradigm Model for Flexibility of Rural Entrepreneurial Businesses in Dealing With the COVID-19 Crisis; Application of Grounded Theory in Western of Iran. *Frontiers in Public Health, 10,* 833909. Advance online publication. doi:10.3389/fpubh.2022.833909

Zahedi, A., & Otterpohl, R. (2015). Towards sustainable development by creation of green social entrepreneur's communities. *Procedia CIRP, 26,* 196–201. doi:10.1016/j.procir.2014.07.037

Zahra, S. A., & Covin, J. G. (1995). Contextual influences on the corporate entrepreneurship performance relationship: A longitudinal analysis. *Journal of Business Venturing, 10*(1), 43–58. doi:10.1016/0883-9026(94)00004-E

Zahra, S. A., Korri, J. S., & Yu, J. (2005). Cognition and international entrepreneurship: Implications for research on international opportunity recognition and exploitation. *International Business Review, 14*(2), 129–146. doi:10.1016/j.ibusrev.2004.04.005

Zahra, S. A., Sapienza, H. J., & Davidsson, P. (2006). Entrepreneurship and Dynamic Capabilities: A review, model, and research agenda. *Journal of Management Studies, 43*(4), 917–955. doi:10.1111/j.1467-6486.2006.00616.x

Zander, A. (1993). *Making boards effective: The dynamics of nonprofit governing boards.* Jossey-Bass.

Zawislak, P., Alves, C., Tello-Gamarra, J., Barbieux, D., & Reichert, F. (2012). Innovation capability: From technology development to transaction capability. *Journal of Technology Management & Innovation, 7*(2), 14–27. doi:10.4067/S0718-27242012000200002

Zeng, J., & Ren, J. (2022). How does green entrepreneurship affect environmental improvement? Empirical findings from 293 enterprises. *The International Entrepreneurship and Management Journal, 18*(1), 409–434. doi:10.100711365-021-00780-4

Zhao, H., Hills, G. E., & Siebert, S. E. (2005). The mediating role of self-efficacy in the development of entrepreneurial intentions. *The Journal of Applied Psychology, 90*(6), 1265–1272. doi:10.1037/0021-9010.90.6.1265 PMID:16316279

Zollo, M., & Winter, S. G. (2002). Deliberate learning and the evolution of dynamic capabilities [June.]. *Organization Science, 13*(3), 339–351. doi:10.1287/orsc.13.3.339.2780

Żur, A. (2021). Entrepreneurial identity and social-business tensions–the experience of social entrepreneurs. *Journal of Social Entrepreneurship, 12*(3), 438–461. doi:10.1080/19420676.2020.1740297

About the Contributors

Mohammed El Amine Abdelli is a researcher at the University of Salamanca. He is a reviewer of several indexed journals (Scopus, Web of Science) and reviewer books in (IGI GLOBAL,Taylor & Francis)..

* * *

Muhammad Mahboob Ali In Dhaka School of Economics, at Entrepreneurship Economics Programme, Prof. Dr. Muhammad Mahboob Ali, MPhil in Financial Economics, PhD in Macroeconomics and Post-doctoral in Entrepreneurial management from Naresuan University, Thailand, is contributing as a coordinator and also pioneer in the field of entrepreneurship development. As Professor Ali got training in AIT on outcome-based education as well as inductive learning and also in UGC, Bangladesh, he tried to do something unique following the path of the honourable Prime Minister Sheikh Hasina whom he treats her as perfect statesman. Prof. Ali during establishing the Programmes got various training, field trip support from the PKSF. His super goal is to create self-employed and income generating creative and innovative people to serve the country which was independent by the Bangabandhu Sheikh Mujibur Rahman. Muhammad Mahboob Ali is not only macroeconomist of the country but also financial economist, IT expert and entrepreneurial expert. He is also a literator. He was ex Vice Chancellor of Presidency University, Bangladesh. He started his career in the banking sector and then switched to academia. Muhammad Mahboob Ali wrote research-based book Novel, lyrics, poems, short-stories and 23 books for children. He wrote 150 research-based articles which was published in peer reviewed journals including SCOPUS indexed and ABDC indexed journals. He is associated with total 27 journals as a member of the editorial board out of which 4 is SCOPUS indexed. However, during COVID-19, he wrote following articles in different books and journals (2020 to 2022, March): José G. Vargas-Hernández and Muhammad Mahboob Ali (2022, March). Sustainability and Green Socio-Ecosystem Resilience: A Conceptual View, International Journal of Environmental Sustainability and Green Technologies, 13 (1), DOI: 10.4018/IJESGT.292453; Muhammad

Mahboob Ali (2022, February). Bilateral Cooperation Between Australia and Bangladesh in Diverse Areas: An Analysis to Cope With the COVID-19 Aftermath, in the Book: Strategic Cooperation and Partnerships Between Australia and South Asia, DOI: 10.4018/978-1-7998-8657-0.ch006, Anita Medhekar, Sreeparna Saha Farooq Haq (Editors), IGI Global; José G. Vargas-Hernández and Muhammad Mahboob Ali (2022, March). Servant Leadership Styles as a Challenge to Develop Innovation in Resilient Environments: A Conceptual View, January 2022 DOI: 10.4018/978-1-7998-8820-8.ch005, In the book: Key Factors and Use Cases of Servant Leadership Driving Organizational Performance, Maria Present in (editor), IGI Global; Muhammad Mahboob Ali and Anita Medhekar, (Jul 30, 2021). The BIMSTEC Free Trade Area: Economic Cooperation, Opportunities, and Challenges, DOI: 10.4018/978-1-7998-5774-7.ch006, in the book: Evaluating Trade and Economic Relations Between India and Southeast Asia, Venkataramanaiah Malepati, Anita Medhekar, Harpreet Kaur (editors), IGI Global; José G. Vargas-Hernández and Muhammad Mahboob Ali (November, 2021). Organizational Culture, Knowledge, Learning Organizations, and Innovation on Sustainable Organizations: Strategic Implications, DOI: 10.4018/978-1-7998-7785-1.ch013,in the Book: Smart Cities, Citizen Welfare, and the Implementation of Sustainable Development Goals, IGI Global, Ana Cristina Pego (Editor); Ali, Muhammad Mahboob (September, 2021). Digital opportunities in the healthcare enterprises during COVID-19: An empirical analysis of the developing country. Corporate Governance and Organizational Behavior Review, 5(2), 44–55. (SCOPUS INDEXED JOURNAL); Ali, Muhammad Mahboob (July-December, 2020). Bangabandhu Sheikh Mujibur Rahman: A Magnetic and Excellent Statesman in Bangladesh, DOI: 10.46333/ijtc/9/2/4, International Journal of Trade and Commerce-IIARTC, July-December 2020, Volume 9, No.2; Ali, Muhammad Mahboob (October, 2020). Digitization of the emerging economy: An exploratory and explanatory case study, Journal of Governance & Regulation, 9(4), 25-36. (SCOPUS INDEXED JOURNAL); Ali, Muhammad Mahboob (2019-2020). Grim situation of the world due to COVID19: Economic perspective, , Geopolitics under Globalization, 3(1):24-29. On 12 December, 2021 award in recognition of contribution in creating new entrepreneurs in the country by The Global Nation was received by Prof. Dr. Muhammad Mahboob Ali, DScE. He also earlier received award for being outstanding educationalist of foreign origin Entreprnrueship-2019 by Global Entrepreneurship Grid (GEG) India. Prof. Dr. Muhammad Mahboob Ali in the International virtual webinar series " Quest for Insight Beyond Boundaries" on "Social Entrepreneurship" organized by Institute of Management & Technology, Faridabad, India on 7th June, 2021. Prof. Dr. Muhammad Mahboob Ali was a session Chair, D2P10 Education and learning in the 2nd AIUB International conference on Business and Management 2021 organized by Faculty of Business Administration, American International University- Bangladesh virtually on 29 and

30 October, 2021. As a speaker Prof. Dr. Muhammad Mahboob Ali worked at the call for paper University as Pendidikan National entitled “Optimizing a role of the younger generation to be a savvy in Industrial revolution. On 11th May, 2022 as a session chair in the 5th International conference 2022 on “Digital Transformation and sustainability in business practices” on April 7- 8, 2022 organized by Amity college of commerce and Finance, Amity University, Uttar Pradesh, India. Prof. Dr. Muhammad Mahboob Ali attended virtually a seminar on “Decentralized Finance and Technology Block chain “on 9 October, 2022 organized by Rangsit University, Thailand. On 6th August, 2020 Prof. Dr. Muhammad Mahboob Ali gave a lecture on Sustainable business strategies under the new normal at KV Institute of Management and information studies (KVM Business School), India. Prof. Dr. Muhammad Mahboob Ali received foreign origin Entrepreneurship award -2019 by the Global Entrepreneurship grid on 2 February, 2019. Muhammad Mahboob Ali got literary award different times.

Ayansola Ayandibu holds a BSc Hons in Accounting, Master of Business Administration, and a PhD. in Leadership Studies (Strategy, Innovation, and Entrepreneurship). He worked in the corporate environment for 8 years in Nigeria before relocating to South Africa. In 2012, Dr Ayandibu worked for Lieutenant Consulting, in Midrand, Johannesburg as an accountant/economist. He lectured at the University of KwaZulu-Natal from February 2013 to January 2021 in the discipline of Management and Entrepreneurship. Dr Ayandibu has lectured Accounting, Management, and Entrepreneurship modules at the University of KwaZulu-Natal. He has also published articles in accredited journals, published book chapters, and edited a book on entrepreneurship. Dr. Ayandibu has attended international conferences at the University of London, UK, Harvard University (USA), and Ryerson University, Toronto Canada. He lectures Banking and Financial Management modules. Dr Ayandibu has supervised several honours students, master’s and PhD candidates. Dr. Ayansola Ayandibu is a member of the South African Institute of Management (SAIM), South African Institute of Management Scientists (SAIMS), South African Institute of Business Accountants (SAIBA), and Institute of Chartered Economists of Nigeria (ICEN).

Nicoletta Cangiano is a Ph.D. student in “Entrepreneurship and Innovation” at the University of Naples Parthenope. Her current research approaches how firms could adopt antifragility to tackle grand societal challenges, i.e., black swans, such as economic crises, pandemics, wars, etc. Beyond this, she also undertakes qualitative and conceptual research on entrepreneurial and innovation ecosystems, deepening the role of government as a key actor that affects the development and evolution of the ecosystem. In 2020 she became a member of the Erich Fromm Study Center, and since 2021 he has been a member of the editorial board.

Paula Danby has a strong interest in business management and leadership. She leads a team of academics in the area of leadership, human resource management and enterprise facilitating academic development and focusing on the student experience. She is also Co-Lead for the Business School Research Centre, where she contribute and support academics to enhance the research culture and promote an inclusive, diverse, and multi-disciplinary research environment. She is a Senior Fellow of the Higher Education Academy. Her research interests relate to innovative leadership practices, wellbeing, developing effective relationships, equality, diversity and inclusion.

Bhim Jyoti has been working with V.C.S.G., UUHF, College of Forestry, Ranichauri, Tehri Garhwal, Uttarakhand, India as Assistant Professor of Seed and Technology. She received MSc in Seed and Technology from CCS University Meerut and PhD in Seed and Technology from G. B. Pant University of Agriculture, Pantnagar, Uttarakhand. She has published several research articles in the seed and technology, plant growth, seed vigour, genetic variability, Biotechnological approaches, climate change and agricultural productivity.

Farhan Mirza is a graduate assistant at the Department of Management and Humanities, Universiti Teknologi PETRONAS, Malaysia. He has seven years of working experience in various academic and research institutions. His research interest is in customer experience and digital marketing.

Samuel Olutuase holds a PhD in Management with specialisation in Entrepreneurship. He has published works in peer reviewed journal to credit. Samuel has research experience and expertise in entrepreneurship, management and administration research, with 13years of teaching and supervision experience at universities in Nigeria and South Africa. His research experience includes: socio-economic data to determine Nigeria's poverty level for UNDP. He has also served as data analyst on various research projects: City Cape Town project (Exploring unemployed women's economic survival in Kayelitsha); German Technical Cooperation (GTZ) and MDG projects in Plateau state. Samuel has expertise in both quantitative and qualitative research tools.

Ana Pinto Borges PhD in Economics, Faculty of Economics, University of Porto. Coordinating Professor and Pedagogical President at ISAG - European Business School. Assumes the Executive Coordination of ISAG Research Centre of ISAG (NIDISAG) between 2014 - 2021 and scientific coordinator of the Center in Business Sciences and Tourism (CICET - FCVC), since 2020. Author of more than 40 publications in indexed international scientific journals. Participation in presentations in various national and international congresses and member of the Scientific Committees in academic events. Editor and one of the founding members of the European Journal of Applied Business and Management (EJABM). Former Accenture consultant in the financial area. Economist at the Health Regulatory Entity since 2010.

Ahsan Riaz graduated from the Asia Pacific University of Technology & Innovation, Malaysia holding a Ph.D. in corporate finance with a merit award. Currently, Dr. Ahsan Riaz serves as Assistant Professor at Lyallpur Business School GC University Faisalabad, Pakistan. He has vast teaching and research experience of more than 12 years in Accounting and Finance. He has the author of many research articles and an editorial board member of the Asian Institute of Research journal Economics and Business Quarterly Reviews. He is also a reviewer of many reputable journals like Asian Social Science, International Business Research, and the International Journal of Economics and Finance of the Canadian Center of Science and Education (CCSE). He is an expert in quantitative analysis and a professional Eviews and Sos-Viewer trainer.

Khuram Shahzad is a behavioral scientist and development expert, with 15+ years of international experience with the industry, development agencies, and academia. Dr. Shahzad has received his PhD in Management from RMIT University, Australia along with special training from the National University of Singapore (NUS), New York University (NYU), Nottingham Trent University, UK, and Asian Development Bank (ADB). He has been engaged with RMIT Australia as ad-hoc faculty to teach capstone courses of Human Resource Management, Entrepreneurship, and New Venture Creation. He is a Monitoring & Evaluation consultant for Asian Development Bank (ADB) and Better Cotton Initiative (BCI) UK. As a professional consultant and trainer, he has developed the leadership and team-building capacity of diverse groups of working professionals in government and private sector organizations. His expertise ranges from organizational and management diagnostics to transformational leadership skills necessary to modify and shape up organizational culture and behaviours.

Ajay K. Singh is working as an Assistant Professor (Economics) in the School of Liberal Arts & Management, DIT University Dehradun. He did Post-Doctorate Research with EDI of India, Ahmedabad, Gujarat (India). He received MPhil (Economics) from Devi Ahilya University Indore (India), and PhD (Economics) from IIT Indore (India). He has published research papers in the area of climate change and agricultural productivity, assessment of food security; estimation of GFSI, assessment of environmental sustainability index and its association with socio-economic indicators; implications of entrepreneurship ecosystem on economic development; and implications of digitalization on economic development at national and global level.

Ding Hooi Ting is an Associate Professor at the Department of Management & Humanities, Universiti Teknologi PETRONAS, Malaysia. He also serves as the Cluster Leader for the Business and Management Cluster. His research interests are in consumer behavior and behavioral change.

Shajara Ul-Durar is an Associate Professor in Management and Organisational Behaviour at the University of Sunderland, UK. The researcher is an emerging early career researcher with expertise in Business Ethics. She is UN PRME SDGs Regional Head/Chapter Lead for Pakistan. Shajara has experience leading Postgraduate and Undergraduate courses at several high-ranked Higher Education Institutes in the UK, including Nottingham Business School, Southampton Business School, Leicester Business School and Coventry Business School. She is the projects' lead of the Association of Physicians and Surgeons of the UK. She holds memberships of Higher Education Academy as a Fellow, Chartered Management Institute as CMgr MCMI, Chartered Association of Business Schools as Certified Management and Business Educator, Academic Associated CIPD, Professional Member Young Professionals' Society and a member of The British Academy of Management. She is an enthusiastic interdisciplinary researcher who wants to create an impact through research. She is experienced in cross-cultural research. She has won several research grants/projects including PRME and British Council and has published in high-profile international academic journals.

Index

I

M

N

O

P

R

S

T

V

W

Ensure Quality Research is Introduced to the Academic Community

Become an Evaluator for IGI Global Authored Book Projects

The overall success of an authored book project is dependent on quality and timely manuscript evaluations.

Applications and Inquiries may be sent to:
development@igi-global.com

Applicants must have a doctorate (or equivalent degree) as well as publishing, research, and reviewing experience. Authored Book Evaluators are appointed for one-year terms and are expected to complete at least three evaluations per term. Upon successful completion of this term, evaluators can be considered for an additional term.

If you have a colleague that may be interested in this opportunity, we encourage you to share this information with them.

www.ingramcontent.com/pod-product-compliance
Lightning Source LLC
LaVergne TN
LVHW081344300926
849161LV00008B/2058